The 'Scientific Revolution' of the sixteenth and seventeenth centuries continues to command attention in historical debate. What was its nature? How did it develop? Controversy still rages about the extent to which it was essentially a 'revolution of the mind', or how far it must also be explained by wider considerations, social, economic, political and cultural.

In this volume, leading scholars of early modern science argue the importance of specifically national contexts for understanding the transformation in natural philosophy between Copernicus and Newton. Distinct social, political, religious, cultural and linguistic formations shaped scientific interests and concerns differently in Italy, France, Britain, the Germanies, Spain, and so on, and throw light on different levels of scientific intensity. Questions of economic and institutional development, and of the transmission of scientific ideas, are also addressed. The emphasis upon national determinants makes this volume an entirely original contribution to the study of the Scientific Revolution.

Contributors: MARIO BIAGIOLI, L. W. B. BROCKLISS, WILLIAM CLARK, HAROLD J. COOK, JERZY DOBRZYCKI, DAVID GOODMAN, JOHN HENRY, JOSEF SMOLKA, SVEN WIDMALM, PAUL WOOD

THE SCIENTIFIC REVOLUTION
IN NATIONAL CONTEXT

THE
SCIENTIFIC REVOLUTION
IN NATIONAL CONTEXT

EDITED BY

ROY PORTER

Senior Lecturer in the Social History of Medicine,
Wellcome Institute

MIKULÁŠ TEICH

Emeritus Fellow, Robinson College, Cambridge

CAMBRIDGE
UNIVERSITY PRESS

Published by the Press Syndicate of the University of Cambridge
The Pitt Building, Trumpington Street, Cambridge CB2 1RP
40 West 20th Street, New York, NY 10011-4211, USA
10 Stamford Road, Oakleigh, Victoria 3166, Australia

First published 1992

Printed in Great Britain at the University Press, Cambridge

A catalogue record for this book is available from the British Library

Library of Congress cataloguing in publication data

The Scientific Revolution in national context/edited by Roy Porter
and Mikuláš Teich.
    p.   cm.
Includes index.
ISBN 0 521 39510 0 (hardback). – ISBN 0 521 39699 9 (paperback)
1. Science – Europe – History – 16th century. 2. Science – Europe –
History – 17th century. I. Porter, Roy. 1946–   . II. Teich,
Mikuláš.
Q127.E8S36 1992
509.4′031 – dc20   91–34348   CIP

ISBN 0521 39510 0 hardback
ISBN 0521 39699 9 paperback

CONTENTS

CONTRIBUTORS

MARIO BIAGIOLI teaches history of early modern science at the University of California, Los Angeles. His *Galileo Courtier* is to be published by the University of Chicago Press.

L. W. B. BROCKLISS is Fellow and Tutor in Modern History at Magdalen College, Oxford. He is the author of *French Higher Education in the Seventeenth and Eighteenth Centuries: A Cultural History* (Oxford, 1987), and of many articles on aspects of the history of education, medicine and science in early modern France. He is also editor of the annual journal *History of Universities*.

WILLIAM CLARK currently teaches at the Institut für Wissenschaftsgeschichte, at Göttingen University. He is working on *The Doctor of Philosophy* (*Homo Academicus Germanicus*), which will be published by the University of California Press.

HAROLD J. COOK, an Associate Professor of the History of Medicine and History of Science at the University of Wisconsin-Madison, has published a number of works on seventeenth-century English medicine and science, including *The Decline of the Old Medical Regime in Stuart London* (Ithaca, N.Y., 1986). In recent years, with the support of the Fulbright Commission and the National Endowment for the Humanities, he has embarked upon a study of late-seventeenth-century Dutch medicine and natural history.

JERZY DOBRZYCKI has for many years been a leading historian of science in Poland, specializing in Copernican studies. He is the editor of *Complete Works of Nicholas Copernicus*, II: *On the Revolutions*, and of *The Reception of Copernicus' Heliocentric Theory: Proceedings of a Symposium Organized by the Nicolas Copernicus Committee of the International Union of the History and Philosophy of Science, Toruń, Poland, 1973* (Dordrecht, 1972).

DAVID GOODMAN was Visiting Assistant Professor in History of Science at the Johns Hopkins University, Baltimore, and is currently Lecturer in History of Science and Technology at the Open University. His research is concentrated on science and technology in early modern Spain. His *Power and Penury: Government, Science and Technology in Philip II's Spain* was published by the Cambridge University Press in 1988. He is now preparing a book on the Spanish navy in the seventeenth century.

JOHN HENRY lectures on the history of science and medicine in the Science Studies Unit at the University of Edinburgh. He has published a number of articles on late Renaissance and early modern science and medicine, and is joint editor (with Sarah Hutton) of *New Perspectives on Renaissance Thought* (London, 1990), and joint author (with Barry Barnes and David Bloor) of *Scientific Knowledge: A Sociological Analysis* (London, 1992).

JOSEF SMOLKA was born in Prague in 1929, and studied mathematics and physics at the Charles University. His doctoral thesis was on the philosophy of Bernard Bolzano. Later he devoted himself to the problems of the history of science in the seventeenth and eighteenth centuries, publishing variously on Procopius Diviš and his lightning rod (1754), on Stepling and on Boscovich. With L. Nový, he produced a scientific biography of Isaac Newton. One of his particular interests has been Johannes Marcus Marci, the main personality in the development of Czech science in the seventeenth century.

SVEN WIDMALM studied physics and the history of science and ideas at Uppsala University and at the University of Michigan, Ann Arbor. He is currently Assistant Professor in the Department of History of Science and Ideas at Uppsala University. His thesis, published in 1990, deals with eighteenth- and nineteenth-century geodesy, surveying and cartography. He has published several articles on eighteenth-century science and has also written on the politics of high-energy physics in Sweden in the 1960s. He is currently working on the relationship between military, science and information technology *c.* 1850–1950.

PAUL WOOD teaches in the Department of History, University of Victoria. He has published papers on the early Royal Society and on science and philosophy in the Scottish Enlightenment. He is the author of *Aberdeen and the Enlightenment: The Curriculum of the Aberdeen Colleges 1717–1800* (Aberdeen, 1991), and his edition of Thomas Reid's scientific manuscripts is forthcoming with Edinburgh University Press.

ACKNOWLEDGEMENTS

GRASPING the relations between the particular and the universal, the interplay of part and whole, is one of the historian's perennial challenges. This book forms part of a series focusing upon major constellations of ideas, culture, and action, and attempting to ascertain their general features, their more local aspects, and the links between them – links which are often complicated and difficult to unravel. The volumes which have already appeared in this series – about the Enlightenment, Romanticism, the *fin de siècle* and the Renaissance – have shown how each of those key moments in European culture possessed certain unifying characteristics, a programme jointly held by, or spreading amongst, thinkers and activists from many lands; but they have also shown that their manifestations and meanings were different in (say) Spain and Sweden, Bohemia and Britain, determined by local circumstances and distinctive ideological needs. This account of the Scientific Revolution constitutes a further exploration of this viewpoint. The editors are most grateful to William Davies at the Cambridge University Press for his lasting support for this series – a support which now dates back more than a decade – and to the contributors for sharing our faith in this historical perspective. Thanks too to Frieda Houser for the administrative backup which has made editing this volume a pleasure and to Dorothy Dosanjh for her splendid index.

INTRODUCTION

ROY PORTER AND MIKULÁŠ TEICH

MODERN science proclaims itself objective, rational and international: the periodic table of the elements hangs upon the chemistry laboratory wall in Berkeley, Berlin and Beijing, the writ of Boyle's Law runs all around the globe. Science is said to be a universal language or culture, transcending national boundaries and nationalistic rivalries.[1] To a fair degree this is true. A profusion of poetries, philosophies, aesthetics and theologies litters the continents, but there is only one scientific enterprise in the commonly accepted sense.[2] When an Indian scientist changes places with an Italian, or an Argentinian with an Austrian, no conceptual problems are posed. Nobel Prizes symbolize the unity of science today.[3]

This quality of universality is much prized and celebrated. It is therefore hardly surprising that historical accounts have sought to demonstrate that the pursuit of natural knowledge in earlier centuries was equally independent of, and superior to, subjective, personal, local and other essentially contingent factors. Science (we are often told) owed its progress to a commitment to strict scientific method (whether that be induction, deduction, experimentalism, or whatever) and, above all perhaps, to genius, the Odyssey of the brilliant Mind, lost in thought, confronting the external realities of Nature. Thus, in explaining Copernicus' rejection of geocentrism and espousal of a heliocentric astronomy, Imre Lakatos and Elie Zahar have written:

> Our account is a narrowly internalist one. No place in this account for the Renaissance spirit so dear to Kuhn's heart; for the turmoil of Reformation and Counter-Reformation, no impact of the Churchman; no sign of any effect from the alleged or real rise of capitalism in the 16th century: no motivation from the needs of navigation so much cherished by Bernal. The whole development is narrowly internal; its progressive part could have taken place at any time, given a Copernican genius between Aristotle and Ptolemy, or in any year, say, after the 1175 translation of the

I

Almagest into Latin, or for that matter, by an Arab astronomer in the 9th century. External history *in this case* is not only secondary; it is nearly redundant. Of course, the system of patronage of astronomy through Church sinecures played a role; but studying it will contribute nothing to our understanding of the Copernican scientific revolution.[4]

The aim of the present book is to argue the opposite of these claims: that the practice of science has, in reality, been profoundly dependent upon a variety of specific contexts to be explored below. The following essays do not especially engage with Lakatos and Zahar's peculiar idea that the Copernican Revolution could have taken place at almost any *time*, even before the flowers had withered on Ptolemy's grave. After all, history is about understanding why things happened when they did, not how they might have happened – but didn't – at sundry other times; and even the great majority of 'intellectual' historians of science have accepted the notion of the ripeness of time. Rather, this book will amplify a more challenging and novel case: that it is at our peril that historians of science neglect the geo-cultural element. Study of the rise of modern science, this book aims to show, needs to take into account not merely the Renaissance, the Reformation and the Counter-Reformation, not merely the problems of navigation and the needs of capitalism; and not merely various other so-called 'external' factors that the proudly 'internalist' Lakatos and Zahar do not mention: magic, hermetism, the occult tradition, the discovery of the New World, technological developments such as the invention of the microscope, the telescope and the printing press, the reform of the university, the exigencies of war, and so forth.[5] It also specifically needs to evaluate the role of particular and disparate national and cultural traditions of thinking and mental work, the patterns of education, the channels of intellectual communication, the opportunities for, or restrictions upon, free thought and expression that operated within discrete language groups and under distinctive political jurisdictions. We will not gain a full grasp of the special filiation of that much-maligned but still useful beast of historical burden, the Scientific Revolution – roughly, the vast transformation in ways of thinking about Nature wrought between the early sixteenth century and the close of the seventeenth – until we take account of its *where*, as well as its when and how; or, in other words, as Josef Smolka neatly puts it below, the Classical unities of time and place apply to the dramas of science no less than to the tragedies of the theatre.[6]

Cultural topography and geo-politics are, not surprisingly, almost totally neglected in the great synoptic histories of the Scientific Revolution that appeared in the decades after the War, the works of Alexandre Koyré, Herbert Butterfield, A. R. Hall and Marie Boas Hall,

Charles Gillispie, and others, works that accented the inner adventures of ideas and their transformation.[7] For intellectual historians of this kind, the Scientific Revolution was a revolution in and of the mind; if there was a geography of thought, it was to be traced on maps that were metaphysical, *metaphorical*.

Yet neither did the so-called 'externalist'[8] histories of science that rose to popularity from the mid-sixties pay much more attention to tangible national contexts of thought and frameworks of intellectual production.[9] The writings of Frances Yates and others were more concerned with recovering alternative intellectual traditions long hidden from history – astrology, alchemy, cabalistic magic and Rosicrucianism[10] – but their material base was often left all too vague, sometimes being loosely associated with a folk or underground tradition.[11]

This is not to say that the links between natural knowledge and the operation of the socio-political sphere had always been totally neglected. In an influential, if widely denigrated, paper delivered in 1930, the Soviet scholar, Boris Hessen, explicitly situated Newton's *Principia* in Newton's England (*of course*: it cannot have been irrelevant that Newton became both an MP and Master of the Mint, not to say President of the Royal Society). In his *The Social Function of Science* (1939) and *Science in History* (1954), J. D. Bernal systematically juxtaposed political, social economic and scientific history.[12] By contending that the spirit of modern experimental science was a function of the Calvinist ethos, even the rather Weberian Robert Merton implied in the 1930s in his *Science, Technology and Society in Seventeenth Century England* that it was no accident that the scientific movement was disproportionately associated with Protestant Holland, England and Scotland.[13] And, on the grandest scale of all, Joseph Needham's magisterial *Science and Civilisation in China* (1954–) has aimed to show that, despite her scientific precocity, China failed to pioneer the Scientific Revolution because that empire lacked the socio-political and socio-economic structures and climate of Europe, above all, nascent capitalism.[14]

Certain currents in modern history of science have built upon these insights. Investigations of the (micro-)politics of scientific inquiry have recognized the involvement of men of science in political affairs, as with Shapin and Schaffer's account of Hobbes or James Jacob's biography of Robert Boyle.[15] Margaret Jacob's study of the Boyle Lecturers and their milieu has shown how Newtonian ideology was put to political service in supporting the Whig–Anglican establishment in England after the expulsion of James II.[16] The chauvinistic dimensions of the Newton-Leibniz quarrel, or the long-sustained resistance of French science to Newtonianism (or, in a later century, to Darwinism), have also received

notice.[17] Over the last decade, many comparable cases have been
examined.[18]

Despite such initiatives, however, the relations between the staggering
scientific changes wrought between Copernicus and Newton, and, in the
widest sense, the political diversity and change, the chaos and 'search for
stability' that characterized Europe in the century after the Reformation, remain neglected.[19] And this is so even though every historian of
European politics emphasizes the magnitude of the transformations in
the nature of the state and the bases of princely power that Europe
underwent during the early modern centuries.[20] The history of states
and the history of science are generally studied in isolation from each
other; the excellent Routledge *Companion to the History of Modern Science*
(1990) contains, in all its thousand pages, only one discussion pertaining
to these questions, and that relates exclusively to twentieth-century
scientific internationalism. *Reappraisals of the Scientific Revolution* (1990),
another important revisionist work, barely touches upon the dialectics of
knowledge with political cultures. Only one publication appearing in
English in recent years – *The Emergence of Science in Western Europe* (1975)
– engages with the national basis of early science head-on. And, though
bold for its day, its discussions now appear, nearly twenty years later,
rather narrow and dated.[21]

Because of such neglect, it has seemed worthwhile to produce the
following volume posing the question of the relations between scientific
endeavour and its distinct national contexts,[22] in the hope of throwing
further light upon the social, economic and political dimensions of the
Scientific Revolution. There is no need here to summarize the
contributors' findings in full, but it is worth underlining certain of their
conclusions.

No one would dispute that there was a certain internationalism in the
pursuit of science in the early modern era. There was a shared ancestry:
Greek natural philosophy, passed down *via* scholasticism throughout
Latin Christendom. There was a common language, Latin – and if
Descartes was venturing to write his *Discours de la méthode* in French,
Newton was still publishing the *Principia mathematica philosophiae naturalis*
in 1687 in the old *lingua franca*.[23] And there was much scientific travelling
and migration, some impelled by persecution, as for example the French
Huguenot refugee-scientists who fled from Louis XIV and settled in the
Dutch Republic and in England.

But, alongside this cosmopolitanism, special politico-cultural circumstances produced force-fields shaping natural knowledge in different
ways in different nations. As Mario Biagioli argues in the first essay, the
power of the princely court in post-Renaissance Italy produced not

merely patronage-based scientific networks but a style of intellectual production ('Baroque') that was distinctively rhetorical and theatrical.[24] In France, the authority of the Sun King underwrote a deeply authoritarian style of scientific activity, whereas in England the disturbances of the Civil War and the studied moderation of the Restoration invited the gentlemanly cultivation, and cult of a philosophy that prized facts.

Later essays flesh out, extend and modify some of Biagioli's claims. Laurence Brockliss demonstrates how the sheer populousness and opulence of France helps explain its sudden burst into scientific eminence during the seventeenth century, while showing how *la grande nation*, though Catholic, managed to escape the strangulation of scientific inquiry that overtook post-Galilean Italy and (as David Goodman's essay demonstrates) the Iberian peninsula. The aspect of England which John Henry chooses to emphasize in his contribution is its distinctively Hookerian Anglicanism, a *via media* that embraced an element of doubt, and so laid the epistemological basis of a scientific ethos that valued a certain empirical cast of thought. William Clark contends that features of the economic and political landscape of the German-speaking lands – their well-developed technology, the pedagogical role of the Jesuits and other Catholic teaching orders in southern Germany, the military involvement of princes at the height of the Thirty Years' War – did not merely give special stimulus to certain sciences like chemistry, but provided a distinctive symbolic and ideological seedbed for the mechanical philosophy. Superficially similar, but, at bottom, radically different circumstances in the low countries gave rise to a very different scientific alignment. Like much of Germanic Europe, the United Provinces were urbanized and supported a high level of economic development. But, Harold Cook shows, the liberal–Protestant politics of the Dutch favoured smaller-scale, more empirical scientific activities, such as botany, collecting, microscopy and medical inquiry, rather than the ostentatious system-building of an Athanasius Kircher or a Leibniz.[25]

No nation produced the Scientific Revolution single-handed. That ferment of knowledge was the outcome of complex and intricate cultural-chemical affinities and processes. It may well have been crucial to the development of modern science in Europe – contrast China – that distinct intellectual traditions were able to flourish in a multiplicity of polities. Edward Gibbon was soon to offer the typical Enlightenment reflection that the political pluralism of modern Europe happily prevented the reinstatement of the imperial and intellectual tyrannies of Rome (imperial and Christian) and permitted the seeding of freedom of thought.[26] And – *pace* Lakatos and Zahar – in such processes of intellectual change, time and space both counted, an issue especially tackled below by Josef Smolka in his essay on Bohemia, focusing on the court of Rudolph II. As Jerzy Dobrzycki suggests, early centres of scientific transformation, such as Renaissance Poland – rather like Tycho Brahe's Denmark or Rudolph's Prague – had declined in both political and intellectual importance by the eighteenth century. Josef Smolka's discussion of Bohemia likewise demonstrates that political and military disaster – the Thirty Years' War and the consequent imposition of intellectual uniformity, through recatholicization under the Jesuits – could terminate what had been lively milieux for scientific innovation.

By the eighteenth century, however, other nations had gained economic strength, not least Sweden and Scotland – which, as Sven Widmalm and Paul Wood show in their respective essays, were to play distinguished parts during the Enlightenment era in both consolidating the scientific endeavour through systematic teaching and diffusion, and also in pioneering 'backward' sectors, such as chemistry, natural history and the technological application of science. Above all, Enlightenment ideology increasingly stressed the value of science for national improvement.

Historians commonly wave some dimension of history in front of their readers, claiming that it is the forgotten grand arcanum, the key to Clio's mysteries. It would be foolish to contend that attention to national cultural seedbeds will resolve, once and for all, the ambiguities of the Scientific Revolution. Nevertheless, it is our conviction that the twists and turns of global scientific change will not be understood without regard for questions of indigenous language, education, communication networks, institutions, economics, social relations, politics, religious confession, patronage, and other comparable elements that can be called its 'national context'. It is no accident that the making of the modern state and of modern monarchies formed the background of the tremendous transformations constituting the making of modern science. This volume foregrounds the complex interplay between these factors, differing as they do from country to country – from state to state – and the life of scientific intelligence. We believe the result rectifies imbalances, and provides a richer canvas for viewing the Scientific Revolution.

NOTES

1 The concept 'culture' is used here in the wider, anthropological sense. See C. Geertz, *The Interpretation of Cultures* (New York, 1973). On the language of science, see J. V. Golinski, 'Language, Discourse and Science', in R. C. Olby,

G. N. Cantor, J. R. R. Christie and M. J. S. Hodge (eds.), *Companion to the History of Modern Science* (London, 1990), 110–26; L. Jordanova (ed.), *Languages of Nature: Critical Essays on Science and Literature* (London, 1986).

2 Naturally these claims beg many questions, because there remain tribal societies which operate cognitive systems for understanding and transforming nature that are in no way indebted to the chain of labours from Aristotle and Ptolemy, through Vesalius and Newton, Einstein and Crick and Watson, up to the present. For discussion of rival rationalities, see John Ziman, *Public Knowledge* (Cambridge, 1968); Michael MacDonald, 'Anthropological Perspectives on the History of Science and Medicine', in P. Corsi and P. Weindling (eds.), *Information Sources in the History of Science and Medicine* (London, 1983), 61–96.

3 And naturally this is not to deny the presence of ferocious national scientific rivalries. The point is that such rivalries take place against the background of a cosmopolitan, cooperationist ideology.

4 Imre Lakatos and Elie Zahar, 'Why Did Copernicus's Research Program Supersede Ptolemy's?', in Robert S. Westman (ed.), *The Copernican Achievement* (Berkeley, 1975), 354–83, quotation from p. 380. The historical background to Copernicus is discussed in Dobrzycki's essay in the present volume and in Robert S. Westman, 'Proof, Poetics and Patronage: Copernicus's Preface to *De revolutionibus*', in David C. Lindberg and Robert S. Westman (eds.), *Reappraisals of the Scientific Revolution* (Cambridge, 1990), 167–205. The works of Kuhn alluded to are T. S. Kuhn, *The Copernican Revolution* (Cambridge, Mass., 1957); and *idem*, *The Structure of Scientific Revolutions* (Chicago, 1962). For Bernal, see below, note 12. Our disagreement with Lakatos and Zahar is not meant to imply that we deny or minimize the importance of transformations in scientific method in the Scientific Revolution. Changes in theories and practice of observation, classification, systematization, experimentation, quantification and so forth were immense. We merely demur from the implication that these are somehow 'timeless' and merely 'in the mind'.

5 For some introduction to such factors, see, for instance, E. Eisenstein, *The Printing Press as an Agent of Change*, 2 vols. (Cambridge, 1979); William Eamon, 'From the Secrets of Nature to Public Knowledge', in Lindberg and Westman, *Reappraisals*, 333–65; Paolo L. Rossi, 'Society, Culture and the Dissemination of Learning', in Stephen Pumfrey, Paolo L. Rossi and Mauric Slawinski (eds.), *Science, Culture and Popular Belief in Renaissance Europe* (Manchester, 1991), 143–75; Michael Adas, *Machines as the Measure of Men: Science, Technology, and Ideologies of Western Dominance* (Ithaca, N.Y., 1989); John Gascoigne, 'A Reappraisal of the Role of the Universities in the Scientific Revolution', in Lindberg and Westman, *Reappraisals*, 207–60; Roger Emerson, 'The Organization of Science and its Pursuit in Early Modern Europe', in Olby, Cantor, Christie and Hodge, *Companion*, 960–79.

6 Whether the transformations in science in this period are best called a 'revolution' is a crucial question but not the central issue of this volume. For recent discussions of the value of the concept of scientific revolution and of *the* Scientific Revolution, see John A. Schuster, 'The Scientific Revolution', in Olby, Cantor, Christie and Hodge, *Companion*, 217–43; I. B. Cohen, *Revolution in Science* (Cambridge, Mass., 1985); Roy Porter, 'The Scientific Revolution: A

Spoke in the Wheel?', in Roy Porter and Mikuláš Teich (eds.), *Revolution and History* (Cambridge, 1986), 297–316; *idem*, 'Introduction' to Pumfrey, Rossi and Slawinski, *Science, Culture and Popular Belief*, 1–15; David C. Lindberg, 'Conceptions of the Scientific Revolution from Bacon to Butterfield: A Preliminary Sketch', in Lindberg and Westman, *Reappraisals*, 1–26.

7 Herbert Butterfield, *The Origins of Modern Science, 1300–1800* (London, 1950); C. C. Gillispie, *The Edge of Objectivity: An Essay in the History of Scientific Ideas* (Princeton, 1960); A. R. Hall, *The Scientific Revolution, 1500–1800* (London, 1954); *idem*, 'Merton Revisited, or Science and Society in the Seventeenth Century', *History of Science* 2 (1963), 1–16; *idem*, 'On Whiggism', *History of Science* 21 (1983), 45–59; M. B. Hall, *The Scientific Renaissance* (London, 1962); Alexandre Koyré, *From the Closed World to the Infinite Universe* (Baltimore, 1957).

8 For the 'internalist/externalist' debate, see H. Kragh, *An Introduction to the Historiography of Science* (Cambridge, 1987); Steven Shapin, 'Social Uses of Science', in G. S. Rousseau and Roy Porter (eds.), *The Ferment of Knowledge: Perspectives on Scholarship of Eighteenth Century Science* (Cambridge, 1980), 93–142.

9 Scientific developments in national context pertaining to Soviet-type socialist countries have received largely uncritical attention by indigenous historians. This does not apply to the broad-ranging history of astronomy, mathematics, physics and chemistry in Bohemia and Moravia by J. Folta, Z. Horský, L. Nový, I. Seidlerová, J. Smolka and M. Teich, *Dějiny exaktních věd v českých zemích do konce 19 století* ['History of science in the Czech lands to the end of the nineteenth century'] (Prague, 1961). There is a summary in English.

10 See Frances Yates, *Giordano Bruno and the Hermetic Tradition* (London, 1964); I. Couliano, *Eros and Magic in the Renaissance*, trans. by Margaret Cook (Chicago and London, 1987); Patrick Curry (ed.), *Astrology, Science and Society: Historical Essays* (Woodbridge, Suffolk, 1987); *idem, Prophecy and Power: Astrology in Early Modern England* (Cambridge, 1989); *idem*, 'Astrology in Early Modern England: The Making of a Vulgar Knowledge', in Pumfrey, Rossi and Slawinski, *Science, Culture and Popular Belief*, 274–92; for magic, see Keith Thomas, *Religion and the Decline of Magic: Studies in Popular Beliefs in Sixteenth and Seventeenth Century England* (London, 1971; repr. Harmondsworth, 1978); John Henry, 'Magic and Science in the Sixteenth and Seventeenth Centuries', in Olby, Cantor, Christie and Hodge, 583–96; Brian P. Copenhaver, 'Natural Magic, Hermetism, and Occultism in Early Modern Science', in Lindberg and Westman, 261–302; H. Leventhal, *In the Shadow of the Enlightenment: Occultism and Renaissance Science in Eighteenth-Century America* (New York, 1976); Robert Darnton, *Mesmerism and the End of the Enlightenment in France* (Cambridge, Mass., 1968); M. J. T. Dobbs, *The Foundations of Newton's Alchemy* (Cambridge, 1975); Germana Ernst, 'Astrology, Religion and Politics in Counter-Reformation Rome', in Pumfrey, Rossi and Slawinski, *Science, Culture and Popular Belief*, 249–73; Keith Hutchison, 'What Happened to Occult Qualities in the Scientific Revolution?', *Isis* 73 (1982), 233–53; Michael MacDonald, 'Science, Magic and Folklore', in J. F. Andrews (ed.), *William Shakespeare: His World, His Work, His Influence*, 1 (New York, 1985), 175–94; Brian Vickers (ed.), *Occult and Scientific Mentalities in the Renaissance* (Cambridge, 1984).

11 See, for instance, for a popular cosmology, C. Ginzburg, *The Cheese and the*

Worms: the Cosmos of the Sixteenth Century (London, 1980); or, for the intertwining of natural knowledge with social knowledge, David Warren Sabean, *Power in the Blood: Popular Culture and Village Discourse in Early Modern Germany* (Cambridge, 1984); Peter Burke, *Popular Culture in Early Modern Europe* (London, 1978).

12 See Mikuláš Teich, 'Reflecting on the Golden Jubilee of Bernal's *The Social Function of Science*', *History of Science* 28 (1990), 411–18; J. D. Bernal, *The Social Function of Science* (London, 1939); *idem, Science in History* (London, 1954); Boris Hessen, 'The Social and Economic Roots of Newton's *Principia*', in *Science at the Crossroads* (1931; repr. London, 1971).

13 Robert K. Merton, *Science, Technology and Society in Seventeenth Century England* (New York, 2nd edn., 1970). For further attempts to relate science and religious thought, see R. Hooykaas, *Religion and the Rise of Modern Science* (Edinburgh, 1973); S. Jaki, *The Road of Science and the Ways to God* (Edinburgh, 1978). For the theological underpinnings see Amos Funkenstein, *Theology and the Scientific Imagination from the Middle Ages to the Seventeenth Century* (Princeton, 1986); and, for surveys of this field, Pietro Corsi, 'History of Science, History of Philosophy, and History of Theology', in P. Corsi and P. Weindling (eds.), *Information Sources in the History of Science and Medicine* (London, 1983), 3–28; and John Hedley Brooke, 'Science and Religion', in Olby, Cantor, Christie and Hodge, *Companion*, 763–82.

14 J. Needham, *Science and Civilisation in China* (Cambridge, 1954–); for evaluation, see Nathan Sivin, 'Why the Scientific Revolution did not take place in China – or didn't it?', in E. Mendelsohn (ed.), *Transformation and Tradition in the Sciences* (Cambridge, 1985), 531–4.

15 See Steven Shapin and Simon Schaffer, *Leviathan and the Air Pump* (Princeton, 1985); James Jacob, *Robert Boyle and the English Revolution* (New York, 1977). For the politics of micro-science, see Bruno Latour, *Science in Action* (Milton Keynes, 1987).

16 M. C. Jacob, *The Newtonians and the English Revolution, 1689–1720* (Ithaca, N.Y. 1976); see also *idem, The Radical Enlightenment: Pantheists, Freemasons and Republicans* (London, 1981).

17 A. R. Hall, *Philosophers at War: The Quarrel Between Newton and Leibniz* (Cambridge, 1980); S. Shapin, 'Of Gods and Kings: Natural Philosophy and Politics in the Leibniz-Clarke Disputes', *Isis* 72 (1981), 187–215; Henry Guerlac, 'Some Areas for Further Newtonian Studies', *History of Science* 17 (1979), 75–101.

18 For instance, in *The Great Instauration: Science, Medicine and Reform, 1626–1660* (London, 1975) Charles Webster links scientific developments to the Puritan revolution. Underpinning much recent work on the politics of scientific knowledge has been the tradition of the sociology of knowledge associated with the 'Edinburgh strong programme'. See for instance D. Bloor, *Knowledge and Social Imagery* (London, 1976); H. Collins, *Changing Order. Replication and Induction in Scientific Practice* (Beverly Hills and London, 1985); B. Barnes, *Interests and the Growth of Knowledge* (London, 1977). The writings of Michel Foucault have equally drawn attention to the relations between science/knowledge and power. See Michel Foucault, *Power/Knowledge: Selected Interviews and Other Writings 1972–1977* (Brighton, 1977).

19 T. Rabb, *The Struggle for Stability in Early Modern Europe* (New York, 1975).

20 See V. Kiernan, *State and Society in Europe 1550–1650* (Oxford, 1980); J. Shennan, *Liberty and Order in Early Modern Europe: The Subject and the State, 1650–1800* (London, 1986); Perry Anderson, *Lineages of the Absolutist State* (London, 1974); F. Braudel, *Civilization and Capitalism, 15th–18th Century*, I: *The Structures of Everyday Life*; II: *The Wheels of Commerce*; III: *The Perspective of the World* (New York, 1985); J. De Vries, *European Urbanization, 1500–1800* (Cambridge, Mass., 1984). On the relative failure of historians of science and general historians to talk to each other, see Roy Porter, 'The History of Science and the History of Society', in Olby, Cantor, Christie and Hodge, *Companion*, 32–46.

21 Olby, Cantor, Christie and Hodge, *Companion* – the essay referred to is Brigitte Schroeder-Gudehus, 'Nationalism and Internationalism', 909–19; Lindberg and Westman, *Reappraisals*; M. Crosland (ed.), *The Emergence of Science in Western Europe* (London, 1975). An older work that brings out national differences in style of scientific thought is John T. Merz, *History of European Thought in the Nineteenth Century*, 4 vols. (Edinburgh, 1896–1914).

22 It is recognized, of course, that the notion of 'nation' in the early modern era is fraught with historiographical difficulties. See the Foreword and Introduction respectively to Mikuláš Teich and Roy Porter (eds.), *The National Question in European Historical Context* (Cambridge, 1993) and *The Renaissance in National Context* (Cambridge, 1991).

23 Peter Burke, '*Heu Domine, Adsunt Turcae*: A Sketch for the Social History of Post-Medieval Latin', in Peter Burke and Roy Porter (eds.), *Language, Self and Society: the Social History of Language* (Cambridge, 1991), 23–49.

24 See further Mario Biagioli, 'Galileo and Patronage', *History of Science* 28 (1990), 1–62.

25 For the material background that underpins Cook's reading of Dutch culture, see Simon Schama, *The Embarrassment of Riches: An Interpretation of Dutch Culture in the Golden Age* (London, 1988).

26 See Roy Porter, *Edward Gibbon: Making History* (London, 1988), Conclusion.

SCIENTIFIC REVOLUTION, SOCIAL BRICOLAGE, AND ETIQUETTE

MARIO BIAGIOLI

EARLY modern Italian science has received and continues to receive so much attention that no summary or synopsis could do justice to the available historiography.[1] Therefore, this essay does not try to offer a synthetic picture of the development of the various scientific disciplines in Italy between 1500 and 1700. Instead, taking the title of this book seriously, I will try to locate some of the conditions that framed the development and subsequent crisis of Italian science during the Scientific Revolution. Some comparison of the cultural and political contexts of Italy and other European countries will help identify possible connections between different national contexts and different aspects or phases of the Scientific Revolution.[2] The essay concludes by suggesting a range of homologies between the development of scientific discourse, authorship and institutionalization during the Scientific Revolution and what Norbert Elias has called the 'civilizing process' – the development of court society, political absolutism and the modern state.[3]

DECLINE OR MARGINALIZATION?

For some time, the crisis of Italian science after Galileo's death was conveniently explained away by the religious obscurantism that was claimed to have set in after his trial in 1633. The attribution of such a central causal role to the trial reflects a tendency in the older historiography to turn Galileo's career (with its brilliant start and abrupt ending) into the epitome of Italian modern national science. While older histories of English and French science may reflect a Whiggish orientation stemming at least to some extent from the authors' appreciation of the successes of their modern national science, in the case of Italy Galileo (rather than the state of modern Italian science) became a mythical point of historiographical reference.[4] Rather than writing the

history of science as leading to a successful present, the older Italian
historiography tended to present late seventeenth-century science as
sucked back in time by the black hole of Galileo's trial.

Recent work has shown that such a simple explanation will not do:
late seventeenth-century Italian science cannot be reified into a 'scuola
galileiana' that sank with its hero.[5] True, Italian science did become
increasingly marginalized from the European scene after 1670 or so, yet
this crisis was not as drastic as previously suggested nor did it affect all
scientific disciplines. For instance, the Church's condemnation of Galileo
did not affect disciplines whose subject matter did not impinge on
cosmology and theology, and it has been recently argued that even its
influence on astronomy was less severe than previously assumed.[6]
Moreover, observational astronomy boomed during the later seventeenth century (mostly due to the new astronomical telescopes produced
by the Italian instrument-makers Fontana, Divini, and Campani) and
Giovanni Domenico Cassini was arguably the leading figure of this sub-
discipline.[7] Similar scenarios of non-declining scientific productivity can
be observed in disciplines as diverse as medicine and electricity.[8]

Then, if we consider the geographical distribution of scientific activity,
we notice that it spread more evenly over the Italian peninsula
(especially in the centre and south) during the seventeenth century.[9]
Similarly, institutional support of scientific activities does not seem to
have declined in Italy after the death of Galileo. Not only did Prince
Leopold de' Medici begin to gather, in 1657, the Accademia del
Cimento (perhaps the first scientific academy dedicated to experimental
practices), but it seems that the Italian branch of the Society of Jesus
maintained its support for science during the rest of the century.[10] In
short, not only did science not leave Italy after 1633, but if we look at the
statistics of Italian publications in the mathematical sciences during the
seventeenth century, we notice that productivity peaked in the period
1661–70.[11]

This said, I am not trying to depict a polemically rosy picture of post-
Galilean Italian science. It is undeniable that, by 1680, the centres of
European science were no longer Padua or Florence, but Paris and
London. Nevertheless, evidence of the continuing development of Italian
science illustrates the problems of notions such as 'decline' or 'progress'
– notions that imply the use of Whiggish (or nostalgic) terms of reference.
Instead, by thinking of scientific change as an open-ended and non-
directed process, we may avoid the problems posed by notions such as
'progress' or 'decline' while acknowledging that the differentiated
development of science may reflect the different environments (the
regional and national contexts) in which it happened to be situated.[12] I

propose to analyse some of these processes and to identify some of the features of the seventeenth-century Italian context that were responsible for that pattern of scientific change that (when viewed from our present point of view) appears as the 'decline' or 'marginalization' of Italian science at the end of the Scientific Revolution.

THE NEW CONTEXT

Economic and political historians agree on the drastic decline of Italy's importance after 1600. By the beginning of the seventeenth century, the duchy of Milan had long lost its independence and had become a territory controlled by Spain. Tuscany was still rich but it was also turning into a provincial and agricultural state with little international relevance. The Florence where Galileo died in 1642 was much poorer (and much less populated) than the city where he grew up. The income of the Medici grand dukes in 1625 seems to have been about half of what it was in 1590.[13]

Urbino – once the seat of the prestigious court described in Castiglione's *Book of the Courtier* – experienced a sharp economic decline at the end of the sixteenth century and disappeared from the political map in 1631 when it was finally incorporated in the Papal State. After having been one of the most sophisticated Italian courts in the fifteenth and sixteenth centuries, Mantua (the court to which Galileo tried to migrate in 1604) lost its importance and eventually its independence around 1629.[14] Venice remained quite powerful, yet it too was experiencing a sharp decline in wealth and political relevance.[15]

Venice's decline was exemplified by its reduced control over the central and eastern Mediterranean – a sea that used to be the busy freeway of east-west trade.[16] Writing to Galileo in 1611, Giovanfrancesco Sagredo told him that, in returning from Syria where he had been residing as the Venetian ambassador, he had to land in Marseilles because the Venetian navy could no longer keep the Adriatic Sea free of pirates.[17] In any case, the commercial importance of the Mediterranean was quickly declining as a result of the opening of oceanic trade routes. Galileo's system of determining longitude at sea, which relied on the satellites of Jupiter as astronomical clocks, was not put to use by his Medici patrons, whose fleet was largely symbolic. Instead, he tried, with his patrons' help, to sell his method first to Spain and then to the Netherlands – two countries that, because of their interest in oceanic trading, had advertised large prizes for the solution of the problem of determining longitude at sea.[18]

Only the Papal State was able to delay its participation in the overall decline of the political and economic relevance of the Italian peninsula; it actually grew (temporarily) stronger with its annexations of various smaller states. However, by about 1650, even the popes had to face a sharp decline in their international power. As shown by Urban VIII's troubles during the Thirty Years' War (troubles that contributed significantly to the context of Galileo's trial), the Pope could no longer even act as the diplomatic arbiter between the great European rulers.

The marginalization of Italian science in this period and the contemporary emergence of France and England as the new scientific centres was linked to these broad politico-economical changes. This is supported by a comparable crisis in other aspects of Italian culture. Francis Haskell has described the decline of Italian and Roman art and artistic patronage after the death of Urban VIII in 1644, and its subsequent migration toward northern Europe. Such a decline was epitomized, in the 1660s, by the (temporary) move to Paris of the symbol of the Roman baroque: Gian Lorenzo Bernini.[19] As many Italian and Roman artists were quick to realize, Louis XIV, rather than the Pope, was the new great patron.[20] Tellingly, Louis XIV was able to summon to Paris in the same years the best Italian sculptor and architect (Bernini) and the best astronomer (Cassini).[21]

LEGITIMIZING THE NEW SCIENCE

Although these considerations suggest a strong link between Italy's politico-economic decline and the crisis of its science during the later part of the seventeenth century, one should not assume a direct causal relationship between the development of science and the presence of cash-abundant patrons or of thriving manufactures. Without denying that such a relationship holds true in many cases, we should not forget that patrons tended to be particularly concerned with (and to spend to maintain) the visibility of their *magnificentia* precisely when their economic status was declining. In seventeenth-century Italy, we find that the most interesting scientific authors and activities were sponsored by economically declining patrons.

It was not Ferdinand I – the last grand duke of Tuscany with a strong militaristic, colonial, and technological bent – who patronized Galileo, but his son Cosimo II – the ruler under whom Tuscany became a provincial agricultural state.[22] Similarly, Prince Leopold de' Medici sponsored the Accademia del Cimento (as well as a remarkable art-collecting programme) at a time when Florence's power had drastically (and permanently) declined.[23] Federico Cesi – the founder of the Accademia dei Lincei in 1603 – embarked in a costly enterprise just when his family (like all the other families of the Roman baronage) was being bled to financial ruin by the increasing concentration of political and financial power in the hands of the new papal families.[24]

Therefore, rather than seek a simple relationship between general categories like 'science', 'economy', 'culture' and 'politics', we may try to break down these categories and consider the *processes* through which *different* types of science fitted *specific* audiences and patrons and, second, how these *different* scientific practices needed *specific* institutional settings, forms of social legitimation and financial support. In doing so, I will try to indicate how the development of political absolutism and of the related power-image of the prince framed science's options for patronage and social legitimation.

The earliest scientific institutions we know of (the botanical gardens and the theatres of anatomy that emerged in several Italian cities in the mid-sixteenth century), or the early technical corps (like the *capitani di parte* operating in Florence from Dante's time), were public institutions sponsored primarily because of their usefulness to medicine or to the technico-military needs of the *community*.[25] Other scientific practices, by contrast, were much more appealing to *individual* princely patrons not primarily because of their practical usefulness but because they could effectively contribute to the patrons' status and image.[26]

In 1610, for instance, the Medici did not offer Galileo an unusually well-paid position at court because of the usefulness or Copernican relevance of his astronomical discoveries. They gave him a stipend of a thousand *scudi* a year and the title of Philosopher and Mathematician of the Grand Duke because he was able to present his discoveries as emblems of Medici power and dynastic continuity.[27] In short, Galileo's unusual success reflected his ability to offer the Medici something that was not a *generic* service (that could have been delivered by anybody) but something that was *exclusively* distinctive of the Medici's image and status.

This type of scientific patronage cannot be dismissed as historically insignificant, a mere sign of the frivolousness of baroque princes. On the contrary, a scientific practitioner's ability to play on aristocratic codes of distinction and present discoveries and practices within that discourse was crucial in overcoming the lower social and cognitive status of innovative scientific disciplines like astronomy and anatomy. Being represented as inferior in social and epistemological status to philosophy and medicine (respectively), astronomy and anatomy were seen as unable to challenge the traditional views held by those more respected disciplines. However, the 'status gap' that hindered the acceptance of scientific innovation could be effectively bridged by obtaining the patronage of high-status patrons like the Medici – a patronage relationship that could lift the social status of the client.[28]

As was first indicated by Robert Westman, the legitimation of Copernican astronomy entailed a re-drawing of the boundary and hierarchy between technical astronomy, natural philosophy, and theology – the 'Queen of the liberal arts'.[29] The Copernicans did not limit themselves to a mathematical *description* of the cosmos (the traditional domain of technical astronomy) but made claims about its *physical structure* and about the *causes* of some celestial phenomena (claims that traditionally pertained to the natural philosopher). By relying on the higher status and epistemological credibility conferred upon them by the received disciplinary hierarchy, the philosophers countered what they perceived as the astronomers' 'disciplinary trespassing' by dismissing the legitimacy of their claims and methodology, arguing that the astronomers had applied their tools to a domain that was not their own. Analogous tensions, perceived invasions and methodological disputes took place in other fields where the domains of natural philosophy and mathematics overlapped, such as in mechanics and hydrostatics.[30]

A strategy often adopted by astronomers and mathematicians to circumvent the status gap between themselves and the philosophers was simply to move to a different institution – to a different social space where the social and cognitive status of their discipline could be freed from the constraints of traditional disciplinary hierarchies. As shown by the careers of some German and Italian Copernicans, the princely court was such an institution.[31] At court, one's social status and credibility depended less on one's discipline and more on one's favour with the prince. This higher socio-disciplinary status could then help the mathematicians-astronomers defend their new hierarchy-disrupting world-views.

A comparable gap in social status and cognitive authority existed between theoretical medicine and surgery. Several of the medical achievements of the Scientific Revolution were connected to the sixteenth-century revival of the investigative study of anatomy (quite conspicuous in Italian universities) and of its teaching through dissection. Before then, anatomy was treated as a subsidiary component of medical training. It was seen as a means to illustrate and demonstrate the physicians' doctrine rather than as a tool for discovery. As shown by several frontispieces of late medieval anatomy texts, the surgeon was usually not seen as an independent researcher but rather as the physician's manual assistant.

The development of investigative anatomy was not unproblematic. To practise 'hands-on' anatomy, one needed to be skilled in surgery – a discipline that, because of its mechanical connotation, had a low social and cognitive status.[32] Like philosophers who claimed for themselves the right to *explain* the causes of the astronomical phenomena *described* by technical astronomers, physicians – by relying on the hierarchy of medical practices – acted as if they alone could *explain* what the surgeons had *observed* through their manual skills. Quite simply, physicians (or philosophers) were the head and surgeons (or astronomers) were the hand. Or, to put it differently, both astronomy and surgery stopped at the 'surface' of natural processes, while philosophers and physicians (endowed with 'theory') could go much 'deeper' and uncover the real causes of the observable phenomena.[33]

The analogy between astronomy and anatomy can also be traced at the level of the tactics adopted by their practitioners in order to legitimize themselves and their disciplines. Like Galileo who managed to transform himself into a philosopher by representing the satellites of Jupiter as a dynastic emblem of the Medici, the leaders of the revival of anatomy tried to improve the status of their discipline by representing their practices as fitting the codes of gentlemanly and aristocratic culture.[34] John Stephen of Calcar's large and artistically etched anatomical illustrations for Vesalius' *De humani corporis fabrica* (which he published in 1543 while he was *explicator chirurgiae* at Padua) reflects, I think, strategies comparable to Galileo's.[35] By depicting skeletons and skinned bodies as elegant Classical sculptures placed against an appropriate backdrop of ruins, Vesalius and his cohorts were trying to bring about a radical change in the social connotation of their profession.[36] Judging from the size (a folio volume of 663 pages), quality and cost of Vesalius' masterpiece, it was not only a scientific text, but also a status-statement and a patronage artefact.[37] Just as the increased social status of the court Copernicans was a resource they could use to legitimize their new theories (and new socio-professional identities), the higher status anatomists could obtain by representing themselves as *virtuosi* (rather than barbers) was crucial in establishing investigative anatomy as a cognitively legitimate branch of medicine.[38]

To summarize, the Scientific Revolution was at least two revolutions in one. Together with the radical conceptual changes that took place in the fields of astronomy, physics, medicine and methodology, a new disciplinary hierarchy that legitimized the new theories and methods was slowly established. The restructuring of disciplinary boundaries, hierarchies and status was made possible both by the practitioners' migrating to institutions that allowed for higher social status and mobility, and by the establishment of new social spaces (such as scientific academies) through which practitioners could legitimize their activities and emerging socio-professional identities.

OPTIONS AND CONSTRAINTS

The acceptance of new world-views depended also on the social legitimation they derived from the 'matches' between the practices of the scientific practitioners and their patrons' cultural taste and 'distinction' – a process that has been carefully studied by Pierre Bourdieu in the modern period.[39] However, such matches were difficult to come by. Gaining support and legitimation for a new theory or discipline implied an often opportunistic rearrangement of elements of pre-existing social scenarios. Let me sketch a few examples of these 'social bricolages'.

Quite probably, the cities and universities of Bologna and Padua viewed anatomy theatres and botanical gardens primarily as educational facilities. However, these institutions also had other social meanings. Not only were they signs of the university's status as a leading academic centre, but they were also city 'monuments' and 'mirabilia' that quickly found their way into tourist guides.[40] Moreover, anatomy theatres tended to become sites of important civic rituals. For instance, in Pisa, Rome, Ferrara, Bologna and (less frequently) Padua, public anatomy lessons took place during the carnival festivities. As shown by Giovanna Ferrari, the Bolognese public dissections (performed in the anatomy theatre) were also a civic ritual through which the government and the university publicly recognized and confirmed each other's role and jurisdictions.[41]

These scientific institutions had further meanings for the practitioners. Although botanical gardens and anatomy theatres were professionally important institutions that provided financial long-term support for the practitioners in charge of them (a support no longer tied to the accidents of an individual patron's life), their establishment was even more important because of the status they could confer on the disciplines they housed. In short, they were much more than buildings accommodating students and providing instructors with possibly adequate teaching facilities and decent salaries. As publicly supported institutions, anatomy theatres and botanical gardens legitimized and stabilized emerging (or previously less legitimate) branches of medicine.[42]

The establishment, around 1595, of the anatomy theatre at Bologna offers an interesting analogy with the institutional migrations of Copernicans from universities to courts outlined above. As shown by

Ferrari, the anatomy theatre was founded at a time when the city was trying to restrict the privileges of the university. By establishing and funding the theatre, the city was also trying to wrest control over the public anatomy lesson away from the university of scholars. Teachers of anatomy (who had often been marginalized within the university of scholars) profited from this institutional struggle and, like Copernicans who gained higher socio-professional status and credibility by moving to court and becoming clients of a prince, they welcomed the new and more distinguished patron.[43] What these examples have in common is that the migration to a new institution made possible the re-negotiation of the practitioners' socio-professional status through their playing into some sort of *raison d'état* – be it the celebration of the image of the absolutist prince or the support of the state's attempt to extend its centralized control over formerly independent institutions.

Just as princely courts made it possible for sophisticated mathematicians like Galileo to improve their social status by displaying dialectical and courtly skills during court disputations, anatomy theatres provided practitioners with a stage where they could perform their 'anatomical plays' and present themselves as *virtuosi* by displaying their *surgical nonchalance*. In a sense, public dissections were the performative equivalent of the artistic etchings of dissected bodies in Vesalius' *Fabrica*.[44] Reporting on the dissections performed by Niels Steno (who would later be employed at the Medici court) in a Parisian scientific academy, a French *virtuoso* wrote to a friend that 'M. Steno is the rage here' and

> When I called us apprentices next to M. Steno, I had reason, for I have never seen such dexterity. He made us see everything there is to see in the construction of the eye – without putting either the eye, the scissors, or his one other small instrument anywhere but on his one hand, which he kept constantly exposed to the gathered company.[45]

The anatomy theatre was also a 'sacred space' – a space in which a disturbing and usually unacceptable practice like human dissection could have its social connotation inverted. What was a crime outside the theatre became science once it entered it. Once in the theatre, the dissected corpse was no longer a defiled body but rather some sort of 'monument' (almost a 'sacrifice') to the new science of anatomy.[46] That such a 'sacralization' of the 'profane' was a process involving major rearrangements of social taxonomies and values may be deduced from the customary scheduling of public anatomies during the carnival, that is, in a period in which society was already 'upside-down'.

The drastic inside-outside distinction cast by the boundaries of that space mirrored the distinction between the professional insiders and outsiders. In this sense, the theatre was a tangible image of anatomy as a profession and of its social and cognitive legitimacy.[47] This relationship between space and professional legitimation may explain why – in the Bologna case studied by Ferrari – some of the audience watched the dissection wearing carnival masks. It may be that the mask-wearing spectators did not have medical credentials and therefore – lacking the professional 'virtue' to transform the profane into the sacred – they had to watch the dissection *incognito*.[48] Wearing masks while participating in an activity that, under normal circumstances, would have been inappropriate to one's status was a standard option of etiquette discussed in Castiglione's *The Book of the Courtier*.[49]

Similar links between scientific practices, status dynamics, and institutions can be found in another of the earliest sites of science: the museum of natural history. As shown by Paula Findlen and Giuseppe Olmi, collecting was a deeply status-laden practice.[50] Museums were nodes within networks of exchange and patronage in which collectors, clients and patrons reproduced and negotiated their status as they exchanged natural specimens as gifts.[51] As Findlen puts it: 'We can imagine the museum as a social diagram whose contents concretely expressed the nature of the relations between patrons and clients, donors and recipients.'[52] In a sense, museums were 'banks of status' in and around which gifts–specimens were displayed or exchanged in the same way that money is deposited in and circulated by modern banks. Like Galileo, who gained social status by contributing to the Medici's image through his donation to them of his astronomical discoveries, smaller collectors gained status by contributing to the great collector's image, that is, by donating their specimens and having them exhibited in his museum. However, there were important differences in the practices and options of social legitimation of Galileo, the anatomists and the natural history collectors.

As Galileo was quick to realize, his scientific discoveries could be best rewarded by an *individual* absolute prince rather than by *corporate* patrons like republics or cities.[53] By fitting his *exceptional* discoveries into the codes of courtly patronage, he managed to enter into a *personal* relationship with a great patron. Because of this 'closeness' to an absolute prince, his social and epistemological status could be increased more effectively than through the patronage of an impersonal patron like the republic of Venice – Galileo's former employer. However, if such a personal patronage relationship (based on an *exceptional* discovery) made it possible for the client to go up in the socio-professional scale, it also made it very difficult (if not impossible) to institutionalize that patronage and extend it to non-exceptional scientific practices.[54]

Moreover, although the Bolognese anatomists, the natural history collectors and Galileo all gained status from contributing to the image of their patrons, Galileo's 'gifts' could not be delivered routinely at every carnival (as with the anatomists) nor could they be included in a museum (as with the collectors). His gifts to the Medici could not be produced, shelved and exposed at will. Far from being a problem, their non-ready-madeness confirmed their exceptionality: this, in turn, made them fit the image of an absolute (i.e., eminently *distinct*) prince. In fact, the 'museum' where the Medicean Stars were exhibited was the cosmos itself, and only absolute rulers provided with suitably dynastic mythologies linking them to celestial gods could represent that space as 'their own'.[55] Consequently, Galileo's gifts would have been 'above the head' (and outside the patronage space) of most patrons.[56] Only a very few patrons were socially equipped to squeeze image out of Galileo's discoveries.[57]

In short, although the 'social bricolage' achieved by anatomists and natural history collectors was structured by the same dynamics that framed Galileo's negotiations with the Medici, the resulting bricolages were quite different. The type of science they practised (and the way the world was) demarcated what type of 'gifts' they could produce. In turn, those 'gifts' matched the patronage possibilities of specific patrons and shaped the type of patronage relations (institutional or personal) that would ensue. To use a chemical analogy, different patrons, disciplines (at different stages of articulation) and scientific practices had different patronage 'valences'.

Although it may be impossible to produce some sort of 'Mendeleev Table' mapping the relationship between different types of scientific practices, disciplinary hierarchies, types of patrons and patronage, institutional spaces and social status, these examples have indicated some of the protocols of 'social bricolage' through which emerging scientific practices tried to gain socio-epistemological legitimation. Let me now turn to analyse some of the ways in which these processes were played out in the politico-economical scenarios of late seventeenth-century Italy.

PROVINCIAL ABSOLUTISM AND THE LEGITIMATION OF SCIENCE

The scientific practices whose legitimacy and public usefulness had been long established and recognized through institutionalization were not drastically affected by the new politico-economic conjuncture. For instance, it does not seem that the decline of the Italian economy caused the closing down of botanical gardens or anatomy theatres. That Italian medicine continued to produce top-rank scientists like Francesco Redi and Marcello Malpighi (and, later, Lazzaro Spallanzani) may confirm the relative stability of the 'ecological' and institutional niche that medicine had established for itself.[58]

More unstable were the scenarios faced by the practitioners of those disciplines that – like astronomy – had not yet been given an institutional setting outside of the university but had seen *individual* practitioners sponsored by *individual* princes. Moreover, no Italian mathematician after Galileo managed to maintain the important title of 'philosopher' (a crucial resource for the cognitive legitimation of the mathematical analysis of physical phenomena) which he had obtained from the Medici in 1610. When, for instance, after 1642, Evangelista Torricelli was chosen as Galileo's successor, Ferdinand II gave him only the title of '*Mathematician* of the Grand Duke'.

That no other Italian astronomer managed to reproduce a bricolage similar to Galileo's is not only a matter of princely taste. In fact, the constitution of the solar system made it impossible for other astronomers to come up with discoveries as *spectacular* as Galileo's.[59] Moreover, his discoveries – being many, stunning, concentrated in a short period of time, and happening when nobody expected them – had made patrons and audiences less impressed by further discoveries. Although the debate on Saturn's rings attracted much attention, prince Leopold de' Medici – the patron to whom Huygens dedicated his *Systema Saturnium* (1659) – did not react to it nearly as enthusiastically as his father had welcomed Galileo's discoveries of 1610.[60] Similarly, the finding of the first satellite of Saturn by Huygens in 1655, and Cassini's finding of more in 1671/2 and 1684, produced little patronage interest.[61]

Moreover, although many observational astronomers continued to scan the sky with increasingly powerful telescopes (these by 1665 could be as long as twelve metres), the causes of planetary motion was the theoretical problem at the centre of many astronomers' and mathematicians' attention. And this was a technical problem that could not have been turned easily into a courtly marvel. For instance, Newton's mechanics as presented in the *Principia* could not easily have been turned into something as eminently dedicable (and tailored to a specific great patron) as the satellites of Jupiter.[62] In short, after Galileo, the conditions for 'bricolage' between astronomy and the image of the princely patrons were no longer there partly because of the way the solar system happened to be and because of the direction taken by astronomical work. Finally, because Italian princes were not the rulers of large, commercially or militarily active states, they probably did not see a good investment in establishing scientific academies whose members could also act as technico-scientific consultants.

To summarize, Italian princely patrons declined to patronize the newer trends in astronomy because these seemed less than spectacular; they could not reward observational astronomy (as they had done in Galileo's time) because spectacular discoveries were exceedingly hard to come by; and they were not interested in patronizing science in general because the states they were ruling did not need such technico-scientific expertise. Let me now test this analysis against the evidence provided by a different national context: late seventeenth-century France.

FROM COSIMO II TO LOUIS XIV

Louis XIV's decision to create the Académie des Sciences in 1666 was not exclusively motivated by his belief that science would solve the technical problems of his kingdom and foster its manufactures. In any case, the Académie did not distinguish itself for the practical usefulness of its activities and findings during the early decades of its activity.[63]

By establishing the Académie, Louis XIV did not offer an institutional setting to *one specific science* (like an anatomy theatre), nor did he reward one *individual* practitioner for producing an astonishing discovery and representing it as an effective emblem of royal power (like the Medici with Galileo). Because of the representation of himself as *the* absolute and all-powerful sovereign, Louis XIV's image would not have benefited much from receiving the dedication of a scientific discovery from an individual client unless it was *absolutely* marvellous and *absolutely* suited to his own image. Unfortunately, the solar system did not provide astronomers with the resources (lily-shaped sunspots, say) to produce such an absolutely fitting image.[64] Louis XIV's power image could be enhanced only by artefacts (paintings, histories, poems) *representing himself* and his absolute power and not just *dedicated to him*. Louis' own image was the sole adequate representation of his power.[65]

Instead, Louis' grand patronage gesture toward science can be better understood by viewing it as indissolubly tied to the 'academic package' that Colbert proposed him, and by looking at how Colbert's project perfectly fitted the representation of the Roi Soleil's absolute power.[66] In fact, since he was trying to present himself as the most powerful and absolute of all sovereigns, it was best for him to be perceived as controlling *all* sciences and major arts by institutionalizing them under his protection. This was a strategy that suited his power image much better than the patronage of *one* specific (though possibly exceptionally conspicuous) practitioner of *one specific* science. In short, by establishing the Académie des Sciences together with the other royal academies, Louis presented himself as having conquered one more realm: the *republic of letters*.

Therefore, the shift from the reward of *a specific and well-fitting marvel* and its producer (or the institutionalization of *one specific scientific discipline*) to the establishment of a scientific corporation comprehending *all sciences* was also caused by the changes in the codes of representations of princely power resulting from the formation of large and increasingly centralized states like France. The 'patronage valence' of the great prince had changed between Cosimo II and Louis XIV. Let me expand on this.

The Medici patronized Galileo because of the remarkable dynastic monuments he had made out of his astronomical discoveries, but were not interested in sponsoring any long-term Copernican 'research programme'. Dynastic monuments would enhance the Medici's image; Copernican astronomy would not. Although the politics of representation of princely power that informed Louis XIV's image were quite similar to those that framed that of the Medici rulers, the specificity of the French context led to a very different scenario of scientific patronage. As shown by the monumental astronomical observatory Louis had built at the outskirts of Paris, he viewed the Académie des Sciences as a monument to himself and to his own power (to the point where the monumentality of the building collided with the practical needs of the working scientists).[67] Similarly, Louis wanted to include all the sciences under his patronage so as to demonstrate his 'absolute' control over them. This gesture resulted in an institution because only a conspicuously walled institution could act (and last) as a monument to his power.

The Medici rewarded Galileo because he helped to 'naturalize' their rule by showing that it had been 'written in the sky'. Louis behaved as if he did not need naturalizing representations of his power.[68] The naturalness of his power was an axiom and not something in need of demonstration. Consequently, he did not need a scientist to contribute (*via* nature) to his image. Louis' founding of the Académie des Sciences was not a recognition of a 'gift' received from a scientist – as it had been with the Medici. Louis did everything by himself, unsolicited, like an unmoved mover. He gave an institution to the scientists because, by doing so, he was not returning a gift but simply displaying his own absolute power. He was obliged by his greatness.

Louis' necessity to present himself as endowed with absolute power and therefore owing nothing to anybody is exemplified by the medal he ordered to be struck to celebrate Cassini's discovery of the satellites of

Saturn. Interestingly, Cassini's name is nowhere to be found on that medal. Instead, the discovery was attributed to the 'learned men whom the King maintained at the Observatory'. Through this erasure of the individual author and his replacement with an anonymous collective identified only in terms of its dependence on the Roi Soleil, Louis was represented as the ultimate author (in the sense of source of legitimation) of the discovery. The medal's audience was expected to perceive Cassini and the other academicians not as free authors but as Louis' agents. The erasure of Cassini's name is not a sign of royal unfairness but rather of Louis' *noblesse oblige* toward himself.[69] In a sense, being the absolute ruler, he has to represent himself also as the 'absolute author'. The erasure of Cassini's name was a matter of royal etiquette.[70]

What is new about the French scenario is that – although the usefulness of the sciences was an unlikely prime cause for Louis' establishment of the Académie – he eventually happened to reap technical benefits from it. By contrast with the small Italian princely states, the construction of the prince's power-image in France was not at odds with the solution of state technological and bureaucratic problems, but actually merged with it. The establishment of the Académie may have been a largely image-oriented gesture, yet that institution eventually turned out to be useful because France was large and centralized enough to make use of a corps of scientific and technical specialists.

This coincidence between image and utility was, I think, not accidental. In fact, a state (large and centralized) that could use the technical services of an institution like the Académie was precisely a state (large and centralized) that could allow its king to develop a representation of his power as absolute. In turn, this type of royal image was one that would make the establishment of the Académie an image-smart gesture. In short, an institution like the Académie des Sciences fitted perfectly into the programme of state control and centralization that allowed Louis to rule as the absolute king he represented himself as being.

Let me now suggest how the analysis of Louis XIV's patronage of science may be brought to bear on the late seventeenth-century Italian scenario.

AN ACADEMY *IN INCOGNITO*

Prince Leopold de' Medici's sponsoring of what is usually considered Europe's first academy of experimental science may seem to contradict my previous claims about the unsuitability of Italian princely patronage for the institutionalization of science.[71] I will try to show that the existence of the Accademia del Cimento between 1657 and 1667 does not subvert the previous analysis but supports it.

As noticed by several historians, Leopold never provided his academy with a legal charter. He called it into session or suspended its activity whenever he desired. He set its experimental agenda, paid for the experimental apparatus from his own purse, and tended to draw his academicians from mathematicians and philosophers who were already on the Medici payroll. It seems that the very name of 'Accademia del Cimento' was a retrospective invention connected to the publication, in 1667, of the *Saggi* – a book presenting a selection of experiments conducted at the (by then) defunct academy. Finally, the academy was neither formally established nor disbanded. It began to meet around 1657, slowed down its activities after 1662, and stopped convening after 1667 when Leopold became cardinal and moved temporarily to Rome. As one academician remarked, the academy was nothing more than an expression of the 'prince's whims'.[72]

The Cimento's status as an unofficial academy was, I think, a direct result of Leopold's participation in it. A prince of Leopold's rank could easily taint his image by working together in an *official* context with his subjects (some of whom were of quite low social background).[73] Things were made even more complicated by the Cimento's commitment to experiments, that is, to a practice involving the use of mechanical devices. People of high social status could *observe* such activities only within settings that provided appropriate 'status shields'. An appropriate etiquette had to be followed. For instance, in the Bolognese public anatomy lessons analysed by Ferrari, a secret compartment was built into the anatomy theatre so that 'authorities, ladies or other persons' could watch the mechanically-connoted dissection without being seen.[74] People of higher social status could be polluted by much less. Pope Gregory XV could not participate openly even in a semi-private academy gathered in the Vatican Palace by the cardinal nephew to listen to orations on biblical subjects. As reported by an observer, the pope 'participated' only *in incognito*, 'remaining retired in a small chapel' attached to the cardinal's room where the gathering took place.[75]

Leopold controlled the possibilities of status-pollution in various ways. First, as shown by the preface to the *Saggi*, he tried to make sure he would be perceived as a princely supervisor rather than an active hands-on participant. Second, he presented the academy as something belonging to his private sphere.[76] In fact, a prince could display himself naked to his servants in the privacy of his bath, but he could not do so in a more public space. Therefore, the participants to the Cimento could not become 'academicians' in the sense of being members of an official corporate body. Leopold's status required them to be his 'scientific servants'. In fact, they were not allowed to display their association to the academy by using titles such as 'Accademico del Cimento'. They had no official relationship with Leopold except as his subjects.

The same issues of status that made Leopold keep the academy as a fully private enterprise prevented him from entering into scientific disputes. In fact, disputes belonged to people who had an axe to grind – like members of the ignorant and self-interested lower classes.[77] The academy's vocal commitment to the experimental method – one that led to accurate descriptions of experimentally (re)produced effects rather than to the explanation of their causes – was not only a result of Leopold's desire to keep clear of possible conflicts with theologians: it reflected the politeness of the philosophical etiquette to which he was bound by his own status.[78]

By having his 'academicians' perform and describe experiments rather than seek their causes, Leopold made sure that the activity of the Cimento would not lead to status-tainting disputes. For analogous reasons, Leopold was exceedingly cautious of having himself invoked as the judge in scientific disputes. When that happened – as with Huygens and Fabri on Saturn's rings – he passed the matter to his academicians. They were instructed to perform careful experiments and, without passing any final judgement, to report what their experiments (based on *models*) suggested about the tenability of the contenders' claims (which the Cimento considered only as *hypotheses*).[79]

Similarly, in the *Saggi* (the text through which the Cimento 'went public' in 1667) Leopold made sure that the academy's activity was represented as having unrolled as smoothly as possible, undisturbed by internal disputes. The frequently strong tensions and explicit disagreements recorded in the academicians' private correspondence were made invisible in the *Saggi*. Moreover, the book was written in a collective voice. No voice of any academician, except that of the Secretary who wrote the report, is ever made explicit. On several occasions, the text's cautiousness to avoid signs of individual authorship went so far as to try to 'objectify' the narrative by adopting the passive of the third person singular ('it was taken', 'it was seen', 'it was thought', 'it was provided').[80]

There is more to the connection between the book's voice and Leopold's status than his attempt to present the academy as a haven of consensus and a space where only non-disputational knowledge was produced. For instance, it is significant that Leopold did not try to publicize his academy by opening up its meetings to many qualified visitors (as the London's Royal Society tended to do), but by distributing (without selling[81]) an elegantly illustrated book presenting a selection of its experiments.[82]

By doing so Leopold was probably trying to kill two birds with one stone. Through the *Saggi*'s textual strategies he managed to efface himself sufficiently from the academy's activities to preserve his princely status and yet not enough to delegitimize the academy's results. Unlike Robert Boyle and the Royal Society who bound themselves to certify knowledge through 'competent' and 'open' witnessing managed through a fairly intricate etiquette,[83] the Cimento's results were presented as credible simply because they had been certified by somebody of Leopold's status.[84]

Because of Leopold's effaced but effective presence, the *Saggi* did not need to reproduce the names of the witnesses and experimenters nor any other specific circumstantial information about the execution of the experiments. In general, the *Saggi* presented neither complete reports of individual experiments nor the 'typical' experiment, but a collage-like narrative composed by various narrative segments taken from different experiments – a procedure that would have not met the strict requirements of what Shapin has called Boyle's 'literary technology'.[85]

In a sense, the present and yet invisible Leopold was the *incognito* certifier of the academy's work. But, because the *Saggi* did not mention any academician in particular, the credit for the work of the academy fell by 'default' on the prince. Leopold became the author *in absentia* – the only way in which he could be an author and enhance (rather than jeopardize) his image. The Cimento's unnamed academicians resemble Boyle's technicians studied by Shapin. They were indispensable as *workers*, but were not legitimate enough to 'make knowledge', that is, to be *authors*.[86] However, unlike Boyle, Leopold did not utilize the academicians' involvement in the experiments to blame them for possible failures. This was not a result of Leopold's good nature but of his very high social status. No embarrassing failure could be represented in a princely experimental narrative.[87] To Leopold, any such accident was equivalent to an embarrassing etiquette blunder at court.

Unlike Boyle, Leopold had the writer of the *Saggi* give his subjects full credit for having *performed* the experiments. However, despite the apparent differences, there is an underlying similarity between Leopold's and Boyle's textual strategies. For instance, in Boyle's case, the assistants were represented as nameless and unable to produce knowledge because it was the patron who had to be presented as the author. It was Boyle who had the status and credibility necessary to 'make knowledge'. The assistants 'collaborated' with him only in the sense that they took care of mechanical tasks that could not be dealt with by somebody of Boyle's status. Leopold's case was different and yet structurally homologous to Boyle's. Having a higher status than Boyle, Leopold was bound to a lower threshold of pollution.[88] Consequently, he could not present himself as participating in scientific activities as much as Boyle could. It was because of this that Leopold's academicians received more credit than Boyle's assistants. However, giving some credit to the academicians did not deprive Leopold of authorship. In fact, because his academicians–subjects were kept nameless and because Leopold was the ultimate source of the academy's credibility, the credit reverted to the prince. Leopold was an author in the only way he could be one: *in incognito*. The peculiar voice of the *Saggi* provided a skilful solution to a problem of etiquette: to allow Leopold to fashion himself as author while remaining unpolluted by the status-tainting features of the knowledge-making process.

The namelessness of Leopold's academicians may reflect the same dynamics of princely power-image that led to the replacement of Cassini's name on the medal celebrating his astronomical discoveries with the 'learned men whom the King maintained at the Observatory'. More generally, one may suggest that the anonymity of some of the early published works of the Académie des Sciences should not be seen just as a sign of allegiance to a Baconian ideal, but may be seen also as reflecting the logic of the image of its royal patron.[89] Symmetrically, the Royal Society's acceptance of the individual authorship of their members may also have reflected the English king's lesser involvement and interest in that institution. That the Royal Society as an institution could dissociate itself from the views of its individual members may be read also as a sign of its relative independence from the king.[90] Because of the relative 'distance' between the king and the Society, his image was not directly at stake in its members' printed work. This estrangement of the royal patron, I think, made it possible for the fellows to emerge as individual authors. For individualism to emerge, the absolute monarch had to go.

This analysis has mapped out some of the specific status dynamics that governed Leopold's relationship with the Cimento and has suggested how similar dynamics may have framed the notion of scientific authorship in other European scientific institutions, but it has not addressed explicitly what Leopold's motives may have been in gathering and sponsoring an experimental academy. Practical usefulness and national technological development do not seem to have been a high-priority concern for Leopold – a junior prince of a small and increasingly agricultural state. Nor could spectacle have played much of a role in Leopold's decisions. Although the activities of the Cimento were rhetorically presented as the heritage of Galileo's science, they could not compare with the spectacularity of his discoveries.[91] As indicated by the *Saggi*, the subject matter of the academy's investigations belonged to the category of *curiosità* rather than *meraviglie*.[92]

The Cimento's activity suited Leopold's image because its experimental discourse (like that of Boyle's experimental philosophy) presented a non-contentious type of knowledge – one appropriate to a prince of post-Reformation Italy. Moreover, the Cimento's activities were quite well suited to the codes of courtly *sprezzatura*. No sweat-inducing machines (like air-pumps) but plenty of elegant glasswork (frequently destroyed during the experiments with truly aristocratic nonchalance) populated its experimental space. Moreover, several of the 'experiences' were not produced in the academy's various meeting places, but observed in the field. They resembled botanizing and collecting (or courtly *conversazioni*[93]) as much as laboratory practices.

Academicians used the artillery pieces of the fortress of Livorno (not operated by themselves but by low-class gunners) to prove Galileo's claims about the parabolic trajectory of projectiles. They stayed up at night somewhere in Palazzo Pitti (probably in courtly late-night gatherings like those described in the *Book of the Courtier*) watching the formation of elegant ice crystals in water containers. On other nights, they busied themselves determining the speed of sound by watching the flare of faraway guns and measuring the time it took to the sound of the firings to reach them.[94] Therefore, the experiments of the Cimento were not part of a 'laboratory life'. Rather, they resembled those courtly activities – like dancing or fencing – that characterized the daily life of a prince. The meetings of the Cimento did not demarcate a modern professional space but took place in the private sphere of the prince. As shown by the sometimes very frequent and unscheduled meetings, its activities were closely connected to the varying schedule of Leopold's daily life. He called its meetings as he would have called a hunting expedition.[95]

That the Cimento did not meet regularly and never received a legal charter was not a sign of Leopold's casual attitude (on the contrary, he was exceedingly orderly and a great organizer) but rather of his status. A fixed schedule and a statute would have been an intolerable restriction of his freedom.[96] To engage in something like the Cimento, Leopold had to keep it as something completely private. It needed to be something that was perceived to be completely his own, something he could fully control and display his power and status by controlling.

At the same time, because of its private character, this setting would provide him with an 'informal' space in which he could participate in (and legitimize) the academy in ways which would have been impossible if the Cimento had happened to be an official institution. In fact, had the Cimento been an official body, Leopold would have had to behave according to the strict etiquette that regulated the public life of a prince like himself – an etiquette that would have prevented him from mingling with technicians. The textual strategies of the *Saggi* reflected similar concerns: they conveyed Leopold's familiarity with (and yet distance from) the Cimento. Those techniques were the textual analogues of the informal formality that surrounded the activities of the academy.

These considerations suggest a relationship between privateness and publicness, participation and distance. Leopold's example indicated that a junior prince could participate in scientific activity only if this was presented as a strictly private enterprise. The case of Louis XIV suggested that an absolute monarch's public involvement in science could be only accompanied by his not participating in the scientific activities he was publicly legitimizing and supporting. In fact, Louis XIV visited the Académie at the Observatory only once, in 1682, during a purely ceremonial event. From the available evidence, it does not seem that Charles II – the king of England who chartered the Royal Society in 1662 – ever visited that institution.[97]

Leopold's concern with fitting his academy into the codes of country life is confirmed by his attention to the literary style of the *Saggi*. First of all, it is telling that he selected Count Lorenzo Magalotti (a sophisticated *virtuoso* and *letterato*) rather than Giovanni Borelli (his most brilliant but not-so-polished academician) as secretary of the academy and writer of the *Saggi*. Then, when the manuscript of the *Saggi* was finally completed, Leopold made sure it was reviewed for the elegance of its style as much as for the accuracy (and religious orthodoxy) of its scientific content.[98] Also, Leopold must have been concerned with the potential tediousness of the *Saggi* since – halfway through the text – Magalotti felt compelled to include a disclaimer about the necessary dullness of the description of the experiments.[99] Because of his status and culture, Leopold could not quite accept the apparent pedantry of Boyle's 'literary technology' without worrying about his own image.

To conclude, I think that the case of the Cimento does not contradict the analysis of the relationship between princely image and the patronage of science outlined earlier in this paper. Although the type of scientific patronage embodied by the Cimento was very different from Cosimo II's patronage of Galileo and from Louis XIV's establishment of the Académie des Sciences, it shared in the image and power dynamics that framed those other two cases. Everything in the Cimento (methodology, 'research programme', experimental activity, organization, etiquette and public representation) was closely tied to the necessities of Leopold's status.[100] In short, the Cimento was not the toy of a rich, provincial, junior prince tired of the occupations of court life. Whatever our evaluation of the science done by the Cimento, it exemplifies the structural features of Italian princely patronage of science at the end of the seventeenth century. Because Italy's political scenario (from the small size of the states to the princes' power-image dynamics) could not accommodate the institutional formats that were developing in other European countries, and because a discipline like astronomy was becoming less spectacular than it had been at the beginning of the century, there were fewer options for social bricolage between the resources of individual scientific practitioners and those of the princely patrons. The Cimento and the other informal academies developed around Roman cardinals and prelates were among the few venues within that scenario.[101]

CIVILITY AND OBJECTIVITY: AN HYPOTHESIS

Although Boyle has been mentioned often in this essay, my narrative has ignored England – the country in which the Scientific Revolution is represented as having reached its culmination. Such a gap is not accidental but reflects this paper's focus on the relationship between the Scientific Revolution and political absolutism – a feature of the emerging modern state that was not prominent in England after 1642. Although this is not the place for a (much needed) comparative analysis of the relationship between political discourses and the legitimation of early modern science in continental Europe and England, I want to suggest ways in which the development of experimental philosophy in England may reflect status dynamics like those encountered with Galileo, the Cimento and the Académie des Sciences.

Unlike France and Italy, England displayed less pronounced social and disciplinary hierarchies.[102] In particular, the mercantile classes had a relatively larger socio-political role there than on the continent. Then – although during the Restoration royal power tried to develop absolutist traits – the seventeenth-century English kings never managed to develop a power comparable to that of the French absolute monarchs. Consequently, the English royal court was not the cultural and political centre it was on the continent, and court society was not the synonym of 'le monde'. Coffee houses, gentlemen's salons, craftsmen's workshops, professional corporations like the Royal College of Physicians, and quasi-private scientific academies like the Royal Society were England's scientific sites. The typology of the Royal Society's membership, its funding and its programme mirrored the English socio-political scenario very closely.[103]

In such an environment, scientists were not primarily concerned with tuning their activities to the codes of patronage of an absolute prince. First of all, the need of major leaps in social status in order to overcome received disciplinary hierarchies was not felt as acutely in England as elsewhere on the continent. Moreover, the king was not the crucial source of legitimation as he was in the rest of Europe. Although the monarch played an important role in legitimizing the Royal Society by granting it a royal charter, his financial support and input into the Society's programme was minimal. The status and image of the gentleman rather than of the absolute monarch was the source of socio-cognitive legitimation sought by the practitioners of the Royal Society.[104]

Consequently, in England (as opposed to the Italian courts) a scientific practitioner did not need to be spectacular. Galileo might have remained unemployed there.[105] Although the Royal Society needed to inject some spectacularity in its experimental practices not least to sustain its membership, the type of spectacle produced there was more a matter of gentlemanly *curiosity* (though possibly a philosophically relevant one) than princely *magnificentia*.[106] Because of this environment, low-key, technical, and potentially 'boring' (in the Boylean sense) work was not only acceptable but eminently legitimate. Boyle's 'literary technology' may have seemed pedantic to continental courtiers yet, because of the English political and religious scenario, it would appeal to the English *virtuosi*. Actually, by drawing on the specific features of the English socio-cultural context, Boyle could turn the tables and equate being 'showy' to being 'unethical'.[107]

However, I would suggest that Boyle's potentially boring 'literary technology' and the complicated ceremonial that regulated the Royal Society's meetings reflected processes not unlike those that framed Galileo's princely representation of his scientific discoveries, the private nature of the Cimento, or Louis' establishment of the Académie des Sciences.[108] The different scientific discourses and institutional structures that we encounter in these cases are reflections of the different types of socio-political order (and related venues for social legitimation) that characterized late seventeenth-century England, France and Italy.

Consider a crucial difference between the English and Italian scientific styles. As shown by Steven Shapin and Simon Schaffer, the English experimental philosophers' strategies for cognitive legitimation were much less aggressive than those of Galileo. In particular, while Galileo built a career partly on his spectacular duel-*like* exchanges with other philosophers and mathematicians, Boyle condemned such activities and put forward a form of scientific discourse aimed at preventing 'philosophical duels': kinds of behaviour he saw as philosophically sterile and socially disruptive.[109]

However, we can detect some homology beneath the conspicuous differences between Galileo's and Boyle's scientific discourses. Boyle tuned his programme for experimental philosophy to the English socio-political context by presenting his polite solution to the problem of scientific knowledge as closely linked to the political politeness necessary to the maintenance of social order – an issue of great political concern after the Civil War.[110] Galileo's tactics in representing his astronomical discoveries as fitting the Medici's dynastic mythology, and his engaging in spectacular courtly disputes, reflected a similar perception of the possibility of legitimizing the new science by playing the codes of *raison d'état* as embodied, in this case, in court culture.

In short, the very different argumentative styles of Galileo and Boyle may be traced to the different political power structures of Italy and England at that time. Although with the development of political absolutism real duels became prohibited both in Italy and France, duel-*like* fictional performances such as tournaments, jousts and *barriere* were very common and well-received within court culture.[111] When safely kept in the domain of *fiction* or courtly *spectacle*, the duel was perceived as an acceptable and even honourable 'social trope'.[112] In fact, while reminding the courtiers of the (sometimes mythical) knightly roots of princely power, duel-like performances provided aristocrats with a courtly tool for sublimating their aggressive, knightly drives.[113] In short, duel-like performances were not seen as threatening to the absolutist ruler and they actually helped him domesticate (Elias would say 'civilize') the formerly politically threatening feudal lords.

This may explain why Galileo's aggressive, duel-like scientific disputations were not seen as impolite or improper by the sophisticated audiences of the Florentine and Roman courts as, by contrast, they would have been in England. Galileo's performances were welcome and rewarded because – as shown by Cosimo II's attitude during the dispute on buoyancy of 1612 – they were perceived as akin to theatrical plays.[114] Similarly, in publishing his texts, Galileo tended (or was pressed) to use fictional genres like the dialogue (among imaginary or real but deceased actors) or 'soft' genres like the letter and the discourse. By doing so, his frequently harsh attacks on the adversaries *could* be represented as not being real challenges leading to real (philosophical) duels. Evidently, I am not saying that Galileo thought of his work as a philosophical comedy. On the contrary, the trial of 1633 showed how strongly he believed in the reality of the Copernican cosmos. More simply, I suggest that Galileo's textual strategies provided his patrons with a safety valve through which they could prevent putting their honour on the line and having to be defended as a result of their client's engaging in philosophical duel-like tournaments. If necessary, they could regard Galileo's texts or performances as 'carnivalesque' challenges rather than *ex-professo* statements.[115]

On the other hand, in England, which had just undergone a bloody civil war and where royal power was slowly restoring itself, duel-like behaviour was likely to be perceived as socio-political anathema. Unlike continental absolute rulers, English monarchs were far from being so secure on their thrones as to turn potentially threatening social tropes into domesticated courtly games that ended up confirming their power. That was a trick only well-established absolute princes could pull. Once seen in this context, Boyle's duel-preventing experimental philosophy appears as reflecting English Restoration *raison d'état* as much as Galileo's duel-like courtly scientific performances incorporated the discourse of Italian political absolutism.[116]

One may also try to push this hypothesis further and try to relate the differing English and continental notions of scientific authorship and facts to those countries' different socio-political structures and discourses. As we have seen, the different role of the sovereign in legitimizing the scientists' practices tended to set the conditions of possibility of scientific authorship. To use a spatial metaphor, the 'distance' between the sovereign and his 'scientific subjects' tended to frame the latters' ability to present themselves as knowledge-producing authors. For instance, the prince's relative 'closeness' to his practitioners tended to prevent them from being represented as legitimate *individual* authors. Such a scenario could result either from a junior prince participating in the subjects' scientific practices (as in the case of Leopold) or from a powerful absolute monarch (Louis) legitimizing them at a distance but linking his image and honour to their activities. In both cases, the prince's investment in the scientific activities of his subjects tended to render them 'nameless'. As has been noted, the effacing of the scientific authors was a matter of princely etiquette.

Although Galileo was far from being represented as a nameless author, his case may fit this model too. True, Galileo was a conspicuous individual author but, as we have seen, his princely patrons had the option to represent his arguments as spectacles or fictional narratives. In short, his closeness to the prince did not produce an effacement of his authorial individuality (as in the case of the Cimento and, to a lesser extent, of the Académie) but it tended to 'efface' his claims. In fact, the effacement of the scientific author or the fictionalization of his claims were etiquette-bound strategies reflecting a common goal: the need to preserve the honour of the princely patron; this, in turn, legitimized the scientist's activity.[117] In England, on the other hand, where the sovereign was relatively 'far' from his scientific subjects and did not constitute the fundamental source of the legitimation of their knowledge-claims, the practitioners could claim some level of *individual* authorship of *non-fictional* knowledge.[118]

To summarize, the scientific practitioner had to be 'close' enough to the source of legitimation in order to be perceived as credible, reliable, etc. However, the 'closer' (and potentially more legitimate) one became, the more one's individual authorship tended to shrink as the prince's power and honour became increasingly implicated in the client's claims. Ultimately, the practitioner might either be absorbed by the black hole of princely power and lose his name and authorship or see his arguments represented as fictions.[119]

However, the practitioners could not select the optimal blend of legitimacy and authorship and then locate themselves at the desired 'distance' from the prince. Far from being unlimited, the practitioners' options were framed by the specific socio-political power structures surrounding them. And, as shown by the different scenarios provided by England, France and Italy, the space where one could be a legitimate author was framed differently by different political power structures.

What is particularly original and significant about the English case is that the king's reduced power and role in legitimizing scientific practices produced a social space in which different forms of scientific etiquette could be articulated. Or, to put it differently, because the 'pull' of prince-centred legitimation was lower in England than elsewhere, a wider and less 'tense' social space was provided in which one could manage to be both an individual and a legitimate author. Experimental philosophy was a scientific etiquette that happened to develop in and reflect this specific social space.

Because the king's honour was not directly at stake in their claims, the members of the Royal Society could represent themselves as authors and their knowledge claims as non-fictional. They produced 'matters of fact', not philosophical comedies. However, this does not mean that they were able to produce knowledge 'freely'. Simply, a different but equally serious set of constraints had resulted from the replacement of the honour of an absolute prince with that of many gentlemen as the source of legitimation of scientific authorship and knowledge. Experimental philosophy was the apparatus of scientific etiquette through which Boyle managed to negotiate these new constraints in ways that could allow for the production of legitimate knowledge claims.

On the continent, knowledge claims and scientific authors could be represented as fictional or nameless so as not to threaten the prince's honour and not to undermine their ultimate source of legitimacy. Because a gentleman's honour was lower than that of an absolute prince (though still perfectly legitimate by English standards), the *virtuosi* could produce non-fictional knowledge claims. In short, that they could make non-fictional claims resulted from their higher threshold of 'pollution' which in turn resulted from being less 'honourable' than an absolute monarch. However, although the English *virtuosi* could produce non-fictional knowledge claims, they could not be dogmatic, that is, they could not present their claims as rigidly unnegotiable.[120] Dogmatic claims would have undermined the process of knowledge legitimation by threatening the honour of those who were supposed to legitimize these claims: the other gentlemen.

The necessity of casting claims in ways that would prevent 'philosophical duels' from developing among *virtuosi* was particularly strongly felt because the gentlemen's honour was less powerful at legitimizing knowledge than that of an absolute prince and, consequently, *virtuosi* needed to 'group together' in order to produce publicly legitimate knowledge. Not surprisingly, although the experimental philosophers were real authors, they needed to rely on each other to certify what they had done. *They could be legitimate individual authors only in so far as they were members of a gentlemanly corporation* (like the Royal Society).

To summarize, while the Cimento and Galileo could be represented either as *nameless authors* or as producers of *fictional claims* as a result of their reliance on the status of one *individual absolute prince* in order to legitimize themselves and their knowledge, the English *virtuosi* could represent themselves as *individual authors* producing '*matters of fact*' because they relied on the social status of a *corporation of gentlemen* as the source of the legitimation of their knowledge.

More precisely, to use Elias' terminology, the Royal Society was a 'figuration' of *interdependent* authors. The etiquette-like dimensions of experimental philosophy and of the Royal Society's protocols of corporate interaction resulted from the need to regulate this interdependence in constructive ways, that is, by making sure that nobody's honour would be threatened by the process of knowledge certification.[121]

The striking difference between Galileo's aggressive style and Boyle's polite one is a result of the different contexts framing the 'civilizing process'. Boyle's experimental philosophy was polite because it aimed at constituting (and depended on) a community of interdependent knowers. Galileo's aggressive style, by contrast, reflected an authorial identity fashioned by an absolutist court where he was perceived and rewarded as a producer of court spectacles – spectacles that had to be both duel-like in accordance with the codes of court culture and fictional so as not to embarrass or threaten his patron's honour. Although Galileo's scientific discourse was polite by Florentine or Roman court standards, it was informed by an etiquette much different from the one that structured Boyle's experimental philosophy. Galileo's etiquette was prince-oriented while Boyle's was targeted at an interdependent group of gentlemen and *virtuosi*.

It is in this context that we may understand the etiquette dimensions of Boyle's notion of 'matter of fact'. As has been noted, the experimental philosophers could not make knowledge claims that threatened the honour of those who were supposed to engage in the collective process of their legitimation. One had to produce honour-friendly claims without 'softening' them, that is, without turning them into fictions. Boyle's matter of fact was a type of empirical claim that could solve this problem. Matters of fact were non-threatening and yet non-fictional. However, we should not perceive matters of fact merely as 'lower' or 'reduced' forms of empirical claims. The success of Boyle's programme did not result from watering down or fictionalizing empirical claims but by tying their production (their 'fashioning') to the codes of gentlemanly identity. Matters of fact were neither *weak* nor *fictional*: they were *civilized*. True, matters of fact were *produced*, but the modalities of their production were homologous to those structuring the social constitution of gentlemanly identity, that is, of the source of social and cognitive legitimation. Self-fashioning was world-fashioning.[122]

In short, by engaging in experimental philosophy, gentlemen fashioned matters of fact as they were fashioning themselves as gentlemen. Or, to put it differently, matters of fact were 'disciplined' statements that *incorporated* a collective scientific etiquette in their very constitution. Matters of fact did not 'insult' anybody because everybody was supposed to have co-operated (actually or virtually) in their production.[123] And it was by not threatening the honour of anybody and by involving everybody legitimate in the process of their fashioning that matters of fact became legitimate, that is, that they became 'objective' knowledge.[124] Etiquette, then, was the common key to the production of both civility and objectivity.[125]

To conclude, the difference between the scientific styles of Boyle, Galileo and the Cimento may reflect the different political power structures that *framed their conditions of legitimacy*.[126] Although Italy and England displayed different political power structures, the *processes of legitimation* connecting scientific styles to political power structures were, I think, quite comparable. In particular, I have suggested that the legitimation of one's identity and knowledge claims necessitated some source of status, credibility, honour, power. However, the stronger the power/honour one tapped into to legitimize one's identity and knowledge claims, the greater the danger of it backfiring and 'erasing' either the claim or the author.

Because of the analogy between these processes and those of courtly and gentlemanly self-fashioning, I have used the term 'etiquette' to refer to the protocols through which one interacted with the power/honour one needed to legitimize one's claims and identity while avoiding false steps that might trigger its backfiring. I hope to have shown that different political power frameworks allowed for the articulation of different types of scientific etiquette. As a result, the fundamental tension between the need to legitimize power/honour and the need to control its possible backfiring were articulated by different etiquettes in different countries. However, not all these different scientific etiquettes managed to survive. Some disappeared with the political systems that had framed them. That today's scientific practices resemble Boyle's scientific etiquette more than Galileo's suggests that modern Western political systems resemble seventeenth-century parliamentarian England more closely than granducal Florence or papal Rome.

NOTES

Thanks to Roger Hahn, David Harden, Nancy Salzer, Michael Segre, Steve Shapin, Jay Tribby, Norton Wise, and especially Julian Martin for their comments and to Paula Findlen for all the useful references.

1 I will try to use the footnotes as some sort of fragmented bibliographical essay. Although *Isis*' Critical Bibliography remains the best general bibliographical source, a more comprehensive survey of works on the history of Italian science can be found in Massimo Bucciantini and Anna C. Citernesi (eds.), *Bibliografia italiana di Storia della Scienza*, (Florence).

2 For reasons that will become apparent in the course of the argument, the scope of this essay is quite narrow. It does not consider (or claim to put forward arguments applicable to) a wide range of disciplines and practitioners. Instead, it focuses only on scientific practices supported by the state or by princely patrons.

3 Norbert Elias, *The Court Society*, (New York, 1983), *Power and Civility*, (New York, 1983) and *The History of Manners*, (New York, 1983).

4 This view goes back at least to the eighteenth century (Paolo Frisi, *Elogi* (Livorno, 1774). I have used the reprint (Rome, 1985), pp. 92, 170–1). Through the subsequent casting of Galileo as the emblem of Italian free-thinking, lay Italian culture has helped solidify this historiographical picture (Pietro Redondi, *Galileo eretico*, (Turin, 1983), pp. 407–9).

5 On the historiographical trope of the 'scuola galileiana', see Ugo Baldini, 'La scuola galileiana', in Gianni Micheli (ed.), *Scienza e tecnica, Annali* III, (Turin, 1980), pp. 383–8 [This volume is part of Ruggiero Romano and Corrado Vivanti (eds.), *Storia d'Italia*]. Among the more recent historiography of seventeenth-century and early eighteenth-century Italian science, see Michael Segre, *In the Wake of Galileo*, (New Brunswick, N.J., 1991); *idem*, 'Science at the Tuscan Court, 1642–1667', in Sabetai Unguru (ed.), *Physics, Cosmology and Astronomy* (Dordrecht and Boston, 1991, 295–308; Ugo Baldini, 'L'attività scientifica del primo settecento', in Micheli, *Scienza e tecnica*, 467–545; Clelia Pighetti, *L'influsso scientifico di Robert Boyle nel tardo '600 italiano* (Milan, 1988); Mario dal Pra *et al.*, *Le edizioni dei testi filosofici e scientifici de '500 e del '600* (Milan, 1986); Claudio Manzoni, *I cartesiani italiani* (Udine, 1984); G. Arrighi *et al.*, *La scuola galileiana: prospettive di ricerca* (Florence, 1979); Marta Cavazza, *Settecento inquieto* (Bologna, 1990); *idem*, 'Bologna and the Royal Society in the Seventeenth Century', *Notes and Records of the Royal Society* 35 (1980), 105–23; Bruno Basile, *L'invenzione del vero* (Rome, 1987). See also Paolo Casini's various works on the reception of Newton in Italy. More recent literature on seventeenth-century Italian science is given in later footnotes.

6 John Russell, SJ, 'Catholic Astronomers and the Copernical System after the Condemnation of Galileo', *Annals of Science* 46 (1989), 365–93.

7 Albert Van Helden, 'The Telescope in the Seventeenth Century', *Isis* 65 (1974), 38–58; Maria Luisa Righini Bonelli and Albert Van Helden, *Divini and Campani: A Forgotten Chapter in the History of the Accademia del Cimento* (Florence, 1981) (published as a supplement to the 1981 issue of *Annali dell'Istituto e Museo di Storia della Scienza*).

8 On the work of electricity in early modern Italy, see John Heilbron, *Electricity in the Seventeenth and Eighteenth Centuries* (Berkeley, 1979), pp. 180–208. For bibliographical references on seventeenth-century medicine see: Guido Panseri, 'Medicina e scienze naturali nei secoli XVI e XVII', in Micheli, *Scienza e tecnica*, 343–80.

9 See Maurizio Torrini, *Tommaso Cornelio e la ricostruzione della scienza* (Naples 1977); Fabrizio Lomonaco and Maurizio Torrini (eds.), *Galileo e Napoli* (Naples 1987) (especially the essays by Olmi, Galluzzi, Torrini, Palladino and Borrelli); Corrado Dollo, *Filosofia e scienze in Sicilia* (Padua 1979); Maurizio Torrini, 'L'Accademia degli Investiganti. Napoli 1663–1670', *Quaderni storici* 16 (1981), 845–81; Silvio Suppa, *L'Accademia di Medinacoeli* (Naples 1971); W. E. Knowles Middleton, 'Science in Rome, 1675–1700, and the Accademia Fisicomatematica of Giovanni Giustino Ciampini', *The British Journal for the History of Science* 8 (1975), 138–54; Lina Montalto, 'Un Ateneo internazionale vagheggiato in Roma sulla fine del sec. XVII', *Studi romani* 10 (1962), 660–73. However, the spread of scientific activities over the peninsula did not reflect a permanent pattern. By the eighteenth century, most Italian scientific centres were in the north, along the Turin-Bologna-Venice axis. On the decline of science in the south see Giuseppe Galasso, 'Scienze, istituzioni e attrezzature scientifiche nella Napoli del Settecento', in *L'Età dei Lumi. Studi storici sul settecento europeo in onore di Franco Venturi*, (Napoli, 1985), 193–228.

10 Heilbron, *Electricity* pp. 101–14, 180–208; *idem*, 'Science in the Church', *Science*

in Context 3 (1989), 9–28; Maurizio Torrini, *Dopo Galileo. Una polemica scientifica (1684–1711)*, (Florence, 1979); C. Costantini, *Baliani e i Gesuiti* (Florence, 1969); Ugo Baldini, 'La Chiesa e le scienze. La scienza gesuitica', in Micheli, *Scienza e tecnica*, 513–26. See also the sizeable literature on the scientific activities of Father Athanasius Kircher in Rome.

11 Baldini, 'L'attività scientifica del primo settecento', pp. 532–3.

12 For a different but related reading of the crisis of Italian science, see Baldini, 'La scuola galileiana', p. 437.

13 According to the ambassadors from Lucca, the grand duke's income was as high as 1.5 million *scudi* around 1590, but it fell to 800,000 around 1625. Amedeo Pellegrini (ed.), *Relazioni inedite di ambasciatori lucchesi alle corti di Firenze, Genova, Milano, Modena, Parma, Torino* (Lucca, 1901), pp. 124, 153. On the decline of Florentine economy in this period see Paolo Malanima, *La decadenza di un'economia cittadina* (Bologna 1982).

14 Ferrara did not even last that long. By 1598 it was annexed to the Papal State, and what used to be the site of an elegant court which just a few decades earlier had hosted, among others, Ludovico Ariosto, quickly decayed to the status of a provincial city.

15 It is quite ironic that it was at the command of Zaccaria Sagredo (the brother of Galileo's close friend Giovanfrancesco) that, in 1630, the Venetian army was badly defeated during the Italian episode of the Thirty Years' War – an event that marked the eclipse of Venice's role in European politics. It was from the battlefield at Valeggio that – just before this historical debacle – Zaccaria wrote to Galileo authorizing him to use Giovanfrancesco's name in the *Dialogue on the Two Chief World Systems*. Galileo Galilei, *Opere*, (ed. Antonio Favaro, Florence, 1890–1909), XIV, pp. 95, 97. Soon afterward, the Venetian army collapsed and Zaccaria was so fast in retreating from the battlefield that his army could not keep up with him. He arrived at the Peschiera camp four hours ahead of his soldiers. See Maria Francesca Tiepolo, 'Una lettera inedita di Galileo', *La cultura* 17 (1979), p. 66.

16 Jan De Vries, *The Economy of Europe in an Age of Crisis, 1600–1750* (Cambridge, 1976), pp. 26–7.

17 Galileo, *Opere*, XI, p. 170.

18 Silvio A. Bedini, 'The Galilean Jovilabe', *Nuncius* 1 (1986), 30–6; G. Vampaemel, 'Science Disdained: Galileo and the Problem of Longitude', in C. S. Maffioli and L. C. Palm (eds.), *Italian Scientists in the Low Countries in the Seventeenth and Eighteenth Centuries* (Amsterdam, 1989), 111–29.

19 Francis Haskell, *Patrons and Painters* (New Haven, 1980), pp. 146–53, 187–90.

20 However, France was not the only focus of emigrating Italian artists. For instance, others opted for England, *ibidem*, pp. 192–9.

21 'Eloge de Monsieur Cassini', in Bernard de Fontenelle, *Eloges des academiciens* (The Hague, 1740), I, 273–312 (esp. pp. 296–7). The parallel between the migrations of Bernini and Cassini can be pushed further. Both of them were at the centre of Louis XIV's academic projects. Cassini – together with Huygens – was treated as the foreign star of the emerging Académie des Sciences. Although Louis was eventually unable to keep Bernini in Paris, he was at least

able to convince him to open (in 1666) the French Academy in Rome; Haskell, *Patrons and Painters*, pp. 188–9.

22 G. Uzielli, *Cenni storici sulle imprese marittime e coloniali di Ferdinando I, Granduca di Toscana* (Florence, 1901), and Furio Diaz, *Il Granducato di Toscana* (Turin, 1976), pp. 280–363.

23 Edward Goldberg, *Patterns in Late Medici Art Patronage* (Princeton, 1983); *idem*, *After Vasari. History, Art, and Patronage in Late Medici Florence* (Princeton, 1988).

24 On the financial decline of the Roman baronage see Carlo Mistruzzi, 'La nobiltà nello Stato Pontificio', *Rassegna degli Archivi di Stato* 23 (1963), 206–44, and Jean Delumeau, *Vie économique et sociale de Rome dans la seconde moitié du XVIe siècle* (Paris, 1959), I, pp. 153–5, 434–8, 467, 471–2. The Accademia dei Lincei has attracted much attention and the resulting bibliography is too vast to be reduced to a few references. Enrica Schettini Piazza's *Bibliografia storica dell'Accademia Nazionale dei Lincei* (Florence, 1980), pp. 21–72, lists most of the relevant (though not the most recent) literature.

25 The first university-connected botanical gardens were established in Padua and Pisa in 1545. Within a few decades they spread to other countries: Leiden (1577), Paris (1590) and Oxford (1621). On the early Italian botanical gardens see Margherita Azzi Visentini, 'Il giardino dei semplici di Padova: un prodotto della cultura del Rinascimento', *Comunità* 34 (1980), 259–338; *idem*, *L'Orto Botanico di Padova e il giardino del rinascimento* (Milano, 1984); Carlo Maccagni, 'Le raccolte e i musei di storia naturale e gli orti botanici come istituzioni alternative e complementari rispetto alla cultura delle università e delle Accademie', in Laetitia Boehn and Ezio Raimondi (eds.), *Università, accademie e società scientifiche in Italia e in Germania dal cinquecento al settecento* (Bologna, 1981); Giuseppe Olmi, 'Le scienze naturali nella prima età moderna', in Gian Paolo Brizzi (ed.), *L'università a Bologna* (Bologna, 1988), 141–52.
The anatomy theatre in Padua was built between 1584 and 1594; Ferrara's in 1588; Pisa's before 1569, and Pavia's before then. Bologna built its first permanent anatomy theatre shortly after 1595, but had been using temporary ones for some time. On anatomical theatres see Giovanna Ferrari, 'Public Anatomy Lessons and the Carnival: The Anatomy Theater of Bologna', *Past and Present* 117 (1987), 50–117; A. Favaro, 'L'insegnamento anatomico di G. Fabrici d'Acquapendente', in *Monografie Storiche sullo Studio di Padova* (Venice, 1922); and G. Richter, *Das anatomische Theater* (Berlin, 1936).
On the *capitani di parte* see Giorgio Spini (ed.), *Architettura e Politica da Cosimo I a Ferdinando I*, (Florence, 1976). On the history of mathematics-based technological practices in early modern Italy, see the indexed bibliography in Mario Biagioli, 'The Social Status of Italian Mathematicians, 1450–1600', *History of Science* 27 (1989), 69–95.

26 Biagioli, 'Italian Mathematicians', pp. 42–56.

27 Mario Biagioli, 'Galileo the Emblem Maker', *Isis* 81 (1990), 230–58.

28 Peter Dear, '*Totius in verba*: Rhetoric and Authority in the Early Royal Society', *Isis* 76 (1985), 145–61; Steven Shapin and Simon Schaffer, *Leviathan and the Air Pump*, (Princeton, 1985), esp. pp. 58–9, 66; Steven Shapin, 'The House of Experiment in Seventeenth-Century England', *Isis* 79 (1988), 373–404; Mario Biagioli, 'The Anthropology of Incommensurability', *Studies in*

History and Philosophy of Science 21 (1990), 183–209. See also Robert Westman's article listed in the next footnote.

29 Robert Westman, 'The Astronomer's Role in the Sixteenth Century: A Preliminary Study', *History of Science* 18 (1980), 105–147; *idem*, 'The Copernicans and the Churches', in David Lindberg and Ronald Numbers (eds.), *God and Nature* (Berkeley, 1986), 76–113; *idem*, 'Proof, Poetics, and Patronage: Copernicus' Preface to De Revolutionibus', in David Lindberg and Robert Westman (eds.), *Reappraisals of the Scientific Revolution* (Cambridge, 1990), 167–205.

30 Biagioli, 'The Anthropology of Incommensurability'.

31 Richard S. Westfall, 'Scientific Patronage: Galileo and the Telescope', *Isis* 76 (1985), 1–31; Westman, 'The Astronomer's Role'; *idem*, 'Proof, Poetics, and Patronage'; Bruce Moran, 'Christoph Rothmann, the Copernican Theory, and Institutional and Technical Influences on the Criticism of Aristotelian Cosmology', *Sixteenth Century Journal* 13 (1982), 85–108; Biagioli, 'Galileo the Emblem Maker'; *idem*, 'Galileo's System of Patronage', *History of Science* 28 (1990), 1–62; *idem*, *Galileo Courtier* (1992).

32 On this topic, see R. K. French, 'Berengario da Carpi and the Use of Commentary in Anatomical Teaching' and V. Nutton, 'Humanistic Surgery', in A. Wear, R. K. French and I. M. Lonie (eds.), *The Medical Renaissance of the Sixteenth Century* (Cambridge, 1985), 42–74 (esp. pp. 46 8) and 75 99 (esp. pp. 84–95). See also Nancy Siraisi, *Medieval and Renaissance Medicine* (Chicago, 1990), pp. 78–114, 153–86.

33 This provides a further analogy between the predicament of Galileo and those who, like Vesalius, wanted to legitimize investigative anatomy. Both of them wanted to 'take over' the cognitive status of the superior discipline (philosophy and medicine) while, at the same time, distancing themselves from their low-status colleagues (applied mathematicians and surgeons). In a sense the socio-professional hybrid proposed by Galileo (the 'philosophical mathematician') shares much with the figure (proposed by Vesalius) of a surgeon who (by developing an investigative surgery) wants to 'take over' the domain of the higher discipline (medicine). The disciplinary tensions between the physicians who taught anatomy from texts and the surgeons who were expected to demonstrate the physicians' claims through the dissected body are beautifully recorded in the discussions/challenges between Vesalius and Curtius during the former's visit to Bologna to perform an anatomy; Ruben Ericksson (ed.), *Andreas Vesalius' First Public Anatomy at Bologna, 1540: An Eyewitness Report* (Uppsala and Stockholm, 1959), esp. pp. 273.

34 Another homology between mathematicians and surgeons may be found in the strategic use of humanism so as to represent their discipline and profession as having Classical (i.e. legitimate) ancestors. Compare, for instance, the strategies discussed by Nutton in 'Humanistic Surgery' and my analysis of some mathematicians' use of Archimedes in 'Italian Mathematicians', pp. 56–67.

35 On the intricate debate over the authorship of the Fabrica's plates and on the relationship between Vesalius and John Stephen, see William Ivins, 'What About the "Fabrica" of Vesalius?', in S. W. Lambert *et al.* (eds.), *Three Vesalian*

Essays (New York, 1952), 45–99; A. Hyatt Mayor, *Artists and Anatomists* (New York, 1984), pp. 97–115.

36 On the link between the social legitimation of anatomy and the anatomists' reference to tropes of court culture see Daniel Brownstein's 'The Production of Anatomical Meaning', a paper delivered at the Northern California Renaissance Association Meeting, Spring 1990, to be included in his forthcoming dissertation, 'Revealing Anatomy: Anatomists and the Medical Space in Italy, 1520–1640', University of California, Berkeley. On Vesalius' pictorial strategies see also Glenn Harcourt, 'Andreas Vesalius and the Anatomy of Antique Sculpture', *Representations* 17 (1987), 28–61. Harcourt's argument is somewhat different from but commensurable with the one presented here. He stresses the connection between Vesalius' anatomical illustrations and Classical sculptures as a way of overcoming the connotation of anatomy as a discipline whose knowledge was rooted in routine violation of bodies. Although I am more concerned with anatomy's low social status because of its mechanical connotation rather than because of its image as a body-violating image, I think that the evidence presented by Harcourt supports my point as well as his.

37 Vesalius published a much shorter, smaller, and less expensive *Epitome* for students' use. It was also published, as the *Fabrica*, in 1543. Illustrations from the *Fabrica* are reproduced in J. B. de C. M. Saunders and Charles D. O'Malley (eds.), *The Illustrations from the Works of Andreas Vesalius of Brussels* (New York, 1973).

38 On Vesalius see C. D. O'Malley, *Andreas Vesalius of Brussels* (Berkeley, 1964). For a survey and bibliographical references on the Padua school of anatomy see Giuseppe Ongaro, 'La medicina nello Studio di Padova e nel Veneto', in G. Arnaldi and M. Pastore Stocchi (eds.), *Storia della cultura veneta*, III, pt. 3 (Vicenza, 1981), 75–134. On anatomy at Bologna see G. Martinotti, *L'insegnamento dell'anatomia a Bologna prima del secolo XIX* (Bologna, 1911). On anatomy at Pisa, see A. Corsini, *Andrea Vesalio nello Studio di Pisa* (Siena, 1915). On the continuing tensions between surgeons and physicians around the teaching of anatomy at the beginning of the eighteenth century, see Elena Brambilla, 'La medicina del settecento: dal monopolio dogmatico alla professione scientifica', in Franco Della Peruta (ed.), *Malattia e Medicina*, Annali VII (Turin, 1984), 5–147 (esp. pp. 5–15).

39 Pierre Bourdieu, *Distinction* (Cambridge, Mass., 1984).

40 Gerrari, 'Public Anatomy Lessons', pp. 76, 81, 89–90. On the Padua botanical garden as a tourist attraction, see Azzi Visentini, 'Il Giardino dei Semplici di Padova', p. 268. On the botanical gardens of Pisa and Florence as symbols of Medici power, see Paolo Galluzzi, 'Il mecenatismo mediceo e le scienze', in Cesare Vasoli (ed.), *Idee, istituzioni, scienza ed arti nella Firenze dei Medici* (Florence, 1980), p. 196.

41 Ferrari, 'Public Anatomy Lessons', pp. 50–106, esp. 97.

42 Confirming the close relationship between institutionalization and socio-disciplinary status, Ferrari argues that the establishment of the theatre of anatomy at Bologna in the 1590s was also tied to the awareness that temporary theatres (something that Bologna had been using until then) had become

'something of a stain on the honor of a discipline that by this time had gained a fine reputation', *ibidem*, p. 72.

43 *ibidem*, p. 66–74, esp. 72–3. Ferrari quotes Aranzio, a Bolognese teacher of anatomy and surgery, as saying in 1586 that: '...I should no longer depend in any way on the scholars, but should recognize as patrons only the distinguished senators; it was therefore concluded that I should be inscribed in the roll of anatomy, and thus insured, and freed from the election of the scholars.' *ibidem*, p. 68. Although this quote dates nine years before the project of the theatre, it lays out very explicitly the anatomists' stakes in the establishment of a city-controlled theatre of anatomy.

44 On dissections as spectacle, see *ibidem*, pp. 56–9, 82–93, and Brownstein, 'The Production of Anatomical Meaning'.

45 André Graindorge to Pierre-Daniel Huet (19 May 1665), quoted in David S. Lux, *Patronage and Royal Science in Seventeenth-Century France* (Ithaca, 1989), p. 40. The translation is Lux's.

46 Michael Lynch has put forward a similar claim about the fate of laboratory rats in 'Sacrifice and the Transformation of the Animal Body into a Scientific Object: Laboratory Culture and Ritual Practice in the Neurosciences', *Social Studies of Science* 18 (1988), 265–89. For related considerations, see also Stefan Hirschauer, 'The Manufacturer of Bodies in Surgery', *Social Studies of Science* 21 (1991), 279–319.

47 These issues maintained a crucial importance later on with the development of experimental philosophy and of experimental sites where only so-called legitimate witnesses would be admitted. On seventeenth-century experimental spaces see Steven Shapin, 'The House of Experiment in Seventeenth-Century England', *Isis* 79 (1988), 373–404.

48 Ferrari, 'Public Anatomy Lessons', p. 52.

49 Baldessarre Castiglione, *The Book of the Courtier*, Book II, ch. 11.

50 Paula Findlen, 'Museums, Collecting, and Scientific Culture in Early Modern Italy' (Ph.D. dissertation, University of California, Berkeley, 1989); *idem*, 'The Economy of Scientific Exchange in Early Modern Europe: Italy', in Bruce Moran (ed.), *Patronage and Institutions* (forthcoming); Giuseppe Olmi, 'Ordine e fama: il museo naturalistico in Italia nei secoli XVI e XVII', *Annali dell'Istituto Storico Italo-Germanico in Trento* 8 (1982), 105–81; *idem*, 'Alle origini della politica culturale dello stato moderno: dal collezionismo privato al "Cabinet du Roi"', *La cultura* 16 (1978), 471–84; *idem*, Ulisse Aldrovandi: scienza e natura nel secondo cinquecento (Trento, 1976). See also Dario A. Franchini *et al.*, *Scienza a corte. Collezionismo eclettico, natura e immagine a Mantova fra rinascimento e manierismo* (Rome, 1979); Gigliola Fragnito, *In museo e in villa* (Venice, 1988); Giorgio Fulco, 'Per il "museo" dei fratelli Della Porta', in Maria Cristina Cafisse (ed.), *Rinascimento meridionale e altri studi* (Naples, 1987), 105–175; Oliver Impey and Arthur MacGregor (eds.), *The Origins of Museums* (Oxford 1985), pp. 5–28; Aimi Antonio, Vincenzo De Michele and Alessandro Morandotti, *Musaeum Septalianum: una collezione scientifica nella Milano del seicento* (Milan, 1984); Maristella Casciato, Maria Grazia Iannello and Maria Vitale (eds.), *Enciclopedismo in roma barocca. Athanasius Kircher e il Museo del Collegio Romano tra Wunderkammer e museo scientifico* (Venice, 1986); Adalgisa Lugli,

Naturalia et mirabilia (Milan, 1983); *idem*, 'Inquiry as Collection', *RES* 12 (1986), 109–124; Krzysztof Pomian, *Collectionneurs, amateurs et curieux. Paris, Venise: XVIe–XVIIe siècle*, (Paris, 1987). On recent anthropological interpretations of collecting and museums, see James Clifford, *The Predicament of Culture* (Cambridge, Mass., 1988), pp. 215–51, and George Stocking (ed.), *Objects and Others*, (Madison, 1985).

51 The classic text on gift exchange is Marcel Mauss, *The Gift* (New York, 1967). On the role of gift exchange in early modern science see Biagioli, 'Galileo's System of Patronage', pp. 18–25 and Findlen, 'The Economy of Scientific Exchange'.

52 Findlen, 'Museums, Collecting, and Scientific Culture', p. 390.

53 Biagioli, 'Galileo's System of Patronage', pp. 38–41.

54 Biagioli, 'Galileo the Emblem Maker', pp. 253–4.

55 *Ibid.*, pp. 232–6.

56 Thanks to their royal status and to the dynastic theogony-style mythologies they had developed since the mid-sixteenth century, the Medici could (mythologically) represent themselves as being linked to the 'other gods' of the cosmos. Such a self-representation was not available to the nobility and patriciate. Natural history collecting and the museum were activities and spaces more appropriate to their status. Galileo's discoveries (as he had represented them) were 'above their heads'. Through the museum – a space perceived as an encyclopaedic picture of the entire world – the gentlemen could still represent themselves as being 'in touch' with the cosmos. However, the connection that the museum was able to establish between the collector and the cosmos was a 'generic' one. The macrocosm-microcosm analogy was one that fitted anybody and nobody in particular. In a sense, all museums were pictures of the cosmos. Instead, Galileo had managed to establish a *personal* relationship between the Medici and Jupiter.

57 This argument is informed by Pierre Bourdieu's work on the dynamics of social distinction as present in his *Distinction*, esp. pp. 11–96.

58 That the vast majority of Italian active foreign members of the Royal Society during the late seventeenth and the eighteenth centuries were physicians seems to support this point (Marie Boas Hall, 'The Royal Society and Italy, 1667–1795', *Notes and Records of the Royal Society* 37 (1982), 63–81; p. 70).

59 Galileo's inability to produce exceptional discoveries on a routine basis was not necessarily a liability. Although this may have prevented the Medici from developing an astronomical observatory, the very rarity of court-fitting astronomical discoveries, that made science's institutionalization unappealing to the Medici, provided Galileo with the possibility of an exceptional career by presenting his exceptionally rare discoveries as eminently 'exclusive' – that is as fitting the codes of taste of an absolutist prince.

60 However, one may argue that Louis XIV's recruitment of Huygens to Paris to direct the newly-founded Académie des Sciences in 1666 may also be a result of the high international visibility he had gained through his work on Saturn's system.

61 On the debate on Saturn's rings, see Albert Van Helden, 'The Accademia del

Cimento and Saturn's Ring', *Physis* 15 (1975), 244–59. On astronomical discoveries after 1650 see *idem*, 'The Telescope in the Seventeenth Century'.

62 In fact, as shown by Margaret Jacob, Newton's philosophy gained an emblematic significance for a socio-religious group (the 'latitudinarians'), not for an absolute prince; *The Newtonians and the English Revolution, 1689–1720* (Ithaca, 1976). See also Julian Martin, 'Explaining John Freind's *History of Physick*', *Studies in History and Philosophy of Science* 19 (1988), 399–418.

63 Roger Hahn, *The Anatomy of a Scientific Institution: The Paris Academy of Sciences, 1666–1803* (Berkeley, 1971), pp. 1–57; Alice Stroup, *A Company of Scientists* (Berkeley, 1990), pp. 46–61, 103–16, 169–79. For a recent interpretation of Louis' support of science, see Roger Hahn, 'Louis XIV and Science Policy', in David L. Rubin (ed.), *Sun King: The Ascendancy of French Culture during the Reign of Louis XIV* (Washington, 1991), 195–206.

64 Actually Gian Domenico Cassini, after having discovered two additional satellites of Saturn in 1671–2, quickly realized that the number of known planets and satellites (fourteen) matched Louis' dynastic order. Although the king appreciated the 'gift', he did not go out of his way to demonstrate his gratitude to Cassini, who was not even mentioned in the medal that was struck in 1686 to commemorate the event; I. B. Cohen, 'G. D. Cassini and the Number of the Planets', in Trevor H. Levere and William R. Shea (eds.), *Nature, Experiment, and the Sciences* (Dordrecht and Boston, 1990), 199–205.

65 Louis Marin, *Portrait of the King* (Minneapolis, 1988), pp. 121–37. Louis Marin's work has informed several aspects of the analysis of political absolutism presented here.

66 Jean-Marie Apostolidès, *Le Roi machine* (Paris, 1981), esp. ch. 2, 'L'organization de la culture', and Rubin, *Sun King*.

67 The observatory's monumentality reflected Colbert's plan (never quite fulfilled) that it would serve as the headquarters of the Académie – it was supposed to become Louis' 'House of Solomon'. On the conflicts between the architect Perrault and the astronomer Cassini, see C. Wolf, *Histoire de l'Observatoire de Paris de sa fondation à 1973* (Paris, 1902), pp. 19–27. That the observatory was actually perceived as a monument is confirmed by Wolf who writes that: 'Avant même que la construction du grand bâtiment fut terminée, l'Observatoire devint un but de promenade pour les seigneurs et les dames de la Cour…', promenades that flattered Cassini but disrupted his working schedule (*ibidem*, p. 115).

68 Actually, such representations may have been counter-productive in that they may have implied that Louis was in need of that type of legitimation.

69 Cohen, 'G. D. Cassini and the Number of the Planets', p. 204. See also n. 63.

70 See also n. 89.

71 The standard sources on the Accademia del Cimento are: Giovanni Targioni Tozzetti, *Notizie degli aggrandimenti delle scienze fisiche accaduti in Toscana nel corso di anni LX del secolo XVII* (Florence, 1780; repr. Bologna, 1970); W. E. Knowles Middleton, *The Experimenters* (Baltimore, 1971). See also the very insightful article by Paolo Galluzzi, 'L'Accademia del Cimento: "gusti" del principe, filosofia e ideologia dell'esperimento', *Quaderni storici* 16 (1981), 788–844.

72 Galluzzi, 'L'Accademia del Cimento', p. 823.

73 For brief biographical sketches of the participants to the Cimento, see Knowles Middleton, *The Experimenters*, pp. 26–40. On Antonio Uliva – the most 'picturesque' of the academicians – see Ugo Baldini, *Un libertino accademico del Cimento: Antonio Uliva* (Florence, 1977).

74 Ferrari, 'Public Anatomy Lessons', p. 80.

75 Venceslao Santi, 'La Storia nella *Secchia Rapita*', *Memorie della Reale Accademia di Scienze, Lettere, e Arti in Modena* 3:9 (1910), pp. 263–4.

76 This, in fact, is how Leopold was presented in the preface to the *Saggi*; Giorgio Abetti and Pietro Pagnini (eds.), *L'Accademia del Cimento* (Florence, 1942), p. 85.

77 Shapin, 'The House of Experiment', pp. 395–9. The concern with the development of a gentlemanly discourse of science is one of the leitmotifs of Shapin and Schaffer, *Leviathan and the Air Pump*.

78 Abetti and Pagnini, *L'Accademia del Cimento*, pp. 83–7, 124. See also my 'Galileo's System of Patronage', pp. 36–8. An analysis of the relationship between scientific discourses that do not search for ultimate causes and the political discourse of absolutism as embodied in court culture is presented in my 'Courtly Comets', ch. 5 of *Galileo Courtier* (Chicago, 1992).

79 Van Helden, 'The Accademia del Cimento and Saturn's Ring', *Physis* 15 (1975), 244–59. A similar attempt on Leopold's side to get off the hook by introducing experimental protocols of evaluation rather than pass judgements on the disputants' claims is also reflected in the Cimento's involvement in the dispute between Divini and Campani on the relative quality of their telescopes; Maria Luisa Righini Bonelli and Albert Van Helden, *Divini and Campani: A Forgotten Chapter in the History of the Accademia del Cimento* (Florence, 1981).

80 In his 'Of Conversational Dispositions and the *Saggi*'s Proem', in Elizabeth Cropper (ed.), *Documentary Culture: Florence and Rome from Grand Duke Ferdinand I to Pope Alexander VII* (Florence, forthcoming), Jay Tribby has convincingly argued that this type of discourse should not be seen as reflecting a modern concern with scientific 'objectivity' but rather a paradigmatic example of seventeenth-century courtly *sprezzatura*.

81 Galluzzi, 'L'Accademia del Cimento', p. 798. That the *Saggi* could not be bought was a result of Leopold's high status. However, this also helped the credibility of the scientific work described in the volume. In fact, by not being on sale, the *Saggi* were represented as being the result of a disinterested and therefore objective enterprise.

82 Shapin, 'The House of Experiment', pp. 383–95, 399–404. That the academy's closure *vis-à-vis* non-members was related to Leopold's princely status is supported by a similar pattern we encounter in France. In fact, the Académie des Sciences (another academy founded by a prince), too, was much less open to outsiders than the Royal Society. Finally, although Leopold's academy received a few visitors, I suspect that these visits were strategically planned rather than routine events. For instance, the only documented visit to the Cimento is by the *English* ambassador to Florence – a visit that happened at a time when Leopold was trying to prove the Torricellian priority over the vacuum experiments, the prime subject matter of *Boyle*'s work. Targioni Tozzetti, *Notizie degli aggrandimenti* II, pt. 1, pp. 333–6.

83 Michael Hunter, *Science and Society in Restoration England*, (Cambridge, 1981), p.

36; Shapin, 'The House of Experiment', p. 392. As noticed by Norbert Elias, etiquette tends to become more intricate when the risks of status-pollution rise higher. Consequently, Leopold's academy's lack of a specific ceremonial reflects its private character – a context which reduced considerably the possibility of status-pollution.

84 The diary of the Accademia del Cimento presents a picture of the certification process strikingly similar to that adopted by the Royal Society. On 31 July 1662, 'The Academy met at Sig. Lorenzo Magalotti's house, about repeating some experiments that appeared most necessary to the finishing of the work that is to be printed. *All of these, when they have been made easy by practice, have to be done again in the presence of His Highness.*' (quoted in Middleton, *The Experimenters*, p. 57, emphasis mine). The procedure is very similar to that described by Shapin, in which the experiments were tried and de-bugged at Hooke's house/ laboratory and then re-produced in front of the Society's certifying membership (Shapin, 'The House of Experiment', pp. 400–2). The structure of the certifying process is identical in the two cases; what changes is only the certifying persona.

85 Steven Shapin, 'Pump and Circumstance: Robert Boyle's Literary Technology', *Social Studies of Science* 14 (1984), 481–520. In 'Cooking (with) Clio and Cleo: Eloquence and Experiment in Seventeenth-Century Florence', *Journal of the History of Ideas* 52 (1991), 417–39, Jay Tribby discusses the experimental narratives of Francesco Redi and of the Cimento in terms of courtly conversation with ancient authors who had written on similar topics.

86 Shapin, 'The House of Experiment', pp. 373–404; *idem*, 'The Invisible Technician', *American Scientist* 77 (November–December 1989), 554–63.

87 Similarly – as shown by the lengthy review process of the manuscript – Leopold showed himself extremely worried about the possibility of somebody finding errors in the *Saggi*.

88 It may be that the Cimento's apparent lack of interest in building an air pump could have been related to Leopold's status. A sweat-inducing machine may have been too much for Leopold. On the devices introduced to keep sweaty operators of air-pumps out of the gaze of the aristocratic virtuoso, see Steven Shapin, 'The Invisible Technician'.

89 However, one may try to argue that Bacon's natural philosophy – having been developed by a high court official in a period in which royal power in England was moving toward political absolutism – may have reflected some of the features that would later become typical of the political discourse of continental absolutism.

The Académie's official acceptance of individually authored publications (still reviewed collectively by the Académie) took place only in 1699; Hahn, *Anatomy of a Scientific Institution*, pp. 19–20, and Léon Aucoc, *L'Institut de France. Lois, statuts et règlements concernant les anciennes Académies et l'Institut de 1635 à 1889* (Paris, 1889), pp. 87, 89. On the Académie's secretive attitudes about internal proceedings and discussions, concern with controlling the publications of academicians, and tensions resulting between these practices and the individual academicians' aspirations, see Stroup, *A Company of Scientists*, pp. 204–9. I tend to see these issues as related to the king's need to present the Académie as

'royal', that is, as his own (hence the secrecy about its proceedings). The
Académie was not just another gathering. It was an official one; it involved the
king's name and honour in its activities and products (hence the careful
collective review, censorship, and occasional anonymity of its texts).

90 On the Royal Society's publishing policies, see Margery Purver, *The Royal
Society: Concept and Creation* (Cambridge, Mass., 1967), p. 179.

91 The parallels between Leopold's policy for science and the visual arts are quite
interesting. As shown by Edward Goldberg's *After Vasari. History, Art, and
Patronage in Late Medici Florence* (Princeton, 1988), Leopold structured his
patronage of the arts on the conscious realization that Florence (and the
Medici) had played a crucial role in the development of the visual arts in Italy
and Europe. Probably because Florence was now losing its role as the trend-
setter in the visual arts, it was time to begin to celebrate the *history* of the
relationship between the Medici and the arts. Leopold's sponsorship of Filippo
Baldinucci's strictly Florence-centred monumental continuation of Vasari's
Lives of the Artists is part of this design. The establishment of a Gallery in the
Uffizi exclusively dedicated to celebrating the *artists* who had worked for the
Medici (and not only their works) is another part of this programme. I think
that the Cimento (and especially its *Saggi*) fit this picture very well. They are the
scientific equivalent of Leopold's celebration of the Medici historical role in the
development of the arts. In fact, if one remembers that the Medici had
supported Galileo and Torricelli (whose experiments on the vacuum kept busy
European *virtuosi* for much of the seventeenth century) it is not far-fetched to
imagine that Leopold could perceive his House as having supported 'all
science' in the same way they had patronized all that counted in the visual arts.

92 On this issue, see also n. 56.

93 The link between courtly science and *conversazione* has been introduced by Jay
Tribby in his studies of seventeenth-century Tuscan, Italian and French courtly
and gentlemanly science. On the subject, see his 'Of Conversational Dispositions and the *Saggi*'s Proem', in Cropper, *Documentary Culture*; idem, 'Con-
versing the *museo Cospiano*', forthcoming in *Rhetorica*; and idem, 'Cooking (with)
Clio and Cleo'. On courtly science as *conversazione*, see also Mario Biagioli,
Galileo Courtier, ch. 3.

94 Several of their 'experimental objects' had a definite high-status connotation.
For instance, the academicians observed *thick gold* containers exploded by the
expansion of ice, experimented with the dissolution of *pearls*, and studied the
properties of *diamonds*.

95 On the Cimento as a prince-driven enterprise, see Galluzzi, 'L'Accademia del
Cimento', pp. 796–7. That the Cimento was not a practitioner-driven body is
made clear by the dissatisfaction with its 'research programme' expressed by
some of its best members like Borelli. In particular, he was frustrated by three
features of the academy. First, the academy – being bound by Leopold's
concern with avoiding interpretations – was not producing interesting claims.
Second, the collective voice with which it was presenting its results destroyed
the authorship of its most able members. Third, the experiments were not
targeted at a specific research programme (a programme that could not exist

given Leopold's status-investment) but wandered in all directions or focused for too long on what Borelli perceived as irrelevant problems.

96 That calling meetings without warning was a sign of power is confirmed by Louis XIV's practices. In his memoires, he recalled calling up his ministers 'when they least expected it'. (quoted in James E. King, *Science and Rationalism in the Government of Louis XIV, 1661–1683*, (Baltimore, 1949), p. 86).

97 Judging from contemporary reports reproduced by Wolf, the Dauphin's visit to the Académie in 1677 and that of Louis in 1681 were highly ceremonial events and the royal guests did not participate in any scientific activity (Wolf, *Histoire de l'Observatoire*, pp. 117–18). See also Stroup's brief but insightful remarks on Le Clerc's engraving of the (imaginary) visit of Louis to the Académie in 1671, *A Company of Scientists*, pp. 5–8. On the Royal Society expectations about Charles II's visit, see Shapin and Schaffer, *Leviathan and the Air Pump*, pp. 31–2, and Simon Schaffer, 'Wallification: Thomas Hobbes on School Divinity and Experimental Pneumatics', *Studies in History and Philosophy of Science* 19 (1988), pp. 294–5. On the way the 'distance' between the patron and the client frames the forms of scientific discourse and their legitimacy, see Biagioli, 'Galileo's System of Patronage', pp. 36–8. I am developing this theme at greater length in my forthcoming 'Absolutism, the Modern State, and the Development of Scientific Manners'.

98 On the literary dimension of the *Saggi*, see Teresa Poggi Salani, 'Tra Accademia della Crusca e Accademia del Cimento', in V. Branca (ed.), *Letteratura e scienza* (Palermo, 1978), 519–28.

99 Abetti and Pagnini, *L'Accademia del Cimento*, p. 144.

100 For instance, his brother Ferdinand II – the grand duke – could not have adopted such a patronage strategy. In fact, although for many years Ferdinand gathered an academy resembling Leopold's, his status prevented him from giving it any public visibility. Ferdinand's academy was never represented through something like the *Saggi*.

101 W. E. Knowles Middleton, 'Science in Rome, 1675–1700, and the Accademia Fisicomatematica of Giovanni Giustino Ciampini', *The British Journal for the History of Science* 8 (1975), 138–54.

102 At least, disciplinary boundaries and hierarchies are not conspicuous categories in the historiography of English early modern science.

103 Michael Hunter, *The Royal Society and Its Fellows 1660–1700: The Morphology of an Early Scientific Institution* (Chalfont St Giles, 1985).

104 On the difficult synthesis of the roles of the gentleman and the experimental philosopher, see Steven Shapin, '"A Scholar and a Gentleman": The Problematic Identity of the Scientific Practitioner in Early Modern England', *History of Science* (1991), 279–327.

105 For instance, although the English astronomer Harriot used the telescope for astronomical observations before Galileo, he does not seem to have thought of the reward he could have received by a courtly representation of those 'marvels'.

106 On the role of spectacular experiments in maintaining the Royal Society's membership, see John Heilbron, *Physics at the Royal Society during Newton's Presidency* (Berkeley, 1983).

107 For instance, upon receiving the Cimento's *Saggi*, Oldenburg referred to it as
     'the pompous book of their experiments', R. D. Waller, 'Lorenzo Magalotti in
     England, 1668–9', *Italian Studies* 1 (1937), p. 60.
108 The similarities between the corporate etiquette of the Royal Society and that
     of the House of Commons has already been noted by Steven Shapin in 'The
     House of Experiment', pp. 392–3.
109 Shapin and Schaffer, *Leviathan and the Air Pump*, pp. 22–79; Shapin, 'The House
     of Experiment'. Issues of trust, credibility, and non-disruptive, 'duel-pre-
     venting' forms of scientific discourse are being analysed by Steven Shapin in his
     forthcoming book, *The Social History of Truth*.
110 Shapin and Schaffer, *Leviathan and the Air Pump*, pp. 80–1, 282–3.
111 On the prohibition of duels see Richard Herr, 'Honor Versus Absolutism:
     Richelieu's Fight Against Dueling', *The Journal of Modern History* 27 (1955),
     281–5; Frederick R. Bryson, *The Sixteenth-Century Italian Duel* (Chicago, 1938),
     pp. 102–3; V. G. Kiernan, *The Duel in European History* (Oxford, 1989), esp. pp.
     68–96; François Billacois, *The Duel: Its Rise and Fall in Early Modern France* (New
     Haven, 1990), pp. 40–6, 95–105. For an interesting analysis of the transition
     from aristocratic views of duels to more 'civilized' ones informed by considera-
     tions of absolutist reason of state, see Giancarlo Angelozzi, 'Cultura dell'onore,
     codici di comportamento nobiliari e stato nella Bologna pontificia: un'ipotesi di
     lavoro', *Annali dell'Istituto storico italo-germanico in Trento* 8 (1982), 305–24. On
     the transition, in Italy, from fighting duels to talking about them, that is, to the
     emergence of the 'scienza cavalleresca' partly as a form of courtly conversation
     at the end of the sixteenth century, see Francesco Erspamer, *La biblioteca di Don
     Ferrante. Duello e onore nella cultura del cinquecento* (Rome, 1982), pp. 56–7, 69–73.
     On duel-like theatrical court spectacles, see, for instance, Alois Maria Nagler,
     Theatre Festivals of the Medici (New Haven, 1964) and Elias, *Court Society*, pp.
     148–9.
112 It is important to remember that the literary genres used by the courtly Galileo
     tended to be *fictional*. For instance, he did not write *treatises* (a genre in which the
     author speaks with *ex-professo* authority and, consequently, 'gives the lie' to
     opponents) but worked within the fictional genre of the *dialogue* (Campanella
     called the *Dialogue on the Two Chief World Systems* a 'philosophical comedy'), the
     discourse (a genre in which arguments are presented and debated without
     reaching ultimate truths), and *letters* (addressed to a third party rather than to
     the interlocutor whose positions he was challenging). Similarly, in the *Assayer*
     – one of Galileo's most abrasive works – he did not debate against a real person
     but insulted a *mask* (in that debate, the Jesuit Grassi was represented as a
     fictional character – Lotario Sarsi). As Galileo mentioned at the beginning of
     the *Assayer*, by wearing a mask, one makes him/herself liable to insults because
     his/her real identity and status (the *sine qua non* for a challenge) become
     undetectable. The apparent exception presented by the two published texts
     where he made extensive use of geometrical propositions can be explained. One,
     the *Discourse on the Two New Sciences*, was published after his fall, in the
     Netherlands, and allegedly without his permission. The other, the *Discourse on
     Bodies in Water*, was largely a dialectical argument that contained only a few
     geometrical propositions. Its relatively dogmatic character can be seen as a

result of Galileo's attempt to restore his credibility with the grand duke after he had been vocally attacked by a number of Tuscan philosophers and had been criticized by the grand duke for his impolite behaviour during the dispute. In short, Galileo was 'philosophically violent' because he had been 'given the lie' by his opponents. Nevertheless, it is interesting that his 'dogmatic' style was criticized by his friend Sagredo and by the Jesuit Griemberger.

113 It is also interesting to see that, in time, jousts and tournaments shed their aggressive features and turned into polite theatrical genres and equestrian ballets; Elias, *Court Society*, pp. 148–9.

114 Biagioli, 'Galileo's System of Patronage', p. 30.

115 Galileo's trial should not be seen as an exception to this pattern. The patron's ability to represent the client's claims as fictional should be evaluated contextually. For instance, because of his delicate political position in 1632, Urban VIII could not quite act as if Galileo's *Dialogue* were a hypothetical piece (as it was supposed to be).

116 A much more extensive and detailed comparative analysis of these issues is provided in my 'Absolutism, the Modern State, and Scientific Manners' (forthcoming in *Critical Inquiry*), and in *Galileo Courtier*, ch. 1 and Epilogue.

117 The patron's honour could be threatened in a number of ways: by binding it to knowledge claims that may turn out to be wrong; by tying it to an author whose aggressive argumentative style may be represented as a breach of polite etiquette; or – in the case of an absolute prince – by intimating that the practitioners' knowledge was produced independently from the legitimation they had received from the prince.

118 However, one could not increase the 'distance' between the practitioners and the princely source of legitimation indefinitely without delegitimizing the scientific enterprise. In fact, were the 'distance' to increase too much, then the scientific disciplines may be perceived as illegitimate, unreliable, etc., like self-interested artisans.

119 This phenomenon reflects well-known patronage scenarios. As Francesco Liberati put it in *Il perfetto Maestro di Casa*, (Rome, Bernabò, 1658), 'Lodasi però più tosto il non intrigarsi troppo co i signori, massimamemte co i Principi grandi, li quali sono simili al fuoco, che posto in debita distanza riscalda, & illumina, e troppo vicino abbrugia, e toglie la vista,' p. 9.

120 Some of these issues are analysed in ch. 2 of Steven Shapin's forthcoming book, *A Social History of Truth*.

121 Shapin, 'The House of Experiment', pp. 397–8.

122 I owe this felicitous phrase to Steven Shapin.

123 On the relationship between 'neutral facts', etiquette and objectivity, see also Lorraine Daston, 'Baconian Facts, Academic Civility, and the Prehistory of Objectivity', forthcoming in *Annals of Scholarship*.

124 By 'involving' I mean both direct and virtual involvement. Virtual involvement refers to the fact that, by resembling the ritualized forms of interaction that structured the gentlemen's lives and identities, experimental philosophy may have seemed 'natural' to them. In short, an entire culture (and not just the set of gentlemen involved in the production of one specific matter of fact) was represented in that 'scientific etiquette'.

125 Expanding on Shapin's and Schaffer's crucial but somewhat Durkheimian
    point that solutions to the problem of knowledge are solutions to the problem of
    social order, I would say that the notion of etiquette may help bring those two
    domains together by pointing to the process through which both knowledge
    and social order are produced and maintained: self-fashioning.

126 However, I am not at all dismissing the role played by England's specific socio-
    economic context in the development of its science. On the contrary, I believe
    that those considerations could be easily reconciled with the picture presented
    here. In fact, the specific English political structure and discourse that frames
    my interpretation is closely connected to the specific socio-economical scenario
    of seventeenth-century England.

2

THE SCIENTIFIC REVOLUTION IN FRANCE

L. W. B. BROCKLISS

THE AGE OF THE UNIVERSITY

IN the second half of the sixteenth and in the early seventeenth centuries the large majority of the French social and cultural elite showed scant interest in unravelling nature's secrets. The socially dominant *noblesse d'épée* seldom received a sophisticated education in the classical humanities and philosophy and often could read no other language but French. Their physically exacting existence left little time to contemplate God's creation and the few who did so found a soldier's comfort in the sceptical wisdom of Montaigne.[1] The highly-educated members of the liberal professions, on the other hand, had usually studied natural philosophy as part of their professional training. But they too showed little interest in later life in gaining a fuller acquaintance with the natural world. Although many clerics and lawyers were extraordinarily learned, by and large their erudition was focused on the burning religious and political problems of the day, not on the mysteries of nature.[2] Even medical physicians paid scant attention to the philosophy of nature on which their professional activities were supposedly based. Whatever they might claim, the majority were empirical practitioners.

Apart from the odd figure at court the only Frenchmen who had more than a passing interest in the science of nature in the era of the Wars of Religion were likely to be professors of philosophy and medicine. In their case they had little choice, for physics or natural philosophy was part of their teaching brief. France in the early seventeenth century was well-endowed with institutions of higher education, possessing sixteen universities and some hundred *collèges de plein exercice* which taught the classical humanities and philosophy. As a result the teachers of physics formed a coterie several hundred strong, to whose number must be added the philosophy professors attached to many regular convents. Yet if the professors were forced by their charge to have some sort of expertise in natural philosophy, only a handful had a permanent and passionate interest in the science of nature. Colleges were increasingly in the hands of the regular orders, especially the Jesuits, who seldom employed a professor in the same capacity for more than a couple of years, while medical faculties outside the Midi lacked endowed chairs and appointed lecturers on short-term contracts. In fact, dedicated students of nature were usually to be found only in the capital. In the early seventeenth century Paris possessed some ten *collèges de plein exercice* staffed by seculars who often held their post for several decades. It was also the site of the Collège Royal, an elite institution founded by François I containing endowed chairs in philosophy, medicine and mathematics (a subject at this date otherwise largely neglected).[3]

The natural philosophy nurtured in the universities, colleges and convents of early Bourbon France was a causal science. The large majority of professors were not interested in increasing the amount of data mankind possessed about the natural world but in explaining everyday experiences in the light of a series of axioms. This natural philosophy was also primarily an historical and textual science. The professors did not see their task as one of developing a personal statement about the natural world. Rather they saw themselves as the explicators of a philosophical enterprise which stretched back through their scholastic forebears to the ancient Greeks. Their role, as seekers after truth, was to locate among the ancient philosophers the man whose conception of the principles of physics was self-evidently right, then to evaluate in the light of those principles the various explanations of natural phenomena that he, his followers and even dissident philosophers had subsequently offered. In other words the early Bourbon natural philosopher saw himself as a judge, who passed sentence on the arguments of his predecessors, not an explorer.

Among the various physical philosophies of antiquity the professors considered only the formulations of Aristotle and Galen worthy of consideration. The professors never believed that antiquity should be slavishly followed, and some even cited the Horatian tag 'in nullius verba'.[4] Nevertheless all were unequivocal supporters of the Peripatetic School. Similarly, Renaissance critics of Aristotle and Galen received scant attention. Ramus, a Paris professor until his murder in 1572, was largely ignored even by Protestant colleagues, while Paracelsus and his followers were the object of permanent vilification. It was only among medical practitioners outside the university world that supporters of hermetic or iatrochemical cosmologies were to be found. When Giordano Bruno attempted to outline his ideas at the University of Paris in 1585 he had to make an unscheduled and ignominious departure through a window to escape the wrath of his audience.[5] The professors' prejudice was strengthened by the growing support they received from the Catholic Church and secular authority. Both Henri III and Henri IV tolerated and even welcomed philosophical dissidents, such as Bruno, at court. The Catholic Church and its allies in the judicial bureaucracy, however, saw opponents of Aristotelianism (often quite rightly) as the allies of Protestantism. After the assassination of Henri IV in 1610 the court, too, succumbed to this Counter-Reformation paranoia and it became unwise to parade heterodox philosophical opinions openly. Not surprisingly, committed Paracelsian physicians left the country. The Protestant Turquet de Mayerne, for instance, crossed the Channel to the court of King James. Those who attempted to flout establishment opinion were quickly silenced. When in 1624 the chemist Etienne de Clave and two friends attempted to hold a public debate in defence of atomist principles, the Paris Parlement banned the mooted *séance*, expelled the three offenders from the jurisdiction of the court (one-third of France), and forbade in the future 'any person on pain of death to hold or teach any maxim contrary to ancient and approved authors'.[6] Most heterodox thinkers lay low and waited for court opinion to change. This was only to happen once the eirenicist Richelieu was firmly in control after 1630.[7]

However, although the professors were imprisoned within an Aristotelian framework, it must not be thought that their natural philosophy lacked vitality. Admittedly, they were expected to work within a scholastic Aristotelian tradition. They were not free to imitate their Paduan colleagues and develop a purely rational Aristotelian science of nature that ignored the truths of the Christian faith.[8] All the same, there had never been a single scholastic *via* in the late middle ages and on contentious issues the professors were relatively free to choose between the different schools. They were not constrained, like colleagues in some Catholic states, to promote a particular scholastic position.[9] Moreover, many were advocates of philosophical eclecticism who denounced alternative traditions as philosophical heresies but freely incorporated the opinions of Aristotle's opponents and enemies within their natural science.

Some professors, for instance, were interested in Plato on account of his semi-Christian view of the soul and on a number of occasions Paris professors, notably Jacques Charpentier, lectured on the compendium of Alcinous.[10] Others, especially medical professors, demonstrated a sympathy for certain Paracelsian and hermetic ideas. The inspiration behind this particular development seems to have been the mid-sixteenth century Paris physician, Jean Fernel, whose extremely influential

Galenic synthesis laid idiosyncratic stress on the role of occult powers and faculties rather than elemental qualities in explaining natural phenomena.[11] Fernel's authority became the justification for accepting the validity of many Paracelsian homeopathic remedies that had no justification in Aristotelo-Galenic theory. One professor of philosophy and doctor of medicine, the Swiss Janus Caecilius Frey, had no difficulty even in accepting the idea of the doctrine of signatures in explaining the shape and characteristics of minerals.[12]

A third group of professors, however, found Fernel's eclecticism unacceptable. From the turn of the seventeenth century a growing number of physicians attached to the Paris faculty attempted to outlaw any remedy whose use could not be justified rationally. The recourse to occult explanations was denounced as a justification for therapeutic empiricism. As a result a new form of Aristotelianism developed in the capital whose advocates had certain points in common with contemporary sceptics. They stressed the limitations of human knowledge and warned against the acceptance of praeter-natural phenomena, such as possession, which had no obvious Aristotelian foundation. Their leading light in the second quarter of the seventeenth century, Gui Patin, came close in his private correspondence towards the end of his life to seeing even the devil as a human creation. Satan was a mere bugaboo, 'a hideous black beast with no white to his eye, whose ugliness is used by monks to frighten us all'.[13]

Despite the vitality of French Aristotelianism in the late sixteenth and early seventeenth centuries it must be stressed that the professors added little to the sum of human knowledge. Their chief contribution was exegetical. Several of their number produced scholarly editions of important or little known classical texts, continuing a tradition which had begun in the late fifteenth century with Guillaume Cop, the Latin translator of a large proportion of the classical medical inheritance. Thus, at the end of the sixteenth century, Henri de Monantheuil published a Latin version of the *Mechanics* of the pseudo-Aristotle; in 1619 Guillaume Duval produced a Greek and Latin edition of the complete works of Aristotle; and René Chartier spent the second quarter of the seventeenth century producing a similar bilingual edition of the complete works of Galen and Hippocrates.[14]

The handful of professors who actually did devote some of their time to observing the natural world, rather than just commenting on the opinions of their predecessors, were no more productive. The majority of these were anatomists. The medical faculties of Montpellier and Paris at the turn of the seventeenth century were the heirs to a significant sixteenth-century anatomical tradition. The Paris anatomist Jacques

Sylvius had trained Vesalius; the Montpellier anatomist Rondelet had pioneered comparative anatomy. The early-seventeenth century faculties retained their reputations as centres of anatomical excellence. Jean Riolan II who dissected at Paris for the first three decades of the century was renowned as the most skilful anatomist in Europe. But no French anatomist before 1630 made any notable anatomical discovery. Jean Riolan is credited with the identification of several muscles and valves but he is chiefly remembered for his opposition to Harvey. Riolan might have been more innovative if his facilities had been better. Unlike his English contemporary he received little aid from his colleagues or sovereign. Until 1617 the Paris faculty did not even have an anatomical theatre. As a result Riolan anatomized in the open air at the mercy of the rain and snow.[15]

THE EMERGENCE OF A COMMUNITY OF EXPERIMENTAL PHILOSOPHERS

From what has been said, it is evident that France played little part in the birth of the New Science at the turn of the seventeenth century. Natural philosophy remained the property of university and college professors whose interests were predominantly textual. There is little sign either that before 1620 the professors were even aware that in other parts of Europe, notably in northern Italy, there were natural philosophers at work who had a very different approach to the natural world. Contemporary attempts elsewhere to observe nature more closely and describe the behaviour of natural phenomena mathematically seem to have gone largely unnoticed, whatever the philosophical bias of the individuals concerned. In the second decade of the seventeenth century professors teaching natural philosophy at the University of Paris, for instance, had no detailed knowledge of Galileo's astronomical observations recorded in the *Sidereus nuncius* of 1610. The Paris professor Jean Crassot, whose course was published in 1618, was aware of the invention of the telescope and its potential as an astronomical instrument, but he showed no knowledge of its use by Galileo. Unable to reach a satisfactory conclusion as to the nature of moon-spots, his suggestion for solving the conundrum only betrayed his ignorance: 'Let the ocular instrument be used for a better comprehension of this sort of blemish.'[16]

In the decades after 1620, however, French interest in the new experimental philosophy expanded rapidly. In every part of the kingdom by the mid-seventeenth century individuals were to be found busy imitating and developing the observations and experiments of their counterparts in other countries. Some of these *érudits* made important contributions to the burgeoning experimental philosophy. The anatomist Jean Pecquet discovered the role of the lacteal vessels in sanguification; Descartes and Fermat made pioneering studies of optics; Mersenne was the author of a significant study on harmonics; while Pascal and his brother-in-law Florion Périer have gained lasting recognition for their experimental confirmation of the existence of air-pressure. These, however, were only the famous names whose shades have found a permanent place in the Pantheon of the Scientific Revolution. They were merely the elite corps of a fast-growing army. By the 1660s there may have been few people in France seriously interested in the new science of dynamics, but astronomers, chemists and anatomists were legion.[17]

Many of these experimental philosophers were still connected to the world of the university and college. Most professors continued to be traditionalist natural philosophers whose primary interest in the new science lay in reconciling contemporary discoveries, primarily in astronomy, with Aristotelian physical principles. A typical example was the Caen Jesuit Pierre Gautruche, whose textbook published in 1656 demonstrated a sophisticated reading knowledge of contemporary experimental philosophy, but no obvious hands-on experience.[18] A hard core of professors, however, became committed experimental philosophers. Many, unsurprisingly, were attached to the medical faculties, but a growing number were professors of mathematics. At the turn of the seventeenth century there had been comparatively few mathematics chairs in France, but their number steadily increased over the century as a knowledge of mathematics came to be seen as a professional necessity for army officers, surveyors and master mariners. In the period 1620–60 the mathematics chairs at the Paris Collège Royal supported a succession of experimental philosophers, notably Gilles de Roberval and, towards the end of his life, Pierre Gassendi. So too did many of the chairs attached to Jesuit colleges. In 1633–4 the mathematics professor at Avignon was none other than one of the leading figures in the early history of magnetism, Athanasius Kircher. In fact the Jesuit Order in various capacities supported a considerable proportion of France's experimental philosophers in the mid-seventeenth century. Before 1660 at least a dozen colleges in the kingdom had been the site of astronomical observations and the college at Avignon (later to be followed by its Paris counterpart) had been endowed with a permanent observatory.[19] In the first half of the 1640s, moreover, the Jesuits possessed, in the person of Honoré Fabri, professor of mathematics and philosophy at Lyons, arguably the most skilful experimentalist in mechanics in the country.

Unfortunately for France, in 1646 he was summoned permanently to Rome.[20]

In contrast to the earlier period, however, a significant coterie of these experimental philosophers had no connection with the academic world. Some had lucrative positions in the Church, such as the astronomer Jean Tardeus, vicar-general of the diocese of Sarlat, whose anxiety to save the Aristotelian doctrine of the incorruptibility of the heavens led him to conclude that the sun-spots that he viewed through his telescope were solar satellites. These he loyally christened Bourbons.[21] Others were lawyers by training, a group which began to produce a growing number of experimental enthusiasts. Peiresc, Gassendi's original patron, was an Aix *parlementaire*;[22] Fermat belonged to the Toulouse bar; Descartes, too, had been intended for the judiciary until lured by a life in the army.[23] A handful did not belong to the liberal professions at all and had not attended any institution of higher education. This was true of Pascal, who to all intents and purposes was an autodidact. It was equally true of one of the few members of the *noblesse d'épée* who took a serious interest in the new science in the mid-seventeenth century: Gaston d'Orléans, Louis XIII's wayward brother. Whatever their background, moreover, many of these experimental philosophers had no professional preparation for their scientific work. Most anatomists and chemists were understandably medical practitioners, but certainly not all. Descartes and Gassendi were just two 'amateur' dissectors who became interested in anatomy with no prior medical training.

The number of experimental philosophers in mid-seventeenth century France, however, should not be exaggerated. Even within the liberal professions, theirs was only a minority enthusiasm in an age when religious and political issues still dominated the minds of most educated people. There must have been many, too, like Pascal, who ended up forswearing the contemplation of nature for the contemplation of God.[24] As a result many experimental philosophers were solitaries, even in the university and college context, pursuing their passion in the midst of a sea of indifference. Before 1650 only a handful, if often the most productive, belonged to a scientific coterie. Peiresc headed one at Aix to which Gassendi became attached; there were others at Dijon and Rouen (Pascal's home town). In Paris Mersenne in his convent (he was a Minim) played host to a gathering of experimental philosophers; Richelieu's gazetteer, the hermeticist Théophraste Renaudot, presided over another.[25] But such circles were often impermanent and dissolved once the leading light or patron moved elsewhere for business or health reasons. For those unwilling or unable to travel, the chief way of keeping in touch with fellow enthusiasts and getting to know what was being published in France and elsewhere was through correspondence.

Given the vagaries of the French postal service in the seventeenth century and the eternal dilatoriness of letter writers, it is surprising that this form of communication was to be the key to the rapid creation of a national community of experimental philosophers. That this proved the case was solely due to the efforts of Mersenne. The Paris Minim in the 1630s and 40s became a national postbox. Experimental philosophers throughout the state, both Protestant and Catholic, clerics and laymen, were encouraged to keep him informed of their work and he in turn passed on the details of striking experiments and claims to other interested parties. Mersenne was also the most important conduit for news from abroad, thereby tying in the fledgling French community of experimental philosophers with their colleagues elsewhere. Descartes, a Frenchman in virtually permanent self-imposed exile in the United Provinces during these two decades, proved a particularly useful source of foreign developments. Thanks to Mersenne the French scientific community began to knit together and its members to stimulate each other's research. When in September 1648 Pascal's brother-in-law, Périer, confirmed the existence of air-pressure by demonstrating that the height of a suspended column of mercury was lower at the summit of Puy-de-Dôme than at ground level, the crucial experiment had been suggested by Descartes.[26]

Mersenne, however, died in 1648 and nobody took his place. The tyro national community began to fall apart again, even though its leading lights, like Gassendi, had by now been drawn to the capital. Fortunately, by this date the correspondence network was in one respect no longer so vital. After the Minim's death, the social and cultural isolation of French experimental philosophers was not as acute, so the important morale-boosting function of his network became superfluous. In Paris, at least, experimental philosophers began to be viewed with a new respect by the court aristocracy and the urban elite. This was largely due to a successful campaign of self-promotion in the 1650s and 60s with the foundation in the capital of a number of scientific salons. Established in imitation of the literary salons that had brought together the aristocracy and the *gens de lettres* in the reign of Louis XIII, the private scientific academies of the mid-seventeenth century provided an ideal forum in which Parisian experimental philosophers could demonstrate their practical skills and expatiate on their discoveries before a wider audience. The most famous was the academy of the *robin* Henry-Louis Habert de Montmort which from 1657 had a definite constitution. Patronized by English exiles, it became, according to Fontenelle, the inspiration for the Royal Society.[27]

Not surprisingly, in the years after the Fronde the French government viewed these gatherings of intellectuals and aristocrats with suspicion. The Protestant experimental philosopher, Samuel Sorbière, secretary to the Montmort academy, seems to have been a government spy who sent detailed accounts of each *séance* to Mazarin.[28]

The French government, on the other hand, was not hostile to the experimental philosophy *per se*. From the 1630s attention began to be paid to the utilitarian rhetoric of its philosophers and individuals received government patronage. Richelieu's interest in the new science was demonstrated by the support he gave the chemist Gui de la Brosse in the establishment in 1641 of the Paris Jardin du Roi, an independent institute for practical instruction in botany and anatomy.[29] Government interest automatically raised the experimental philosopher's stock and helped as much as the development of the scientific salon in popularizing the new science among the elite. Until 1660, however, this interest was muted. It was only once Colbert came to dominate the government in the 1660s that the new science became a significant state concern. Colbert believed that every aspect of French intellectual and artistic life should be brought under state control in order to bring ever more honour and glory to his royal master. The experimental philosophy was no exception. Colbert's policy quickly resulted in the creation in 1666 of a unique seventeenth-century institution, the Académie royale des Sciences. This was a small incorporated society of experimental philosophers with twenty to thirty members, subsidized and equipped by government money, who were expected to direct their efforts to 'useful' co-operative projects, such as discovering a way to measure longitude at sea. Its members were all government appointees, state scientists *avant la lettre*. With the creation of the Académie the experimental philosophy had gained the ultimate endorsement of the French absolute state. The government aimed to make the Academy the centre of the experimental philosophy in Europe. From its inception its exclusive membership included some of the most active and original minds of the century, notably the Dutchman Huygens and the Italian J. D. Cassini, lured by the promise of a handsome pension and proper research facilities.[30]

THE DEVELOPMENT OF THE MECHANICAL PHILOSOPHY

In the period *c.* 1620 to *c.* 1660 the experimental philosophy in France clearly experienced a period of 'take-off'. Initially the property of a handful of university and college professors, it had become the enthusiasm of a cross-section of the social and cultural elite, its devotees loosely organized into a national community enjoying state support and recognition. At the same time there ceased to be any consensus as to its philosophical underpinning. Within the university and college world the large majority of experimental philosophers remained committed Aristotelians, even if their Aristotelianism was not always of the kind a Gui Patin would have approved of. Many, like J. B. Morin, professor of mathematics at the Collège Royal, were dedicated believers in the existence of occult virtues and qualities, which in his case justified an enthusiasm for astrology.[31] Outside the academic milieu, on the other hand, many experimental philosophers broke completely with Aristotelianism. Indeed, a few, notably Mersenne and Pascal, rejected the idea of a causal physics altogether.

Mersenne seems to have concluded that the study of traditional natural philosophy was unscientific and purposeless because it was impossible to obtain a certain knowledge of the essence of matter. Arguments about the cause of natural phenomena were inevitably species of rhetoric. Natural philosophers should therefore abandon their traditional interest and limit their activities to the mathematical observation of natural phenomena. God, Mersenne believed, had constructed the world harmonically. This harmony was revealed by uncovering the mathematical ratios to which the behaviour of all natural phenomena could be reduced. This was an enterprise, moreover, favoured by the Creator to the extent that its pursuit would encourage religious devotion.[32]

Pascal believed that the primary role of the natural philosopher was to throw light on the 'mysteries' [his word] of nature by the formulation of fertile *expériences*. In the preface to his *Traité du vide* (posthumously published in 1663) he differentiated between two types of knowledge. Truths of history and faith were dependent on textual authorities; truths of the natural world on reason and experience. It was as illegitimate for the natural philosopher to swear by the ideas of the ancients as it was for the Christian theologian to rely on his reason. Knowledge of the natural world was cumulative. The ancients had believed that nature abhorred a vacuum because they lacked the *expériences* available to Pascal and his contemporaries. The natural philosopher should not worship the ancients but follow their example:

> Just as they [the ancients] made use of their inheritance only as a means to gain new knowledge, and just as their boldness opened the road to great advances, so we must handle what they have passed down to us in a similar manner, treating their knowledge as a means not an end of our studies, and thus try to surpass them.[33]

The most common allegiance of the opponents of Aristotelianism was to some form of hermetic or Paracelsian philosophy, an allegiance in the mid-seventeenth century no longer dangerous to affirm. Gui de la Brosse was a committed Paracelsian; so too were most of the other leading experimental chemists of the period, such as Nicolas Lefèvre.[34] Many of the correspondents of Mersenne were clearly hermetically inclined, although the Minim himself found hermeticism the seedbed of atheism and materialism.[35] A handful of independently-minded experimental philosophers, on the other hand, rejected the scholastic and Renaissance philosophical inheritance in all its forms and embraced a contemporary physical philosophy still in the first stages of its development: atomism. The idea that natural phenomena could be explained in terms of the shape and motion of unobservable particles had been originally suggested by Democritus and Epicurus. Their views, however, remained little known before the Renaissance recovery of Lucretius' *De rerum natura* and won few supporters before the turn of the seventeenth century, when they were embraced among others by Galileo in his *Assayer* of 1623. Atomist ideas, we have seen, were championed in France by De Clave and his friends the following year, but it was only in the 1640s and 1650s that the doctrine began to attract a solid core of adherents.

By the mid-seventeenth century there were two forms of atomism current in France and vying for support: one articulated by Descartes, chiefly in his *Principia philosophiae* of 1644, and the other by Gassendi in his posthumous *Syntagma philosophicum* of 1658. The two statements were very different. Gassendi intentionally attempted to replace Aristotelianism by an alternative classical tradition. In his eyes natural philosophy was still an historical and textually-based discipline.[36] As a result his atomism was deliberately Epicurean, founded on a concept of hard, indivisible particles moving in a vacuum. Epicurus' physical philosophy was merely adjusted to fit the requirements of Christian theology and the difficulties of explaining all natural phenomena in terms of matter in motion. Like the Aristotelians, Gassendi continued to believe, for instance, that the development and behaviour of organic matter was determined by some form of soul.[37] He also, as was befitting a natural philosopher in the humanist tradition, wrote specifically for a classically educated audience. Writing almost exclusively in Latin, his Epicureanism was intended to be consumed by the liberal professional elite, to which he himself belonged as a churchman (he was canon of Digne) and college professor (as a young man at Aix, in old age at Paris).

Descartes, in contrast, was a radical innovator, whose atomist philosophy was deliberately solipsistic. His scorn for any classical tradition was made abundantly clear in his first published work, the

Discourse on Method of 1637, where he presented an idealized reconstruction of his own intellectual odyssey:

> ...having learnt from the time I was at school that there is nothing one can
> imagine so strange or so unbelievable that has not been said by one or
> other of the philosophers...I could not choose anyone whose opinions
> seemed to me I ought to prefer to those of others, and I found myself
> constrained, as it were, to undertake my own guidance.[38]

Starting from the fundamental conclusion of his own existence,
Descartes was ultimately led to posit the existence of two totally separate
substances, mind and matter, and that material natural phenomena
could be explained only in mechanical terms. Unlike Gassendi's,
however, Descartes' atomism was built on a conception of matter that
was indefinitely divisible and a universe that was entirely material,
albeit largely filled with invisible subtle particles, much finer than the
terrestrial particles from which natural phenomena were actually
constructed. Furthermore Descartes applied his physical philosophy
universally. Even the most complex physiological processes, including
reproduction, were explained in terms of matter in motion.[39]

Descartes also aimed at a much wider audience than Gassendi.
Although the *Principia* was first published in Latin, a French translation
appeared three years later; and the earlier *Discourse on Method* and its
accompanying treatises on *Geometry*, *Dioptrics* and *Meteorology* were
presented in the vernacular from the beginning. Descartes, however
much he sought the approval of the Jesuits and the Paris Faculty of
Theology for his work, seems to have hoped that his philosophy would be
consumed by literate people generally, whatever their sex or background. Natural philosophy was no longer to be the exclusive property
of the liberal professional elite but of everyman. Admittedly, Descartes
was not the first to publish a work of natural philosophy in French. In
the course of the sixteenth and early seventeenth centuries several
classical texts had been translated, notably Pliny and Dioscorides by
Antoine du Pinet in 1562 and 1572, and from the 1620s a number of
contemporary scientific treatises appeared in the vernacular after an
initial Latin edition.[40] Descartes' publications, however, were paramount in establishing French as a suitable language for natural
philosophy, just as Galileo had demonstrated the possibilities of Italian.
Other experimental philosophers, like Pascal, quickly followed Descartes' lead. From the mid-seventeenth century the use of French in
scientific discourse was commonplace; it was the language of the *salon*,
the Academy and scientific publication. If Newton had been a
Frenchman he would not have published his *Principia* in Latin.

As the son of a *conseiller de parlement* who had deserted the family profession for a life of arms, Descartes' commitment to publishing in the vernacular was quite understandable. It was a contribution to ending the cultural divide within the French elite. Descartes' aim, expressed in the *Discourse*, was to create an entirely new kind of educated man, one whose knowledge of the natural world would not be based on book-learning but on personal exploration. Descartes was convinced of the apodictic status of the principles at least of his physical philosophy, but he believed that each individual should uncover those principles himself by following the correct (i.e. Cartesian) method of investigation. Indeed, he argued that he would never have found out as much as he had done, had someone else given him his physical principles:

> I am persuaded that if I had been taught from youth all the truths of which I have since sought demonstration, and had had no trouble in learning them, I might never have known any others; at least I should never have acquired the habit and facility which I think I have of discovering new truths, according as I apply myself to looking for them.[41]

The *Discourse* was thus a new type of scientific work, an invitation to a philosophical adventure. Each man was to be his own natural philosopher, testing and verifying his deductions about the way the world worked in the light of his observations of natural phenomena. As a result the experimental philosophy was not, in Descartes' eyes, some great collaborationist enterprise, an attempt *à la* Mersenne or Pascal to describe the behaviour of natural phenomena more and more carefully by devising complex experiments for collecting mathematical data. Rather, it was a personal, isolated and unsophisticated investigation of nature to confirm or falsify physical theories. To Descartes the experimental philosophy had no independent status: it was the handmaid of a natural philosophical science of causes. For this reason he has been described as an 'innovative Aristotelian'.[42]

Descartes' conception of the natural-philosophical enterprise was exemplified in his personal biography. He seems to have first become interested in atomism on encountering the Dutchman, Beeckman, while serving in the army of Maurice of Nassau as a volunteer in 1618.[43] Although Descartes' thoughts on an alternative physical philosophy developed throughout the 1620s, it was only in 1628 on the urging of his spiritual advisor, the Christian Platonist Cardinal Bérulle, that he decided to commit his life to the quest.[44] Descartes pursued his goal in deliberate isolation. Like a monk taking the cowl, he abandoned his Parisian friends and the nascent French scientific community, choosing instead to live for the next twenty years in the United Provinces. The

province of Holland was a natural haven because of its relative religious
and intellectual freedom but Descartes' initial decision to go into exile
was the consequence of his rigorous solipsism.

THE AGE OF THE ACADÉMIE DES SCIENCES

While the middle decades of the seventeenth century in France witnessed
a burgeoning interest in the experimental philosophy, the period of the
personal rule of Louis XIV saw that interest become a general
enthusiasm, almost a mania. Star-gazers, appropriately enough in the
age of the Sun King, were particularly prolific. In Provence alone it has
been possible to locate as many practising astronomers in the fifty years
1680–1730 as in the whole of France in the first sixty years of the
seventeenth century.[45] As before much of the serious research was in the
hands of institutions or representatives of social groups already associated
with the new science. The Jesuits in particular continued to produce
extremely proficient experimental philosophers, like Ignace-Gaston de
Pardies who was one of the first men on the continent to attempt the
colour experiments of Newton.[46] Indeed, their contribution in this
period was no longer restricted by the loss of their most talented
experimenters to Rome. In the highly charged Gallican atmosphere of
the reign the Society in France was careful to avoid the accusation of
dancing to an Ultramontane tune.

A dilettante interest in the experimental philosophy, on the other
hand, was the preserve of a much more extended social field than
hitherto. The monastery and the château, as much as the college and the
municipal hôtel, were now the locus of scientific activity, if admittedly
the interest of the devotees of the new science among the old regular
orders and the provincial *noblesse d'épée* lay principally in natural history
and chemistry rather than astronomy and mechanics. This was the
period of the birth of the natural history cabinet all over France.[47] By the
early-eighteenth century the enthusiasm for collecting fossils, dried
plants and other mummified curiosities was so great that Parisian-based
entrepreneurs had stepped in to supply the market. Serious botanists
and chemists found this commercialization of the experimental philosophy distasteful. In 1739 the Paris chemist-apothecary Claude-Joseph
Geoffroy was forced to supply one such entrepreneur, a merchant called
Gersin, with a letter of introduction to the greatest collector of them all,
Hans Sloane in London. In a subsequent communication with the
Secretary to the Royal Society Geoffroy vented his spleen at Gersin's
unsavoury trade: 'He is a merchant who has turned his hand to

gathering natural curiosities for those willing to buy them from him and he makes a pretty penny out of it.'[48]

The widespread enthusiasm for the experimental philosophy in the reign of Louis XIV had nothing to do with the Sun King himself. The royal Bourbon line showed no interest in the new science, unlike the junior Orléanist branch of the family. Louis XIV visited the Académie des Sciences only once, in December 1681, and then unwillingly.[49] Rather, the broad constituency for the new science reflected a highly successful campaign of popularization. In the first place, the liberal professional elite now received a sound introduction to the experimental philosophy in the physics part of their college philosophy course. The teaching of physics by the end of the seventeenth century occupied virtually a half of the two-year course and detailed descriptions of contemporary experimental work in areas such as pneumatics were integrated into the traditional framework of the study of the causes of natural phenomena. Until the turn of the eighteenth century this introduction was admittedly aural, although some professors do seem to have had diagrams of experimental apparatus printed and distributed. From 1700, however, private teachers of experimental philosophy, such as Pierre Polinière, were doing the rounds of the Paris *collèges de plein exercice* at least offering extra-curricular courses in practical experimental physics.[50] Similar private courses, moreover, were given in Paris and other French towns throughout the period of personal rule. Any member of the elite, therefore, male or female, who wanted to learn more about the experimental philosophy, was now in a much better position to do so. The most famous *conférences* were those given by the Cartesians, Rohault and Régis. Rohault started lecturing in the capital in the mid-1650s and seems to have continued to do so until his death in 1672; his pupil Régis toured the provinces between 1665 and 1680, beginning with a five-year stint at Toulouse. In terms of their audience the *séances* of the two Cartesians attracted the same amateur clientele as the earlier private academies of Montmort *et al.* In their case, however, they made no pretence to be bringing together the experimental philosopher and high society. Rather they were clever showmen who used the experimental philosophy to illustrate and vindicate Cartesian mechanism. Essentially, they gave a series of structured practical lectures in Cartesian physics to anyone willing to pay the entrance fee.[51]

Rohault and Régis also ensured that their course in Cartesian experimental physics would reach a wider audience by publishing their vernacular lectures in the form of an illustrated manual.[52] In so doing they demonstrated their perspicacity. In the age of Louis XIV the vernacular printing press played a vital role in introducing the new science and the different competing physical philosophies to a wider audience. Descartes had grasped the potential of presenting his ideas in French but his printed vernacular works were intended to inform, not entertain: they made no allowance for the casual or infrequent reader. In the final decades of the seventeenth century, in contrast, a number of experimental philosophers turned their attention to penning easy and elegant introductions to contemporary scientific debates. The most successful publication was Fontenelle's *Entretiens sur la pluralité des mondes*, a Cartesian and Copernican account of the new astronomy, which deployed a variety of literary devices to titillate the reader and hold his or her attention. First published in 1686 it had reached its seventh edition by 1714. Fontenelle aimed in particular at a female readership:

> I have placed in these *Entretiens* a woman who is being educated and who has never previously heard of the subjects discussed therein. I felt that this fiction would help me make the work more enjoyable and encourage ladies. My heroine has no supernatural character; nor does she divest herself of the limitations of a person who has no tincture of scientific knowledge; yet she has no problem in understanding everything said.[53]

The vernacular printing press was also an important vehicle in keeping interested but amateur experimental philosophers abreast of the latest developments. In 1665 Sallo established the *Journal des Sçavans* as a periodical (the first of its kind) dedicated to the brief review of learned publications all over Europe. In the hands of its second editor, the *académicien* Jean Gallois, the *Journal* quickly became a popular, weekly, French institution. In many respects it was a more important publication for the popularization of the new science than the *Philosophical Transactions*, for its articles demanded little of its readers and news about the experimental philosophy was mixed with reviews of works of history and theology. The journal had a strong editorial voice, Gallois in particular appending critical observations to his digests. On 21 March 1672, for instance, the review of the *Observationes anatomicae* of the Danish anatomist, Kerkringius, was followed by an incisive discussion of the reality of the ovist claims it contained. Gallois was dismissive of the assertion that the tiny vessels discovered in the ovaries of female animals were in reality eggs which on conception were transferred to the womb, insisting that 'in the animals dissected in great numbers at the Académie royale des Sciences, these tiny vessels have never been discovered in a detached state.'[54] It was this strong editorial voice, as much as the periodical's popularity, which accounted for the eventual appearance of a rival publication. In the first decade of the eighteenth century, the Jesuits set up their own *Mémoires pour l'histoire des sciences et des beaux-arts*, printed at Trévoux.

While the constituency for the new science broadened significantly during the period 1660 to 1715, creative experimental activity became located exclusively in the capital. Paris at the turn of the eighteenth century was renowned throughout Europe as a centre of excellence in virtually every field of the experimental philosophy: anatomy, botany, astronomy, chemistry, dynamics. But the rest of France made little positive contribution to the sum of human knowledge. The provinces were filled with enthusiastic experimenters but their work was pedestrian. This was in complete contrast to the middle decades of the seventeenth century when France's most innovative scientific minds were either based primarily in the provinces, like Pecquet and Pascal, or lived mainly outside the kingdom altogether, like Descartes. The growing centralization of the most dynamic aspects of French science in the reign of Louis XIV was reflected in the itinerary of foreign visitors to the country interested in the new science. Thus in the 1670s Locke travelled throughout France, going as far south as Montpellier; Martin Lister on the other hand in the late 1690s visited only the capital.[55]

The reason for the concentration of creative activity in the French capital can largely be attributed to the development of the French absolute state and the magnetic effect of the court and administration permanently based at Paris-Versailles. In the first half of the seventeenth century France was little more than a series of regional societies. Admittedly, this remained the case until the Revolution to some degree, but there can be little doubt that from the reign of Louis XIV anybody with talent and ambition was ineluctably drawn to the capital. Paris was henceforth the centre of French culture *tout court*. Nationally-organized institutions, such as the regular orders, which had traditionally made powerful contributions to the cultural life of the country, only helped to consolidate the development. Quickly seeing which way the wind was blowing, they summoned their best minds to the capital and turned their Paris establishments into intellectual power-houses.[56] It was for this reason that the focal point of Jesuit scientific activity after 1660 switched from Lyons to the Paris Collège de Clermont, deferentially renamed in the early 1680s the Collège Louis-le-Grand. It was there, for instance, that Ignace-Gaston Pardies spent his final years, teaching mathematics.

The contribution of Paris to French experimental philosophy was all the greater in that it was in the capital that, inevitably, the Académie des Sciences was established. The *académiciens*, we saw, were a relatively small group of people. In the years 1666 to 1699 only sixty-two appointments were made. The *académiciens*, however, were the most productive and innovative members of the country's community of experimental philosophers. Admittedly, the co-operative projects which formed the *raison d'être* of the Academy's existence seldom bore fruit. The attempt to write a natural history of French plants, based around chemical analysis, was a particularly spectacular failure.[57] Nevertheless, the experimental work of particular individuals was frequently of the highest quality: Mariotte's enunciation of the laws of shock, Huygens' work with pendulums, J. D. Cassini's discovery of a second satellite orbiting Saturn: these are just three of the many major contributions made by the *académiciens* to the new science in the reign of Louis XIV. In part the quality of their work was the simple manifestation of their talent: the Académie des Sciences, despite or perhaps because of the fact that its members were government appointees, was definitely filled with committed and creative experimental philosophers (both foreigners and Frenchmen). On the other hand, before 1699 at any rate, many talented experimenters were excluded from its midst, for it was the policy of Colbert and his successors that dogmatic supporters of the various competing natural philosophies could not be admitted. Jesuit Aristotelians, then, as well as doctrinaire Cartesian mechanists were always passed over for appointment, however good their experimental qualifications. Part of the reason for the productivity of the *académiciens*, therefore, must lie in the facilities membership put at their disposal. Members had access to a purpose-built observatory, the Academy had its own dissecting theatre and chemical laboratory, as well as the use of the theatres at the Jardin du roi, and the royal zoo and palace gardens kept the *académiciens* endlessly supplied with specimens. Moreover, seminal works, such as Tournefort's pioneering *Elémens de botanique*, which set out a new system of plant classification, were printed at the Academy's expense.

The presence of the *académiciens* in the capital guaranteed that any aspiring experimental philosopher would be lured to Paris, regardless of the city's general attraction as the dynamic heart of the nation's culture. Although the activities of the *Académie des Sciences* were supposedly secret, its members seem to have been more than willing to discuss their personal research with outsiders. Just as in the middle decades of the century, a number of private scientific academies continued to flourish in Paris where the *académiciens* mingled freely with interested amateurs and aspiring young experimental philosophers. Typical was the one run in the 1690s by the apothecary father of Claude-Joseph Geoffroy, attended among others by Cassini and the chemist *académicien* Homburg.[58] In these circumstances the only way that the domination of Paris could have been undermined was if the crown had incorporated rivals to the Académie des Sciences in the provinces, which could have become the focus of regional pride and research. The elevation of the status of

Paris was still recent (early in his reign, the Jesuits had even suggested to Louis XIV that he move the capital to Lyons) and many provincial cities were of sufficient size and wealth to build on previous traditions of cultural independence.

To a certain degree provincial science did gain an institutional embodiment. Louis XIV and his ministers were not wholeheartedly committed to the concentration of French culture in Paris, as long as the arts and sciences were strictly under state control. The French absolute state of Louis XIV was not a centralized polity but a series of distinctive entities welded into a homogeneous whole by a bureaucratized central will. From the beginning of the period of personal rule, therefore, the crown did not prevent the establishment of rival royal academies. In 1667, only one year after the foundation of the Académie des Sciences, Colbert arranged the incorporation of the provincial circle of experimental philosophers at Caen, which met under the patronage of Pierre-Daniel Huet, Bishop of Avranches.[59] The royal Académie de Physique of Caen was admittedly short-lived but other more permanent foundations followed towards the end of the reign in other provincial towns. Most of these were dedicated to the promotion of the arts as well as the sciences (although it should be remembered that this was also Colbert's intention for the Paris Academy), but in 1706 a second purely scientific academy was founded at Montpellier. In the long term, however, none of these academies proved a threat to the dominance of the Paris foundation and their strictly scientific work was imitative rather than original. This was not surprising. Provincial *académiciens* did not receive a stipend and their institutional bases often had few facilities for research. Throughout the eighteenth century they were primarily filled with amateur enthusiasts drawn from the local professional elite, whose experimental activities played second fiddle to their career.[60]

Moreover, from 1699 the Académie des Sciences underwent a significant reorganization. From the turn of the eighteenth century experimental philosophers were no longer excluded because of their doctrinaire philosophical allegiance and a number of dogmatic Cartesians, like the Oratorian Malebranche, gained admission. As a result, any possibility that such figures might have become the leading lights of rival provincial academies was dispelled. Thereafter the Paris academy really did contain the cream of the French experimental community and inevitably admission became the goal of all serious experimental philosophers (and the not-so-serious like Voltaire). By establishing an annual essay prize and encouraging members of the experimental community to forward their discoveries to the Academy for validation, it was guaranteed that the Parisian institution would be the focal point of French scientific activity. In the eighteenth century French science became even more centralized, a tendency only reinforced during the Revolution and maintained ever since.[61]

The centralization of French science was accompanied by the re-establishment of a consensus among the experimental community as to the fundamental principles of natural philosophy. In the middle decades of the century experimental philosophers in France had been an ideologically heterogeneous group, embracing a variety of physical philosophies and divided even as to the purpose and form of experimental activity. Mersenne and Descartes were clearly poles apart. By the turn of the eighteenth century, in contrast, the experimental community once more sailed under the same flag, although the ensign that was flown from the collective mast-head bore the device of matter in motion not matter and form. There was general agreement that natural philosophy remained a causal science and that the activity of observing and measuring natural phenomena was ultimately intended to aid the construction of an apodictic physics. There was now a consensus throughout the community, however, that the only plausible natural philosophy was one founded on mechanist principles, not Aristotelian qualities. In the early eighteenth century this view was shared by laymen and clerics alike, even by Jesuit experimental philosophers who belonged to an order traditionally passionately attached to Aristotle. Indeed, it was a Jesuit mathematician, Nicolas Regnault, who produced in imitation of Galileo's Copernican *Dialogue* the most famous vernacular popularization of the mechanical philosophy, the *Entretiens physiques d'Aristote et d'Eudoxe*.[62] Furthermore, this ideological revolution was not simply limited to the community of experimental philosophers. It also embraced the entire community of professors of philosophy, mathematics and medicine to which many experimental philosophers were still professionally attached. Until 1690 the large majority of university and college professors remained as always dedicated Aristotelians. By 1720, however, there was scarcely a single advocate of qualitative physics amongst them. The last Aristotelian physics textbook was published by the Jesuit, Gaspard Buhon, in 1723.[63]

This ideological revolution remains very difficult to explain. Before the final quarter of the seventeenth century there was little sign that the community of experimental philosophers would embrace the mechanical philosophy. For a large part of the seventeenth century those who attempted to relate the findings of the new science to the traditional concerns of natural philosophy had few problems in integrating the work of experimental philosophers into an Aristotelian framework. Aristotelian natural philosophy in France was definitely refined in consequence but never proved demonstrably inadequate. Where research suggested that traditional opinions were obsolete, such as a belief in the reality of planetary spheres, then the dependent theory was adjusted. Aristotelian natural philosophers proved remarkably adept at adapting time-honoured viewpoints while maintaining fundamental positions such as the distinction between the sub- and super-lunary universe. Sometimes they even turned experimental work to their advantage. The French Jesuit Grandami, for instance, who taught at the prestigious Collège de la Flèche (attended by both Mersenne and Descartes), accepted, as did several other prominent figures in his Order, that Gilbert had successfully demonstrated that the earth was a magnet. Grandami used this discovery, however, to argue in opposition to Gilbert that the earth was immobile.[64] In contrast, the alternative physical philosophies on offer were no more compelling as interpretations of observed fact. Many assumptions about the behaviour of natural phenomena Descartes deduced from his principles, such as the instantaneous transmission of light, proved just as wrongheaded on examination as traditional Aristotelian sacred cows. Not surprisingly, therefore, many of the first generation of *académiciens* were Aristotelian fellow-travellers, like Roberval, or Aristotelian revisionists, like J. B. du Hamel, the Academy's first secretary.[65]

In addition, it made good political sense for a French experimental philosopher in the reign of Louis XIV to remain an Aristotelian. Paracelsianism and iatrochemistry, it will be recalled, had been identified with heresy and irreligion. The same fate befell the new mechanical philosophy. Gassendist atomism, despite the orthodox protestations of its author, was immediately damned by the French Church as atheistical. Gassendi's attempt to establish an alternative classical tradition of natural philosophy met with scant sympathy in the circles of the Counter-Reformation when the founding-father of the tradition was Epicurus. Descartes' personal formulation of the mechanical philosophy was greeted just as coolly. The Church accepted that Descartes was a sincere Catholic but insisted that his philosophy had heretical implications. If mind and matter were distinctive substances, there seemed no rational explanation of transubstantiation, despite the valiant efforts of Descartes and his henchmen to invent one.[66] Cartesianism appeared to the Church as a Protestant ramp, a supposition subsequently vindicated by its eventual enthusiastic reception in the universities of Geneva and the United Provinces.[67] Furthermore, among the first Catholics to embrace Cartesianism in France were figures such as Antoine Arnauld, who were adherents of a predestinarian theology developed by the Augustinian bishop of Ypres, Jansen, that was declared heretical by the pope in 1653.[68] As the Jansenists, too, were associated, however unfairly, with the Fronde, it is scarcely surprising that the state as well as the Church viewed Cartesianism with suspicion. In consequence, from the beginning of the 1670s there was a definite attempt to stop the philosophy from taking root in the country's universities, colleges and convents.[69]

For various reasons, therefore, the mechanical philosophy should have made only slow inroads into France in the years after 1660. Its obvious supporters, as in the case of Paracelsianism, ought to have been found only among freethinkers and Protestants, and there were few of either category among the French elite resident in France once Louis turned *dévot* and revoked the Edict of Nantes in 1685. The fact that the reality was very different is perplexing. As the mechanical philosophy in some form spread all over Europe in the second half of the seventeenth century and not just in Protestant countries, this is evidently a development that cannot be studied simply in terms of the French experience. A complete explanation will only be possible once much more is known about the substitution of a mechanist for a qualitative physics across the continent. Unfortunately, this is a problem which has only just begun to be seriously studied.[70] Nevertheless, it is possible to make several observations about the French case.

The position of pre-eminence that the mechanical philosophy had attained by the turn of the eighteenth century would have been impossible without the conversion of the Académie des Sciences. From its inception, some of the members of the Académie, notably Huygens, Mariotte and Perrault, had been enthusiastic supporters of a mechanist physics. But initially they were an isolated coterie. It was only once the older members of the original promotion had died that the philosophical allegiance of the Academy swung radically in a mechanist direction. By the end of the century the transformation was complete, irrespective of the *académicien*'s speciality. Even the chemists displayed mechanist credentials. The conversion of the Academy was crucial. As the focal point of French experimental philosophy, its voice was authoritative within the wider scientific community. Other experimental philosophers ineluctably followed the *académiciens*' lead, regardless of the anathema of the Church.

The conversion of the Academy was made possible by the relative independence of the crown's ministers. Louis himself, especially after 1680, was closely associated with the Church's hostility to mechanism. However, the king's lack of interest in the Académie permitted his agents to elevate to its ranks any experimental philosopher who in their eyes would contribute to the greater glory and strength of the kingdom.

Philosophical allegiance (provided it was not stridently voiced) was unimportant. All the same, Louis was never totally the plaything of his 'bourgeois' ministers, whatever the disgruntled Saint-Simon might have maintained.[71] It is unlikely so many mechanists would have been appointed to the Academy, had not the leading experimental philo-sophers in the kingdom wisely adopted a form of mechanism best suited to assuage the tender religious conscience.

Of the two alternatives, the *académiciens* plumped for the Cartesian version of the mechanical philosophy, not Gassendist atomism. In so doing they obviously opted for the theologically safer philosophy. If Descartes was viewed unsympathetically by the Catholic Church, at least he was not accused of deliberately encouraging materialism and free thought. The *académiciens'* choice was not just the result of simple political calculation. To a large degree it reflected contemporary enthusiasm for the Cartesian philosophy which had been cleverly orchestrated by Descartes' original French supporters. While Descartes had lived, his version of the mechanical philosophy had received little positive endorsement from the French scientific community, even from those attracted to atomist explanations. Gassendi, less dogmatic and towards the end of his life strategically placed in Paris, undoubtedly had the larger following. However, on Descartes' death in 1650 (at the court of Queen Christina of Sweden) a small group of acolytes led by Clerselier dedicated their lives to preserving and extending a knowledge of his work among his fellow countrymen. This was done in a variety of ways: by publishing the great man's letters, translating and reissuing works already in print, editing unpublished works (notably *Le Monde* and *De l'homme* in 1664), organizing Cartesian *conférences*, and above all by the repatriation of the hero's body. When Descartes' remains were returned to France in 1666, Clerselier cemented fifteen years of proselytization by a brilliant *coup de théâtre*. Descartes was accorded an unofficial state funeral. After his body had been dramatically interred in the church of Sainte Geneviève du Mont (symbolically in the heart of the university), Clerselier held a celebratory banquet for a bevy of experimental philosophers and their patrons.[72] Descartes, the self-imposed exile, was clearly turned into, if not a martyr, definitely an icon of the new science. Gassendi, in contrast, had no such propaganda machine working in his favour. On his death in 1655, Gassendi's closest disciple was François Bernier. The latter might have played a role similar to Clerselier's, but he immediately disappeared to the court of the Great Moghul, only returning in 1669. When Bernier finally published a Gassendist textbook in 1678 it was by then too late to recover the initiative.[73] Descartes' acolytes, moreover, not only placed their hero firmly in the public eye.

In popularizing his philosophy they did their best to play down its more radical and offensive features by placing Descartes within a classical tradition. Thus Rohault in the preface to his Cartesian textbook deliberately engaged the sympathy of his readers by insisting that he had taken 'all the general notions [therein] from Aristotle for establishing both the principles of natural things as well as their chief properties.'[74]

The *académiciens*, therefore, had little choice but to take up the Cartesian alternative of the mechanical philosophy. In their hands, however, the work of redefinition was taken significantly further. Unlike dogmatic Cartesians they steered clear of metaphysics and distanced themselves from the burning issue of the essence of matter. Descartes' mechanist approach to physics and his assertion that the universe was a plenum consisting of three types of matter were not treated as apodictic. Rather, the approach was judged commonsensical and the recourse to subtle matter a useful explanatory strategy. Careful distinction, moreover, was drawn between inert and living matter. Most *académiciens* would have agreed with Perrault's definition of an animal as 'a being which has feeling and which is capable of exercising the functions of life by dint of a principle which we call a soul.'[75]

Thereby the potential tension between Church and state was successfully diffused and the mechanical philosophy deemed theologically safe.[76] In the long term, however, the strategy was not a happy one. In the early eighteenth century what was essentially a heuristic device hardened into an orthodoxy, especially with Fontenelle at the Academy's helm.[77] As a result the *académiciens* took fifty years to grant the legitimacy of Newtonian physics. Their best mathematicians had no difficulty in grasping the significance of the *Principia* and from the 1690s Varignon accepted the validity of the inverse-square law in the single instance of a body orbiting the sun. No *académicien* before Maupertuis in the 1730s, however, would grant the existence of an inexplicable, mutually-acting, interplanetary, gravitational force. The French insisted that the heavenly bodies must be sustained in their orbits by the pressure of circulating subtle matter and turned their attention to saving Cartesian vortex-theory.[78] For the first four decades of the eighteenth century the best scientific minds of the country devoted their energies to the pursuit of a chimera. It was only in the middle decades of the century that the scientific community finally bowed to the strength of the observational evidence in favour of Newton (some of which ironically the French themselves had provided) and accepted the existence of universal attraction. Even then, though, many refused to accept that attraction was a property of matter and insisted that ultimately all occult forces were mechanical.[79] Admittedly, there was one positive result to this sorry saga. Attempts to save the Cartesian theory were necessarily mathematical, for Newton's analysis of planetary motion began with a mathematical demonstration of the inadequacy of a vortex explanation. As a result, French experimental philosophers became expert mathematicians and mathematical manipulation of data rather than creative experiment became the peculiar characteristic of French physical science. Thereby the foundations were laid for the explosion of scientific creativity which accompanied the Revolutionary and Napoleonic eras. The Newtonian Laplace, although he might not have realized it, owed a great deal to the defensive campaign fought by his Cartesian predecessors.

CONCLUDING REMARKS

No-one, least of all contemporaries, has ever doubted that the French contribution to the new science of the seventeenth century was a commanding one. Put simply, the Scientific Revolution can be reduced to two fundamental shifts in the conception of natural philosophy. On the one hand, while the study of the natural world remained a science of causes, a novel interest came to be taken in the observation of natural phenomena, to such an extent that for some the experimental philosophy became an autonomous enquiry. On the other hand, the concept of what constituted a legitimate explanation of a natural phenomenon came to be radically altered as the formalistic and qualitative explanations of the scholastic Aristotelians were replaced by a commitment in principle to a mechanist universe. Frenchmen played a significant role in the development of both of these fundamental conceptual changes. From the 1630s a continuous line of French *savants* helped not just to validate but to shape the experimental philosophy through their observations of the behaviour of natural phenomena. Above all they played a major role in establishing the importance of mathematics as the language of experimental philosophy. At the same time, two of their number, Gassendi and Descartes, were the key creators of the physical philosophy which in many different forms would eventually replace the principles of scholastic Aristotelianism as the epistemological basis of natural philosophy. So central was the French role in the development of the new science in the last thirty years of the seventeenth century that there were few enthusiastic experimental philosophers elsewhere in Europe who did not visit the country to pay homage to the leading lights of its scientific community. One of Newton's many peculiarities was that he never visited France (unlike Huygens and Leibniz).

The reasons for the centrality of the French contribution to the Scientific Revolution were several. Blessed with clear summer skies in the

Midi, France was obviously better placed initially than other countries in northern Europe to replicate and develop the work of Galileo and his disciples. France, too, was a populous and relatively wealthy pre-industrial society with an extremely developed state apparatus. More than other countries, France possessed a large pool of well-to-do, university-educated, professional people – professors, clerics, lawyers and medical men – just those groups from which the majority of serious experimental philosophers were drawn. Furthermore, in the second half of the seventeenth century France was the most powerful and culturally influential country in Europe. The work of her best experimental philosophers received attention and applause in part because they were the subjects of Louis XIV. The Académie des Sciences became the arbiter of Europe's scientific taste just as the other royal academies influenced tastes in literature, art and architecture. Creative experimental philosophers in a minor principality, even one whose government protected and promoted natural philosophy, would not have attracted the same notice.

These reasons help us to understand why the new science in France was able to blossom and gain an international reputation. They do not explain why it took root in the first place; nor why France was the birthplace of the mechanical philosophy. Neither was inevitable. After all, many of the characteristics outlined above were shared by Spain in the first half of the seventeenth century, but the Hispanic peninsular is remarkable only for the paucity of its contribution to the Scientific Revolution. Moreover, Spain's lack of interest in the new science can largely be attributed to the stifling tendencies of a militant Counter-Reformation culture. As France too was the home of a militant Counter-Reformation church, it might have been expected that her Catholic allegiance would have condemned her in turn to a place on the scientific touchline. Certainly elsewhere in Catholic Europe the Church did little to promote the new science. Among the regular orders in the vanguard of the Counter-Reformation only the Jesuits seem to have shown a genuine interest in the experimental philosophy, albeit as Aristotelians.[80]

In France, however, the Counter-Reformation Church exercised no such negative voice. On the contrary, paradoxically, its role was a creative one. This was due to the peculiar position the Catholic Church occupied in the life of the country. There can be little doubt that many French clerics viewed the observational activities of experimental philosophers with suspicion and that the Church as a body decried all anti-Aristotelian natural philosophies. Only Jansenist clerics who had a theological quarrel with the Church wholeheartedly embraced the mechanical philosophy before the end of the century. Orthodox

Churchmen who had been initially enthusiastic supporters of the mechanical philosophy, like Pierre-Daniel Huet, quickly recanted once they sensed its potential as a Protestant ramp.[81] Nevertheless, although the majority of seventeenth-century Frenchmen were Catholics and the crown in principle supported the Counter-Reformation, the Church's power to control any aspect of French culture was limited.

Until the late seventeenth century France had an important Protestant minority, protected by law, with a powerful voice in commerce and the professions. Whatever the views of the bishops the French crown was unwilling to eradicate the Huguenots as long as France's foreign policy was based on an alliance with Protestant powers.[82] The Huguenots, then, were free to participate in the burgeoning scientific movement if they cared to do so. Many did, especially as chemists.[83] Furthermore, the Church had limited power even over the faithful. There was no Inquisition and the judiciary, heirs to a Gallican tradition that went back to the early fourteenth century, maintained that the state not the Church should control moral and ideological delinquency. In France censorship was a civil matter.[84] As a result, except for the period 1610 to 1630, Catholic natural philosophers ran little danger in expressing heterodox ideas. Only members of the regular clergy who were subject to the internal discipline of their order were likely to be harassed if they broke with Aristotle, like the Oratorians of Angers who in the early 1670s showed too great an enthusiasm for Cartesianism.[85] Descartes did not live in exile because he feared for his life. Exile suited his solipsistic, idiosyncratic concept of the new science. Even when Louis XIV turned *dévot* and expelled the Huguenots in 1685 the Catholic Church never gained a controlling voice over the New Science, for the crown's ministers, if not the crown, continued to deny the Church the right to intrude in many areas in which it claimed a moral and ideological interest. Natural philosophy was henceforth under the more benign control of a purely secular institution, the Académie des Sciences.

The Catholic Church could not, therefore, stop the experimental philosophy taking root in France as it arguably did in Spain. Once, after 1630, the *politique* view of the relative independence of the state from the Church had become the unquestionable position of the crown and its ministers, experimental philosophers had space to breath. On the other hand, the French Catholic Church was far from being a toothless tiger. It certainly had far more power than the Dutch Calvinist Church, an institution which would similarly have liked to control all aspects of thought.[86] Among the faithful it had a great moral authority, if nothing else, and it had enough friends in high places ultimately to end toleration for Huguenots. In consequence, the Catholic Church had an important influence on the way the new science developed in France. Throughout the century no sincere Catholic could easily subscribe to neo-Platonic, hermetic or Paracelsian beliefs, given the Church's hostility. Catholics who did so were often converts, like Renaudot. Catholic experimental philosophers, therefore, who no longer found an Aristotelian approach to the natural world convincing, either moved away from a causal physics altogether, like Mersenne, or were forced to discover a novel, alternative epistemology. It was no coincidence that the canon Gassendi and the Jesuit-educated Descartes moved towards the mechanical philosophy. Whatever the basis for their inspiration (and it is difficult to believe that Descartes really did create his universe *ex nihilo*), both were attempting to fashion a theologically acceptable anti-Aristotelian alternative philosophy. Descartes pointedly dedicated his analysis of the metaphysical basis of his physics, the *Meditations* of 1641, to the Paris Faculty of Theology.[87]

Of course, the Catholic Church found the mechanical philosophy no more acceptable than hermeticism. The first reaction of the devotees of mechanism was to try to defend it. Descartes and his supporters vainly tried to show that transubstantiation could still be defended rationally, if matter was defined by extension. The second generation of mechanists recognized the power of the Church and were more obedient. They transformed Cartesian mechanical philosophy into a heuristic device. This time the attempt to formulate an alternative physical philosophy to Aristotle's proved acceptable to the hierarchy and at the turn of the eighteenth century Cartesianism, suitably sanitized, entered the college curriculum. Thus, the French Catholic Church not only aided the formulation of the mechanical philosophy; it also encouraged its dissemination in a non-dogmatic, probabilist form. To the extent that it was in this form that the mechanical philosophy tended to spread all over Europe, the French Catholic Church was a powerful influence on the Scientific Revolution *tout court*.

NOTES

I would like to thank Ann Blair of Harvard and Maarten Ultee of Tuscaloosa, Alabama, for their helpful comments on an earlier version of this chapter.

1 For the most recent appraisal of the educational attainments of the French nobility, see Mark Motley, *Becoming a French Aristocrat. The Education of the Court Nobility 1580–1715* (Princeton, 1990), ch. 2.

2 Cf. the case of the Paris *parlementaire* and *politique* historian, Jacques-Auguste de Thou, who died in 1617 leaving a library of 8,000 books.

3 L. W. B. Brockliss, *French Higher Education in the Seventeenth and Eighteenth Centuries* (Oxford, 1987), ch. 1; R. Chartier, M. M. Compère and D. Julia, *L'Education en France du XVIe au XVIIIe siècle* (Paris, 1976), ch. 5 and pp. 186–7. The *collèges*

de plein exercice were new institutions of the sixteenth century, sometimes affiliated to the universities, and they swiftly usurped the teaching role of the faculties of arts. The sobriquet 'de plein exercice' refers to the fact that these colleges taught a complete course in the arts. Other French colleges taught only Latin and Greek grammar, not philosophy.

4 E.g. Jacques du Chevreul (1595–1649), professor at the Paris Collège de Harcourt: see Bibliothèque Municipale Cherbourg, MS 24, fos. 334–5, transcription of his physics course, 1629.

5 Frances Yates, *Giordano Bruno and the Hermetic Tradition* (London, 1964), chs. 15 and 16.

6 Charles Duplessis d'Argentré, *Collectio judiciorum de novis erroribus qui ab initio duodecim saeculi ... in Ecclesia proscripta sunt*, 3 vols. (Paris, 1728–31), II, pp. 146–7: *arrêt* 4 Sept. 1624. Forbidden 'à toutes personnes à peine de la vie tenir ni enseigner aucunes maximes contre les Auteurs anciens et approvez.'

7 Richelieu wished to reunite Christendom but believed that Protestants should be won over by argument not force: see P. Blet, 'Le Plan de Richelieu pour la réunion des protestants', *Gregorianum* 48 (1967), 100–29. The more tolerant atmosphere of the 1630s brought Campanella, among others, to the capital.

8 For an introduction to this school which flourished until 1630 and whose most famous representative was Pomponazzi, see J. H. Randall, *The School of Padua and the Emergence of Modern Science* (Padua, 1961).

9 E.g. Spain. According to the 1625 statutes of the University of Salamanca Aristotelian natural philosophy had to be taught specifically from the sixteenth-century commentaries of De Soto, Báñes and Toledo. See M. Fernández Alvarez *et al.* (eds.), *La Universidad de Salamanca*, 3 vols. (Salamanca, 1990), II, pp. 172–3. Admittedly, the Jesuits as an order were supposed to follow a Thomist line, but there is no evidence that they did so exclusively in France.

10 Jacques Charpentier (d. 1574), *Platonis cum Aristotele in universa philosophia comparatio* (Paris, 1573): an Aristotelian's justification for the study of Plato. Further details in Brockliss, *French Higher Education*, pp. 339–40.

11 See especially his *De abditis rerum causis libri duo* (Paris, 1551).

12 J. C. Frey, *Universae philosophiae compendium* (Paris, 1633), pp. 263–4. Posthumously published: he died in 1631. Frey taught philosophy in the 1610s, but a manuscript transcription of his course suggests he initially kept quiet about his Paracelsian enthusiasm.

13 Gui Patin (d. 1672), *Lettres*, ed. J. H. Réveillé-Parise, 3 vols. (Paris, 1846), II, pp. 211–12, letter to Falconet 11 May 1660: '... une vilaine bête noire, qui n'a point de blanc en œil, de la laideur duquel se servent les moines à faire peur au monde'. For further details on this new form of Aristotelianism, see L. W. B. Brockliss, 'Seeing and Believing. Contrasting Attitudes towards Observational Autonomy among French Galenists in the First Half of the Seventeenth Century', in W. F. Bynum and Roy Porter (eds.), *Medicine and the Five Senses* (Cambridge, 1992).

14 Only published in its entirety in 1679. Monantheuil (d. 1606), Du Val (d. 1646), and Chartier (d. 1654) were professors of mathematics, philosophy, and surgery at the Paris Collège Royal: biographical notices in Cl. P. Goujet,

Mémoire historique et littéraire sur le Collège Royal de France, 3 vols. (Paris, 1758), *sub disciplina*.

15 Cf. his complaints to the faculty in Bibliothèque de la Faculté de Médecine, Paris, MS 11, fo. 123, faculty minute 22 Nov. 1614. For Riolan's career, see R. Tabuteau, *Deux anatomistes français: les Riolan* (Paris, 1929). Riolan's most important work was his *Osteologia* (Paris, 1614). He died in 1657.

16 J. Crassot, *Physica* (Paris, 1618), p. 309: 'Adhibeatur etiam oculare instrumentum ad feliciorem maculae illius perceptionem.' A posthumous publication. Crassot died in 1616. Spy-glasses were on sale in Paris from the spring of 1609: see Galileo Galilei, *Siderius Nuncius or the Sidereal Messenger*, trans. and ed. A. van Helden (London, 1989), p. 4.

17 On the astronomical work, see P. Humbert, 'Les astronomes français de 1610 à 1667. Etude d'ensemble et répertoire alphabétique', *Mémoires de la société d'études de Draguignan* 63 (1942); G. Bigourdan, 'Sur les observations astronomiques faites en France avant la fondation de l'académie des sciences', *Comptes rendus de l'Académie des Sciences* 161 (1915), 289–92, 469–75, 500–6, 513–19 (on Peiresc and his circle).

18 P. Gautruche (1602–81), *Physica universalis; physica particularis*, 2 vols. (Caen, 1656); another edn. Caen 1665. For an idea of how successfully Aristotelians integrated the new science into their qualitative physics, see Brockliss, *French Higher Education*, pp. 337–50.

19 Strictly speaking Avignon was not part of France, as it remained a papal enclave until the Revolution.

20 Details in François de Dainville, 'L'Enseignement des mathématiques dans les collèges jésuites de France du seizième au dix-huitième siècle', in *idem*, *L'Education des jésuites (XVIe–XVIIIe siècles)*, ed. M. M. Compère (Paris, 1978), 323–54.

21 J. Tardeus, *Borbonia sidera, id est planetae qui solis limina circumvolitant motu proprio ac regulari* (Paris, 1620); French trans. 1622. Tardeus (*c.* 1561–1636) had met Galileo in 1614, discussed sun-spots with him, then spent five years observing them.

22 Peiresc was probably the first Frenchman to use a telescope for studying the heavens; he had acquired an instrument, on hearing of Galileo's work, as early as Nov. 1610.

23 Descartes definitely took a law degree at Poitiers: see J. R. Armogathe *et al.*, 'La Licence en droit de Descartes: Un placard inédit de 1616', *Nouvelles de la République des Lettres* 2 (1988), 123–45.

24 Pascal had close links with the Jansenist community of Port-Royal and after a second, permanent 'conversion' on 23 June 1654 gave up his scientific work completely.

25 Howard M. Solomon, *Public Welfare, Science and Propaganda in Seventeenth Century France. The Innovations of Théophraste Renaudot* (Princeton, 1973), ch. 3. Renaudot's circle did not just discuss natural philosophy; Campanella was one of the group.

26 R. Descartes, *Œuvres et lettres*, ed. A. Bridoux (Paris, 1953), p. 1289: Descartes to Mersenne, 13 Dec. 1647. It seems likely that Descartes suggested the crucial experiment in conversations with Pascal on 23–4 September 1647.

27 Fontenelle, *Histoire de l'Académie royale des Sciences*, I (Paris, 1733), Aii v°. The new academies are discussed in Harcourt Brown, *Scientific Organizations in Seventeenth-Century France* (Baltimore, 1934), esp. chs. 4–7.

28 Personal communication by Wendy Perkins, University of Birmingham, who works on Sorbière. Her 'Samuel Sorbière: Writings on Medicine', *Seventeenth-Century French Studies* 8 (1986), 217–28, gives a good account of Pecquet's lectures at the Montmort Academy.

29 See R. C. Howard, 'Guy de la Brosse: The Founder of the Jardin des Plantes in Paris', Ph. D. dissertation, Cornell, 1974, ch. 2.

30 Details in Alice Stroup, *A Company of Scientists. Botany, Patronage, and Community at the Seventeenth-Century Parisian Royal Academy of Sciences* (Berkeley, 1990), part ii and appendix. Although its foreign stars were well-supported, the Académie was not handsomely endowed; its income was equivalent to that of one of the richest French abbeys.

31 Cf. his *Astrologia gallica* (The Hague, 1661). Posthumous publication; Morin died in 1656. Richelieu was one of his astrological clients.

32 This is the argument in Peter Dear, *Mersenne and the Learning of the Schools* (Ithaca, N.Y., 1988).

33 B. Pascal, *Œuvres complètes*, ed. L. Lafuma (Paris, 1963), p. 231: 'Comme ils ne sont servis de celles qui leur avaient été laissées que comme de moyens pour en avoir de nouvelles, et que cette hardiesse leur avait ouvert le chemin aux grandes choses, nous devons prendre celles qu'ils nous ont acquises de la même sorte, et à leur exemple en faire les moyens et non pas la fin de notre étude, et ainsi tâcher de les surpasser.'

34 Author of a *Traité de chimie* (Paris, 1660). For the chief chemical philosophers of the period, see H. Metzger, *Les Doctrines chimiques en France du début du XVIIᵉ siècle à la fin du XVIIIᵉ siècle* (Paris, 1969), chs. 1–3.

35 R. Lenoble, *Mersenne ou la naissance du mécanisme* (Paris, 1643), esp. ch. 3.

36 This point is brilliantly developed in Lynn Sumida Joy, *Gassendi the Atomist. Advocate of History in an Age of Science* (Cambridge, 1987), esp. pt. 2.

37 Gassendi's biology was teleological but in contrast to contemporary scholastic Aristotelians his conception of the soul was a materialist one. He believed that humans possessed both a material and an immaterial soul. See O. R. Bloch, *La Philosophie de Gassendi* (Paris, 1971), esp. pp. 362–8.

38 R. Descartes, *Discourse on Method and the Meditations*, trans. and intro. F. E. Sutcliffe (Harmondsworth, 1971), p. 39.

39 For his mechanist embryology, see 'La Description du corps humain et de toutes ses fonctions' (pt. 4), in Descartes, *Œuvres*, ed. Ch. Adam and P. Tannery, 12 vols. (Paris, 1897–1913), XI, pp. 252–62. First published in 1664.

40 E.g. the astronomical speculations of Jean Tardeus: see note 21 above.

41 *Discourse on Method*, p. 86.

42 Desmond Clarke, *Descartes' Philosophy of Science* (Manchester, 1982), ch. 8. This book contains the best study of Descartes' attitude towards experimentation, see ch. 2.

43 Descartes spent about five years as a soldier fighting in the Thirty Years' War. It was while serving in the army of the Duke of Bavaria in 1619 that he had his

famous 'oven' experience. The best source for his life is A. Baillet, *La Vie de Monsieur Descartes*, 2 vols. (Paris, 1691).

44 Howard Wickes of Newcastle Polytechnic has argued in an unpublished article for a strong Platonist influence on Descartes in his early work, notably in his *Le Monde*, completed but not published in 1633.

45 J. B. Homet, *Astronomes et astronomie en Provence 1680–1730* (Aix-en-Provence, 1982).

46 August Ziggelaar, SJ, *Le Physicien Ignace-Gaston Pardies SJ (1636–1673)*, *Acta historica scientiarum naturalium et medicinalium* 26 (Copenhagen, 1971).

47 This remains as yet a poorly researched subject but see E. Lamy, *Les Cabinets d'histoire naturelle en France au XVIIIe siècle et le Cabinet du roi 1635–1793* (Paris, 1930). Also the interesting details about collections in Paris in Kryzstof Pomian, *Collectionneurs, amateurs et curieux. Paris, Venise: XVIe–XVIIIe siècle* (Paris, 1987), pp. 142–62.

48 British Library, MS Sloane, 4056, fos. 73–4, letter 12 April 1739. 'Cest un marchand qui sest mis a ramasser les curiosites naturelles pour ceux qui les veulent bien rachepter de luy et il y trouve bien son compte.' Gersin was probably the art and curiosities dealer Gersaint.

49 Stroup, *A Company of Scientists*, pp. 5–8.

50 Brockliss, *French Higher Education*, pp. 189–90.

51 On Rohault's activity, see Pierre Clair, *Jacques Rohault 1618–1672* (Paris, 1978), pp. 42–56. For Régis, see Brown, *Scientific Organizations*, pp. 212–13.

52 Jacques Rohault, *Traité de physique*, 2 vols. in 1 (Paris, 1671); Pierre-Sylvain Régis, *Système de la philosophie*, 2 vols. (Paris, 1690). Rohault's textbook was printed in Paris until 1730; there was a Latin edition published at Geneva in 1674; and an English translation printed in 1723.

53 'J'ay mis dans ces Entretiens une Femme que l'on instruit, et qui n'a jamias oüy parler de ces choses-là. J'ay crû que cette fiction me serviroit et à rendre l'Ouvrage plus susceptible d'agrément, et à encourager les Dames par l'exemple d'une Femme, qui n'ayant point de tout un caractere surnaturel, et ne sortant jamais des bornes d'une personne qui n'a nulle teinture de Science, ne laisse pas d'entendre ce qu'on luy dit.' B. Fontenelle, *Entretiens sur la pluralité des mondes* (Amsterdam, 1689), Preface, A4.

54 *Journal des Scavans* 21 March 1672, 'discours des œufs...', p. 42: '...dans les animaux qui ont été dissequez en tres grand nombre à l'Académie Royalle des sciences, on n'a jamias trouvé de vesicules actuellement détachées.'

55 *Locke's Travels in France, 1675–1679, as Related in his Journals, Correspondence and Other Papers*, ed. J. Lough (Cambridge, 1953); Martin Lister, *A Journey to Paris in the Year 1698* (London, 1699).

56 The most famous monastic centre of scholarship in the capital at the end of the century was the Benedictine abbey of Saint-Germain-des-Prés, whose Maurist monks pioneered the scholarly study of the Middle Ages. See M. Ultee, *The Abbey of St.-Germain-des-Prés in the Seventeenth Century* (New Haven and London, 1981).

57 Stroup, *A Company of Scientists*, esp. pp. 70–87.

58 B. de Fontenelle, *Eloge d'Etienne-François Geoffroy* in *Histoire de l'Académie Royale*

des Sciences, I (1733), pp. 93–100. For private Paris academies in the 1670s and 1680s, see Brown, *Scientific Organizations*, ch. 11.

59 David S. Lux, *Patronage and Royal Science in Seventeenth-Century France. The Académie de Physique in Caen* (Ithaca, N.Y., 1989), esp. ch. 4.

60 D. Roche, *Le Siècle des lumières en province: académies et académiciens provinciaux 1680–1789*, 2 vols. (Paris, 1978), I, esp. chs. 1, 4 and 6.

61 The best account of the organization of French science in the eighteenth century is Roger Hahn, *The Anatomy of a Scientific Institution: The Paris Academy of Sciences 1666–1803* (Berkeley, 1971).

62 First edn. 3 vols. Paris 1729; eighth edn. by 1755. There was also an English version in 1731.

63 G. Buhon, *Philosophia ad morem gymnasiorum, finemque accommodata*, 4 vols. (Lyons, 1723), II and III. Details of the transformation in institutions of higher education in Brockliss, *French Higher Education*, esp. pp. 350–9, 404–8.

64 Stephen Pumfrey, 'Neo-Aristotelianism and the Magnetic Philosophy', in John Henry and Sarah Hutton (eds.), *New Perspectives on Renaissance Thought* (London, 1990), 177–89.

65 Author of a variety of neo-Aristotelian textbooks, most notably *Philosophia vetus et nova ad usum scholae accommodata* (Paris, 1681). I have used the third edn., 2 vols. (Paris, 1685).

66 Most recently discussed in Desmond Clarke, *Occult Powers and Hypotheses. Cartesian Natural Philosophy under Louis XIV* (Oxford, 1989), ch. 1.

67 M. Heyd, *Between Orthodoxy and the Enlightenment. Jean-Robert Chouet and the Introduction of Cartesian Science in the Academy of Geneva* (The Hague, 1982); E. G. Ruestow, *Physics at Seventeenth-Century Leiden. Philosophy and the New Science in the University* (The Hague, 1973), chs. 3–6. Initially Dutch Protestants at Leiden condemned Cartesianism.

68 On the linkage, see: Henri Gouhier, *Cartésianisme et augustinisme au XVIIᵉ siècle* (Paris, 1978), chs. 4 and 5; G. Rodis-Lewis, 'Augustinisme et cartésianisme à Port-Royal', in E. J. Dijkerstuis *et al.* (eds.), *Descartes et le cartésianisme hollandais* (Paris, 1950), pp. 131–82. The predestinarian theology condemned by the pope consisted of five propositions supposedly found in Jansen's *Augustinus* (1640). Jansen's supporters acknowledged the propositions to be heretical but denied that they could be found in the bishop's book. Hence the Jansenists believed that Jansen's real views were orthodox.

69 See the account given in 'Quaedam recentiorum philosophorum ac praesertim Cartesii propositiones damnatae ac prohibitae', in J. Du Hamel (not to be mistaken for J.B.), *Philosophia universalis sive commentarius in universam Aristotelis philosophiam ad usum scholarum comparata*, 5 vols. (Paris, 1705), V, appendix, pp. 1–45.

70 The disappearance of Aristotle was not even considered a problem until recently when scholars began to appreciate the plasticity and vitality of Peripatetic philosophy in the Renaissance. For the reappraisal, see in particular: C. B. Schmitt, 'Towards a Reassessment of Renaissance Aristotelianism', *History of Science* 11 (1973), 159–93; Edward Grant, 'Aristotelianism and the Longevity of the Medieval World View', *History of Science* 16 (1978),

93–166; Christia Mercer, 'The Vitality and Importance of Early-Modern Aristotelianism' (to appear).

71 A view most forcibly expressed in his 'Lettre anonyme au roi'. See Saint-Simon, *Mémoires*, ed. Gonzague Truc, 7 vols. (Paris, 1948–61), iii, pp. 1238–79.

72 Baillet, *Vie de Descartes*, bk. 7, ch. 23. The funeral took place on 24 June 1667. The university's chancellor was forbidden by the state to give a funeral oration.

73 Fr. Bernier, *Abrégé de la philosophie de Mr. Gassendi*, 2 pts. in 1 vol. (Lyons, 1674). The complete work appeared only in 1678 (8 books in 7 vols.). Before Bernier's publication, Gassendi also suffered in comparison because his views were not rigorously ordered in a textbook fashion.

74 *Traité de physique*, 1, Preface, unpaginated. I have used the Amsterdam edn. of 1672. 'J'ay pris d'Aristote toutes les notions generales, soit pour l'établissement des principes des choses naturelles, soit aussi pour ce qui regarde leurs principales proprietez.'

75 Cl. Perrault, *Essais de physique ou recueil de plusieurs traitez touchants les choses naturelles*, 4 vols. (Paris, 1680–8), iii, p. 1: '...j'entens par animal un estre qui a du sentiment, et qui est capable d'exercer les fonctions de la vie par un principe que l'on appelle Ame.'

76 I build here on the argument contained in T. McClaughlin, 'Censorship and Defenders of the Cartesian Faith in Mid-Seventeenth Century France', *Journal of the History of Ideas* 40 (1976), 563–81.

77 L. M. Marsak, 'Bernard de Fontenelle: The Idea of Science in the French Enlightenment', *Transactions of the American Philosophical Society* NS 49 (1959), 3–64.

78 P. Brunet, *L'Introduction des théories de Newton en France au XVIIIe siécle avant 1738* (Paris, 1931); *idem*, *Maupertuis*, 2 vols. (Paris, 1929); H. Guerlac, 'Newton in France: The Delayed Acceptance of his Theory of Colour', in *idem*, *Newton on the Continent* (London, 1981), ch. 5.

79 J. Ehrard, *L'Idée de la nature en France dans la première moitié du 18e siècle* (Paris, 1963), pt. 1, ch. 3; Brockliss, *French Higher Education*, pp. 336–71 (on the nature of Newtonian physics in the colleges post-1760).

80 Outside France, the contribution of the Jesuits to the experimental philosophy is only now beginning to be seriously studied. For a positive account of their role, see J. L. Heilbron, *Elements of Early-Modern Physics* (Berkeley, 1982), pp. 93–107. Also several articles in the special issue of *Science in Context* 3:1 (1989), 'After Merton: Protestant and Catholic Science in Seventeenth-Century Europe'. The detrimental effect that the Counter-Reformation seems to have had on the creativity of natural philosophy is illustrated by the history of the Scientific Revolution in Bohemia. While Rudolph II promoted religious pluralism in the country, Prague was one of the leading centres of the new science. After the Battle of the White Mountain in 1620 Bohemia was subjected to a violent campaign of religious indoctrination and the burgeoning scientific movement collapsed. See Robert Evans, *Rudolf II and his World. A Study in Intellectual History 1576–1612* (Oxford, 1973).

81 In his later life Huet penned a famous anti-Cartesian tract: *Censura philosophiae Cartesianae* (Paris, 1689).

82 The Church's official line on the Huguenot problem can be charted across the

century in P. Blet, *Le Clergé de France et la monarchie. Etude sur les Assemblées du Clergé de 1615 à 1666* (Rome, 1959); and *Les Assemblées du clergé de Louis XIV de 1660 à 1693* (Rome, 1972); *passim.*

83 E.g. *académicien* Samuel Duclos.

84 The Church (through the Assembly of the Clergy which met every five years) and the universities could censor works but their judgements had no force of law. As a result of this powerful Gallican tradition, even the decrees of the Council of Trent had no force of law. Gallican lawyers did not like the boost that the Council gave to papal power.

85 In their case, too, the chief count against them was embracing heterodox ethical and political ideas: see Fr. Babin, *Journal ou rélation fidèlle de tout ce qui s'est passé dans l'Université d'Angers au sujet de la philosophie de Des Cartes en exécution des ordres du roy pendant les années 1675, 1676, 1677 et 1678* (1678).

86 The relationship between Church and state was *the* great debate in France 1560–1630: hence the fact that all the leading lawyers and churchmen in this period were preoccupied with what was essentially a religious issue, as was said at the beginning of the article. For a recent exemplary exposition of the two possible positions, see R. C. Clay, 'The Political Vocabulary of the Politiques', D. Phil. thesis, Oxford 1987.

87 'A Messieurs les doyens et docteurs de la sacrée faculté de théologie de Paris': see Descartes, *Œuvres philosophiques*, ed. F. Alquié, 3 vols. (Paris, 1963–73), II, pp. 383–9.

3

THE SCIENTIFIC REVOLUTION IN THE GERMAN NATIONS

WILLIAM CLARK

Historia von D. Johann Fausten (Frankfurt-am-Main, 1587) tells the sad story of a Wittenberg alumnus. Faust, an astrologer, a doctor of theology and medicine, who studied night and day, despaired finally of the knowledge in books. He sold his soul to Satan for twenty-four years of real power, in order to fulfil academic male fantasies. But, like a good German, Faust continued working for eight years after the pact. With Mephistopheles he journeyed through the celestial spheres, and from these observations produced the best calendars and prognostications. Through satanic arts, he was able to dominate nature, emblematized by food, peasants and women. He travelled much, and demonstrated his abilities for many audiences, including the imperial court. His fame spread. (In later editions of his *Historia*, other universities will woo him from Wittenberg.) By magic he fêted his colleagues on free food, as if a job search committee were in permanent session. He slept with a new woman every night. But he perished wretchedly, and went to hell.

Faust's *Historia* is a German testament to a male intellectual crisis of the early modern era: desire for more power and knowledge over heaven and earth than were contained in the traditional philosophy's books. That is the motif for my analysis of the Scientific Revolution, which has this structure: instruments and experimentalism; mathematics and heliocentrism; *mechanica mundi et harmonia mundi*. The first two sections discuss central strands of the Scientific Revolution, the third their attempted unification through the *mechanica mundi*, which in the German Nations was seen by some as needing to be complemented by the *harmonia mundi*. Following Robert Westman, I attempt to fix intellectual history within socio-political and aesthetic-psychological dimensions. But first some remarks about the scene: the German nations.

In the Renaissance, Baroque and Enlightenment, the 'Holy Roman Empire of German Nations' constituted less than an empire, but more than a nation. More or less defining 'central Europe', the German

Nations embodied central European problems in the age of the nation state. An essential German Nation (Prussia) was not part of the Empire; an essential part of the Empire (Bohemia, treated in another essay) was not a German Nation. The Swiss cantons left the Empire (*c.* 1477) to form a nation of Germans, French and Italians (Switzerland). Located in the centre of Europe, the Empire had border disputes with many other nations, and thus the question of what was or was not a German Nation (Bohemia? Switzerland? Franche-Comté? Alsace? Brabant? Schleswig? Silesia?) often became a question about European nationality *per se.* The Empire itself was divided by a common religion (Christianity), which the central socio-political event of the early modern era, the Thirty Years' War (1618–48), certified. The large northern and central territories (Prussia, Brandenburg, Brunswick, Saxony, Hessen, Württemberg, the Swiss cantons) became Protestant, while the southern and eastern (Austria, Bavaria, the Palatinate, Silesia) remained predominantly Catholic. In between, particularly in the west and centre, were sprinkled a plethora of independent and impossible political entities, some big, some small, and of various religious confessions.

In 1500 the Empire had sixteen universities, which had grown by 1700 to about thirty-six, sixteen of which were Catholic, and all but two of those dominated by the Jesuits. Given Franz Eulenberg's figures (which omit Vienna and Louvain), the largest universities, in the sixteenth century, were Wittenberg and Leipzig, with about seven to eight hundred students annually; third in size, Helmstedt had about half that. In the seventeenth century, Leipzig was the largest, with about seven hundred per year, then Jena, about six hundred, then Wittenberg, about four hundred and fifty; Duisburg, last, had about ninety. The largest and richest universities doubtless shaped the orthodoxies of the age; but those whom we see as scientific 'revolutionaries' or 'progressives' worked, if not in court towns, then often at the very small and humble universities, some of which had less money than some English colleges.

Like this, so much in the Holy Roman Empire of German Nations seemed backwards, upside-down, both more and less than it was, unified in disunity. The large number of universities, a seeming strength, really embodied a weakness: the socio-political disunity of knowledge's territorialization. Every territory, however small, wanted its own university, however small. German scholars were, at least, united by a common language (Latin); but no cultural capital existed, in the manner of a Paris or London. Berlin was a swamp, and in the middle of nowhere. Munich was famous for its monasteries, beer and radishes. And Vienna was not really 'Vienna' until 1683, when its first café opened. The imperial and princely courts were important; but German intellectual life revolved mostly around the universities, on the whole seated in provincial towns. In the absence of a cultural metropolis, intellectual life thus dwelt in the ideal realm of a 'cosmo-polis', and in the material realm of the provinces – German intellectuals were ideally always the best 'Holy Romans', or Europeans, or *Weltbürger*, but often practically the worst provincials. An emblem of the age and the nation, Leibniz, who began his education at the two most important universities, Leipzig ('Little-Paris') and Jena, finished it in 1667 at Altdorf, small and in the provinces. As Leibniz wandered from place to place in the Empire, he, like so many other Germans, found himself obsessed by the question of the relation between the supposed whole and the parts. What was the spiritual 'harmony' behind the material elements of the German Nations? 'Das liebe heil'ge Röm'sche Reich, Wie hält's nur noch zusammen?'

INSTRUMENTS AND EXPERIMENTALISM

Leibniz writes in 1669 (or maybe 1670), 'It is not laudable that we Germans were the first in the invention of mechanical, natural, and other arts and sciences, but are now the last in their expansion and betterment.'[1] The fault lay, he held, not with artisans, but rather philosophers, who had falsely separated practice and theory. Leibniz, scholastic Aristotelianism's last champion, was himself a figure of the Baroque, a modern, for whom knowledge of nature rested on instruments.

Scholastic Aristotelianism had entailed separation of art and nature, as well as *technē* and *epistēme*, *praxis* and *theōria*. Aristotelian physics was theoretical knowledge (*scientia*) of nature, which disclosed nature's universal structures, the four causes. In this contemplative work, material instruments were inappropriate, since they produced only knowledge of manufactured nature, an artefact, alien to knowledge of nature's true causes. Aristotelian physics, while without significance for craft, proved, however, able to perform an important social role.

Jean-François Lyotard, in *La Condition postmoderne* (1979; English trans., 1984), has argued that narrative plays a fundamental part in maintaining the social bond. It seems to me that the structure of Aristotelian nature, the four causes (material, efficient, formal, final), is homomorphic with the structure of narrative (scene, actor, plot, end). Aristotelian physics renders nature transparent *qua* narrative form.[2] This did not mean the physicist actually composed narratives, any more than the critic did; rather, like the critic, the physicist facilitated the comprehension of obscure narrative forms. The poetic structure of Aristotelian nature authorized a 'critical' discourse, which made nature *qua* narrative intelligible within and facilitative of social praxis.

While the Classical world took the poetic structure of nature as spectacle without author, the Christian world took it as authored play, a Book.[3] That did not relieve the Christian, the scholastic physicist, from Aristotelian *empeiria*, observation of nature's spectacle; but, for the scholastic physicist *qua* critic, observation was itself *hermeneia*, reading of nature's Author. Observation of nature, the realm of visibility itself, lay within the domain of the legibility of the Book of Nature. Most essential to scholastic physics was, therefore, not the critique of spectacles, but rather the reconciliation of readings.

The scholastic physicist, the reconciler of nature's readings, worked in lecture and disputation. The latter, scholastic disputation, embodied forensic theatre, a trial, which enacted the reconciliation of readings. This theatre of disputation, like western judicial procedure in general, itself had a narrative structure (topos, disputants, case, resolution).[4] While the physicist functioned in lecture as critic, aiding the comprehension of narrative forms, in disputation the physicist and fellow players actually enacted a narrative form, which constituted the academic social bond. The disputational order of knowledge (dialectics), and the causal order of nature (physics), were an analogically structured couple, both made transparent by narrative forms. The perennial attraction of Aristotelian nature and scholastic disputation to academics and courtiers lay within this forensic-poetic coupling, not within any 'organicism', perhaps alluring to rustics.

During the Renaissance, the German dynasties took control of the universities, with the Catholic dynasties handing control to the Jesuits by 1622. Protestant ministries and the Jesuit *ratio studiorum* enjoined the teaching of Aristotelian physics and scholastic disputation. This policy continued throughout the Baroque, even at new places, like the University of Rinteln, founded in 1671, and at progressive places, like the University of Altdorf, reprimanded by its patron in 1678 for departing from Aristotle. Regardless of disposition, physics professors were to remain Aristotelian scholastics by statute or court injunction. By statutory office, enforced or not, the physicist did not provide instrumental knowledge of nature for craft, but rather reconciled readings of the Book of Nature in the latinate theatre of disputation.

Conflicting forces existed, however, between university and court. The imperial court had supported makers of scientific instruments since the early Renaissance. By the onset of the Baroque, princely support of instrument makers is attested for every major German Nation, Catholic and Protestant.[5] Interest in practical applications stood behind this support; but it helped erode the academic distinctions between practice and theory, already under fire from an anti-academic critique.

Let us delimit the field of anti-academic critique, in the German Renaissance, with the figures of Agrippa, Agricola and Paracelsus, each of whom questioned the divorce of instruments and knowledge. As base and emblem of the anti-academic field, we may see that most German of all sites, next to the university, namely the mine, with which all three figures were intimately associated. Agrippa and Agricola assailed alchemists, but let us consider the anti-academic critique as centred intellectually around an alchemical view. Agrippa and Agricola sat at the extremes, the former at that of the purely occult, the latter at that of the purely technical. Agrippa denounced academic knowledge as vain and fruitless in comparison with the magical arts.[6] And Agricola, in his *De re metallica* (1556), presented a powerful picture of the mine as non-textualized nature made fast by the mechanical arts.

Paracelsus ('Cacophrastus' and the 'Lutherus medicorum'), a wanderer like Leibniz later, occupied the central position in the anti-academic critique. Paracelsus' *Paragranum* (1529/30) concerned physics and astronomy, which were to be 'married' by alchemy. He wished to replace, or at least complement, the Aristotelian cosmos with one bound together by 'sympathy' and 'antipathy', forces which linked the human body (the microcosm) to the cosmos (the macrocosm). No mere theorist, he held one must unite theory and practice, put down books and dirty one's hands. Traditional learning is full of shit, and 'shit [*Dreck*] is its best part', since that is actually on earth, as opposed to the constipations in books. Paracelsus adopted as positive metaphor that form of manual labour perhaps most abhorrent, by its proximity, to academics: cooking.[7]

The critique of the 'little books of men' (written in ink), in favour of the 'great Book of Nature' (read through instruments), occurred when books were first becoming relatively plentiful, familiarity breeding contempt, as it were, after the German invention of the printing press *c.* 1450.[8] The alchemists held that knowledge of nature lay, not within a critical or textual domain, but rather an instrumental one. Alchemists spoke of the Book of Nature, but advanced an anti-Aristotelian view of nature as non-poetic spectacle. This denied neither vitality, nor semiosis, as inherent in nature. Paracelsus, as well as Agrippa and Agricola, saw nature as alive, and full of signs. The alchemist worked, however, not like a critic or spectator seeking discursive knowledge about a textual or poetic nature, but rather like a physician or miner seeking instrumental power over an animistic and signatured nature.

Paracelsus' writings attracted a notable following in the late Renaissance, which continued the attack on academics, and reached a high watermark in Oswald Croll's *Basilica chymica* (1609).[9] But alchemy, as such, could not advance beyond a counter-culture. With its animistic and secretive practices, alchemy had anti-Christian and anti-social overtones. Alchemical laboratories were present at some courts, but propagation of the Paracelsian position seems unlikely from princes who enforced an Aristotelian ideal of knowledge at the universities. To move the alchemical view from the margins, the work of Andreas Libavius, especially his *Alchemia* (1597), served better. Owen Hannaway has argued that Libavius set out to disenchant alchemy, reform its language and make it safe for the established order.[10] This gains more significance given the appearance of Faust's *Historia* in 1587.

Let the work of a Protestant divine mark the divide. In Johann Andreae's *Reipublicae Christianopolitanae descriptio* (1619), the instrumental view of knowledge had become, not the path to hell, but rather the basis of Utopia. The theatre of the laboratory, in place of disputation, became the privileged site for the production of knowledge: a physics laboratory for the earth (§xlvii); a mathematics laboratory for the heavens (§§xlix–l); a chemical laboratory, on good Paracelsian principles, for the marriage of heaven and earth (§xliv). 'If you do not analyse matter through experiment, if you do not improve knowledge through better instruments, you are worthless' (§xi). In the Baroque, a theology of the instrument arose, the laboratory as temple of knowledge. This theology grew into a new field of knowledge called 'technology'. And, doubtless due to the Thirty Years' War (1618–48), dark but inverted Faustian images soon coloured technology's field.

In 1649, Johann Alsted, a Helmstedt professor, saw it as a domain of 'lapsed' female nature. Nature, as upright daughter of God, was superior to art, and ought be approached in a contemplative, non-instrumental manner. But nature, as lapsed daughter of God, fell into the grasp of technology. 'Since [she] is corrupted by her lapse, ... sordid vestments contaminate this daughter of God ... [Thus] art is a surer ruler than nature, because it can remedy nature's defects.'[11] Instrumental knowledge did not occasion a lapsed (male) nature, as in Faust's *Historia*. A lapsed (female) nature necessitated instrumental knowledge. Alsted's *technologia* transformed Andreae's soteriology of instruments into a sort of penology of nature. Late-Baroque German scholars seem to have shared Alsted's vision, but to have rejected his Manichaean views, and come to the conclusion that (female) nature was generally lapsed. By the time of Leibniz, many thought the judicial stripping of nature's vestments laid the basis for science and society. 'After the Scientific Revolution, *Natura* no longer complains that her garments of modesty are being torn by the wrongful thrusts of man.'[12]

This made sense to those living in the scholarly state of nature. The Thirty Years' War had debased the etiquettes of court and university, undermined Christianity as the basis of social order, and destroyed the 'good life'. Economically threatened individuals could no longer afford the aristocratic ideal of a life divorced from practice. The liberal would now need to reconcile themselves with the manual arts. The alchemists' instrumental ideal of knowledge, an animistic counter-culture in 1550, christianized around 1600, emerged commercialized after 1650: technology as the new basis for social order.[13] Intellectual heir to Agrippa, Agricola and Paracelsus, Johann Glauber saw the shape of things to come, and pitched technology as a panacea for German ills in his *Des Teutschlandts Wolfahrt* (1656–61).

The technological ideal of knowledge gained strength from those who, ascending from the scholarly state of nature, founded republics of scholars in the interstices between court and university. The Baroque saw the flowering of the society of scholars, like the alchemical society in Altdorf which Leibniz joined in 1666. Such societies, unlike the universities, dedicated themselves to the marriage of theory and practice. With the foundation in 1652 of the imperial Academia Naturae Curiosorum, the society of scholars moved into the public domain, beside the university. Realizing the pragmatic value of such institutions, Leibniz worked thereafter for the foundation of other princely academies in the German Nations, but succeeded only at Berlin, where a Societas Scientiarum Brandenburgica arose in 1700, with Leibniz as president.

What brought the universities into this expanding empire of the instrumental and technological ideal? What linked the ideals of court and university with each other, and to the nascent domain of private society? What promised to reconcile the old social imperative of narrative with the new one of technology? The Baroque 'experiment' did all this.

The Baroque saw marvellous instruments invented: thermometer, telescope, barometer, microscope, air pump, pendulum clock. In the Germanies, the vogue of instruments arose after the 1630s. The Würzburg Jesuit professors, Kircher, mostly absent, and Schott, together with the Magdeburg engineer and Protestant alderman, Guericke, served as an odd team spreading the vogue.[14] Kircher and Schott worked over the waxing arsenal of instruments, and depicted them in books, which infiltrated even Protestant universities. Guericke published late, but had made a big splash with demonstrations of air pumps and vacua, which he performed for the imperial diet in 1653 and 1654.[15]

After 1670, instruments to reenact 'experiments' structured university physics classes. An adversary of Leibniz, J. C. Sturm, seems to have been the first, with a *collegium experimentale* taught in 1672 at Altdorf, though Schott perhaps predated Sturm here at Würzburg. In any case, classes with experiments soon spread, to Jena and Kiel in the 1670s, Helmstedt by 1680, Marburg *c.* 1682, Rostock by 1698, Freiburg-im-Breisgau in 1698, Gießen 1698/99. Marburg got a professor of experimental physics in 1682, and Kiel in 1693. Such chairs and classes soon became general.[16]

But what is an 'experiment'? The use of instruments left the domain of the technological, like mining or cooking, and became an experiment, when a discursive intentionality arose. Unlike mathematics, this took a narrative structure. An experiment needs scene, actor(s), plot and end. Different modes of emplotment (romance, comedy, tragedy, satire) are also clear. The Baconian canon – the plot's resolution seems accidental, not anteriorly transparent – emplots experiment as comedy, while a judicial rhetoric ('inquisition', 'vexation') may emplot the experiment as tragedy. And the notion of the *experimentum crucis* recurs to romance (epic), where heroes usually possess marvellous instruments and undertake crucial trials of skill. The experiment's narrative form, especially when emplotted as comedy, lets it replace the disputation, which had established the academic social bond.[17]

The new *collegium experimentale* displaced many of the classes in which disputation on physics had taken place. J. C. Sturm announced his class at Altdorf as offering, not 'vain and subtle disputation', but rather examination of nature itself, and not merely 'narrated', but exhibited to the 'spectator's eyes'.[18] As basis of the academic social bond, the theatre of critical readings would give way to that of spectacular sights. The new experimental physics soon acquired a liturgical form, as the textbooks tied the reenacting of experiments, perhaps variously emplotted, to an annual calendar. And the instruments of this new liturgy or theatre can be seen as manifestations of kitsch.

'Kitsch' is an interpretive and relational concept, not a substantive or essentialist one, so there's no matter of fact about this. But, at the least, a noteworthy analogy exists between kitsch and the demonstration instruments of experimental physics. They originate in the same period (the Baroque), have similar cultural forms (syntheses of the wonderfully rare and mechanically replicable), and serve similar ends (reenforcement of order in a consumer culture).

José Maravall in *La cultura del Barroco* (1975; English trans., 1986) has argued that the emergence of a 'culture industry', which invented kitsch, constitutes a defining moment of the Baroque. This culture industry arose from a crisis: how to relate elite, latinate cultures – court and university – to the popular or mass culture, the 'public', arising from the breakdown of traditional order in the new urban milieu. Elites, within the bureaucracy and bourgeoisie, required new techniques to control the 'public', who became conceived as consumers, moved more by products and spectacle than argument or sermon. The emerging culture industry, according to Maravall, sponsored quasi-mechanized production of newly standardized cultural objects (plays, broadsheets, crucifixes, clocks, telescopes) for the public, who were best moved, controlled, by objects inspiring awe. The production of replicable and consumable visual wonders, kitsch, definitive of the Baroque, was mastered most of all by the Jesuits. The Jesuits' fondness for experimental instruments, masterfully displayed in their textbooks, is but one instance of their deployment of kitsch.[19] And, unlike the kitsch in Catholic churches, these Baroque creations conquered Protestant sensibilities.

Since 'kitsch' is not a substantive, but rather a relational concept, no object is *per se* kitsch. An instrument possessed by an aristocrat (say, Boyle), or by an alchemist (say, Paracelsus) might not be kitsch, while a precise replica, possessed by a middle-class physics professor, might be. The demonstration instrument becomes kitsch only through relation to certain other objects of consumer culture, and through the object's envisaged use, as when in a *Programm* of 1 July 1697, the Marburg physics professor, Dorsten, advertises:

> As Kircher holds, natural science is meaningless, deceitful, and worthless, if not supported by experiments... I shall follow this path, and thereby lift the veil of secrecy from many wonders... I announce a *collegium experimentale*, wherein with the help of costly machines (the likes of which up to now have not been seen in Germany) all things will be exhibited to the eyes with such variety and clarity...

The Baroque remade the latinate, elitist, disputational world of scholastic philosophers, remade the secretive, anti-social, instrumental world of Renaissance alchemists, into the visible, public, experimental world of Enlightenment scientists. As technological narrative, as a consumer society's privileged mode of rendering nature transparent, as a sort of Comedy of Kitsch, the instrumental demonstration experiment bound court and university to each other, and to the non-latinate 'public'. But this only translates a version of Simon Schaffer's thesis about the Enlightenment back into the Baroque.[20]

MATHEMATICS AND HELIOCENTRISM

Of Luther's *Tischreden*, along with 855 and 4638 (1539), which ridicule heliocentrism, recall also 2919a (1533): 'Astronomy is to be rejected, when it predicts the future for each person, but to be accepted...when it remains in its bounds.' As Robert Westman has shown, astronomy's dilemma came from transgression of disciplinary bounds, from confusions and role reversals, a kind of disciplinary cross-dressing.[21] In the Germanies, the problem of astronomy, part of mathematics, concerned the bad habits of the mathematician as astrologer and cosmologist.

The mathematician as astrologer knew intimate details about the heavens. The planets had minds, individuated by gender and by the four temperaments. From the female Earth, the planets built a gendered hierarchy. Moon, Mercury and Venus, were, like Earth, 'inferior' and female, excepting Mercury, who was bisexual. The Sun was male, as were the 'superior' planets, Mars, Jupiter and Saturn. The genders led to celestial romances. Venus liked all the planets, and they all liked her, excepting Saturn, who was friends with Jupiter, Sun and Moon, but hated Mars and Venus. Mars liked Venus, but hated everyone else, and most of all Jupiter and Sun. The latter liked Jupiter and Venus, but hated Mars, Mercury and Moon. You need experts to keep it straight.[22]

The temperaments and romances of the stars, inscrutable to many here below, move us. 'The heavens affect us... Each of the planets has its own appearance, signature and offspring in us...'[23] The weather and the body's humours feel the influence of planetary conjunctions and transits through the zodiac and celestial houses. The mathematician as astrologer had knowledge of all this in advance, thus had a potentially lucrative role as meteorologist (calendar- and almanac-maker), and as medical consultant, if a physician had not learnt the mathematics to cast patients' horoscopes. And, as court astrologer, the mathematician became a political consultant, when he cast the prince's horoscope.

Some belief in astrology seems the norm in the Renaissance.[24] Even Luther's comment only concerned the bounds of mathematical prediction, how much was fated by the stars. But theologians seemed concerned about the influence of mathematicians and physicians. The Protestant *Historia* of 1587 has Faust's downfall begin when he 'wished no longer to call himself a theologian,...called himself a doctor of medicine, became an astrologer and mathematician,...became a physician' (§i). After the satanic pact, Faust's political career took off, for he could warn princes they would be beset, 'this one by inflation, that one by war, another by death' (§xviii). A papal bull of 5 January 1586, 'Contra exercentes artem astrologiae iudicariae', shows like concern amongst the Catholics. While allowing prediction of events under 'natural causes', in agriculture, navigation and medicine, the bull decreed that, though necessity ruled the heavens, chance (*fortuna*) existed here below, and forbade horoscopic prediction of the fortuitous as satanic. This denied mathematicians their political ambitions.

The Renaissance mathematician as astrologer posed a problem, which the mathematician as cosmologist did not. Cosmology lay outside the purview of mathematics (astronomy), and within that of theology, metaphysics and physics. In 1543 an astronomical work, Copernicus' *De revolutionibus*, committed a disciplinary transgression. It posited an heliocentric cosmos, in place of the Aristotelian/Ptolemaic geocentric cosmos endorsed by theology, metaphysics and physics. As Westman's work shows, no great problems arose, for few took Copernicus seriously. Up to 1600, only four avowed Copernicans existed in the Germanies: Georg J. Rheticus, astrologer and sometime mathematics professor at Wittenberg and Leipzig; Christopher Rothmann, mathematician-astrologer to the Landgrave of Hesse-Cassel; Michael Mästlin, mathematics professor at Tübingen; and Johannes Kepler, imperial mathematician-astrologer.

In the Catholic lands, alarm had been defused by Copernicus' rhetorical and political skills. Heliocentrism, though not accepted, was eventually acknowledged, in 1581, in the much-used textbooks of the erstwhile Bamberger Jesuit, Christopher Clavius.[25] In the Protestant Germanies, what Westman has termed the 'Wittenberg Interpretation' of heliocentrism predominated, at least up to the 1570s. Formulated at Wittenberg by Luther's righthand man, Philipp Melanchthon, and taught by the latter's disciples, this interpretation adopted Copernicus' new (equantless) mathematical models into a geocentric framework; it embraced Copernicus the mathematician, but ignored the cosmologist.[26]

After 1570, as Westman and Jardine have shown, things became more complex.[27] Better appreciation of Copernicus' cosmology emerged, while more precise observations of comets placed them above the lunar orb, where they ought not be, given physicists' doctrines. The incidence of unorthodox cosmological assertions increased amongst mathematicians; Tycho's geo-heliocentric theory stood as an epitome of this, and as a gateway to the Baroque. Those professionally concerned with astrology, especially court mathematicians and physicians, helped alter mentalities. 'Certainly true astrology, which is part of physics, investigating the heavens', gives us knowledge of the causes of terrestrial events.[28] As astrologer casting horoscopes, the mathematician, like it or not, moved in the domain of physics, and thus cosmology. But if heliocentrism and astrology worked jointly to put the cosmologist's hat, Copernican or not, on the mathematician, they soon proved unsuited for collaboration.

To find a cosmology for heliocentricism, and to redeem astrology, unified and gave much of the strangeness to Kepler's work. Kepler published prognostications, and defended a reformed astrology.[29] 'The office of the mathematician is commonly (*vulgo*) thought to be the annual production of prognostications.' Indeed, 'no book under the sun sells as many copies…as the calendars and prognostications of a talented astrologer.' Beyond meteorology, the astrologer attained a role as medical and political consultant, for 'in matters of politics and war, the astrologer has justifiably some say.'[30] Kepler's astrology moved, from the desultory chapters 9 to 12 of his *Mysterium cosmographicum* (1596), to the crux of his *Harmonice mundi* (1619). But, alas, his *Astronomia nova* (1605) revealed the problem of heliocentric astrology.

Heliocentrism disarrayed the heavens' gendered hierarchy, as the female Earth switched places with the male Sun. Kepler solved this problem by degendering celestial bodies, save perhaps the Sun and Earth. 'You'll not find the wife [*coniunx*, that is, the female] in the stars, [for only] Earth brings forth this kind of animal. *Fortuna* is her name.'[31] Denying temperaments and romances seemed logical, since he had lobotomized the planets, removed their souls.[32] In the *Astronomia nova*, the old system of crystalline spheres and planetary intelligences, the 'motor souls', became a solar system of dispirited planets governed by one motor soul, or magnetic force, in the (male) Sun. The Sun's rotation produced a magnetic vortex, which, in conjunction with circular inertia and the magnetic polarities in each planet, provided a physical basis for Kepler's two mathematical laws of planetary motion (the law of elliptical motion, and the law of equal areas in equal times).

To forge a physico-mathematical cosmology for heliocentrism, Kepler disenchanted the heavens, a development which had been underway, if not for centuries, then at least since 1570.[33] But a basis for astrology now seems to be lost. How could such stupid stars move us here below? Kepler answered: celestial romance becomes celestial harmonics, to which the human soul is attuned. The marvellous theory of celestial harmonic proportions in the *Harmonice mundi* saved astrology, linked the metaphysics (the relation of the five regular solids to planetary orbits) in the *Mysterium cosmographicum* with the physico-mathematics of the *Astronomia nova*, and gave Kepler his third planetary law (the constancy of the proportions of the squares of the periodic times and the cubes of the mean distances of the planets). In the *Harmonice mundi*, much of traditional astrology disappeared, but enough survived to preserve something of the mathematician's political role.[34]

Kepler's project – to link metaphysics, physics, mathematics and astrology within an harmonic heliocentric cosmos   had little effect. Kircher paid him the rare compliment of disputing his theories, but said,

'Our Kepler, Imperial Mathematician...: as mathematician, no one is better or more subtle; as physicist, no one is worse.'[35] Into the 1670s, most cosmologies remained non-Copernican altogether. (I presume the geocentric system was used in 'The Seven Planets', a ballet produced at Dresden in 1671.) Progressive Protestants and Catholics, Sturm and the Kircher/Schott team, adhered to the Tychonic theory into the 1680s. And Guericke, the most famous German heliocentrist between Kepler and Leibniz, saw no sense in Kepler's laws.[36] Until Leibniz's reconstruction of him, Kepler was a great mathematician gone crazy.

Newton's *Philosophiae naturalis principia mathematica* (1687) was reviewed in 1688 by the *Acta eruditorum* (founded in 1682 at Leipzig, and for two generations the preeminent academic journal in the Germanies). The lengthy review referred to Newton's Copernican heliocentrism with elliptical orbits, but made no reference to Kepler. Two years later the journal reviewed Johann Zimmermann's *Exercitatio theoricorum Copernico-coelestium mathematico-physico-theologica* (1689), and tied elliptical orbits with heliocentrism to Newton and Kepler. Between these two reviews, two articles by Leibniz had appeared in the journal. Regarding elliptical orbits, they invoked the name of Kepler, but not Newton, and intimated that Copernicus' and Tycho's systems had been replaced by Kepler's.[37] Leibniz began the invention of the new, improved 'Kepler'.

Though heliocentrism and Kepler had influential adherents by the 1680s, the German Baroque did not witness the triumph of Copernicanism. Into the eighteenth century, heliocentric cosmologies could ignore Kepler, and remained opposed by the Catholic Church and by Protestant ministers.[38] Disciplinary changes had, however, occurred. As Westman noted, those professionally interested in astrology – mathematicians and physicians – had crossed over into cosmology. This began at the onset of the Baroque, principally with court figures like Tycho, and soon became institutionalized at the universities. Mathematicians and physicians commonly came to hold the professorship of physics, for instance at Altdorf, Basel, Tübingen, Gießen, Marburg, Freiburg-im-Breisgau (before the Jesuits took over), Rinteln, Duisburg and Leipzig. Physics, once bound to metaphysics and theology, would link up with mathematics and medicine (which further explains the rise of instrumentalism in physics). The contest moved within cosmology, to be fought between a physico-mathematical heliocentrism and a theological geo-heliocentrism.

The mathematician's gains as cosmologist seemed, however, bound to losses as astrologer. Kircher and Schott still believed in celestial souls and romances; and, in his *Organum mathematicum* of 1668, intended for elites, Schott removed the new plebeian topics (mechanics) of his *Cursus mathematicus* of 1661, and gave a longer presentation of astrology. But most intellectuals moved in the opposite direction. Baroque metaphysics, especially the mechanistic, made astrology improbable. A much-used Protestant textbook of mid-century said, in eleven editions, stars are mindless.[39] Though defences continued, the mathematician as astrologer became marginalized by intellectuals after the 1680s. After the Baroque, astrology, unlike kitsch, was only for the unenlightened public.[40]

But mathematicians wished not to relinquish their political role. In 1674, Leibniz's mentor, Erhard Weigel, integrated the remnants of astrology into a new mathematical science of society. Males would be represented by odd numbers, females by even, criminals by negative numbers, and the handicapped by fractions. The planetary gendered hierarchy became a metaphor for the social order. The signs of the zodiac represented social types; for example, ♈ signified those without their own means of support: children, paupers, students, prisoners.[41] Instead of horoscopes, a kind of combinatorial art or political arithmetic of the body social might forecast the social order.

Weigel's political science had the same success as Kepler's. More promising seemed the *Statistik* conceived in the late Baroque by the cameralists. Whereas astrology had embraced astronomy and physics in one system, astrology's retreat left 'politics', the terrestrial domain of chance (*fortuna*), separated from 'geometry', the celestial domain of necessity (*fatum*). Two mathematical world systems were in order, one system to govern the heavens, and another to govern the earth, that is, the people. *Statistik* and combinatorics might provide a proto-mathematics for public or social sciences. And, as Lorraine Daston has shown, the late Baroque also witnessed the sudden rise of the insurance industry.[42] Horoscopes would be replaced by the statistics and actuarial tables of social sciences and the insurance industry, which, like the kitsch of the culture industry, constructed a new 'public'.

It is fitting then that Leibniz, while working on the construction of a celestial domain for the non-astrological, a-political 'Keplerian' heliocentric system, also played a part, however small, in creating the new terrestrial domain of insurance plans and mortality tables.[43]

MECHANICA MUNDI ET HARMONIA MUNDI

Leibniz writes, in a letter for the *Acta eruditorum* in 1696 (or maybe 1695), 'Consider two clocks or watches perfectly synchronized. This is possible in three ways. The first consists in the mutual influence of one watch upon the other; the second consists in the care taken by the person keeping them; the third consists in their own [synchronous] exactitude... [which is] my hypothesis, *the way of pre-established harmony.*' Leibniz wrote to the Electress Sophie in 1694, '...Harmony consists in rapport or in consonance, and in the way in which there is point of view in perspective. It is what writers on the art of poetry intend when they require unity of plot in a tragedy.' In a notebook in 1676, he had written, 'To exist is nothing other than to be in harmony.'[44] The Baroque world order, was it the harmony of narrative (poetics), the harmony of horology (mechanics), or not harmony at all?

Antiquity, the Middle Ages and the Renaissance saw the mechanical as artificial, something contrary to nature. Machines, as part of human art, were not part of nature's order. A *mechanica mundi* was not nature. Nonetheless, the 'machine(ry) of the world', the *machina mundi*, served as a metaphor for the heavens throughout the same historical periods.[45] From the heavens, the *machina mundi* worked its way to earth, and the mechanical clock seems to have been the principal vehicle.

From the late Middle Ages, mechanical clocks evolved, from devices to indicate the position of the Sun ('time of day') into astrological devices, with dials for all the planets in relation to the zodiac. Such astrological clocks embodied tangibly mechanical representations of the heavens. Many clocks also acquired *automata*, mechanical figures, which, driven by hidden mechanism, moved in a seemingly lifelike way.[46] The Baroque clock would be both the epitome of the instrument as kitsch, and the protean symbol to mediate the transition from a poetico-astrological to a mechanical world order. But, in the Germanies, the horological *machina mundi*, as *systema mundi*, would relate to the *harmonia mundi*.

Amongst others, Westman and Hallyn have shown the central role of 'harmony' and 'symmetry' for astronomers. Rheticus, Copernicus' first German convert, felt the harmony of heliocentrism, which gave the cosmos system and symmetry, unlike geocentrism. Heliocentric harmony was the musical and political consonance of parts in their proper places in a whole. The Copernican cosmos, a harmoniously designed clock, had no superfluous wheels. The *machina mundi*, as harmonious system, drew upon teleological principles of function and economy in nature.[47]

So must we understand Kepler's remark of 1605, 'My aim would be to say that the celestial machine [*caelestem machinam*] is not like a divine spirit [*animalis*], but rather like a clock.'[48] No opposition exists here between 'mechanism' and 'organicism', for that was invented in the post-Cartesian world. Kepler's astronomy removed alchemical-astrological animism, and mechanized the heavens as 'clock'. But, by remaining in the domain of harmony, his de-animized, horological *machina mundi* stayed in the realm of teleology, which grounded the *systema mundi.* For his system of the world, Kepler employed metaphors not only of horological and musical, but also of political harmony, 'since what else is a Kingdom [*Regnum*] if not Harmony'?[49] The teleological domain of 'harmonic proportions' drew discrete mechanical laws into a systematic unity, and provided the link between the spiritual and the material. Harmonic proportion, as the unity of the world and the soul, exists not as a thing amongst other things, but rather – like the unity of plot in poetics – as the system of relations grasped by the mind attuned to the world (or text). 'The Spirit [*Anima*], the bond of Mind and Body, would be in essence nothing if not Harmony.'[50]

The opposition between mechanism and teleology, which would allow the later distinction between mechanism and organicism, arose through a non-horological, militaristic translation of the mechanical metaphor. Leibniz wrote to Empress Amélie in 1715, 'War is the kingdom of force [*le règne de la force*], and thus of mathematics and mechanics.'[51] The Baroque's militarization of nature seems to have occurred, first through the influence of tactics, and then ballistics, within the *machina mundi.*

From the late Middle Ages through the Renaissance, muskets and cannons made military machines *per se* obsolete, while the army itself became mechanized, as *machina militaris*: the practice of tactical formation of battle-units emerged. Tactical formation arose in the Renaissance and Early Baroque through increasing emphasis on the geometrical formation of units in combat. One Italian tactician, overly influenced by court dance, went so far as to form his units of soldiers into half-moons, ellipses, and even zodiacal figures. The next step, the mechanization of formations, was taken in Maurice of Nassau's army. The counts of Nassau wanted to produce a relatively continuous stream of fire from discontinuous particles (musket-balls). In 1594, Maurice's cousin William had a good idea, and made a drawing like this:

```
a⟍     a⟍     a⟍     a⟍
b ⟩    b ⟩    b ⟩    b ⟩
c )    c )    c )    c )
d )    d )    d )    d )
e ⟋    e ⟋    e ⟋    e ⟋
a⟋     a⟋     a⟋     a⟋
```

The a's shoot their muskets, then fall back behind the e's to reload, while the b's shoot, then fall back behind the a's, and so on, till the e's fire, then fall back, at which point the a's must be ready to refire. (They'll need more guys in the ranks.) This rotational motion was called 'counter-march', and William said it came from a Roman drill. The further mechanizing of counter-march, especially the idea of choreographing the reloading, seems, however, to have come from ballet.

Although it never became central like the clock, dance played a metaphorical role in linking the astrological to the mechanical, and then militaristic, world view. In antiquity, Lucian's *The Dance* (*Peri orcheseōs*) tied the metaphor of dance both to the harmony of the celestial bodies' motions and to the marching of troops to music. In the Renaissance, court dance often interwove the gendered hierarchy of the heavens, and other astrological motifs, with military and political themes. The origins of Classical ballet lie in the 1570s to 1610s, when the first clear indications of choreography emerge, most particularly for the ballet *Circé*, produced at Paris in 1581. In the next decades, choreographers learnt to give formations of dancers the appearance of pre-established harmony, a continuous motion in choreographed unison, by analysing dance mechanically, into numbers of discrete motions, each mastered separately, then recombined in the final presentation.

Military ballet at court, in which officers participated, could have provided the direct entry of these notions into the military. In any case, the choreography – mechanized harmony – of reloading reached perfection in Jacob de Gheyn's *Wapenhandelinghe* (1607), which analysed the loading of a musket into a choreography of forty-three illustrated steps, to be performed as counter-march in ranks. Gheyn's book accelerated the diffusion of counter-march, and the mechanization of tactics generally, which, a step ahead of the mechanical philosophy, diffused in the next decades from Maurice's Dutch army into armies throughout Europe, and in the Germanies particularly, first to Brandenburg c. 1610, then to the Palatinate, Brunswick, Württemberg, Hessen, Baden, Saxony and Holstein.[52] Counter-march in the Dutch army must have been in a high state of harmonious mechanization in 1618, when Descartes served with that army, as his *Discours de la méthode* recounts. (I'm trying to explain how the mechanization of motion overtook the elite.)

But the militarized version of the mechanical philosophy, which soon followed counter-march throughout Europe, dispensed with the notion of 'harmony'. Emphasis moved from tactics, the harmonious mechanization of discrete bodies and particles in motion, to ballistics.[53] The new kingdom of mechanical force, nature as ballistical field, first attained influential advocates in the 1630s, the height of the Thirty Years' War. The ballistical metaphor pushed problems of projectile motion and particle collisions into physics' centre. The revival of atomism came about in step. In the Germanies, Cartesianism would be the most notorious vehicle of the militaristic world order void of harmony.

Descartes' *Discours* and *Meditationes* centre on nice narratives, and his *Principia* spins a poetic, albeit mechanical, cosmogony. Yet it was Descartes who orchestrated the great caesura between narrative and science. As Amos Funkenstein has argued, Cartesianism, fulfilling a project of mediaeval nominalism, cast nature as an aggregate of discrete, mechanically defined singulars.[54] This got rid of teleological principles in nature. As the kingdom of mechanical 'force', ballistical matter in motion, nature left the domain of harmony and poetics. The physicist could not work like a critic, for nature now had neither unity of plot nor choreography. The transparency of nature to knowledge lay not in a narratological domain, nature's poetic construction; it lay in a technological domain, nature's mechanical construction, conceived ultimately as a militaristic domain, and not of tactics, but ballistics.

Cartesianism suffered the ban in the Germanies. The *Index Romanus* forbade Descartes' writings in 1663, sealing their fate in the Catholic lands. In the Protestant lands, decrees that physics professors adhere to Aristotle were essentially directed against Cartesianism, by the late Baroque. Cartesianism and atomism generally, *via* Scaliger, Gassendi and Boyle, penetrated the Germanies nonetheless. Here they displaced, or, more commonly, fused with other natural philosophies, which occupied a spectrum, from scholastic Aristotelianism to Paracelsianism.

Johann Sperling, in his *Synopsis physicae* (Wittenberg, 1649) in eleven reprintings, kept Aristotle's causes and elements, and Paracelsus' *tria prima* (salt, sulphur, mercury), but embraced atomism. Elsewhere he declared, 'The world has no substantial form. For its wholeness is not essential, but rather as an aggregate.'[55] Guericke's *Nova experimenta* (1672) postulated, *contra* Aristotle, the atomists' vacuum, and Joachim Jungius rejected Paracelsianism for a mechanical corpuscularism of qualitatively different atoms.[56] Cartesian versions of mechanism also emerged, for instance at the universities of Marburg, Gießen, Duisburg and Kiel. Johann Sucier in Basel, in his *Compendium physicae Aristotelico-Cartesianae* (1685), grounded the Aristotelian elements and causes upon Cartesian principles of matter and motion. And Altdorf's Sturm presented a vortex corpuscularism of pure Cartesianism.[57] But few Germans were wedded to such unvarnished corpuscular mechanism, and abandonment of teleology *per se* seems rarer. In this regard, let us now consider the positions of Kircher/Schott and Leibniz.

Kircher and Schott, teacher and pupil, and most renowned of Catholic natural philosophers, contributed much to the cult of the machine, seen as 'natural magic'. Their mathematical works integrated new mechanical topics, like Galilean projectile motion (but not impact mechanics, which seems to appear in textbooks only in the eighteenth century). Schott even adopted corpuscularism and Boyle's mechanization of the air, giving it weight and spring. But Kircher and Schott did not set mechanics as physics' foundational discipline. They sought instead a discipline tied to teleology. Kircher's *Musurgia universalis* (1650) aside, they, unlike Kepler, did not find the foundational discipline in harmonics ('acoustics'). Schott favored optics, as did Kircher at one point, who later perhaps switched to a non-mechanical magnetism.[58] Like Kepler, Kircher saw nature's unity in relational categories; and he transformed Aristotle's four elements and qualities into relational forces: assimilation, communication, attraction-repulsion, rarefaction-condensation. A *panspermia* pervaded nature, whose fundament was Paracelsian sympathy-antipathy. Schott had an *aether plenum* unifying nature, and Kircher saw the metaphysical unity of nature as love.[59]

If Kircher and Schott embodied the pre-eminent German Catholic natural philosophers of the late Baroque, Leibniz was the pre-eminent German natural philosopher *simpliciter*. His view of the denouement of the 'Scientific Revolution' – the publication of Newton's *Principia* in 1687 – is evident from a letter to Huygens in 1689, and the articles published in the *Acta eruditorum* in 1689 and 1690.[60] In the articles, Leibniz opposed himself to the Cartesian theory of celestial motion and gravity. Against Descartes, but without mentioning Newton, he returned to a version of Kepler's theory of harmonic motion and magnetic aether vortices. The letter to Huygens shows that Leibniz thought Kepler's theory also preferable to Newton's. The turn to 'harmony' indicates the centrality of Kepler and teleology in Leibniz's self-understanding of his opposition, as a German, to Descartes and Newton. Leibniz's would be the mechanical world of 'pre-established harmony', a vision more at home with the tactical, choreographical metaphor than the ballistical.

Rejecting his youthful Cartesianism, Leibniz laboured thereafter to restore the *mechanica mundi* within a Keplerian *harmonia mundi*. He characterized this variously as the reconciliation of nature and grace, of efficient and final causes, of mechanics and politics, of mechanism and organicism. Against Cartesianism, he returned to the notion that the mechanical, as machine, only made sense within the broader domain of teleological principles of function and economy. Without final causes, in a nature composed only of atoms under ballistical laws, there is no system, no reference structure to make the aggregate a whole.[61]

Even the new fields of projectile motion and impact must follow teleological as well as mechanical principles. Leibniz set his concept of 'force', *vis viva* (mv^2), against the Cartesian 'quantity of motion' (mv), and against Newtonian 'force' (ma). The theory of *vis viva* sought integration of entelechies, the teleological, with the mechanical, but it was long unclear how it might do so. Leibniz invoked the 'economy of motion' not only regarding light (the principle of least time), but also regarding collisions.[62] He once linked system, universal harmony, and economy, with the political notions of 'private' and 'public'. An object (light) considered in its 'private' existence, followed strictly mechanical laws; but, considered in its 'public' existence, systematic principles of harmony and economy obtained.[63] As Mary Terrall and Norton Wise have shown, Leibniz's project – a physics dedicated to the reconciliation of mechanism and harmony, the latter seen as teleology or organicism – lived long in the German Nations.[64]

In expounding his theory of harmony and mechanics, Leibniz, like most Germans concerned with the nature of the Empire, favoured political metaphors. 'The Deity governs souls as a prince governs his subjects, or as a father cares for his children, while He disposes with other substances as an engineer manages his machines.'[65] Might Leibniz have said of the Deity's relation to souls, 'As an author cares for her books'? Could Leibniz, librarian and historian to the duke of Hanover, and scholastic Aristotelianism's champion, have recovered literary metaphors, have rethought 'harmony' as the 'world-as-text', or the 'world-as-library'?[66] For that, the Cartesian disjunction between literature and science was perhaps now too great. Leibniz himself says of Descartes sardonically, 'One will soon forget the lovely novel of physics [*le beau Roman de physique*] which he gave us.'[67] The association of nature with narrative had become something for 'ladies'.

Carolyn Merchant, in *The Death of Nature* (1980), has argued that mechanism led to the death of nature, which had been seen as female. Mechanism led as well to the apotheosis and gendering as masculine of mechanical or analytical thinking. Complementing Merchant's thesis, in so far as it does not essentialize gender, we can say, correlatively, that mechanism gendered narrative as feminine. Nature-as-female became narrative-as-feminine. After the Baroque, the 'woman' would be seen as the consumer *par excellence* of narrative, the reader of novels, and a previously ungendered form of knowledge, narrative, would become gendered as feminine by 'men of science'. The mechanical philosophy denied the poetic basis of nature, and took knowledge based on narrative, criticism, as emasculated, effeminate knowledge. Scientists would speak of the world-as-text with the derogatory tones they reserved for 'science for ladies'. Narrative became knowledge's charwoman.

This brings us to the public again. The two previous moments of the Scientific Revolution, experimentalism and heliocentrism, emerged within the horizon of science's relation to a new public, constructed as consumers of kitsch and as statistics of *fortuna*. Mechanism, the middle term between experimentalism and heliocentrism, emerged within the horizon of science's construction of the 'woman' as rhetorical figure for the public. The woman as the public's figure would be seen as the consumer of scientific narratives. At the close of the Baroque, and throughout the Enlightenment, scientists, from Fontenelle to Euler, would seek to make the mechanical philosophy fit for the public, popular, through letters addressed to and dialogues containing women. And the scientist would approach and seek to dominate the public after his conception of a woman: someone to be seduced, for love or money, by heroic stories.[68]

CONCLUSION

If the Germans have a national character regarding the Scientific Revolution, the names of Paracelsus, Kepler, and Leibniz mark it most distinctly. To the Germans themselves, these three essentially name what it meant to be 'German' in the Renaissance and Baroque. The German *Sonderweg* opposed the hegemony of (ballistical) mechanism in its mediation of experimentalism and heliocentrism. Germans sought a reciprocal relation within science between the technical and the social, the material and spiritual. They looked for this in Paracelsian *sympátheia*, Keplerian *harmonia*, or Leibnizean *dépendance mutuelle*, and expressed it in political metaphors: the elusive unity of the Empire of German Nations. Instead of seeing narrative as the foundation of knowledge as social praxis, they fell with Faust into an essentializing identification of the feminine (*qua Kultur!*) with the social bond. 'Das Ewig-Weibliche zieht uns hinan.'

NOTES

I wrote this paper while Kenan Fellow at the Society of Fellows in Humanities, Columbia University. For their help with various drafts of this paper, I most gratefully thank Lorraine Daston, Anne Higgins, Lisbet Koerner, Pamela Smith, Norton Wise, and, of course, the editors.

1 Gottfried W. Leibniz, *Die Werke*, ed. O. Klopp, 11 vols. (Hanover, 1864–88), 1, p. 133; also *cf.* x, pp. 299–310.

2 Aristotle, *Physics*, bk. II, esp. ii–ii, vii; *Metaphysics*, bk. I, esp. ii–vii. In the latter, Aristotle gives an historical derivation of the four causes (*aitíai*), showing that his predecessors' accounts (*aitíai*) of nature can be reduced to these, and insists that a complete account involves all four (*i.e.* narrative closure). The relation of the Aristotelian causes with the fundamental principles of dramaturgy could be illuminated by extrapolation from Kenneth Burke, *A Grammar of Motives* (Berkeley/Los Angeles, 1969), rendering his five principles into four. For an alternate reading of the poetic basis of Aristotelian nature, see Jürgen Mittelstraß, 'Das Wirken der Natur', in F. Rapp (ed.), *Naturverständnis und Naturbeherrschung* (Munich, 1980), 36–69.

3 Hans Blumenberg, *Die Lesbarkeit der Welt* (Frankfurt, 1981), ch. 5.

4 Many words for 'cause' in the West have their origin in terms for judicial cases: *aitía, causa, Ur-sache*, and, in English, sake. The four causes are the grounds for telling the story of a crime or case, *i.e.* an event within the law's compass, in narrative closure: scene, agent(s), plot, and end. On law, history, and narrative, *cf.* Hayden White, 'The Value of Narrativity in the Representation of Reality', in W. J. T. Mitchell (ed.), *On Narrative* (Chicago, 1981), 1–24.

5 Ernst Zinner, *Deutsche und niederländische Instrumente des 11.–18. Jahrhunderts* (Munich, 1956), pp. 604–5. Bruce Moran, *Science at the Court of Hesse-Kassel* (Hist. Diss., UCLA, 1978), pp. 190–96.

6 Henricus C. Agrippa, *De incertitudine et vanitate scientiarum et artium* (Antwerp, 1531), pp. 9^r–12^r, 41^v–42^r, 53^r, 156^r; *De occulta philosophia* (Cologne, 1533), pp. i–iv, xv–xvi.

7 Paracelsus (Phillipus A. Theophrastus von Hohenheim), *Sämtliche Werke*, ed. K. Sudhoff, pt. 1: 14 vols. (Munich, 1922–33), VIII, pp. 36–43, 48, 138–40, 150–2, 181.

8 See Abbot P. Usher, *A History of Mechanical Inventions* (Cambridge, Mass., 1929/54), ch. 10. Elizabeth Eisenstein, *The Printing Press as an Agent of Change*, 2 vols. in 1 (Cambridge, 1979/80), esp. chs. 5–6.

9 Lynn Thorndike, *A History of Magic and Experimental Science*, 8 vols. (New York, 1923–58), V, ch. 29. Allen Debus, *The Chemical Philosophy*, 2 vols. (New York, 1977), I, chs. 2–3.

10 Owen Hannaway, *The Chemists and the Word* (Baltimore, 1975), esp. chs. 4–6. *Cf.* Jan Golinski, 'Chemistry and the Scientific Revolution', in David Lindberg and Robert Westman (eds.), *Reappraisals of the Scientific Revolution* (Cambridge, 1990), 367–97.

11 Johann Alsted, *Scientiarum omnium encyclopaediae*, 2 vols. (Leiden, 1649), I, p. 59.

12 Carolyn Merchant, *The Death of Nature* (New York, 1980), p. 189.

13 Cf. Pamela Smith, *Alchemy, Credit, and the Commerce of Words and Things: Johann Joachim Becher at the Courts of the Holy Roman Empire* (Hist. Diss., Johns Hopkins University, 1989/90), pp. 337–9, 376, 437.

14 Otto von Guericke, *Experimenta nova* (Amsterdam, 1672). Athanasius Kircher, *Ars magna lucis et umbrae* (Rome, 1646); *Magnes sive de magnetica arte* (Rome, 1654). Kaspar Schott, *Magia universalis naturae et artis*, 4 vols. (Würzburg, 1657–9); *Technica curiosa* (Nuremberg, 1664).

15 On the Germanies generally, see John Heilbron, *Electricity in the Seventeenth and Eighteenth Centuries* (Berkeley, 1979), pp. 183–92, 213–19, 261–75.

16 On the eighteenth century, see Fritz Krafft, 'Der Weg von den Physikern zur Physik…', *Berichte zur Wissenschaftsgeschichte* 1 (1978), 123–62.

17 Many thanks to John Rogers of the Yale English Dept. for referring me on modes of emplotment to Northrop Frye, *Anatomy of Criticism* (Princeton, 1957/71). The *experimentum crucis* makes the experiment similar to alchemy, which is emplotted romantically – on the role of marvellous instruments and crucial trials in Romance, see *ibid.*, pp. 33, 186–206; and V. Propp, *Morphology of the Folktale*, trans. L. Scott (2nd. edn., Austin, 1968), pp. 39–51, 60–5. An easier move from the forensic-poetic cast of disputation would be toward emplotment of experiment as judicial inquisition and penology, *i.e.* toward

tragedy. A rhetoric of judicial torture and inquisition did figure in the Baconian experimental canon – see Merchant, *The Death*, pp. 168–70; and Frye, *Anatomy*, p. 208, notes the co-temporality of tragedy's two great eras with science's: Classical Athens and the Classical Age in Europe. But Frye (*Anatomy*, p. 166) also notes the similarity of comic emplotment to judicial suits, and, as central to comedy, sees the 'integration of society' and the tendency 'to include as many people as possible in its final society' (pp. 43, 165); thus, a comic mode of emplotment would be most sensible for the experiment, seen as basis of an academic social bond. *Cf.* Geoffrey Cantor, 'The Rhetoric of Experiment', in D. Gooding *et al.* (eds.), *The Uses of Experiment* (Cambridge, 1989), 159–80. Cantor's ascription of tragic emplotment (pp. 175–6) would be better seen as comic. On comedy and tragedy generally, see Frye, *Anatomy*, pp. 35–52, 163–86, 206–23.

18 Johann C. Sturm, *Collegium experimentale sive curiosum*, 2 vols. (Nuremberg, 1676–85), I, 'programma invitatorum'.

19 On the Jesuits' fondness for instruments, see Heilbron, *Electricity*, pp. 103–4, whose reading of this is different.

20 Simon Schaffer, 'Natural Philosophy and Public Spectacle in the Eighteenth Century', *History of Science* 21 (1983), 1–43.

21 See Robert S. Westman, 'The Melanchthon Circle, Rheticus, and the Wittenberg Interpretation of the Copernican Theory', *Isis* 66 (1975), 165–93; 'The Astronomer's Role in the Sixteenth Century', *History of Science* 18 (1980), 105–47; 'Nature, Art, and the Psyche:... the Kepler-Fludd Polemic', in Brian Vickers (ed.) *Occult and Scientific Mentalities in the Renaissance* (Cambridge, 1984), pp. 177–229; 'Proof, Poetics, and Patronage: Copernicus's Preface to De revolutionibus', in Lindberg and Westman, *Reappraisals*, pp. 167–205.

22 Valentin Naibod, *Enarratio elementorum astrologiae* (Cologne, 1560), esp. pp. 262, 349.

23 Paracelsus, *Sämtliche Werke*, VIII, pp. 163–4.

24 See Thorndike, *History of Magic*, V, chs. 13–19.

25 See Robert S. Westman, 'The Copernicans and the Churches', in D. C. Lindberg and R. L. Numbers (eds.), *God and Nature* (Berkeley, 1986), pp. 76–113. See esp. pp. 86–95. See also *idem*, 'Proof, Poetics, and Patronage'.

26 Westman, 'The Melanchthon Circle'.

27 Robert S. Westman, 'The Comet and the Cosmos: Kepler, Mästlin and the Copernican Hypothesis', *Studia Copernicana* 5 (1972), 7–30; 'Three Responses to Copernican Theory: Johannes Praetorius, Tycho Brahe, and Michael Maestlin,' in R. S. Westman (ed.), *The Copernican Achievement* (Berkeley, 1975), 285–345; 'The Astronomer's Role'. N. Jardine, *The Birth of the History and Philosophy of Science: Kepler's Defense of Tycho against Ursus* (Cambridge, 1984), ch. 7.

28 Caspar Peucer, *Commentarius de praecipuis divinationum* (Frankfurt, 1593), pp. 644–5, 688, 693. Also Naibod, *Enarratio*, p. 2.

29 Johannes Kepler, *Gesammelte Werke*, ed. Max Caspar, 19 vols. (Munich, 1937–75), I, pp. 314–56; IV, *passim*. *Cf.* Gérard Simon, *Kepler, astronome, astrologue* (Paris, 1979).

30 Kepler, *Gesammelte Werke*, IV, pp. 12, 32, 150.

31 *Ibid.*, xv, p. 464. But *cf. ibid.* vi, pp. 291–3.

32 *Ibid.*, i, p. 70; iii, p. 361; vii, pp. 295–7.

33 For the longer perspective, see Hans Blumenberg, *Die Genesis der kopernikanischen Welt* (Frankfurt-am-Main, 1975), pt. 2, ch. 2.

34 Kepler, *Gesammelte Werke*, vi, pp. 186–205, 264–86.

35 Kircher, *Magnes*, p. 390.

36 See Guericke, *Experimenta*, bk. 1. Athanasius Kircher, *Iter exstaticum coeleste*, ed. Caspar Schott (2nd edn., Würzburg, 1671), pp. 36–9. Johann Sturm, *Physicae conciliatricis* (Nuremberg, 1687), pp. 179–84. Sturm was later avowedly a Copernican.

37 *Acta eruditorum* 7 (1688), 303–15; 8 (1689), 82–96; 9 (1690), 228–39, 258–64.

38 Ernst Zinner, *Entstehung und Ausbreitung der Coppernicanischen Lehre* (Erlangen, 1943), pp. 379–88. Rainer Baasner, *Das Lob der Sternkunst: Astronomie in der deutschen Aufklärung* (Göttingen, 1987).

39 Johann Sperling, *Synopsis physicae* (Wittenberg, 1649), pp. 112–13.

40 On the 'public' and astrology, see Baasner, *Das Lob*, ch. 17.

41 Erhard Weigel, *Arithmetische Beschreibung der Moral-Weissheit von Personen und Sachen* (Jena, 1674), esp. pp. 7–12, 22–6, 39.

42 Lorraine Daston, *Classical Probability in the Enlightenment* (Princeton, 1988), ch. 3.

43 Hans Schmitt-Lermann, *Der Versicherungsgedanke im deutschen Geistesleben des Barock und der Aufklärung* (Munich, 1954), ch. 5.

44 Gottfried W. Leibniz, *Die philosophischen Schriften*, ed. C. I. Gerhardt, 7 vols. (Berlin, 1875–90), iv, pp. 500–1; *Die Werke*, vii, p. 300; *Sämtliche Schriften und Briefe*, 6th series: 6 vols., (Darmstadt, 1923–80), iii, p. 474.

45 Mittelstraß, 'Das Wirken' pp. 44–5, 51–9.

46 See Otto Mayr, *Authority, Liberty and Automatic Machinery in Early Modern Europe* (Baltimore, 1986), chs. 1–3.

47 Georg J. Rheticus, *Narratio prima* (1540), in Kepler, *Gesammelte Werke*, i, pp. 97–104, 131. On harmony in non-Copernicans, see Phillip Melanchthon, *Initia doctrinae physicae* (1549), in *Corpus Reformatorum*, ed. C. G. Breitschneider, 28 vols. (Halle, 1834–60), xiii, p. 266. Erasmus Reinhold, *Theoricae novae planetarum...Purbachii* (Wittenberg, 1542), see the dedication and preface (unpag.).

48 Kepler, *Gesammelte Werke*, xv, p. 146.

49 *Ibid.* vi, p. 10. *Cf.* Fernand Hallyn, *La Structure poétique du monde: Copernic, Kepler* (Paris, 1987), esp. p. 302.

50 Kepler, *Gesammelte Werke*, vi, p. 95; also pp. 211–25; and i, p. 70; iii, pp. 34–5, 361; iv, pp. 22 3, 32 3.

51 Leibniz, *Die Werke* xi, p. 44.

52 On the above, see Henning Eichberg, 'Geometrie als Barocke Verhaltensnorm', *Zeitschrift für Historische Forschung* 4:1 (1977), 17–50, esp. 26–36; Geoffrey Parker, *The Military Revolution* (Cambridge, 1988), esp. pp. 18–21; Max Jähns, *Geschichte der Kriegeswissenschaften vornehmlich in Deutschland*, 3 vols. (Munich, 1889–90), i, esp. pp. 292–4, 702–5. Joseph Gregor, *Kulturgeschichte des Ballets* (Vienna, 1944), pp. 191–8. Tactics, soon a part of mathematics, may have helped revive the atomists' concepts of 'figure', 'size', 'order' as definitive of motion – these are central concepts in tactics. *Cf.* Justus Lipsius, *De militia*

romana (Antwerp, 1598), *passim*, esp. pp. 13, 47; Kaspar Schott, *Cursus mathematicus* (Würzburg, 1661), bk. XXIII, on tactics.

53 The importance of ballistics was, of course, seen long ago in A. R. Hall, *Ballistics in the Seventeenth Century* (Cambridge, 1952).

54 See Amos Funkenstein, *Theology and the Scientific Imagination* (Princeton, 1986), chs 2–3, 5, esp. pp. 184–8, 320–7.

55 Johann Sperling, *Exercitationes physicae* (Wittenberg, 1663), p. 701.

56 Hans Kangro, *Joachim Jungius' Experimente und Gedanken zur Begründung der Chemie als Wissenschaft* (Wiesbaden, 1968).

57 Sturm, *Physicae*, pp. 16–37, 59–60, 90–6, 145–6.

58 Kircher, *Ars*, pp. 5, 31; *Magnes*, pp. 376–80. Schott, *Magia* I, pp. 2–3.

59 Kircher, *Magnes*, pp. 376–80, 407–9, 605–13; *Mundus subterraneus*, 2 vols. (Amsterdam, 1665), II, pp. 6, 328. Schott, *Technia*, pp. 30, 76, 223, 246–58.

60 *Acta eruditorum* 8 (1689), 82–96; 9 (1690), 228–39. Letter to Huygens in Gottfried W. Leibniz, *Mathematische Schriften*, ed. C. I. Gerhardt, 7 vols. (Hanover, 1849–63), II, pp. 187–93.

61 Leibniz, *Die philosophischen Schriften*, IV, pp. 281, 339–40, 390–9, 446–8, 472–80, 562; VI, pp. 149, 542; *Sämtliche Schriften*, II, pp. 246–50, 280; III, p. 394; *Die Werke*, X, p. 255; XI, p. 176; *Mathematische Schriften* II, pp. 241–3.

62 Leibniz, *Sämtliche Schriften*, II, pp. 228–9, 254–5; *Mathematische Schriften* II, pp. 215–31, 236–43; *Die philosophischen Schriften*, IV, pp. 393–400, 446–8, 468–79, 504–16. On the importance of *vis viva* in the eighteenth century, regarding function and economy in the notion of a system, see Terry Reynolds, *Stronger Than a Hundred Men: A History of the Vertical Water Wheel* (Baltimore, 1983). If horology and ballistics constitute the central technological *topoi* for Baroque mechanics, then hydrodynamics constitutes the same for Enlightenment mechanics. The path from the Mechanical to the Thermodynamical World goes by way of the water wheel.

63 Leibniz, *Sämtliche Schriften*, II, pp. 314–15.

64 Mary Terrall, *Maupertuis and Eighteenth Century Scientific Culture* (Hist. Diss., UCLA, 1987), chs. 1–3, esp. pp. 114–15. M. Norton Wise, 'German Concepts of Force, Energy, and the Electromagnetic Ether, 1845–1880', in G. N. Cantor and M. J. S. Hodge (eds.), *Conceptions of the Ether* (Cambridge, 1981), 269–307.

65 Leibniz, *Die philosophischen Schriften*, IV, pp. 479–80.

66 *Ibid.* VII, p. 302. *Cf.* Blumenberg, *Die Lesbarkeit*.

67 Leibniz, *Die philosophischen Schriften*, IV, pp. 302–3.

68 The point is Lyotard's. I have gendered it.

4

THE NEW PHILOSOPHY IN THE
LOW COUNTRIES

HAROLD J. COOK

FROM Gemma Frisius and Simon Stevin to Christiaan Huygens, from Clusius to Hermannus, from Paludanus to Ruysch, from Paauw to De Graaf, from Van Helmont to Sylvius, from Beeckman to Swammerdam and Van Leeuwenhoek, and from Vesalius to Boerhaave, Dutch and Flemish scholars combined excellent educations with investigative enterprise, technical competence, and moral commitment. These and other people of the region achieved wide notice and enduring fame. In the low countries, the intellectual and cultural changes of the late middle ages and Renaissance had not just a broad influence, but a deep one as well. It was a place where local traditions and a patchwork of competing jurisdictions allowed both Humanism and the Enlightenment to prosper in difficult times. It was also a region in which the new science flourished.[1]

Yet when we begin to examine the work of the many scholars of the region who helped to create fundamental changes in the European knowledge of nature, we will be forced to note an important fact: the new science grew mainly by the efforts of people engaged in working out the details of natural history, medicine, chemistry and mathematics. Perhaps the focus of attention people have given to 'philosophers' the likes of Galileo, Descartes, Newton and Leibniz has warped our expectations. To be sure, the Dutch Republic can claim Christiaan Huygens, and perhaps even Descartes, since the latter wrote his most important works in the United Provinces. But more importantly, the very phrase 'Scientific Revolution' was created by mid-twentieth-century scholars to indicate a shift of world view based upon the mathematization, or latterly the mechanization, of nature. Alexandre Koyré and his like wrote brilliantly but polemically about changes in natural philosophy centred upon seemingly revolutionary new ideas of the heavens, of falling bodies and of corpuscles.[2] The scholars of the low countries knew about these new philosophical positions, and even helped to create many of them. What is striking about their work in comparison to their forbears, however, is the intense amount of investigative energy they gave to exploring the natural world, and to getting its details straight: it is the difference between a Sir John Mandeville and a Sir Thomas Browne.

If we take the Scientific Revolution to be this new investment of time and energy in detailed investigations of nature rather than the development of any particular world view, then the scientific enterprises of the scholars of the low countries provide a rich illustration of how deep and wide the network of such scholars was becoming in early modern Europe. The social, economic, political and educational structures of the low countries provided the foundation for an intellectual revolution, but a revolution not so much in the construction of a mechanical world view (with which not everyone agreed) as in the growth of explorations into the details of nature. And as we shall see, many of the most important attempts to explore nature in detail emerged from the medical faculties.

MEDICINE AND MATHEMATICS

At the heart of the intellectual transformation of the low countries lay the many excellent schools in the provinces, supported by piety and practicality, and encouraged by municipal patriotism. The gospel of learning for the laity had made deep inroads in the regional culture. It was not only the region that gave rise to the late medieval 'Modern Devotion', but a region that had given birth to scholars of the rank of Rudolph Agricola and Desiderius Erasmus as well. Long before the revolt, then, local schools had become quite excellent in many of the towns and cities throughout the region, training and supporting some of the most noted northern humanists. In addition to lower schools and Sunday schools for young children, in which teaching was in local vernaculars, one or more Latin schools grew up in almost every large town and city. By the later sixteenth and the seventeenth centuries, some of the Latin schools of the northern provinces were receiving special attention from the municipalities, growing into the 'illustrious schools', or *athenaea*, which amounted to universities in virtually all respects except that they did not have the right to grant degrees. Together with the flourishing of formal education in the low countries went the spread of general literacy, and the printing press. The general regard for learning had become so deeply rooted by the sixteenth century that the dense network of chambers of rhetoric – which not only organized Latin ceremonies for visiting dignitaries but also held organized public competitions with each other even through the seventeenth century – had memberships that included not only some of the social and educational elite but also thatchers of roofs, ship masters, servants of bureaucrats, carpenters and butchers.[3]

In the early- to mid-sixteenth century, a number of fine local schools in the low countries turned out well-educated pupils who became prominent in church, court and city, but only one university existed for the territory. This was Louvain, established in 1425, located in Brabant, near the major southern centres of population and wealth. As at other northern universities, the new humanism of the fifteenth century made inroads at Louvain, where teaching in Greek and Latin grew to be quite excellent. It remained rather scholastic in its philosophical orientation, so that it did not adopt some of the new approaches transforming teaching at Italian universities and even Paris in the early sixteenth century. Andreas Vesalius (1514–64), the famous anatomist, later criticized his medical education at Louvain as remaining stuck in scholastic (and Islamic) ways rather than adopting the humanist (and Greek) medicine of Paris and Italy. Yet it was at Louvain where Vesalius gained his outstanding competency in Latin, and where he learned Greek and Hebrew as well; and it was at Louvain where he resolved to study medicine and received a solid preparation in it before going on to further medical studies in Paris in 1533. It was in Louvain that he witnessed his first autopsy; and it was from outside Louvain's walls that with the help of his admired friend Gemma Frisius he smuggled in his first human skeleton from the corpse of an executed criminal. While his major fame came during his sojourn in Italy from 1537 to 1546 – before he took up imperial service like his father and friends before him – his achievements could not have come about had it not been for Louvain's fine teaching in arts, languages and scholastic medical philosophy.[4]

If Louvain did not adopt some aspects of the latest criticism of established philosophy, professors at Louvain nevertheless promoted other developments, including those in mathematics. Both a professor of medicine at Louvain and the first strong advocate of Copernicanism in the low countries, Vesalius' friend Gemma Frisius (1508–55),[5] displayed a typical set of interests for the period. Like the Italian Girolamo Cardano (1501–76) and so many others of the period, Gemma combined an interest in medicine and mathematics,[6] making Louvain a centre of new astronomical and cosmographical instruction during the time he taught medicine there. His first publication, in 1529, was a new edition of Peter Apianus' *Cosmography*, followed a year later by a geographical, cosmographical and mathematical work of his own; and a year after that, he and Caspar Vander Heyden (or Caspar de Myrica) brought out a 'cosmographic sphere', or globe. Within three years of his taking his medical doctorate in 1536, the regents of the University of Louvain appointed Gemma to a chair of medicine, which he held until his death, teaching the new cosmography and astronomy as well as medicine. One of Gemma's best-known pupils, Gerard Kramer, or Mercator (1512–94), became perhaps the pre-eminent cosmographer of the sixteenth century; another, the young John Dee of England, came to study mathematics with him, and brought back to Trinity College, Cambridge, a brass astronomer's staff invented by Gemma, a new brass astrolabe Gemma designed, and two globes made by Mercator.[7] Gemma's theoretical solution to the problem of finding the longitude would have to wait two hundred years for sufficiently accurate clocks, but his solutions to mapping and measuring local distances *via* triangulation were successfully put to the test within a few decades of his death by Willebrod Snellius.

An early intellectual patron of Gemma's, Johann de Curiis Dantiscus, a humanist bishop born in Gdańsk and representing the king of Poland at Brussels, sent him inside information on new discoveries from the court of Charles V for incorporation into his maps. Through Dantiscus, too, Gemma first heard of and recognized the significance of Copernicus' theories, in or prior to July 1541, for Dantiscus had connections with Copernicus' disciple, Georg Joachim Rheticus (1514–74). In all probability, Dantiscus supplied Gemma with a copy of Copernicus' manuscript *Commentariolus* and Rheticus' interpretation, the *Narratio prima* (1540 and 1541). Gemma clearly understood Copernicus' heliocentric system, soon read Copernicus' *De revolutionibus orbium coelestium* (1543), and defended heliocentrism despite all opposition.[8]

By the sixteenth century, too, new concerns had evidenced themselves throughout the region in the lower schools, cities and aristocratic courts. While the spread of the chemical and occult philosophies in the low countries has not yet received an adequate account, their influences made themselves manifest. The Brussels-born aristocrat Joan Baptista van Helmont (1579–1644) gained an extensive knowledge of mathematics, astronomy and ancient philosophy at Louvain but later decided that academic hair-splitting was not for him, rejecting academic ways for the more active study of medical chemistry.[9] Cornelis Pietersz Schagen brought out a Dutch-language edition of the hermetic *Poimander* in 1607.[10] Earlier, the alchemist and cabalist Cornelius Agrippa served Margaret of Parma's court in the low countries from 1529 to 1532, and had his books printed in Antwerp.[11]

While some of the new ideas never gained acceptance by university scholars, the unity of interests among people of court and university was

more typical than conflict. The developments in natural history provide
a fine example of the breadth of support for new studies. Three of the
most famous naturalists of the later sixteenth century grew up in the low
countries: Rembert Dodoens, or Dodonaeus (1516–85); Matthias de
l'Obel, or Lobelius (1538–1616); and Charles de l'Escluse, or Clusius
(1526–1609). All three came from well-educated and well-to-do families,
and all obtained excellent educations before going on to Louvain for
further studies. All three also embarked upon long journeys in search of
knowledge and experience, travels typical of the period.[12] Before or
during these study tours, all three decided to embark upon medicine as
their major study. And on these tours, all three gained an enthusiasm for
that exciting new branch of study, natural history. For both Lobelius
and Clusius, the personal influence of the renowned natural historian
Guillaume Rondelet – professor of medicine at Montpellier – turned
them to the new subject. After their travels and studies, they all obtained
positions in the low countries as city physicians, posts that made them
part of the governing oligarchies (regenten) of the towns.[13]

Each also gained the patronage of the local and European nobility,
who were quite interested in the new natural history. For Dodoens' first
book on plants, he obtained a privilege from the emperor Charles V to
use the woodcuts of Leonard Fuchs' herbal; he dedicated the book that
led to his greatest renown, his vernacular herbal or Cruydeboeck of 1554,
to the governor of the low countries and Charles' sister, Mary of
Hungary. When the growing religious and political troubles of the
region caused Dodoens to turn down an offer to become a professor at
Louvain, he was able to take up instead a position as court physician to
the Holy Roman Emperor, Maximilian II, and retain it under Rudolph
II. After the worst of the political and military turmoil of the mid-60s
and 70s in the low countries, he resigned his post, travelled slowly back
to the southern Netherlands via Cologne, and settled in Antwerp, until
in 1582 he accepted the position of professor of medicine at the new
University in Leiden, a post obtained only with the blessings of the
curators, who ran their school with a sharp eye.[14] Throughout his
peregrinations, Dodoens continued to publish books on natural history.
Lobelius fled to England after the revolt, just as many others did.
Returning to the low countries about 1572, he published his Plantarum seu
stirpium nova in London in 1576, with a translation into Dutch (the
Kruydtboeck) in 1581. Shortly after the publication of his Latin work he
entered the service of the leader of the revolt, William I, Prince of
Orange. When William was assassinated in 1584, Lobelius moved to
Middelburg, a thriving port in the northern province of Zealand, and
due to his reputation among the regenten of the city, became one of its four

town physicians. In 1596 he moved yet again, back to England, as physician and gardener to Lord Edward Zouch. James I of England granted him the title of Royal Botanograph. Lobelius died in Highgate, north of London, in 1616.[15]

The most famous of the three, Clusius, travelled very widely before he became prefect of the imperial garden in Vienna under Emperor Maximilian in 1573. Because of the expense of Vienna and growing religious tensions at the court of his successor Rudolph II (Clusius being at least a Protestant sympathizer), he left Vienna in 1587, establishing himself first in Frankfurt in 1588, and finally accepting the position as professor of medicine and curator of the new botanical garden at the university in Leiden (but without the obligation of teaching). He moved there in 1593, carrying his exotic plants with him – which helped to cause the tulip craze of the early seventeenth century – where he remained until his death, bringing the university great renown.[16] From Clusius to Hermann Boerhaave (1668–1738), the Leiden *hortus* remained one of the foremost botanical gardens in Europe, assembling specimens from all over the world, partly through the help of university curators connected to the Dutch East and West India Companies.

NATURAL HISTORY, MEDICINE AND MATHEMATICS IN THE EARLY REPUBLIC

The respect for learning possessed by the aristocrats and regents who led the Dutch Revolt caused them to found a number of new universities after it became clear that the rebellion would be a fight for independence. To educate clergymen for the Calvinist church, but also to educate lawyers and physicians and the sons of the well-to-do, the leaders of virtually each of the seven United Provinces established a new university: the provinces of Holland and Zealand founded the University of Leiden (1575); Friesland founded Franeker (1585); Gelderland founded Harderwijk (1600); the states of Groningen set up a university in the city of that name (1614); and the same happened in Utrecht (1636). All these universities included faculties in the arts, theology, medicine and law. Because they were new schools, they incorporated new kinds of teaching based on the latest kinds of studies, especially those being pursued in northern Italy.[17] Consequently, some of these Dutch universities, especially Leiden and Franeker, and later Utrecht, became quite well regarded internationally.

The ways in which teaching in the natural sciences developed at Leiden illustrates the concerns of the Dutch *regenten* to have many of the latest ideas and investigations passed on to their sons. The early curators of Leiden university worked energetically to make their new school a place where the latest studies could be had; and they were well-educated and discerning critics. The curator of the university who negotiated with Clusius, Johan van Hogelande, had already corresponded with him about plants; like Jan van der Does (or Douza, lord of Nordwijk), he had a fierce commitment to making Leiden a centre of humanist learning, helping to attract scholars the likes of Lipsius and Scaliger. He and other curators could not imagine their new university becoming truly excellent without a first-rate botanical garden, so necessary to teaching the natural science of the day. At the University of Pisa a cloister garden had been extended by 1543 to serve the university, Leipzig university had begun its *hortus* about 1542, Padua and Florence theirs about 1550, the university of Bologna had made an older garden of medicinal simples into a *hortus* about 1567. Princes and emperors, nobles and townspeople also established private botanical gardens where they cultivated exotic as well as useful plants. Early in 1587, therefore, the curators of the new university requested from the Leiden burgomasters a plot of ground for a garden next to the former convent that now housed the university; and when the request was granted, they gave one of the medical professors, Geraerdt de Bont, or Bontius (1536–99) a salary increase of fifty gilders to explain herbs in the summer and continue his anatomical lessons in the winter. But Bontius soon ceased his work in botany, so the curators began to approach others.[18]

Although Clusius eventually took the post, he had not been the first choice of Van Hogelande and the other curators of the new university. They had first offered the position to a younger man, Berent ten Broeke, better known as Bernardus Paludanus (1550–1633), a native of Steenwijk, in the north-east province of Drenthe. Like so many others, Paludanus had a firm grounding in languages and various new studies. He, too, had embarked upon travels that led him through Germany, Poland, Lithuania, Italy, Syria, Palestine, Egypt, Malta and Sicily, and he had considered going to Santo Domingo in the Americas. Throughout his travels, Paludanus collected objects, specimens and information, and established a dense network of natural historical correspondence that continued after he became city physician of Zwolle and then Enkhuisen. When in 1591 the curators of Leiden university proposed that he become the head of the new botanical garden, and bring his collections with him, the burgomasters of Enkhuizen would not let this most valuable citizen go – besides, his wife was doubtful about the move.

To have obtained not only the services of Paludanus but his collections would have been an even greater coup for Leiden than getting Clusius and his botanical specimens. Paludanus had assembled a truly wonderful cabinet of natural history and art: fruit, grains and woods from the tropics; the plumage of birds (for example, the bird of paradise of New Guinea); preserved specimens of fish and reptiles; the horns of different animals; insects, shells and corals; several types of earths (including earth of Damascus, said to be the colour of the flesh of Adam), stones, minerals and marbles; precious gems, coins, medals and counters; weapons, clothes and other objects used by 'savages' and foreigners; objects of art done in ivory, rare woods and precious metals; mummies and funerary furnishings from Egypt; and jewels and rings of many kinds. His wide knowledge of natural history can also be seen in the notes he added to accounts of the Indies in the 1596 volume of the *Itinerario* of Jan Huygen van Linschoten (1563–1611), the Hakluyt and Purchas of continental Europe.[19]

Nor is the story of the foundation of the Leiden botanical garden (*hortus*) only a story of being able to attract a Clusius after being turned down by a Paludanus. The experience and expertise of many people lay behind the development of the garden. While the curators exerted themselves to find and attract a scholar of natural history to head the *hortus*, the day-to-day planning of and education in it was carried out by an apothecary from Delft: Dirck Outgaertsz Cluyt (1546–98), well known for his own private garden. Cluyt maintained his own large apothecary shop on the Wijnhaven in Delft, with a well-known large enclosed garden where he raised costly plants for use in medicines. He began work in the Leiden garden in 1591, although because he had no academic qualifications he could not become curator. The elderly Clusius could not work in the garden after his arrival in Leiden in October 1593 because of an injury to his hip incurred earlier that spring; even by the spring of 1594 – the planting season – he was unable to work in the garden. Clusius wrote to the regent Douza that he needed someone to take his place, and so it was that Cluyt set up the garden in the four summer months of 1594, while Clusius gave all his energies to his private garden (especially his tulips), his letters and his publications. Even after Clusius recovered, Cluyt and his son Outgaert gave the lessons to the students in the garden in the summer, and in the winter taught them with a collection of 4,000 simples and illustrated books that Cluyt had assembled.[20]

Along with providing facilities for teaching in natural history, the curators of Leiden university also promoted anatomical studies. In 1592, at the same time that botanical teaching began in the *hortus*, the curators of the university opened an anatomical theatre in a former Beguinage chapel near the main university building. Quite clearly, the curators wished to emulate teaching at Padua; and the first medical professors they hired had studied there. Bontius, the first professor of medicine at Leiden, had begun medical studies at Louvain and completed them at Padua; the second professor, Johannes van Heurne, or Heurnius (1543–1601), had also studied medicine and mathematics at Louvain before travelling on to Paris, Padua and Pavia. The third medical professor, Pieter Paauw (1564–1617), was of the first generation to be educated in the northern Netherlands, studying first under Bontius at Leiden before embarking on his study trip; Aelius Everhardus Vorstius (1565–1624), like Paauw, also studied at Leiden before his fourteen years of travel and study abroad. All were excellent anatomists who turned out generations of students trained in the latest skills and knowledge. The first two generations of medical teachers at Leiden, then, stressed anatomy and botany just as much as professors did in Padua. There were even early attempts to imitate the clinical teaching that had begun to enter the curriculum of Padua, although the university would have to wait until 1636 for such teaching to begin in fact. Going further than Padua, early plans for Leiden included requiring 'the inspection, dissection, dissolution and transmutation of living bodies, plants and metals': chemical teaching as the equal of anatomical and clinical instruction (although such instruction would have to wait until the 1630s).[21]

Like the garden, however, the anatomy theatre was more than a place for inculcating the latest knowledge in students. Many people, not only students, visited both places, where they saw more than the material signs of life. The enclosed garden and the adjoining building's natural history collections came to resemble the garden of paradise, in which all living things existed peacefully side by side. When at the end of the seventeenth century the Englishman William Sherard edited the work of his friend, the Leiden professor Paulus Hermannus (1646–95), he entitled the book *Paradisus batavus* (1698). As for the theatre, anatomical images were rife with moral meanings about the body, the hidden structures of life, the impending death of each of us, and the vanities of this world.[22] For those who might be a bit slow to see this for themselves, during the spring through autumn months when anatomy lessons were not given the theatre was filled with human skeletons. Some held banners with Latin mottoes about the shortness of life, one wore a feathered cap while riding a cow to portray vanity, two held the symbols of Adam and Eve while standing next to a tree, and so forth. The walls beneath were hung with important works of art on various moral themes about this world and the next, many of which are now among the treasures of the Rijksmuseum in Amsterdam.[23] Perhaps the artistic traditions of each city were related to the different ways of pursuing anatomy in each, as well.[24] In short, the study of nature demanded great industry and attention to detail, but it also edified.

Mathematics, too, might be done for purposes of edification and utility as well as for the pleasure of investigation. The leader of the Republic after William the Silent's death, Maurice of Nassau, studied mathematics both as a useful subject and as a way of penetrating God's designs; the same purposes brought the mid-century political leader, Johann de Witt, to become an excellent mathematician. The curators of Leiden university therefore provided for a professorship in mathematics, first held by Rudolph Snellius van Royen (1546–1613). While from the beginning, at Leiden as elsewhere, mathematics had been taught as an ordinary part of the arts programme, Snellius began teaching it as a special course. Born in Oudewater, Snellius embarked upon a study tour before taking up medicine in Pisa and Florence. Probably it was in Heidelberg that Snellius became an exponent of Ramism, for Ramus spent some time lecturing there in 1569. When Snellius returned to the northern Netherlands and became a lecturer at Leiden in 1578, shortly afterwards being promoted to extraordinary professor of mathematics and Hebrew, he brought a commitment to Ramist teachings with him.[25] Rudolph's son, Willebrord Snellius (1546–1626), succeeded his father in the chair of mathematics in the seventeenth century, and became an even more noted mathematician. While the curators of Leiden university tolerated a Ramist on the faculty who taught Hebrew and mathematics, they refused the recommendation of the faculty senate in 1598 to make Snellius the professor of natural philosophy. Instead, they chose the physician Everard Vorstius, an Aristotelian recommended by Scaliger.[26] Snellius would have to settle for becoming an ordinary professor of mathematics three years later.

In addition to Snellius' mathematical teaching, the curators of Leiden allowed for the development of an engineering school, in which the widely regarded mathematician Simon Stevin (1548–1620) taught.[27] Born in Brugge and later employed as a book-keeper for the city, Stevin fled the conflict in the south, settling in Leiden about 1581. He published several major works with the great printing firm of Plantin, all in the new national language of Dutch, which Stevin patriotically considered the best in the world for expressing scientific ideas despite having virtually to invent its scientific vocabulary. His works included an important book of 1585 (*De Thiende*) advocating the use of decimals rather than fractions in arithmetic, later crucial to John Napier's invention of logarithms, and three books published in 1586 on statics, applied statics and hydrostatics. Stevin's work on statics may have considerably influenced Galileo.[28] At the same time, he entered into a partnership with Johan Cornets de Groot (father of Hugo Grotius) to build improved water mills.

These 'practical' interests brought Stevin about 1590 into the service of Prince Maurice of Nassau, the stadholder, and head of the Dutch army. Maurice not only reformed the army in imitation of the Romans, and adopted Lipsius' new views of stoic virtue, he had Stevin teach him mathematics, natural philosophy and the art of fortification: lessons later published by Stevin in Dutch as *Wisconstighe Ghedachtenissen*, or *Mathematical Memoirs* (1608). In them Stevin included a defence of the Copernican system (before Kepler or Galileo had published theirs), which raised concerns among the Calvinist clergy. Stevin's ideas of how to develop a new system of fortifications quickly and cheaply for the emerging nation were of considerable importance for the country, and the science of fortification in turn had a large influence on the development of geometry. He also consulted with Maurice on the construction of mills, locks and harbours. Maurice had Stevin establish a curriculum for an engineering school in Leiden (the 'Nederduytsche Mathematique'), where lessons would be given in Dutch, so that military engineers, surveyors, carpenters and others could study mathematics. While Stevin gave no lessons himself, the protégé of a Delft burgomaster, Ludolph van Ceulen (1540–1610), who gained wider fame for calculating the value of pi to thirty-five decimal places, did.

Willebrord Snellius (son and successor of the mathematics professor Rudolf Snellius) admired the various endeavours of Stevin and van Ceulen. He translated Stevin's works into Latin, took up Gemma Frisius' method of measuring distances by triangulation (working on the region south of Leiden) and, on the basis of these efforts, estimated the circumference of the earth. He also gave lectures in optics at Leiden during 1617 and the winter of 1621–2, discovering in 1621 a law of the refraction of light that still bears his name, despite the fact that Descartes published it as his own in his *Principia* (it is not certain whether Descartes had seen Snellius's work beforehand or not).[29] W. Snellius may also have brought experimental demonstrations into the teaching of natural philosophy when he gave a course for the professor of philosophy Gilbertus Jaccaeus (1578?–1628).

But perhaps the most important teacher of the new investigative methods of nature in the Republic was François dele Boë, Sylvius (1614–72), a chemical physician.[30] During the revolt, his grandfather had fled from the southern Netherlands to Frankfurt; François was born nearby, at Hanau. As a youth, he travelled to many Protestant and iatrochemically-influenced universities in the northern Netherlands, Germany and Switzerland for his education in medicine, graduating from Basel in 1637, a seminary of medical chemistry. After some further travel, he settled briefly in Leiden, where in 1639 and 1649 he gave private lectures in anatomy and physiology in the gallery of the *hortus*, being among the first on the Continent to demonstrate the circulation of the blood and to examine the lymph system.[31] At Leiden he also became well acquainted with Descartes, and he and his students remained generally pro-Cartesian afterwards: although they did not accept all of his doctrine, they were inclined towards a Cartesian-like physiological mechanism, but with chemical reactions providing the energy to drive many processes.[32] When no prospect of a regular teaching post at Leiden appeared, Sylvius took up residence in Amsterdam from 1641 to 1658, where he developed a very successful practice amidst some of the most notable experimental physicians and surgeons of the period. He also befriended in Amsterdam the influential German iatrochemist Johann Glauber (1604–70). He acquired such a great reputation in medical practice and chemical and anatomical knowledge that in 1658 he obtained the offer of a professorship in Leiden at an unusually high salary, where he taught until his death.

Sylvius became renowned for developing clinical teaching in one of the Leiden hospitals (the St Caecilia Gasthuis), where he also performed post-mortem dissections on those who died there, and for teaching chemistry privately.[33] Moreover, he not only enthusiastically prescribed chemical medicines in his practice, but he taught that physiological processes were essentially chemical in nature. Like Van Helmont, he concentrated especially on the idea that fermentation typified the chemical physiology of the body; Sylvius also became one of the strongest advocates of the chemical doctrine that everything could be divided into acids and alkalis. In 1666, he also acquired the formal position of professor of chemistry. His union of excellent anatomical, clinical and chemical knowledge and investigative enterprise came to typify the best of Dutch experimental medicine. A generation of experimental physicians followed him in uniting explorations in chemistry, anatomy and practice: among his most famous students were Niels Stensen, or Steno (1638–86), Jan Swammerdam (1637–80), and Renier de Graaf (1641–73).

Given the wide-ranging interests of people like Stevin and Sylvius, it would seem of little use to try to divide contemporary Dutch 'pure' science from 'applied', or to divide 'craftsmen' from 'scholars'. Not only were all branches of mathematics taught at Leiden (and elsewhere), practitioners easily moved from one branch of study to another, and from mathematics to natural philosophy to chemistry to empirical investigation, without hesitation.

INVESTIGATIONS AND PHILOSOPHY BEYOND THE UNIVERSITY

The ways in which intellectual boundaries were being reformed by people who moved easily between court, city and university is nowhere better illustrated than by the investigations of Isaac Beeckman (1588–1637), who virtually gave birth to early modern atomism.[34] Born into a family of strongly Calvinist candlemakers who fled to Dutch Middelburg from the fighting in the southern Netherlands, Isaac received a sound education in the lower school of Middelburg and in the Latin schools of nearby Arnemuiden and Veere.[35] These were the years when the ingenious Cornelis Drebbel (1572?–1633) lived in Middelburg, inventing the thermometer and microscope, among other things; the years around 1608 when two spectacle-makers of Middelburg, Hans Lipperhey (d. 1619) and Zachiarias Janssen (c. 1580–after 1628), invented the telescope. Beeckman returned to the business of Middelburg candlemaker after a couple of years' study in Leiden, where he learned mathematics and picked up Ramist predilections from Rudolph Snellius. Beeckman tried to improve various parts of the process of candle manufacture and quickly became involved with other projects, too – especially waterworks, laying and improving waterpipes and -pumps not only for local brewers but for wealthy merchants who possessed fountains. He also undertook meteorological investigations. After selling the family business to his apprentice in 1616, Beeckman took up other studies on his own, including medicine.

It may have been Beeckman's reading of the polemics of the French physician Jean Fernel against atomism that led Beeckman to work out a detailed defence of it. He learned medicine well, taking a medical doctorate in 1618 from the university of Caen. After moving to Breda at the end of the same year, he met the young René Descartes, who had come north to study the new military science of Maurice of Nassau. While the story that they met over a public mathematical contest is probably unfounded, the two shared many interests in geometry, music, hydrostatics and falling bodies, among other subjects. The older Beeckman apparently convinced Descartes to take up the study of nature mathematically. In the wake of the purging of the schools of religious Remonstrants, Beeckman secured a series of teaching positions, most importantly at the Latin school in Rotterdam from 1620 to 1627, and in Dordrecht from 1627 to 1637, where he held the post of rector. During his Rotterdam period, Beeckman became known as an expert adviser on practical mechanics and technology, even becoming a central figure in a local society called by its members the 'Mechanical College'. They involved themselves particularly in improving the designs of various kinds of windmills and waterworks. During his period in Dordrecht, Beeckman followed Galileo's ideas and difficulties closely, and introduced them to his friend Descartes.[36]

While this busy candlemaker/engineer/physician/philosopher/ teacher may not immediately seem to be the kind of abstract thinker who would provide a firm foundation for atomism, he did. Beeckman's most noted contribution was to give sound argumentative support to the notion that atomism could work to explain all natural events, and that it could also provide a moral foundation for a Christian life. When Pierre Gassendi met Beeckman in Dordrecht in 1629, it was apparently Beeckman who convinced Gassendi to turn his attention to the natural philosophical side of the philosophy of Epicurus.[37] Gassendi's works in turn became one of the most important sources for the new atomist philosophy in Europe. Beeckman's interest in the 'picturability' of natural events may have been related to his interest in mechanical devices, but it also had strong roots in the Ramism he learned from Rudolph Snellius.

Beeckman's personal acquaintance with Descartes and Gassendi, and with Marin Mersenne and Fabri de Peiresc, illustrates, too, how important the international network of scholars was. Such networks extended from the low countries into Germany and Sweden, Poland and Hungary, Britain, Italy, Spain and the Ottoman Empire. Letters travelled in Dutch ships, diplomatic bags and merchant packs over virtually all of the known world, even into Japan, where the Japanese allowed a Dutch trading post to remain after throwing out all other foreigners from the land. But perhaps the most important intellectual contacts in the early seventeenth century between the low countries and other regions were with France. With war continuing, the southern low countries looked to the Catholic France of Henri IV, Louis XIII, Cardinals Richelieu and Mazarin for support against their neighbours to the north; for their part, the Dutch often looked to France for political and military support against the warring Habsburg provinces wedged between them. (After Louis XIV's invasion of 1672, the side of Dutch politics that had most valued English contacts gained the upper hand.)

So it was that Gassendi made his only journey outside France to the low countries, in 1628–9 and again in 1641–4, at the urging of his patron Peiresc. The people whom Gassendi wished to visit so badly included the Liège Jesuit Jean Roberti (1569–1651), who had come out strongly against Van Helmont; the Louvain scholar Libert Froidmont or Fromundus (1587–1653), who like Gassendi had written on the comet of 1618; the Louvain physician Thomas Feyens or Fienus (1567–1631), who had also written on the comet; Walter Driessens or Valerius

Andreas (1588–1655), the librarian, professor of Hebrew at the Collegium Trilingue in Louvain, and law professor; Erycius Puteanus (1574–1646), Lipsius' successor in the Collegium Trilingue, who also published on the comet of 1618 and had recently issued an edition of Epicurus; Van Helmont, who convinced Gassendi that the philosophers' stone was possible and almost persuaded the vegetarian Gassendi that eating meat was a good and necessary thing; the new Aristotelians of Leiden: Hensius, Vossius, Rivet, Heurnius, Vorstius, Golius and Burgersdijck; Henri Reneri, or Renerius (1593–1639) of Amsterdam, who introduced him to the medical journalist and Rosicrucian Nicolaas Jansz. van Wassenaer (c. 1570–1630); and Beeckman and the noted physician Johan van Beverwyck (1594–1647) in Dordrecht. Given the excellent scholars full of new ideas similar to his own whom he met in the low countries, Gassendi could hardly restrain his excitement about working on Epicureanism when he returned to Paris.[38]

Within two weeks of Gassendi's return to Paris, he also persuaded his friend Mersenne to travel to the north. Mersenne, who took the same route Gassendi had the previous year, also came away deeply impressed by Beeckman, and he also met Descartes on his trip. The work of the Dutch natural investigators apparently gave Mersenne a better sense of the importance of empirical studies. Perhaps equally importantly, Mersenne found that even people of different religious confessions were engaged in serious common purposes.[39] In short, the personal meetings and written exchanges between the Dutch and others helped the new philosophy gather momentum early in the century.

The most controversial natural philosopher of the early seventeenth century who lived in the Netherlands was the French-born René Descartes (1596–1650). In his early twenties, in 1617, he left France for the low countries to learn the art of war; it was in the north that he met Beeckman and shared with him many interests in natural philosophy, becoming convinced by Beeckman to devote his studies to a mathematical approach to nature. After various travels in arms, Descartes returned to France. When more worldly pleasures did not interfere, Descartes turned his attention to medicine, chemistry and optics. Then, in 1627, when the Cardinal de Bérulle urged him to return to his grand plan for a new philosophy, Descartes returned to the Dutch Republic briefly in 1628, and then took up residence there in the spring of 1629, where he stayed twenty years.

Descartes commonly explained to Frenchmen that he needed to get away from family, friends and intellectual rivals to a boring place interested only in trade, but his intellectual project received much encouragement from his Dutch friends. He developed firm intellectual friendships with the professor Henri Reneri, Constantijn Huygens (the secretary to the prince of Orange), and many others, and cultivated the Princess Elizabeth (daughter of the 'Winter Queen', Elizabeth of Bohemia), who held court in The Hague.[40] It was in the Netherlands that Descartes wrote his major philosophical works: Le Monde (completed in 1634 and suppressed by Descartes because of the contemporary condemnation of Galileo), the volume containing his La Géométrie, Dioptrique, and Météores, prefaced by the famous Discours de la méthode (1637), Meditationes de prima philosophia (1641), Principia philosophiae (1644), and Les Passions de l'âme (1649). In his last years, Descartes attempted to apply his natural philosophy more directly to ethics and medicine, in which work his Dutch colleagues influenced him heavily.[41]

The Dutch Republic did not just provide a series of places for Descartes to live and write: his encounters with Dutch intellectual colleagues helped shape the development of his philosophy, both for him and for his interpreters. After all, one of the great tenets of Descartes' views has long been held to be his solution to a crucial physiological question, the relation of body and soul, Descartes drawing a firm line between the two. As Phillip Sloan has pointed out, this key element in Descartes' thinking was not developed until after his move to the low countries,[42] where he became very well aware of the latest medical theories from people like Sylvius, including Harvey's idea of the circulation of the blood.

Above all, the way in which the Utrecht medical professor, Henricus Regius (1598–1679), interpreted Descartes' philosophy had fundamental consequences. A neighbour of one of Descartes' oldest Dutch friends, Renerius, Regius became intimate with Descartes, and an advocate of his views. When in the summer of 1641 a student of Regius' (Johannes de Raey) defended a Cartesian thesis, the new Rector Gisbertus Voetius (1589–1676) grew worried. When Regius defended a thesis in December that held the unity of body and soul to be accidental rather than necessary, Descartes immediately recognized the danger and wrote to Regius that he had been misunderstood. But too late: for Voetius had one of his students defend a thesis that attacked Regius' Cartesianism as Socinian and leading to atheism, going on to attack Copernicanism. Voetius had been among the Contraremonstrant theologians to define orthodoxy at the Synod of Dordrecht or Dort (1618–19), helping to make Aristotelianism the basis for Calvinist theology.[43] When Regius replied to Voetius' student in print, Voetius used his position as rector and head of the Utrecht church to attack Regius personally. From then on, the debate about Descartes' philosophy took various turns down a dangerous polemical road. Not even

Descartes himself could get his interpreters wholly back on the track he thought they should take, and this resulted in formal condemnations and prohibitions against his teachings.[44]

The Dutch response to Cartesianism must be read in the light of three facts: almost all of the formal philosophical teaching in the low countries remained rooted in Peripatetic doctrines, but no single kind of 'Aristotelianism' can be defined;[45] Descartes and his ideas had many supporters among those outside the philosophical and theological faculties, including the *regenten* and the physicians; and, because of local prerogatives, no central authority could everywhere prevent the teaching or printing of unpopular doctrines. The 'Aristotelians' were not immune from ideas revived from other ancient systems of thought such as Stoicism and Scepticism: and the first of these, especially, became associated with teaching in the low countries because of the neo-Stoic Louvain and Leiden professor, Justus Lipsius.[46] The importance of Stoic ideas for natural philosophy in the low countries has not yet been well explored, but Lipsius himself had emphasized the importance of the Stoic doctrines of natural philosophy for investigating natural law – including the idea of a world soul based on *rationes seminales*.[47] Nor were the 'Aristotelians' immune from new philosophical systems, including that of Pierre de la Ramée, or Ramus (1515–72).[48]

Coupled with this mixture of philosophical opinion among the professors in the low countries was the interest in Descartes' ideas outside the philosophical faculties. When Regius first spoke out, he held a position on the medical faculty at Utrecht. Members of the medical faculties at several universities, especially at Leiden, remained advocates of versions of Cartesian mechanism through the middle decades of the century. Descartes had many advocates and enemies outside the universities, as well. Not everyone who supported or attacked Descartes' ideas did so with a full understanding of what he himself advocated. But the Dutch Republic remained a place where Descartes' works could be printed, along with works such as Gassendi's objections to Descartes: all were printed in Amsterdam. The controversy over Cartesianism could not prevent versions of Descartes' philosophy from being taught, written about, and promulgated in the Republic, although in the mid-1670s, in the stricter religious and political climate that followed upon the French invasion of 1672, it briefly became difficult to defend publicly. After about 1670 Cartesian principles made their way into the curriculum of Louvain, too.[49]

Perhaps the range of support among the educated public for new investigations into nature can be seen best by turning to a look at the rapidly growing city of Amsterdam. The generally tolerant *regenten* of the city not only allowed printing presses that turned out argumentative books on philosophy, politics and religion, they took steps to encourage investigations into nature. They supported a new *athenaeum*,[50] encouraged anatomical investigation, established a public botanic garden, did nothing to discourage chemical studies, and sometimes personally took up natural historical and philosophical pursuits.

The most famous of the Amsterdam scientist-politicians is undoubtedly Nicolaas Tulp (1598–1674), painted by Rembrandt. A member of the Calvinist faction in Amsterdam, he held a seat on the city council for many years and several times gained election as one of the four burgomasters.[51] Instrumental in founding the Collegium Medicum, Tulp organized the first city pharmacopoeia and published many reports of medical and natural historical interest.[52] Tulp also took his place in a line of distinguished anatomy professors of the surgeons' guild. He held several public anatomical demonstrations in the guild's chamber and the anatomy theatre in the weigh-house of the sint-Anthonies-Poort, and then in the chamber and anatomy theatre constructed over the meat market in de Nes. He retired from his post in 1653 (just before becoming a burgomaster).[53] Rembrandt painted Tulp in his capacity of anatomical demonstrator to the surgeons' guild, together with some of his auditors, with all the symbolism of wisdom and moral seriousness that the study required.[54]

More important even than Tulp were the many less famous members of the *regent* class who supported investigations into nature. One such person was the wealthy Johannes Hudde (1628–1704), who served on the Amsterdam city council several times, and between 1672 and his death gained election as one of the four burgomasters eighteen times.[55] He, the renowned Christiaan Huygens (1629–95), the mathematician Hendrik van Heuraet (1633–60?), and the Grand Pensionary of Holland, Johann de Witt (1625–72) had all studied under the committed Cartesian and professor at the Leiden engineering school, Frans van Schooten, Jr (1615–60).[56] They kept up a steady correspondence about mathematics, being particularly interested in probability theory (especially actuarial tables): it was to Hudde that De Witt set out his important conclusions. Hudde also learned the philosophy of Benedictus de Spinoza (1632–77) from the lens-maker's own mouth, and with Christiaan Huygens he undertook a study for the States of Holland of the Nederrijn and IJssel rivers in order to plan how to prevent them from silting up.[57] Hudde used his influence to secure a teaching post in philosophy at Leiden for the Cartesian physician Burchardus de Volder (1643–1709), who became the first in the Netherlands to teach natural philosophy through the use of experimental demonstrations.[58] Hudde also spent time experimenting with developing better microscopes by using a single lens. He taught his technique of making a lens from a drop of glass to Jan Swammerdam, and to Antoni van Leeuwenhoek (1632–1723), both of whom achieved fame through the use of this instrument.[59] Several important Amsterdam investigators dedicated books to Hudde, among them Gerard Blasius (c. 1625–92), chief among the members of the Collegium Medicum Privatum, a group of Amsterdammers that met from the mid–1660s until the early 1670s to carry out investigations into animal anatomy.[60] This group, which also included Swammerdam, has been credited with being among the first in Europe to investigate comparative anatomy.[61]

Another of the burgomasters to whom Blasius dedicated his book on animal anatomy was Coenraad Van Beuningen (1622–93), friend of De Witt's and later chief adviser to the stadholder William III. Like Hudde, Van Beuningen helped Swammerdam carry out his work. Van Beuningen first met Swammerdam in the spring of 1664 when Van Beuningen held the post of ambassador in Paris and Swammerdam visited on a study tour. Through Steno, who had been a fellow medical student under Sylvius, Swammerdam gained an introduction to the private academy for the study of nature of Melchisédec Thévenot. Thévenot and Van Beuningen were friends, so the ambassador had occasion to be introduced to Swammerdam. Van Beuningen remained one of Swammerdam's foremost patrons throughout Swammerdam's life. He may have shared Swammerdam's religious explorations, too, for Van Beuningen belonged to the Rijnsburger Collegianten, who sought new forms of religious expression.[62] Van Beuningen arranged such practical matters as permission for Swammerdam to dissect the bodies of those who died in the Amsterdam hospital (the Pietersgasthuis).[63]

The Amsterdam regenten also helped to establish a botanical garden in their city, which gradually grew to world prominence. The apothecaries and physicians had petitioned the city government for a medicinal garden as early as 1618, which soon thereafter came into being on the east side of the Amstel river. Among the petitioners was Augerius Clutius, the son of the Delft apothecary and Leiden gardener Dirck Outgaertsz Cluyt. Given complicated local politics and fiscal tight-fistedness, the Amsterdam medical garden was at first incorporated into the medical garden in the inner courtyard of the Pietersgasthuis. In 1638, when the physicians established a Collegium Medicum to inspect the apothecaries' shops and oversee the training of their apprentices, they began holding lessons in the hospital garden. In 1645, Johannes Snippendael (b. c. 1616) took over as the unofficial prefect, expanded the garden (his printed catalogue of 1646 contains over 800 plants), gained a salary of 400 gilders per year from the city, and with the support of Dr Schaep, a curator of the Athenaeum (and from 1646 a curator of Leiden University), established an institutional connection to the local school.[64]

Yet, being aware of the glory that a rich botanical garden could bring to the city, the Amsterdam council established a new *hortus medicus* at the end of 1682, situated in 'De Plantage', a new extension of the city, where it remains to this day. Jan Commelin and Joan Huydecoper van Maarseveen became the new 'Commissarissen'. Both men were influential members of the city council and both had their own botanical gardens: Commelin had made his fortune as a wholesaler of pharmaceutical commodities, supplying the Amsterdam hospitals and apothecary shops, but also hospitals elsewhere, like Gouda; the wealthy Huydecoper had good personal contacts with the local rulers of the East and West India Companies. Huydecoper directed the two companies to send interesting specimens from overseas directly to Commelin.[65] The Collegium Medicum supported the garden with fees and fines, regularly amounting to over 1,100 gilders per year in the 1680s and 90s.[66] For the period, this was 'big science', indeed.

An interest in collecting exotica – including strange naturalia – continued among the well-to-do of early modern Europe. The 'tulip mania' and consequent financial crash of the early seventeenth century (following Clusius' importation of the first bulbs from Anatolia) illustrates not only the fragility of contemporary financial arrangements but the kinds of capital people were willing to commit to purchasing exotica: in 1636–7, a house in one town was sold for three rare bulbs, while prices on the market for ordinary specimens fluctuated hourly.[67] As the example of the Amsterdam garden reminds us, too, people in the Dutch Republic could take advantage of the military-colonial system being established in Africa, Asia and the Americas by the East and West India Companies to collect and catalogue rare specimens, living and dead.[68] The Amsterdam dockyards (like the dockyards in so many other Dutch cities) teemed with merchants and sailors selling rare and expensive items from all over the world. The elder Swammerdam (1606–78), who owned an apothecary shop opposite the East India docks in Amsterdam, built up a spectacular cabinet, which contained great hoards of rare items from the natural world.[69] The northern Netherlands became filled with well-to-do collectors.[70] With the support of local governors, Dutch settlers in many parts of the world also undertook detailed investigations of the local flora and fauna. Hendrik Adriaan van Reede tot Drakenstein (1636–91) – a young adventurer from a noble family of Utrecht – organized a worldwide network of local and European scholars to prepare and publish several important volumes on the plants of the south-western coast of India.[71] Georg Everhard Rumphius (1627/8–1702) continued his famous work in Amboina in the Dutch East Indies even after he went blind.[72] Maria Sybilla Merian (1647–1717) spent three years in Surinam with her daughters painting insects together with the plants on which they fed.[73] The books produced from such endeavours – some hand-coloured – served to fill gaps in collections as well as to decorate salons.[74]

By the middle of the seventeenth century, then, at Leiden and Amsterdam, as at Franeker, Utrecht and other Dutch cities, many people had taken up active inquiries into nature, often with the support of the local *regenten*. The merchant of Delft, Antoni van Leeuwenhoek, who did not even possess a good ability to write Latin, made remarkable observations with his tiny microscopes over many decades, and through the good offices of Renier de Graaf obtained an introduction to the Royal Society of London, and later a Fellowship.[75] Jan Swammerdam achieved fame for his collections, his microscopy and his anatomical studies and new methods of preparing specimens, helped by Hudde and Van Beuningen.[76] The anatomical studies of Leeuwenhoek's fellow citizen, Renier de Graaf, including his discovery of the role of the follicles in generation, brought him renown, and would have brought him a chair at Leiden had he not been Catholic. The Leiden professors of anatomy Charles Drelincourt (1635–94) and Anton Nuck (1650–92) carried out remarkable anatomical and physiological work.[77] Like Hermann Boerhaave they studied anatomy, botany and chemistry together, and followed natural philosophical debates with great interest.

The 'big science' of the Dutch Golden Age, then, like that elsewhere in Europe, consisted of laborious and expensive work done in anatomical theatres and backrooms, botanical gardens, and chemical laboratories. When the noted physician and naturalist Cornelis Bontekoe discussed the new kinds of experiments being done, he divided them into four classes: those in anatomy, in chemistry, and in medical practice, and those using physical apparatus, such as the air pump.[78] In the last category, today often called 'physics', Bontekoe had in mind the very new instruction at Leiden by De Volder and Dematius. After his trip to England and contacts with Robert Boyle and other members of the Royal Society in 1674, Burchardus de Volder had asked the Leiden curators to let him teach *physica experimentalis* to support *physica theoretica*, and this they allowed. At the same time, the chemist Carolus de Maets, or Dematius (1640?–90), also got their support to show students physical experiments in the laboratory where he had been teaching through chemical experiments since 1669. Dematius used an air pump of his own design built in 1675 by Samuel van Musschenbroek (1639–81).[79] While by the 1670s, then, one could find Dutch investigators trying out physical experiments and giving demonstrations in private rooms and very occasionally in lecture halls, the number of such investigators remained quite small compared to the natural historians, anatomists, physiologists and chemists.

Even philosophers who thought that examining nature in detail might be important had reservations about whether such work could lead to true science, where demonstrative certainty remained the touchstone of truth. The Leiden professor of philosophy Adrianus Heereboord (1614–61), for example, pleaded in 1641 for looking not only into the books of Aristotle but into the book of nature, following Francis Bacon in saying that collections of experiments were necessary for bettering human life. Nevertheless, like other philosophers he believed that while experiments could be useful to ordinary human life, certainty could come only from rational inquiry rooted in eternally true principles. Only at the end of the century did natural philosophy blend experimentalism with theory in a way we might recognize as physics. Then, Willem Jacob 'sGravensande (1688–1742) brought Newtonianism back with him in Leiden after a trip to England in 1715; Groningen appointed Johann (I) Bernoulli (1667–1748) as *professor matheseos* in 1694, and he could soon be found teaching *philosophia experimentalis*, for which the university bought him some instruments in 1697; at Harderwijk, Adrianus Reland (1676–1718) gave the first experimental teaching in natural philosophy in 1700; at Franeker it was the Cartesian, Ruardus Andala (1665–1727), who gave the first lessons in experimental philosophy. The influence of Voetius remained strong at Utrecht, with physical experiments creeping into the curriculum there only in the eighteenth century with Petrus Musschenbroek (1692–1761). Experimental physics – which is sometimes confused with 'science' itself – came slowly to the Dutch universities, as it did to much of Europe.

Even the work of Christiaan Huygens shows a similar tendency. His work in mathematics, observations in astronomy and invention of the pendulum clock brought him an appointment to the Paris Academy of Sciences.[80] His mechanical skills and insights were combined with an outstanding mathematical ability and a philosophical sophistication that made him – like so many others – question Cartesianism while at the same time generally remaining a mechanist. As Joella Yoder has recently clearly demonstrated, Huygens' combination of mathematics and experiment privileged the former over the latter because mathematics stemmed from axiomatic truths; the experiments only had not to contradict the theories.[81] That such principles were rooted in certain metaphysical concerns cannot be doubted.[82] But for Huygens, too, demonstrative certainty had to conform to the evidence of experience and experiment.

CONCLUSION

Most Dutch philosophers, natural philosophers included, continued to seek certainty, which could not come through experiment but only through reason, although experiment could supplement reason. Since a true natural philosophy had to have demonstrative certainty, mathematics provided a crucial tool for discovering natural laws. Another tradition of investigation relied more heavily on the senses: this was the medical and natural-historical tradition.[83] The anatomists and botanists, for instance, found it necessary to make active inquiries into the 'thingness' of nature, relying on but constantly examining the 'experiences' obtained by themselves and other reputable people. Many natural investigators of this sort turned to chemistry as an additional analytical tool for separating complex beings into simpler substances. And some of these people, too, like Sylvius, were happy to use mathematical and mechanical concepts where appropriate. The traditions both of mathematical and of natural-historical and medical investigation lay at the heart of the new intellectual enterprises in the low countries, commonly being pursued by one and the same person.[84] Separating the two methods of investigation in order to assign the causes of the 'Scientific Revolution' to either the one or the other might have heuristic value, but does little to illuminate the complexity of the history.[85]

In many ways, then, developments in the low countries illuminate general trends in the 'Scientific Revolution'. Both inside and outside the universities, new work in medicine and mathematics, and in related subjects like astronomy, cosmography, chemistry, anatomy and natural history, led the way. Stimulated by the humanist philologists' attention to detail and pursuit of investigation,[86] as well as an appreciation of the new mechanical devices without which the very economy of the Republic would have been impossible, the well-educated naturalists of the low countries received support for their work from aristocrats and *regenten*. The outbreak of the rebellion hurt the southern Netherlands badly, but after an initial period of brutal sacrifice the northern provinces found renewed strength (if also renewed confusion) in municipal and provincial independence. As the skilled and wealthy population of the south migrated north at the end of the sixteenth century, and as diking and draining, colonial conquest and merchant capitalism brought new sources of wealth, the Dutch Republic produced a host of renowned investigators of nature. As elsewhere in Europe, the most active of them remained the technologically adept, the collectors of natural history reports and specimens, the cultivators of botanical gardens, the experimenters of chemical workshops, the delvers into living and dead bodies and the great numbers of apothecaries, surgeons and physicians who tried out new medicines according to the latest theories.[87] Such people, more than the philosophers, willingly connected their experiences of nature to a loosely defined 'science', which seemed both useful and edifying.

If this description of the so-called Scientific Revolution in the low countries is correct, it fits well with the work that typified the same movement in other countries. Developments in mathematics and medicine, together with natural history, technology and chemistry, characterized Spanish science in the sixteenth century just as well as the science of the low countries.[88] In France, one of the most important scientific institutions in the seventeenth century was the Jardin du Roi, or Jardin des Plantes, which became famous for the natural-historical investigations pioneered there, but which also holds an important place in the development of chemical teaching.[89] The first publication of the Academy of Sciences of Paris was an anonymous work on animals done by the members, later associated with the name of Claude Perrault; the French Academy also undertook very important botanical investigations.[90] The French minister Colbert saw much importance in having the provincial royal academy in Caen map local areas, look into the flow of rivers, dissect fish and otherwise undertake natural historical work.[91] William Eamon has pointed out how central a place medical and natural-historical investigations took in the early Italian scientific societies.[92] The same is true of the Cimento, and the fame of Malpighi soon rivalled that of Galileo. The Royal Society of London also spent most of its time in natural-historical and medical discussions and demonstrations; surveying the *Philosophical Transactions* underlines the point.[93] Further north, one finds the predominately German Academia Naturae Curiosorum established in 1652 by Dr Johann Lorenz Bausch, and the numerous natural-historical publications of its members; and the predominately Danish group centred around Thomas Bartholin in Copenhagen and its publication, the *Acta Medica Hafniensia*.

Every university with any reputation, and many cities as well, had a botanical garden and anatomy theatre and collections of natural history specimens. Not only universities and kings, but private people devoted large amounts of money to such work, and while they could hardly perform human anatomies on their own, at public anatomical demonstrations the front seats were reserved for the magistrates and the general public was admitted as well.[94] Perhaps by the eighteenth century one can begin to speak of a tradition of scientific teaching that looks like our physics: but in the seventeenth century it was natural history and medicine that dominated the scientific curricula as well as the mailbags of the learned, a dominance that continued through the eighteenth century.[95] Medicine and natural history constituted the 'big science' of the period.

While the low countries never developed a scientific institution to rival the Royal Society, the Academy of Sciences or the Cimento in the seventeenth century, we should not forget that a host of smaller formal and informal societies flourished in the cities and universities of the region, in which some of the most renowned natural investigators of the so-called Scientific Revolution laboured cooperatively. The fiercely defended local privileges of the municipalities and provinces in the Dutch Republic would not admit of a national society until the later eighteenth century.[96] But from the surgeons' guild in Delft (which Leeuwenhoek attended), to the Collegium Medicum and Collegium Medicum Privatum in Amsterdam, to the private and municipal botanical gardens, to the many *athenaea* and universities, groups of Dutch and Flemish scholars took on investigations of nature.

The multitude of small groups and individuals pursuing natural-historical investigations can be seen clearly not only in private correspondence, but in the books published by the members of such groups. One person, Stephan Blankaart (1650–1704), an Amsterdam physician and prolific author, even tried to rival the *Acta Eruditorum* of Germany, the *Journal des Sçavans* of France, and the *Philosophical Transactions* of England by bringing out his *Collectanea medico-physica oft Hollands Jaar-Register der geneesen natuurkunde aanmerkingen* in 1680, 1683 and 1686.[97] These volumes printed reports and accompanying illus-trations of medical observations, anatomical and physiological investi-gations, curiosities of nature and occasionally an astronomical or mathematical problem; Blankaart gathered the reports from his own experience, from his friends, from communications sent to him, and from published books and essays not readily available to the general public. While Blankaart's *Collectanea* look today like a strange combination of scientific reporting and tabloid journalism, his short-lived periodical is not very different from the contemporary *Philosophical Transactions* except in one regard: Blankaart relied on an informal network for his reports rather than the members of an institution.

In addition to never generating a national scientific institution, one can note some national differences between Dutch natural investigations and those in other countries. For instance, the Dutch did superb studies of insects, but the French tended to shy away from the close investigation of such vermin. The French, English and Italian virtuosi tended to have the patronage of wealthy aristocrats and royalty; since the Dutch had a less powerful aristocracy, more patronage tended to come from wealthy merchant *regenten*, sometimes privately but often also through their organized support for the schools, gardens, engineering projects and medical societies.

More important than such particulars, however, is the sense that the loose principles of natural theology – or what the Dutch call 'physico-theology' – played a larger part in creating a sense of purpose for Dutch and other Protestant investigators than it did for establishment scientists in Catholic countries. Neil Gillespie has recently noted that for England, natural theology provided an important ideological underpinning for contemporary society;[98] the same could be said of the Netherlands.[99] One of the most widely read natural theologians of Europe was Bernard Nieuwentijt (1654–1718), physician, chemist and *regent* of Purmerend.[100] His *Het Regt Gebruik der Wereltbeschouwingen ter Overtuiginge van Ongodisten en Ongelovigen* (literally, *The Right Use of Inspections of the World for the Overthrow of Atheists and Unbelievers*) had seven Dutch editions between 1715 and 1750, and had many editions in English, French and German. If it is true that natural theology had less significance for Catholics than for Protestants in the early modern period (this might merely reflect the current state of the literature), perhaps the reason has to do with the continuing threat of scepticism. Given Catholic tradition, it was possible to resort to fideism as a defence against radical doubt; but since Protestants relied more on notions of the primitive church, the 'book of nature' (as many referred to it) provided some of the additional support for the 'book of revelation' thought necessary for belief in the face of doubt and possible atheism.[101]

Whatever the truth of such a generalization, the Dutch clearly showed an interest in natural investigations for purposes of edification as well as utility. As is well known, the moral purposes of the new investigations into nature had two publicly proclaimed aims: to better the condition of mankind and to understand some of God's ways. From the anatomists to the 'physicists', people claimed that their work taught moral values. Teaching may no longer have been from 'fables' like those of Aesop; instead, the ways of God and man could be best known through getting the details straight. For Swammerdam, the wisdom of God could be seen in the figure of the louse, but the poetry of the louse demanded close attention to the particulars: 'I present to you herewith the Almighty Finger of God in the anatomy of a louse', he wrote to Melchisédec Thévenot, 'in which you will find wonder piled upon wonder and God's

Wisdom clearly exposed in one minute particle.' For Swammerdam, it was in the details rather than the generalizations that God could be discovered. It has been strongly argued by one recent art historian that the 'art of describing' – the detailed surface depiction of material objects – differentiates Dutch painting from, say, Italian painting of the same period.[102] Simon Schama has attempted to counter by restoring the centrality of iconographic readings of Dutch painting as a part of his attempt to represent the moral culture of the Republic.[103] He also stresses the predominately Calvinist sources of feeling in the northern Netherlands against Alpers' rejection of religious causes for the precision of depictions of things. Both, however, admit the importance in Dutch painting, and in Dutch culture more widely, of seeing the world in terms of detailed concrete images, 'realistic' images that *also* conveyed moral significations.

In Dutch science as in Dutch art, then, getting the details straight had become terribly important; but those details conveyed messages to edify as well as information to use. The very term 'edification' suggests religious language: it conveys the sense of building up character through teaching. In this sense, the religious uses of natural knowledge might appeal to all religious groups, in the low countries as elsewhere. While there have been a few attempts to argue that the mainly Protestant nature of Dutch society is what made it 'scientific', one must view any strong claims along these lines with the same scepticism with which the 'Merton thesis' is treated by historians of English science.[104] Catholics and Jews also exercised great influence in the Republic, and counting people of different religious affiliations does not help to clarify matters, since vigorous Calvinists like Voetius opposed certain aspects of the new science, while Catholics like De Graaf became influential investigators. R. Hooykaas has argued something a bit different from Merton or Weber: that the confrontation between biblicalism and Graeco-Roman culture created modern science, or, put another way, that it was biblical humanism that opened the path to science, something that Protestants, Catholics and Jews might all promote.[105] Traditions of humanism and of learning for the sake of the *vita activa* remained strong.

We live today in a culture that prizes theory highly, not just in the physical sciences but in all parts of the academy. Collectors of information are often considered to be rather low in the learned hierarchies. Clearly, some predecessors of grand theory can be found in the low countries of the early modern period. But equally important – overwhelmingly more important in terms of the numbers of people and amount of money involved – was the often laborious investigation and collection of the details of nature. People clearly felt great excitement

about being able to discover 'matters of fact', about being able to sort
out truth from fiction. Trying to separate the 'internal' from the
'external' forces involved in such efforts would be as pointless as trying
to figure out whether utility or edification played a more important part
in early modern culture. A history of great scientific thinkers might
overlook the many *savants* of the low countries (as has often been the
case). But as we begin to see how many people became involved in the
investigative enterprise, from sailors to great merchants, from apothecaries to medical professors, from candlemakers to the sons of noblemen,
from citizens to *regenten*, the work done in the low countries may begin to
seem instructive about the general shape of the 'Scientific Revolution'
throughout Europe.

NOTES

This essay would not have been possible without the support of the Fulbright
Commission, the National Endowment for the Humanities and the National Library
of Medicine, who together provided a research leave in the Netherlands during
1989–90. I would also like to thank David Lux, Dirk Struik and Michael Shank for
their astute and helpful comments on an earlier draft of this essay.

1 For other discussions of Dutch early modern science, see T. H. Levere,
   'Relations and Rivalry: Interactions between Britain and the Netherlands in
   Eighteenth Century Science and Technology', *History of Science* 9 (1971),
   42–53; W. D. Hackmann, 'The Growth of Science in the Netherlands in the
   Seventeenth and Early Eighteenth Centuries', in M. Crosland (ed.), *The
   Emergence of Science in Western Europe* (London, 1975), 89–109; D. J. Struik, *The
   Land of Stevin and Huygens: A Sketch of Science and Technology in the Dutch Republic
   during the Golden Century* (Dordrecht, 1981; Dutch edn. 1958); H. A. M.
   Snelders, 'Science in the Low Countries during the Sixteenth Century: A
   Survey', *Janus* 70 (1983), 213–27; K. van Berkel, *In het Voetspoor van Stevin:
   geschiedenis van de Natuurwetenschap in Nederland 1580–1940* (Amsterdam, 1985).
2 The literature on the historiography of the Scientific Revolution is large, but for
   one recent overview, see Roy Porter, 'The Scientific Revolution: A Spoke in the
   Wheel?', in Roy Porter and Mikuláš Teich (eds.), *Revolution in History*
   (Cambridge, 1986), 290–316; my own views have been set out in the
   introductory section to 'The New Philosophy and Medicine in Seventeenth-
   Century England', in David Lindberg and Robert Westman (eds.), *Reappraisals
   of the Scientific Revolution* (Cambridge, 1990), 397–436.
3 F. C. van Boheemen and Th. C. J. van der Heijden, *De Westlandse Rederijker-
   skamers in de 16e en 17e Eeuw* (Amsterdam, 1985).
4 C. D. O'Malley, *Andreas Vesalius of Brussels 1514–1564* (Berkeley and Los
   Angeles, 1964).
5 G. Kish, *Medicina, Mensura, Mathematica: The Life and Works of Gemma Frisius,
   1508–1555* (Publication of the Associates of the James Ford Bell Collection, no.
   4, 1967).
6 L. White, Jr, 'Medical Astrologers and Late Medieval Technology', *Viator* 6
   (1975), 295–308; R. S. Westman, 'The Astronomer's Role in the Sixteenth

Century: A Preliminary Study', *History of Science* 18 (1980), 105–47, esp. pp. 117–21.

7 N. H. Clulee, *John Dee's Natural Philosophy: Between Science and Religion* (London, 1989), pp. 26–9.

8 A. de Smet, 'Copernic et les Pays-Bas', *Janus* 60 (1974), 13–23; E. H. Waterblok, 'The "Reception" of Copernicus's Teachings by Gemma Frisius (1508–1555)', *Lias* 1 (1974), 255–42; Struik, *Land of Stevin*, pp. 25–7; Snelders, 'Science in the Low Countries', pp. 213–14.

9 W. Pagel, 'Helmont, Johannes (Joan) Baptista Van', in C. C. Gillispie (ed.), *Dictionary of Scientific Biography* (New York, 1972), VI, 253–9; W. Pagel, *Jean Baptista Van Helmont: Reformer of Science and Medicine* (Cambridge, 1982).

10 Van Berkel, *In het Voetspoor*, p. 28.

11 C. G. Nauert, Jr, *Agrippa and the Crisis of Renaissance Thought* (Urbana, 1965).

12 W. Th. M. Frijhoff, *La Société néerlandaise et ses gradués, 1575–1814: Une recherche sérielle sur le statut des intellectuels à partir des registres universitaires* (Amsterdam, 1981).

13 M. J. van Lieburg, 'Pieter van Foreest en de Rol van de Stadsmedicus in de Noord-Nederlandse Steden van de 16e Eeuw', in H. L. Houtzager (ed.), *Pieter van Foreest: Een Hollands Medicus in de Zestiende Eeuw* (Amsterdam, 1989), 41–72.

14 P. J. van Meerbeeck, *Recherches historiques et critiques sur la vie et les ouvrages de Rembert Dodoens (Dodonaeus)* (Utrecht, 1980; 1st edn. 1841).

15 G. A. Lindeboom, *Dutch Medical Biography: A Biographical Dictionary of Dutch Physicians and Surgeons 1475–1975* (Amsterdam, 1984).

16 F. W. T. Hunger, *Charles de L'Escluse: Carolus Clusius, Nederlandsche Kruidkundige, 1526–1609*, 2 vols. (The Hague, 1927–42); P. Smit, 'Carolus Clusius and the Beginning of Botany in Leiden University', *Janus* 60 (1973), 87–92.

17 H. de Ridder-Symoens, 'Italian and Dutch Universities in the Sixteenth and Seventeenth Centuries', in C. S. Maffioli and L. C. Palm (eds.), *Italian Scientists in the Low Countries in the Seventeenth and Eighteenth centuries* (Amsterdam, 1989), 31–64.

18 W. K. H. Karstens and H. Kleibrink, *De Leidse Hortus: Een Botanische Erfenis* (Uitgeverij Waanders, 1984); H. Veendorp and L. G. M. Baas Becking, *Hortus Academicus Lugduno-Batavus, 1587–1937: The Development of the Gardens of Leyden University* (Harlem, 1938).

19 F. W. T. Hunger, 'Bernardus Paludanus (Berent ten Broecke) (1550–1633)', *Janus* 32 (1928), 353–64; A. Berendts, 'Carolus Clusius (1526–1609) and Bernardus Paludanus (1550–1633): Their Contacts and Correspondence', *Lias* 5 (1978), 49–64.

20 H. A. Bosman-Jelgersma, 'Dirck Outgaertsz Cluyt', *Farmaceutisch Tijdschift voor België* 53 (1976), 525–48; idem, 'Clusius en Clutius', *Kring voor de Geschiedenis van de Pharmacie in Benelux, Bulletin* 64 (1983), 6–10.

21 H. Beukers, 'Clinical Teaching in Leiden from its Beginning until the End of the Eighteenth Century', *Clio Medica* 21 (1987/88), 139–52; pp. 139–40.

22 W. S. Heckscher, *Rembrandt's Anatomy of Dr Nicolaas Tulp: An Iconological Study* (New York, 1958); W. Schupbach, *The Paradox of Rembrandt's Anatomy of Dr. Tulp* (London, 1982).

23 Th. H. Lunsingh Scheurleer, 'Un Amphithéâtre d'anatomie moralisée', in

Th. H. Lunsingh Scheurleer and G. H. M. Posthumus Meyjes (eds.), *Leiden University in the Seventeenth Century: An Exchange of Learning* (Leiden, 1975), 217–77.

24 Jan C. C. Rupp, 'Matters of Life and Death: The Social and Cultural Conditions of the Rise of Anatomical Theatres, with Special Reference to Seventeenth Century Holland', *History of Science* 28 (1990), 263–87.

25 K. van Berkel, *Isaac Beeckman (1588–1637) en de Mechanisering van het Wereldbeeld* (Amsterdam, 1983), pp. 25–6.

26 P. Dibon, *La Philosophie néerlandaise au siècle d'or* (Paris, 1954), p. 28.

27 E. J. Dijksterhuis, *Simon Stevin: Science in the Netherlands around 1600* (The Hague, 1970; Dutch edn., 1943); Van Berkel, *In het Voetspoor*, pp. 16–21.

28 C. Maccagni, 'Mechanics and Hydrostatics in the Late Renaissance: Relations between Italy and the Low Countries', in Maffioli and Palm, *Italian Scientists in the Low Countries*, 79–99.

29 C. de Pater, *Petrus van Musschenbroek (1692–1761): Een Newtoniaans Natuuronderzoeker* (Utrecht, 1979); Struik, *Land of Stevin*, pp. 46–60; Snelders, 'Science in the Low Countries', pp. 220–1.

30 The best single treatment of Sylvius remains E. D. Bauman, *François dele Boë Sylvius* (Leiden, 1949). For a rather unsympathetic summary in English of his major ideas, see Lester S. King, *The Road to Medical Enlightenment, 1650–1695* (New York, 1970), pp. 93–112.

31 On the reception of Harvey's theory in the Netherlands, see M. J. van Lieburg, 'Zacharias Sylvius (1608–1664), Author of the "Praefatio" to the First Rotterdam Edition (1648) of Harvey's "De motu cordis", *Janus* 65 (1978), 241–57; and Van Lieburg, 'Isaac Beeckman and His Diary-Notes on William Harvey's Theory on Bloodcirculation', *Janus* 69 (1982), 161–83.

32 Harm Beukers, 'Mechanistiche principes bij Franciscus dele Boë, Sylvius', *Tijdschrift voor de Geschiedenis der Geneeskunde, Natuurwetenschappen, Wiskunde en Teckniek* 5 (1982), 6–15, emphasizes that the terms 'iatrochemical' and 'iatromechanical' philosophies were coined after the seventeenth century, so that trying to sort out the medical ideas of those like Sylvius into one camp or the other is a false dichotomy.

33 Beukers, 'Clinical Teaching'; *idem*, 'Het laboratorium van Sylvius', *Tijdschrift voor de Geschiedenis der Geneeskunde, Natuurwetenschappen, Wiskunde en Teckniek* 3 (1980), 28–36.

34 H. H. Kubbinga, 'Les premières théories "moléculaires": Isaac Beeckman (1620) et Sébastien Basson (1621): Le concept d'"individu substantiel" et d'"espèce substantielle"', *Revue d'histoire des sciences* 37 (1984), 215–33; *idem*, 'La première spécification dite "moléculaire" de l'atomisme épicurien: Isaac Beeckman (1620) et le concept d'"individu substantiel,"' *Lias* 11 (1984), 287–306.

35 Beeckman's biography and ideas have been given definitive treatment in Van Berkel, *Isaac Beeckman*; I have relied upon it for the account of his life given below. Also see Van Berkel, *In het Voetspoor*, pp. 36–41.

36 K. van Berkel, 'Galileo in Holland before the *Discorsi*: Isaac Beeckman's Reaction to Galileo's Work', in Maffioli and Palm, *Italian Scientists in the Low Countries*, 101–29.

37 Van Berkel, *Isaac Beeckman*, pp. 123–6; L. S. Joy, *Gassendi the Atomist: Advocate of History in an Age of Science* (Cambridge, 1987).

38 F. Sassen, 'De Reis van Pierre Gassendi in de Nederlanden (1628–1629)', *Mededelingen der Koninklijke Nederlandse Akademie van Wetenschappen, afd. Letterkunde, Nieuwe Reeks* 23:10 (Amsterdam, 1960), 263–307.

39 F. Sassen, 'De Reis van Marin Mersenne in de Nederlanden (1630)', *Mededelingen van de Koninklijke Vlaamse Academie voor Wetenschappen, Letteren en Schone Kunsten van België, Klasse der Letteren* 16:4 (Brussels, 1964).

40 M. Néel, *Descartes et la princesse Élisabeth* (Paris, 1946; 1st edn. 1873); L. Petit, *Descartes et la princesse Elisabeth: roman d'amour vécu* (Paris, 1969).

41 G. A. Lindeboom, *Descartes and Medicine* (Amsterdam, 1979); T. Verbeek, 'Les passions et la fièvre: L'idée de la maladie chez Descartes et quelques cartésiens néerlandais', *Tractrix* 1 (1989), 45–61.

42 Phillip Sloan, 'Descartes, the Sceptics, and the Rejection of Vitalism in Seventeenth-Century Physiology', *Studies in the History and Philosophy of Science* 8 (1977), 1–28, esp. pp. 12–15. Also see Th. A. McGahagan, 'Cartesianism in the Netherlands, 1639–1676: The New Science and the Calvinist Counter-Reformation' (Diss., University of Pennsylvania, 1976), pp. 115–17.

43 F. Sassen, *Geschiedenis van de Wijsbegeerte in Nederland* (Amsterdam, 1959), pp. 122–3.

44 C. L. Thijssen-Schoute, 'Le cartésianisme aux pays-bas', in *Descartes et le cartésianisme hollandais: études et documents* (Amsterdam, 1950), 183–260; *idem*, *Nederlands Cartesianisme* (Utrecht, 1989; 1st edn. 1954); A. C. de Hoog, 'Some Currents of Thought in Dutch Natural Philosophy: 1675–1720' (Diss., Oxford University, 1974); E. G. Ruestow, *Physics at Seventeenth and Eighteenth Century Leiden* (The Hague, 1973); McGahagan, 'Cartesianism in the Netherlands'; K. van Berkel, 'Descartes in Debat met Voetius: De Mislukte Introductie van het Cartesianisme aan de Utrechtse Universiteit (1639–1645)', *Tijdschrift voor de Geschiedenis der Geneeskunde, Natuurwetenschappen, Wiskunde en Teckniek* 7 (1984), 4–18; T. Verbeek (ed. and trans.), *La Querelle d'Utrecht: René Descartes et Martin Schoock* (Paris, 1988); R. French, 'Harvey in Holland: Circulation and the Calvinists', in R. French and A. Wear (eds.), *The Medical Revolution of the Seventeenth Century* (Cambridge, 1989), 46–86.

45 C. B. Schmitt, *Studies in Renaissance Philosophy and Science* (London, 1981).

46 Stoicism has recently come in for close attention; for some important works in English, see M. Roberts, *The Military Revolution 1560–1660* (Belfast, 1956); G. Oestreich, *Neostoicism and the Early Modern State*, (ed. B. Oestreich and H. G. Koenigsberger, trans. D. McLintock; Cambridge, 1982); M. L. Colish, *The Stoic Tradition from Antiquity to the Early Middle Ages* (Leiden, 1985); J. H. M. Salmon, 'Stoicism and Roman Example: Seneca and Tacitus in Jacobean England', *Journal of the History of Ideas* 50 (1989), 199–225.

47 Sassen, *Geschiedenis van de Wijsbegeerte*, pp. 111–12; for an account of ancient Stoic natural philosophy, see S. Sambursky, *Physics of the Stoics* (Princeton, 1987; 1st edn. 1959); and Ludwig Edelstein, *The Meaning of Stoicism* (Cambridge, Mass., 1966), pp. 19–44.

48 W. J. Ong, *Ramus and Talon Inventory* (Cambridge, Mass., 1958); W. S. Howell, *Logic and Rhetoric in England, 1500–1700* (New York, 1961; 1st edn. 1956); W. J.

Ong, *Ramus: Method, and the Decay of Dialogue: From the Art of Discourse to the Art of Reason* (Cambridge, Mass., 1983; 1st edn 1958); Van Berkel, *Isaac Beeckman*, pp. 279–90; A. Grafton and L. Jardine, *From Humanism to the Humanities: Education and the Liberal Arts in Fifteenth- and Sixteenth-Century Europe* (Cambridge, 1986).

49 G. Vanpaemel, 'Rohault's "Traité de physique" and the Teaching of Cartesian Physics', *Janus* 71 (1984), 31–40; Vanpaemel, *Echo's van een Wetenschappelijke Revolutie: De Mechanistische Natuurwetenschap aan de Leuvense Artesfaculteit (1650–1797)* (*Verhandelingen van de Koninklijke Academie voor Wetenschappen, Letteren, en Schone Kunsten van België, Klasse der Wetenschappen* 48:183; Brussels, 1986); *idem*, 'Experimental Physics and the Natural Science Curriculum in Eighteenth Century Louvain', *History of Universities* 7 (1988), 175–96.

50 C. L. Heesakkers, 'Foundation and Early Development of the Athenaeum Illustre at Amsterdam', *Lias* 9 (1982), 3–18.

51 J. E. Elias, *Geschiedenis van het Amsterdamsche Regentenpatriciaat* ('s-Gravenhage, 1923), pp. 114–15, 151–2, 158–60, 163, 165.

52 D. A. Wittop Koning, 'De Voorgeschiedenis van het Collegium Medicum te Amsterdam', *Jaarboek Amstelodamum* (1947), 1–16; Wittop Koning, 'De Oorsprong van de Amsterdamse Pharmacopee', *Pharmaceutisch Weekblad* 85 (1950), 801–3; N. Tulp, *Observationes medicae*. (5th edn, Leiden, 1716).

53 H. Brugmans (ed.), *Gedenkboek van het Athenaeum en de Universiteit van Amsterdam 1632–1932* (Amsterdam, 1932), pp. 179–180.

54 Schupbach, *Paradox of Rembrandt's Anatomy*; Heckscher, *Rembrandt's Anatomy of Dr Nicolaas Tulp*.

55 Van Berkel, *In het Voetspoor*, p. 53.

56 Struik, *Land of Stevin*, p. 85.

57 H. H. Rowen, *John de Witt, Grand Pensionary of Holland, 1625–1672* (Princeton, 1978), pp. 417–18, 411, 417.

58 De Pater, *Petrus van Musschenbroek*, p. 5.

59 M. Fournier, 'Jan Swammerdam en de 17e Eeuwse Microscopie', *Tijdschrift voor de Geschiedenis der Geneeskunde, Natuurwetenschappen Wiskunde en Teckniek* 4 (1981), 74–86; G. A. Lindeboom, 'Jan Swammerdam als Microscopist', *ibid.*, 87–110.

60 G. Blasius, *Anatome animalium, terrestrium variorum, volatilium, aquatilium, serpentum, insectorum, ovorumque* (Amsterdam, 1681); G. A. Lindeboom (ed., with intro.), *Observationes anatomicae Collegii Privati Amstelodamensis* (Nieuwkoop, 1975).

61 F. J. Cole, *A History of Comparative Anatomy: From Aristotle to the Eighteenth Century* (London, 1944), pp. 330–69.

62 J. C. van Slee, *De Rijnsburger Collegianten* (Harlem, 1895), pp. 77.

63 G. A. Lindeboom (ed.), *Ontmoeting met Jan Swammerdam* (Kampen, 1980), p. xv.

64 The best account is W. H. van Seters, 'De Voorgeschiedenis der Stichting van de Eerste Amsterdamse Hortus Botanicus', *Zes en Veertigste Jaarboek Genootschap Amstelodamum* (Amsterdam, 1954), 34–45.

65 D. O. Wijnands, *The Botany of the Commelins: A Taxonomical, Nomenclatural and Historical Account of the Plants Depicted in the Moninckx Atlas and in the Four Books by*

Jan and Caspar Commelin on the Plants in the Hortus Medicus Amstelodamensis 1682–1710 (Rotterdam, 1983).

66 Amsterdam Municipal Archive, PA 27/29: 'Register bevattende jaarlijkse rekening en verantwoording aan de commissarissen van de Hortus Medicus, 1683–1793'.

67 J. de Vries, *The Economy of Europe in an Age of Crisis, 1600–1750* (Cambridge, 1976), pp. 225–6.

68 Struik, *Land of Stevin*, pp. 124–31.

69 G. A. Lindeboom (ed.), *Het Cabinet van Jan Swammerdam (1637–1680)* (Amsterdam, 1980).

70 P. Smit (ed., A. P. M. Sanders and J. P. F. van der Veer, collaborators), *Hendrik Engel's Alphabetical List of Dutch Zoological Cabinets and Menageries*, (Amsterdam, 1986); W. S. S. van Benthem Jutting, 'A Brief History of the Conchological Collections at the Zoological Museum of Amsterdam, with some Reflections on 18th Century Shell Cabinets and their Proprietors, on the Occasion of the Centenary of the Royal Zoological Society "Natura Artis Magistra"', *Bijdragen tot de Dierkunde* 27 (1939), 167–246.

71 J. Heniger, *Hendrik Adriaan van Reede tot Drakenstein (1636–1691) and Hortus Malabaricus: A Contribution to the History of Dutch Colonial Botany* (Rotterdam, 1986).

72 P. A. Leupe, *Georgius Everardus Rumphius: Ambonsch Natuurkundige der Zeventiende Eeuw* (Amsterdam, 1871); *Rumphius Gedenkboek, 1702–1902* (Harlem, 1902); H. C. D. de Wit, 'Georgius Everhardus Rumphius', in de Wit (ed.), *Rumphius Memorial Volume* (Baarn, 1959), 1–26.

73 L. Schiebinger, *The Mind Has No Sex? Women in the Origins of Modern Science* (Cambridge, Mass., 1990), pp. 68–79.

74 J. Landwehr, *Studies in Dutch Books with Coloured Plates Published 1662–1875: Natural History, Topography and Travel, Costumes and Uniforms* (The Hague, 1976).

75 C. Dobell, *Antony van Leeuwenhoek and His 'Little Animals'* (New York, 1958); L. C. Palm and H. A. M. Snelders (eds.), *Antoni van Leeuwenhoek 1632–1723: Studies on the Life and Work of the Delft Scientist Commemorating the 350th Anniversary of his Birthday* (Amsterdam, 1982); E. G. Ruestow, 'Images and Ideas: Leeuwenhoek's Perception of the Spermatozoa', *Journal of the History of Biology* 16 (1983), 185–224.

76 Fournier, 'Jan Swammerdam'; Lindeboom, 'Jan Swammerdam'; R. P. W. Visser, 'Theorie en Praktijk van Swammerdams Wetenschappelijke Methode in zijn Entomologie', *Tijdschrift voor de Geschiedenis der Geneeskunde, Natuurwetenschappen, Wiskunde en Teckniek* 4 (1981), 63–73; Lindeboom, *Observationes anatomicae Collegii Privati*; idem, *Ontmoeting met Jan Swammerdam*; idem, 'Jan Swammerdam (1637–1680) and his *Biblia Naturae*', *Clio Medica* 17 (1982), 113–31.

77 G. A. Lindeboom, 'Dog and Frog: Physiological Experiments', in *Leiden University*, 279–93.

78 C. Bontekoe, *Alle de Philosophische, Medicinale en Chymische Werken* (Amsterdam, 1689), p. 55.

79 Ruestow, *Physics at Seventeenth and Eighteenth Century Leiden*; De Pater, *Petrus van Musschenbroek*, pp. 5–14.

80 A. E. Bell, *Christian Huygens and the Development of Science in the Seventeenth Century* (London, 1947).

81 J. G. Yoder, *Unrolling Time: Christiaan Huygens and the Mathematization of Nature* (Cambridge, 1988).

82 As usual, L. Thorndike provides a rounded overview of Huygens' concerns: *A History of Magic and Experimental Science*, (New York, 1958), VII, pp. 622–39.

83 For another angle on this distinction, see Steven Shapin and Simon Schaffer, *Leviathan and the Air Pump: Hobbes, Boyle, and the Experimental Life* (Princeton, 1986).

84 In addition to Struik, *Land of Stevin*, see R. Hooykaas, 'The Rise of Modern Science: When and Why?', *British Journal of the History of Science* 20 (1987), 453–73.

85 Thomas S. Kuhn, 'Mathematical versus Experimental Traditions in the Development of Physical Science', in *The Essential Tension* (Chicago, 1977), 31–65.

86 In recent years, Jerome J. Bylebyl, especially, has pointed to links between humanist philology and medical investigations: see Bylebyl, 'The School of Padua: Humanistic Medicine in the Sixteenth Century', in Charles Webster (ed.), *Health, Medicine and Mortality in the Sixteenth Century* (Cambridge, 1979), 335–70; and 'Medicine, Philosophy, and Humanism in Renaissance Italy', in John W. Shirley and F. David Hoeniger (eds.), *Science and the Arts in the Renaissance* (Washington, D.C., 1985), 27–49. Also see Joy, *Gassendi*; and Peter Dear, *Mersenne and the Learning of the Schools* (Ithaca, 1988).

87 Harold J. Cook, 'Medical Innovation or Medical Malpractice? Or, a Dutch Physician in London: The Case of Joannes Groenevelt, 1694–1700', *Tractrix* 2 (1990), 63–91.

88 David C. Goodman, *Power and Penury: Government, Technology, and Science in Philip II's Spain* (Cambridge, 1988).

89 Rio Howard, 'Guy de La Brosse: Botanique et chemie au début de la révolution scientifique', *Revue d'histoire de science* 31 (1978), 301–26; *idem*, 'Guy de la Brosse and the Jardin des Plantes in Paris', in Harry Woolf (ed.), *The Analytic Spirit* (Ithaca, 1981), 195–224; *idem*, *La Bibliothèque et la laboratoire de Guy de la Brosse au Jardin des Plantes à Paris* (Ecole Pratique des Hautes Etudes, Histoire et civilisation du livre 13; Geneva, 1983).

90 Alice Stroup, *A Company of Scientists: Botany, Patronage, and Community at the Seventeenth-Century Parisian Royal Academy of Sciences* (Berkeley, 1990).

91 David S. Lux, *Patronage and Royal Science in Seventeenth-Century France: The Académie de physique in Caen* (Ithaca, 1989).

92 For example, see William Eamon and Françoise Paheau, 'The Accademia Segreta of Girolamo Ruscelli: A Sixteenth-Century Italian Scientific Society', *Isis* 75 (1984), 327–42.

93 Robert G. Frank, Jr, 'Institutional Structure and Scientific Activity in the Early Royal Society', in *Proceedings of the XIVth International Congress of the History of Science* (Tokyo, 1975), IV, 82–101; 'The Physician as Virtuoso in Seventeenth-Century England', in *English Virtuosi in the Sixteenth and Seventeenth Centuries* (Los Angeles, 1979), 59–114.

94 See, for example, Giovanna Ferrari, 'Public Anatomy Lessons and the

Carnival: The Anatomy Theatre of Bologna', *Past and Present* 117 (1987), 50–106; Rupp, 'Matters of Life and Death'.

95 A point made by P. B. Wood, 'The Natural History of Man in the Scottish Enlightenment', *History of Science* 28 (1990), 89–123; also see R. L. Emerson, 'Sir Robert Sibbald, Kt, the Royal Society of Scotland and the Origins of the Scottish Enlightenment', *Annals of Science* 45 (1988), 41–72; *idem*, 'Science and the Origins and Concerns of the Scottish Enlightenment', *History of Science* 26 (1988), 333–66.

96 For that period, see W. W. Mijnhardt, *Tot Heil van 't Menschdom: Culturele Genootschappen in Nederland, 1750–1815* (Amsterdam, 1988).

97 He explicitly addressed himself to the editors of these other publications in the preface of the 1683 volume.

98 N. C. Gillespie, 'Natural History, Natural Theology, and Social Order: John Ray and the "Newtonian Ideology"', *Journal of the History of Biology* 20 (1987), 1–49.

99 On the moral culture of the eighteenth-century Republic, see Mijnhardt, *Tot Heil van 't Menschdom*.

100 R. H. Vermij, 'Bernard Nieuwentijt als Experimentator', *Tijdschrift voor de Geschiedenis der Geneeskunde, Natuurwetenschappen, Wiskunde en Techniek* 10 (1987), 81–9.

101 For a different twist, see R. Hooykaas, 'Pascal: His Science and His Religion', *Tractrix* 1 (1989), 115–39, who argues that Pascal used empirical science as a counter to rationalism. But see, too, Michael Hunter, 'The Problem of "Atheism" in Early Modern England,' *Transactions of the Royal Historical Society* 35, Series 5 (1985), 135–57; and *idem*, 'Science and Heterodoxy: An Early Modern Problem Reconsidered', in David C. Lindberg and Robert S. Westman, *Reappraisals of the Scientific Revolution* (Cambridge, 1990), 437–60.

102 Svetlana Alpers, *The Art of Describing: Dutch Art in the Seventeenth Century* (Chicago, 1983).

103 Simon Schama, *An Embarrassment of Riches: An Interpretation of Dutch Culture in the Golden Age* (New York, 1987).

104 For a summary of the debate on the Merton thesis, see I. B. Cohen (ed. and intro.), *Puritanism and the Rise of Modern Science: The Merton Thesis* (New Brunswick, N.J., 1990).

105 R. Hooykaas, *Religion and the Rise of Modern Science* (Grand Rapids, Michigan, 1972). The emphasis placed on learning and tolerance by many Dutch historians has an analogy in the 'Latitudinarian' and science argument of several English-speaking historians, among them James R. Jacob and Margaret C. Jacob, 'The Anglican Origins of Modern Science: The Metaphysical Foundations of the Whig Constitution', *Isis* 71 (1980), 251–67.

5

THE SCIENTIFIC REVOLUTION IN POLAND

JERZY DOBRZYCKI

A MAP of the moon, drawn by van Langren in 1644, harmoniously combined its scientific contents with the panegyric form. Dedicated to the king of Spain, the map features a conspicuous *terra dignitatis*, with lunar craters named after the kings, the queens and nobles of European states. A conspicuous crater named in honour of Władysław (Ladislaus) IV Vasa, king of Poland, grand duke of Lithuania, was surrounded by smaller ones, bearing names of higher dignitaries of Poland and Lithuania, the 'Commonwealth of Two Nations'. The topography of these objects, if somewhat peripheral, nevertheless signified a powerful state influencing the course of events on a vast political subcontinent of north-eastern and eastern Europe.

The Commonwealth was involved in struggle with the budding violent expansion of Sweden (striving for supremacy over the Baltic region), directly in conflict with Muscovy over the territorial claims to vast spaces of the eastern lands of the Grand Duchy of Lithuania; in the south/south-east confronting the Ottoman empire. Political and military conflicts had of course the double-sided effect of inducing some amount of cultural exchange, including in matters scientific. It seems that none of the directions of active political interest enriched, and none could enrich, the scientific milieu of Poland in the early part of the Scientific Revolution. The extensive development of the economy could not enhance the scope of cultural communications; this factor was limited largely to the seaport towns, especially Gdańsk (Danzig). The interests and conflicts were directed away from the centres of actual scientific revolution. Besides, any possibility of intellectual exchange was effectively hampered by ideological, mainly confessional differences, which were very marked in the Commonwealth's relations with Protestant Sweden and Orthodox Russia. The insurmountable rift at the frontiers of the Muslim Turkish empire was quite obvious. In earlier stages of the European Scientific Revolution Sweden and Muscovy were only at the beginning of the more or less rapid process of receiving modern scientific ideas. Books were brought from Poland to Sweden (as war loot) rather than vice versa; scientific books in Cyrillic characters were printed on Lithuanian soil for export to Moscow.

The cultural/ideological factors were significant within the complex society of the Commonwealth; this is evident in the story of the Gregorian calendar reform. Following a royal edict, the Gregorian calendar was introduced in Poland at the very date prescribed by the papal reform (October 1582), as attested not only by documents from the king's chancellery but also by town registers from western provinces. The reform was also accepted immediately in the markedly Protestant town of Gdańsk. Here the critique was channelled into subtle astronomical questions of a technical character, discussed by Peter Krüger, professor at the Gdańsk 'Athenaeum Gedanense' (an academic high school) and the teacher of Hevelius. However, strong opposition came from other quarters. In Riga, another rich Baltic seaport and the capital of Livonia, political and religious tensions made the calendar an issue which sparked off a violent revolt, overthrowing the town council and expelling the Jesuit missionaries, the main exponents of the reform. The final outcome was the execution of the rebellion leaders and the forcible imposition of the new calendar in 1589.

Most lasting was the opposition presented by the Orthodox Church, predominant in the eastern provinces of Poland and Lithuania. Its attitude was expressed in the critique offered by a master of the Cracow Academy, Jan Latosz.[1] His writings – shifting the discussion from ecclesiastical politics to technical computations – nevertheless gave rise to violent polemics and the expulsion of Latosz from the Academy. The polemical literature was to go on; a practical solution found by the publishers of calendars in the regions of mixed confessions was (from 1606) to print both calendar modes side by side – a practice which was to last down to the beginning of the twentieth century. This as it were marginal case of a practical issue illustrates but a part of a wider spectrum of factors influencing and, in general, retarding scientific activity.

These factors must have been parallel or similar to those which conditioned the decline of the Republic up to its partitions in the late eighteenth century. Historians often point to the relatively weak position of towns and of the middle class in general, disempowered politically by the ruling landed gentry. The economy, including trade, was heavily conditioned by extensive agriculture, effectively barring outward expansion and enterprise. In addition, it is difficult to overestimate the destruction of the country's infrastructure caused by alien invasions in

the wake of the Thirty Years' War and, again, during the Great
Northern War in the early eighteenth century.

Of primary interest for the national context of modern science are: the
attitude of society to science, the historical tradition of scientific activity
and – embedded in both – the teaching, in schools and elsewhere. The
highest social class of the Republic, the gentry, expected the school to
provide a preparation for a future mature life as a model citizen-
landlord, running his estate within an extensive form of agriculture, his
public life usually limited to regional elections of deputies for the
national parliament. This is documented in instructions to the tutors of
young gentlemen entering school or going abroad for the finishing
touches to their education: the stress was laid on rhetoric, religion and
Latin; in mathematics the requirements were for practical versatility in
elementary arithmetic and geometry. Those priorities remained at odds
with the aims envisaged by the school authorities, mainly the Jesuit
Order (which dominated in the seventeenth century; growing competition from Teatine and Piarist schools was to come in the next
century). The programme of teaching was centred on ethics and
dogmatics, secular subjects like history (including geography) or
astronomy being subordinated to the fundamental aims of education.
This controversy lessened the popular appeal of the full programme of
learning, the tendency being to attend school only for the first years of
rather elementary teaching.

In general the school curricula – within the well-established Aristotelian tradition – led the pupil from the general foundations of the first
substance through teleological causality down to the *scientia curiosa*, with
no traces of, say, the Baconian empirical attitude. The only way the new
science could and did enter the school was through a gradual and
eclectic inclusion of old and new theories, without inducing the pupil to
express his preference. The Lutheran high schools of the Baltic provinces
(i.e. Royal Prussia) were by a long way the first to participate in this
process. Here, in towns like Toruń and Gdańsk, the pupils came from an
active social stratum of burghers, eager to raise their social status,
conscious of the value of learning. Thus the eclectic treatment of natural
philosophy was clearly in evidence by the turn of the century. The
country's Catholic schools were to follow, generally around the middle
of the eighteenth century.

At the beginning of the epoch of Kepler and Galileo, the scientific
tradition in Poland could invoke the international role played by the
Cracow Academy a century before, recalling the school's greatest
alumnus, Copernicus, and a host of scientists contributing to European
science in astronomy, geography or medicine.[2] A century later, though

obviously in retreat, the Cracow Academy could at least preserve, through its leading scholars (such as S. Pudłowski and J. Brozek), direct contacts with intellectual centres abroad, including Galileo's Florence.

The geography of students' peregrinations reflected the contemporary attraction of various centres. From the late sixteenth century the traditional centres, Italy and Paris, were joined by the Low Countries; because of the Thirty Years' War and its aftermath the role of German universities decreased (though links remained throughout the next decades with the Protestant German-speaking communities of northern towns). In general, the Polish Protestant elite was instrumental in keeping up connections with European scientific centres, including not only the Lutheran Protestant but also the various Antitrinitarian denominations. However, as far as modern sciences are concerned, this kind of contact was too much limited to reception and did not induce creative participation (again, this should be qualified in regard to the learned circles of Gdańsk). Moreover, the number of those studying abroad diminished considerably in the early eighteenth century. The country's system of education could not fill up the gap.

In itself, the educational system cannot be considered the only culprit for the slow reception of new ideas.[3] Its retarding influence was markedly enhanced by the lack of, or by the weakness of, independent scientific activity. What was largely wanting was an institutional basis for science. The Cracow Academy, more and more immersed in the stagnancy of mediaeval programmes, textbooks and structures, resisted by effective lobbying several attempts at creating new independent higher schools (the conflict with the Jesuits was especially acute and long-lasting). Modest attempts at founding a scientific society, as in the case of an informal group in the late seventeenth century in Cracow, failed, presumably for lack of a wider response.

More effective, but neither steady nor fully continuous, were royal protection and patronage. Władysław IV Vasa's long-lasting links with Galileo led to attempts to intervene on his behalf in 1637, a rare occurrence among royal houses of the times.[4] At the royal castle in Warsaw, toward the middle of the seventeenth century, science – in a markedly Galilean garb – was represented by visiting or resident scientists. From the royal botanic gardens came a new herbarium (M. B. Bernitz, *Catalogus plantarum* (Gdańsk, 1652). V. Magni's demonstrations of experiments with the vacuum drew wider attention – and an Aristotelian critique from Cracow Academy quarters (*Admiranda demonstratio ocularis de possibilitate vacui* (Warsaw, 1647)). Experimental science was propagated by T. L. Burattini, who professed 'natural magic' and displayed technical prowess in attempts to construct a flying-machine;

he also published a more speculative essay on the universal unit of length – expounding the earlier ideas of S. Pudłowski. Pascal's calculating-machines were brought to Warsaw, thus equipping an early computing centre at the royal castle.

The best example of the royal court's concern with science was the endorsement of Johannes Hevelius. Relations were upheld by three sovereigns in succession and are amply attested by Hevelius' dedication of stellar constellations (the 'Stellae Wladislavianae' and 'Scutum Sobiescianum'). In Hevelius we meet a scientist well within the mainstream of the Scientific Revolution; if he is somewhat conservative in the application of ancient methodology to positional astronomy, he is more modern in his experiments on the limits of the new powerful tool of science, the refracting telescope. Hevelius was also well inside the communication network of science, not without help from the Warsaw royal court in his relations with Paris, and in direct contact (and polemics) with London and with the Royal Society (he was himself a FRS).

So much for astronomy; mathematics of a decent European standard was represented by A. Kochański, a Jesuit college teacher and librarian to King Johannes III Sobieski. Otherwise, scientific literary production was represented by encyclopaedic compendia. Those produced by Protestant authors found publishers and a wider readership abroad.[5] However, these writings did not contribute directly to a break with the traditional philosophy of nature (this holds, too, for the most famous of this group, the pedagogue J. A. Komenský, of the community of Bohemian Brethren).

The low ebb of scientific activities in the first half of the eighteenth century is undisputed. As has been remarked above, this statement should be qualified in respect of the active community of scientists around the academic high school in Gdańsk. In steadier contact with learned centres abroad (especially with German universities), and profiting early on from Wolff's eclectic pragmatism in matters philosophical, the Gdańsk learned circles participated in pan-European scientific activity, whether in experimental research (D. Gralath, *Geschichte der Elektrizitaet* (1733)), in medicine (mainly J. A. Kulmus, author of *Tabulae anatomicae* (12 editions since 1722)) or in natural history (J. R. Forster, a member of Cook's crew). In 1742 the Naturforschende Gesellschaft was formed, enhancing the activities and communications of the Gdańsk circle.

The general change came within the lifetime of a generation, from around 1740 onwards. It came from outside. New conditions were introduced by the intellectual and political elite of the country following the social and political philosophy of the Enlightenment. In Poland this meant a radical change and modernization of the structure and programmes of education. The aims envisaged were practical rather than cognitive: effective economic and technical practices, necessary for the common good, are impossible without profound scientific foundations. The earliest successful attempt at modernization was carried out by the Piarist pedagogue and political writer, Fr. S. Konarski. His new reformed elite school (Collegium Nobilium, 1740) forced competing Jesuit schools to follow suit; a royal school also followed. The actual landslide in education was started in 1773 with the creation, by Parliament, of a national governing body, the Commission for National Education. This new ministry was instrumental in speeding up the process of preparing teachers for new programmes; as a rule good selected candidates were sent abroad to finish their education in European centres of learning. Previously, these 'postgraduate studies' could be sponsored only by individual benefactors. The Commission took special care to prepare modern textbooks. Mathematical textbooks were translated into Polish from French original texts commissioned specially from the Swiss mathematician l'Huillier (published successively: arithmetic in 1778, geometry in 1780, algebra in 1782).

The efforts of the Commission were crowned by a fundamental reform of higher education. Two universities, the 'Crown Main Schools' in Cracow (for the kingdom of Poland) and the 'Lithuanian Main School' in Vilnius (Wilno) (for the grand duchy of Lithuania), were now using Polish textbooks to teach contemporary science. Newly reformed schools were responsible for setting up modern scientific equipment such as astronomical observatories, botanic gardens (Vilnius, 1782) and university clinics (Cracow).

However pragmatic the primary aims, the results had a deeper effect: the organized efforts of an enlightened political elite, backed by an enlightened monarch, Stanislas August, and by the new generation of well-trained scientists, resulted in the encouragement of scientific research in the reformed and newly created institutions, notwithstanding the loss of the country's independence in 1795. Five years later, men of science and sponsors of science joined their efforts in a newly founded Scientific Society (an institution envisaged by the last king of Poland). The Society counted among its members men of science who were already trained in the new conditions and who belonged to the European community of scientists – men like the geologist and philosopher S. Staszic (a.o. author of a geological study of the Carpathian Mountains), the chemist and biologist Jędrzej Śniadecki (his main work on biochemistry was also published in translation: *Theorie der organischen*

Wesen (Königsberg, 1810); *Théorie des êtres organiques* (Paris, 1825)) and his elder brother Jan Śniadecki. Jan Śniadecki, a leading personality and the main protagonist of the Polish scientific and educational life of the time, exemplifies in his biography the success of the coordinated efforts to restore the nation's place in the international intellectual community.

Already in his earlier, high-school education he was able to profit from a course of modern experimental physics taught in Poznań, by Father J. Rogaliński a Paris-educated scientist. Thanks to a partly private and partly public effort, he was able to polish off his university studies in Cracow with several years of study abroad. From 1776 to 1781 he stayed in Germany, the low countries and especially in Paris, where he attended courses given by the leading mathematicians and scientists of the period. On his return home Śniadecki was appointed to the chair of mathematics and astronomy in Cracow and was thus able to (and did) become the main protagonist of the radical reform of the Academy, lecturing, writing new textbooks and lobbying energetically for the cause when need arose. He set up a new astronomical observatory, and through his work quickly made it a part of the European astronomical network. Śniadecki's role in creating a modern scientific milieu was even more marked and more effective at the other higher school reorganized through the reforms of the Commission for National Education: the University of Vilnius, capital of the grand duchy of Lithuania. Here Śniadecki served for eight years as vice-chancellor (in 1807–15). As a professor he successfully trained a group of students who became scientists of wider repute. His textbooks on physical geography and on mathematics were published in translation in Germany and in Russia. This is a strong if indirect proof that the gap in the pursuit of science was filled in the aftermath of the Scientific Revolution. Teaching and learning in Cracow and Vilnius again became part of the universal paradigm of modern science. Later dramatic changes and vicissitudes could only weaken the amount of effort the nation could devote to scientific research, but they did not break the continuity of the modern scientific tradition.

NOTES

1 An astronomer and astrologer, J. Latosz obtained the degree of doctor of medicine from Padua; in Cracow he gave lectures successively in astrology and medicine.

2 E.g. Matthias de Miechów, *Tractatus de duabus Sarmatiis* (Cracow, 1521); B. Wapowski's maps of central and eastern Europe, Cracow, 1526–28; J. Strusiek, *Sphygmaticae artis libri V* (Basel, 1555).

3 Aristotelian natural philosophy persisted in European schools well into the eighteenth century. For a series of case studies on the dissemination of the

heliocentric theory in various countries, see *Colloquia Copernicana. Etudes sur l'audience de la théorie héliocentrique. Studia Copernicana* v and vi, (Wrocław, 1972–3).

4 For a recent reference see R. S. Westfall, *Essays on the Trial of Galileo* (Vatican City, 1989), pp. 64–5 and n. 73.

5 Two examples of successful publications of this type are J. Jonston, *Theatrum universale*, several volumes of an encyclopedia of the animal world, beginning with *Historia naturalis de quadripedibus* (Frankfurt, 1650; several editions, including translations into Dutch and French); S. Lubieniecki, *Theatrum cometicum* (Amsterdam, 1668).

BIBLIOGRAPHY

General aspects of science and education in Poland are well represented in the historical literature. Presentations range from the short but far from antiquated presentation by A. Brueckner (in his Dzieje kultury polskiej ['History of Culture in Poland'] (2nd edn: 1930)) to an extended essay on science in a wider context by H. Barycz (in *Historia nauki polskiej*, ii: 'Baroque' (Wrocław, 1970). Schools and their changing attitude toward modern scientific trends have been studied more closely by B. and T. Bieńkowski, *Kierunki recepcji nowożytnej myśli naukowej w szkołach polskich* ['Trends in the reception of modern scientific ideas in Polish schools, 1600–1773'] (Wrocław, 1973). Specialized studies should also be mentioned, e.g. that of K. Targosz, on the endorsement of scientific activities at the seventeenth-century royal court: *Uczony dwór Ludwiki Marii Gongazi 1646–1667* ['The learned court of Louise-Marie de Gonzague 1646–67']. A specialized study of wider implications is that of the reception of the heliocentric theory in Poland by B. Bieńkowska, *Kopernik i heliocentryzm w polskiej kulturze umsłowej*, in *Studia Copernicana* iii (Wrocław, 1971).

6

THE SCIENTIFIC REVOLUTION IN
SPAIN AND PORTUGAL

DAVID GOODMAN

THE geographical position of the Iberian peninsula helps to explain why the history of Spain and Portugal has in some respects been so different from the rest of Europe. Situated at the western periphery of Europe and much closer than any other part of the continent to Africa, these were the lands which were most affected by the onslaught of Islam. When in the early eighth century the armies of the Prophet crossed the Straits from north Africa they conquered almost the entire Iberian peninsula and they would remain for centuries, transmitting indelible Arabic cultural infuences, more pronounced than anywhere else in Europe. And that was still perceptible in peninsular science of the early modern period. Geography also partly explains why Portugal and Spain were the first European countries to undertake those voyages of discovery which led to the acquisition of world-wide empires. Proximity to Africa, Europe's westernmost Atlantic seaboard, and the prevalence of favourable winds which would propel Columbus from the southern tip of Spain south-west to the Canaries and Caribbean were geographical advantages which assisted the Iberian navigations. And those navigations as well as the empires which resulted from them provided the strongest stimuli for the development of science in Spain and Portugal.

THE ORIENTAL TRADITIONS

Spain was much more affected by Muslim rule than Portugal. The linguistic inheritance indicates that. The Portuguese language has incorporated some 500 Arabic words; Castilian contains around 4,000. Some of these oriental borrowings were also adopted in other European languages, the consequence of that mediaeval European interest in translations from Arabic science; 'alcohol' and 'azimuth' became permanent additions to the English language. But many other Arabic words were adopted only in Portuguese and Castilian. They include scientific and technical terms which further reveal the importance of the conquering culture's astronomy, alchemy and irrigation works. Portuguese has 'azenha' (= 'water-wheel') and 'alqueire' (a measure of capacity); Castilian vocabulary includes 'azogue' (the metal mercury); 'alquitara' and 'jabeca' (types of distillation vessels); and 'zahorí' (a diviner, practitioner of the occult).

After the Christian reconquest of the peninsula which culminated in the overthrow of the Muslim kingdom of Granada (1492), deeply rooted Arabic science continued to be influential. This is evident from the continued use of those astronomical texts produced in thirteenth-century Toledo under the patronage of Alfonso the Wise, king of Castile and Leon. Based on Arabic originals and written in Castilian, they include the famous *Alfonsine Tables* which, closely following Ptolemy's *Almagest*, allowed the position of the sun, moon and planets to be calculated for particular days or years, as well as the duration of lunar and solar eclipses. Students in the 1560s and 1570s who attended the lectures of Hernando Aguilera, professor of astrology at the university of Salamanca, would have heard him read from the *Alfonsine Tables*. This was a text of European importance, the principal astronomical almanac throughout Europe until the mid-sixteenth century; by the 1540s five editions had been published in Venice and Nuremberg.[1] One of these editions had been bought and used by Copernicus when he was a student at Cracow. Another of the Alfonsine productions, the *Libro del saber de astronomía* ('Book of astronomical knowledge'), aroused interest in sixteenth-century Spain. Around 1560, shortly before construction began on Philip II's Escorial, and before his royal appointment as assistant architect for that huge project, Juan de Herrera was busy sketching geometrical diagrams for a copy of the *Libro del saber de astronomía* being prepared for the king.

There is clear evidence also of sixteenth-century reverence for Arabic medicine. After the fall of Granada, Ferdinand and Isabella broke their promise to allow full toleration of Islam. Soon mosques in the newly conquered territory were being converted to churches and Muslims forcibly converted to Christianity. The principal architect of this policy, Francisco Jiménez de Cisneros, archbishop of Toledo, in a determined effort to eradicate Mohammedanism in Spain, ordered bonfires of Arabic books. But his instructions made exceptions of medical and philosophical texts – these were to be preserved to enrich the library of the new university of Alcalá de Henares which he had just founded (1508). And later in the same century, when the great royal library of the Escorial was being formed, the collections included a large number of Arabic medical and pharmaceutical works. It was partly with a view to securing the benefits of this oriental wisdom that Philip II brought Diego de Urrea, professor of Arabic at Alcalá, to the Escorial to teach the language to the resident monks.[2]

Side by side with this admiration of Arabic culture there was now also disdain. Although Alcalá received Arabic medical works from its founder and employed a professor of Arabic, that university was from the start a humanistic institution, dedicated to the study of Classical languages. The purity of Greek and Latin originals was above all sought by stripping texts of mediaeval accretions, especially due to Arab commentators. In 1518 Antonio de Nebrija, the leading light of Alcalá, used his Classical learning to provide a dictionary of Classical botany, translating the Greek and Latin names of plants into Castilian; it was an appendix to a Latin edition of Dioscorides' *Materia medica*.[3] And during the 1560s the forces of humanism achieved the removal from the curriculum of Avicenna's *Canon*, for centuries the most famous and widely used text of Arabic medicine at European universities; it was replaced by Greek and Latin authors. This was part of a European anti-Arabic movement in medical studies; in sixteenth-century England John Caius and Thomas Linacre were similarly trying to achieve a medicine based on pure Classical texts. Elsewhere in Spain Avicenna's *Canon* remained in the curriculum; at Salamanca there is evidence of its use in 1680.

The Moorish medical practitioners of sixteenth-century Spain were not learned men nurtured on the great Arabic texts of the past; but itinerant quacks and magicians serving large communities of their brethren concentrated in the countryside of Aragon, Valencia and Granada.[4] To contemporary Spaniards these forcibly converted 'New Christians' or 'Moriscos' bore no resemblance to their illustrious ancestors, once admired for their valour in warfare, chivalry and learning. Now this unassimilated minority, popularly called *perros* ('dogs') were despised for their menial occupations, imperfect Arabic and strange dress; they were also feared for their allegiance to Spain's Muslim enemy, the Ottoman Turks. Before the tragedy of their final expulsion from Spain (1609–14), when some 300,000 left, mostly for north Africa, many were persecuted by the Spanish Inquisition for observing Mohammedan rites and some for practising black magic. Recent research has revealed some of the strange remedies and techniques employed by Morisco healers. Some gave the sick moist pieces of paper inscribed with texts from the Koran to swallow; others made prognoses from the patterns formed by molten lead, poured into a vessel of cold water placed on the invalid's head.[5] Mixed into this superstitious and magical medicine was a considerable amount of plant lore based on the Moriscos' familiarity with their rural environment.

There was continuing fear that Morisco healers were out to kill Christians. In the fourteenth century Spain's bishops had warned Christians not to consult Moorish physicians because of the harm they might do. And from the early fifteenth century, statutes of *limpieza de sangre* (purity of blood) were enacted by various cathedral chapters, guilds and university colleges to exclude non-Christians or newly converted Christians from membership. At Huesca (Aragon) in 1487 those of Moorish descent were prohibited from studying medicine. And the same fears were still evident in 1607, shortly before the expulsion of the Moriscos, when the parliament of Castile, the Cortes, heard an address urging the monarch to enforce stronger measures to prevent Moriscos attending medical lectures, because they were infiltrating the medical faculties and plotting to use their knowledge to poison or maim Spain's Christians. Yet there was some ambiguity in the Christian attitude to Morisco healers. Whenever conventional university medicine proved ineffective, Christians at the highest levels of society placed their hopes in fringe practitioners, including Moriscos; Philip II employed two of them to treat his ailing sons.

In addition to Arabic culture, a second powerful oriental scientific tradition had been implanted in the Iberian peninsula with the arrival of the Jews. They had first come, long before the Moors, in the centuries after the Roman destruction of Jerusalem. That diaspora had settled in numerous parts of the world, including Spain. Further waves of medieval migration, especially from north Africa, led to the establishment of large Jewish communities in Portugal and above all in Spain which housed the largest and most influential Jewish community in Europe. No reliable figures have been established for these populations. Portugal in the 1540s is said to have had 60,000 of Jewish descent out of a total population of a million. For Spain historians continue to give varying estimates for the number of Jews at the time of the expulsion, ranging widely from 70,000 to as many as 230,000; the total population of Spain was then around six million. What is not in dispute is the importance of the financial and cultural roles of the Iberian Jews.

In early modern Portuguese and Spanish science the contribution of men of Jewish descent is conspicuous in astronomy and most of all in medicine, where Jews and converted Jews came to dominate the field. Why this should have occurred may have something to do with Judaism itself. Within the Torah, the corpus of Jewish law, there were texts which encouraged the study of the stars and the practice of medicine. The Talmud, with its numerous rabbinic reflections, includes one opinion that the constellations at the time of birth may influence human character. The Zohar, principal text of the Kaballah, the mystical

strand of Judaism, and a product of thirteenth-century Spain, contains
a chapter which asserts that the smallest blade of grass has its appointed
star in heaven, and refers to a statement in the Book of Solomon that
stones fail to develop if they do not receive the light of certain stars. In
the late fifteenth century one of the most learned Spanish astronomers
– he worked in both Spain and Portugal – was a Jew, Abraham Zacut.
In the 1470s he compiled his *Ḥibbur Hagadol* (= 'Great Treatise'), a
Hebrew astronomical work, based on Jewish, Arabic and Greek sources,
including ephemerides; it was published in Portugal and Venice. His
astrological interests led him to write his *Juicio de los eclipses* ('Prediction
from eclipses') and *Tratado de las influencias del cielo* ('Treatise on celestial
influences'), a work on astrological medicine.[6]

The sanctity of the Sabbath has always been one of the fundamentals
of Jewish observance, but above this comes life, and the Torah opens the
way for Jewish physicians to break the Sabbath by working on that day
in order to save life. Distinct echoes of this religious encouragement of
medical practice are discernible in Barcelona's Jewish community in the
early fourteenth century. There the elders had become concerned by the
appeal of non-Jewish secular knowledge, especially Greek philosophy
and science. This was seen as a distraction from the principal object of
study – the Torah – and a dangerous source of heretical ideas. The
rabbi and the community therefore decided to publish a ban prohibiting
Jewish males from studying Greek natural philosophy, at least until they
had reached the age of twenty-five. But the ban revealingly made an
exception of medicine because 'although it is natural science, the Torah
has given the physician permission to practice the art of healing'.[7]

The extraordinary predominance of Jewish physicians in Spain may
also have been assisted by gentiles' expectations of high performance.
The Jews were supposed to possess powerful occult knowledge trans-
mitted from Moses and the prince of wisdom, Solomon. The spurious
Clavicula Salomonis ('Solomon's Key') circulated in sixteenth-century
Spain giving directions for conjuring spirits; communicating knowledge
of the hidden virtues of herbs and stones; and illustrated with magical
diagrams, inscribed with Hebrew letters and words supposed to impart
great powers of recovery from disease. The awe with which Christians
regarded Jewish physicians readily turned into fear at times of social
tension between the two communities. When Henry III of Castile died
at the early age of twenty-seven, rumours soon spread that he had been
poisoned by his Jewish physicians, a myth which was still alive in the
sixteenth century. It was during Henry's reign that *convivencia*, peaceful
co-existence between Christians and the oriental minorities, was broken
by the massacres of Jews in several cities of Castile. This was also when

the first forced conversions of Jews occurred to form that new class in Castilian society, the *conversos* or 'New Christians'. Their difference from the later converts of Moorish origin was the assimilation and intermarriage of many converted Jews. But other *conversos* remained faithful to Judaism beneath a mask of Catholicism, and it was in order to investigate and punish this that the Spanish Inquisition was established by Ferdinand and Isabella in 1478–80. The monarchs' concern that unconverted Jews were impeding the completion of the process of catholicizing *conversos* led eventually to the expulsion of 1492: unconverted Jews were given three months to receive baptism or get out of Spain. Those who chose to remain soon discovered that baptism gave no protection against prejudice. The statutes of *limpieza de sangre* excluded converted Jews from entering the *Colegios Mayores*, those elite institutions of Castilian higher education; and sixteenth-century statutes of colleges of apothecaries in Valencia, Barcelona, Zaragoza and Seville all tried to keep out those of Jewish descent – a regulation of 1529 at Valencia even stipulated that a gentile who married a woman of Jewish ancestry was disqualified from becoming an officer of the college of apothecaries.

Fear mingled with the desire to reduce competition was the motivation. The colleges of apothecaries alleged that they were protecting the population from Jewish malevolence. And in Portugal the same fears produced royal discriminatory legislation. Andrés de Noronha, bishop of Portalegre, had been shown correspondence supposedly revealing a conspiracy between Portuguese *conversos* and their unconverted brethren in Constantinople. Part of the alleged plot was to encourage the *conversos* to study medicine and pharmacy so that they could poison their Christian persecutors. King Sebastian was persuaded to enact a law in 1586 requiring the university of Coimbra to receive thirty medical students of pure Old Christian pedigree.[8]

In theory the statutes of *limpieza* were strict and uncompromising. In practice their application is known to have been less than rigorous for entries into cathedral chapters, membership of municipal authorities and emigration to the Indies, all of which were supposed to exclude *conversos*. It is not known how many *conversos* evaded the statutes to become pharmacists. But it is clear that *converso* physicians managed to reach the highest positions. Francisco López de Villalobos, the *converso* son of a Jewish physician and the author of an early treatise on syphilis, rose to become court physician to King Ferdinand in 1509. His employment was interrupted by three months' imprisonment in the cells of the Inquisition on a charge of securing his royal appointment through black magic; but he was exonerated and resumed his duties at court.

Philip II also employed *converso* physicians. The continuing prominence in Spain of physicians of Jewish ancestry was enhanced by the shortage of Old Christians in the profession. In the 1570s this proved embarrassing for the tribunal of the Inquisition at Logroño. They wanted to consult a skilled physician but could not find one of pure race. They wrote to the Inquisition's central office in Madrid asking if in the circumstances it was permissible to consult an available *converso* physician. The reply from Madrid gave authorization for this on condition that the doctor's title was not recognized.[9] But why was there a shortage of Old Christian physicians? A likely explanation is suggested by some comments of a sixteenth-century Navarrese physician, Juan Huarte de San Juan. He believed that when the Israelites, during the exodus from Egypt and the forty years of wandering in the wilderness, were sustained by manna, the miraculous food dropped from heaven imparted a genius to the race which was still apparent in the outstanding skill of *converso* physicians in sixteenth-century Spain.[10] It could well be that, in a society which gave esteem to those who could establish freedom from Jewish or Moorish descent, the Old Christians avoided the medical profession in case success there might arouse suspicions of Jewish blood.

IBERIAN NAVIGATION AND SCIENCE

A converted Jewish geographer and a prince of Portugal's ruling house of Avis together initiated the first phase of those voyages of discovery which would result in the European domination of the world; at least that is the traditional story. Two shadowy figures of the early fifteenth century, James of Majorca and Prince Henry the Navigator, are supposed to have used science to promote oceanic navigation to discover the source of African gold, secure the lucrative trade in oriental spices and establish a powerful alliance against heretical Islam by finding Prester John, believed to be the mighty monarch of a Christian kingdom somewhere in the east. James may have been Judah Cresques, expert in navigation and geography, and one of the family of Jewish practitioners who had made Majorca a leading centre of cartography in the fourteenth century. Although details are lacking, it is generally accepted that Prince Henry brought an expert from Majorca to teach scientific navigation in Portugal.

Prince Henry the Navigator (1394–1460) has long been one of the great heroes of Portuguese history. He has been generally portrayed as a Renaissance humanist, a scholar and even an expert in astronomy and navigation. In his early twenties, he is supposed to have retired to a villa close to Cape St Vincent on the south-west tip of Portugal (and of

Europe) so that he could better direct his planned series of Atlantic voyages. At nearby Sagres he has been credited with establishing an academy of navigation, staffed by a hired team of the most learned experts. And so he has been seen as the determined scientific projector who originated a master-plan for Portuguese voyages into the Atlantic and to India which after his death was achieved with such remarkable success. One distinguished historian of navigation goes so far as to say that when Prince Henry first began to send his ships south into the unfamiliar waters of west Africa he 'unwittingly started the scientific revolution', because his seamen were forced to resort to observation and experiment to make 'a scientific discovery of the first order', the pattern of prevailing winds in the Atlantic.[11]

This image of Prince Henry has recently been so revised that little remains of his reputation. The new interpretation[12] rejects the alleged expertise in astronomy and instead of a humanist scholar presents him as an impoverished medieval crusader obsessed with the conquest of Morocco to provide booty for his noble retainers. The academy of Sagres is dismissed as a fiction; there is not the slightest evidence for its existence. And his sobriquet 'the Navigator' is attributed to the romantic imagination of a nineteenth-century German historian; apart from the attack on Ceuta, Henry may never have sailed in his life. But he did direct the colonization of Madeira and the Azores, and he did send his corsairs south into African waters.

There is in fact no evidence that Portuguese seamen were using astronomy for navigation until the time of Prince Henry's death. Then around 1460 comes the first evidence of their use of a simple sighting instrument, the marine quadrant, to measure the altitude of the pole-star and so determine position in latitude of ships off the featureless coast of west Africa. It was not the first time this had been done – Norse and Italian seamen had made this measurement before – but with the Portuguese it became systematic and accurate; the earliest Portuguese manuals of navigation show that recorded latitudes could be accurate to one sixth of a degree. As the Portuguese gradually edged their way south along the African coast and approached the equator, the pole-star sank below the horizon, and the midday sun was instead used for establishing latitude. Because the sun's apparent motion is complicated, technical tables are needed to convert solar altitude into latitude, an achievement of Portuguese astronomers.[13] The monarchs João II and Manuel I employed two Jewish astronomers, Abraham Zacut, an exile from Spain, and his Portuguese Jewish pupil, José Vizinho. Together they prepared scientific data and a marine astrolabe for Vasco da Gama's voyage to India (1498).

Lisbon became the world's leading centre of navigational knowledge. The monarchs, eager for its revenues from the trade in eastern pepper and spices, established crown offices, the Casa da Mina and Casa da India, not only for the administration of trade but also for the preparation of maps. From the beginning of the sixteenth century Portuguese cartographers produced the earliest world maps showing the tropics of Cancer and Capricorn, the first accurate representations of the west African coast, and good approximations for the coast of Brazil. Although the crown tried to keep the new maps secret for strategic reasons, bribes and spies from Spain and Italy secured their dissemination. And offers of high payment attracted Portuguese cartographers to England, France and Spain. In Spain the emigrés helped to establish Seville as an even greater centre of navigation than Lisbon. In the 1550s the output of the Portuguese was still impressive and the Jewish connection still evident. Pedro Nuñes, a *converso* originally employed by João III to teach the royal princes mathematics and astronomy, became successively cosmographer royal (1529) and cosmographer major (1547), in charge of navigational teaching and map production in the kingdom; as well as professor of mathematics and astronomy at the university of Coimbra. Before Mercator he tried to find a diagrammatic representation of the earth's surface which allowed for the convergence of meridians towards the poles. His name is still remembered in the 'nonius', a device permitting measurements of fractions of a degree on calibrated navigational instruments, an indication of the heightened sense of accuracy which the experience of navigation brought to science. And this Portuguese reputation was still strong in the 1580s when Philip II drew on their expertise to establish his Academy of Mathematics in Madrid to train Castilians in mathematical sciences. João Lavanha was brought over from Lisbon to organize the teaching of cosmography, geography and matters relating to navigation.

Like the Portuguese, the first Spanish voyages of discovery had not been assisted by celestial observation. Failing to find sponsorship in Portugal the Genoese Columbus had finally been supported by Ferdinand and Isabella of Spain. The Spanish ships and crews which sailed on Columbus' voyage of 1492 were not guided by astronomy; the Caribbean was reached by expert 'dead-reckoning', the use of magnetic compass and observation of currents and winds. But after the discovery of the Caribbean islands the men of science were brought in by the Spanish monarchs to guide navigators on the transatlantic crossing by means of charts and instruments. The Casa de la Contratación (House of Trade) of Seville was founded in 1503 as a royal institution for organizing trade with the Indies and Barbary. But its small staff was later enlarged by scientific and technical personnel. In 1508 the first pilot-major was appointed to examine and license pilots; in 1523 a cosmographer-major became responsible for the manufacture of all nautical instruments and charts; and in 1552 a royal chair of the art of navigation was established to enhance teaching and examining at the Casa. And here also was kept a master-chart, the *padron*, the official standard chart of the Indies, continually corrected by information brought to Seville by returning pilots. This was the institution which so impressed the visiting English navigator Stephen Borough that he called for its imitation in England, though it was not functioning as effectively as he imagined.[14]

Manuals based on teaching at the Casa were published; one of them, Pedro de Medina's *Arte de navegar* (1545), became particularly well known in Europe through translation into French, Dutch, Italian and English. In this way Seville's experts also became the teachers of north European navigators.

An outstanding problem in sixteenth-century navigation was the determination of longitude. It had come to the fore not simply as a requirement for pinpointing a vessel's position at sea, but for political reasons: the competition for territory. In 1493 a Spanish pope, Alexander VI, had declared a line of demarcation running across the world from north to south, one hundred leagues west of the Azores and Cape Verde islands; all territory discovered to the west of this line would be a Spanish preserve. A year later João II improved Portugal's prospects by negotiating the treaty of Tordesillas, by which Ferdinand and Isabella accepted a shift in the demarcation line 270 leagues further west. But these were lines of longitude, impossible to fix because that required accurate measurement of time; the available clocks gained or lost as much as half an hour a day.[15] Consequently the extent of oceans was sometimes intentionally contracted or expanded to claim territory as valuable as the spice islands within the Portuguese or Spanish zone; in that case it was a question of considering the continuation of the Tordesillas line around the other side of the earth into the Pacific. At the beginning of Philip III's reign a large monetary prize of thousands of ducats was offered for a way of determining longitude; the competitors included Galileo; but there was no solution anywhere until the invention, a century and a half later, of John Harrison's marine chronometer. Meanwhile the longitude problem stimulated sixteenth-century Spaniards to observe lunar eclipses in Mexico City, Panama, the Philippines and Madrid, timing their occurrence with inaccurate clocks and deducing longitudes which were far from the truth.

THE EXPERIENCE OF EMPIRE

The Portuguese navigators had enriched science with the discovery of new constellations like the Southern Cross, precise studies of terrestrial magnetism[16] and superior maps. The discovery of the New World – Spanish America and Portuguese Brazil – was for some too great a mental adjustment to accept. Johann von Wendelstein, a geography teacher of sixteenth-century Nuremberg, preferred not to recognize its existence; Bartolomeo Vespucci, professor of astronomy at Padua, continued to hold the classical doctrine that no life could exist in the tropics even though his uncle Amerigo Vespucci had testified to the contrary during his extensive travels in tropical America.[17] But for the Portuguese there was exhilaration over their voyages in the New World and the Old.[18] Their chroniclers and poets praised achievements which put the ancients in the shade; if Ptolemy could only return he would be ashamed at how little geography he knew! This sense of surpassing the ancients is already evident in the mid-fifteenth century when the Portuguese navigators who sailed into equatorial Africa found no shortage of native humans. They said the ancients denied the possibility of life in the torrid zone, but 'we found the contrary'.

This challenge to ancient authority may well have been one of the most important consequences of Iberian navigation: the development of a critical scientific mentality. And this weakening of dependence on Classical authorities is most apparent in the observations over the period 1535–75 on the natural history of the newly acquired overseas territories of the Portuguese and Spanish empires. They show the considerable stimulus those empires gave to science.

Garcia d'Orta's voyage to Goa may well have been an escape from Portugal's intensifying persecution of converted Jews. His parents, Spanish Jews, had settled in Portugal after the expulsion from Spain, only to be faced five years later with the same choice of baptism or expulsion from Manuel I. This time they chose baptism; but their son Garcia would secretly remain a loyal Jew. A physician and professor of natural philosophy at Lisbon, he sailed to Goa in 1534 where he became physician to Portuguese viceroys. And from the base of this capital of Portuguese India he gradually became an expert in far eastern flora, acquiring specimens from agents and growing seeds in his garden. In his *Coloquios dos simples e drogas he cousas mediçinais da India* ('Dialogues on the simples, drugs and materia medica of India', Goa, 1563) he gave the first description by a European of mangoes, coco of the Maldives, the jackfruit and the fruit of the durian trees, as well as the first European account of the symptoms of Asiatic cholera. But more important still was his critical attitude to Dioscorides, the undisputed Classical authority on medicinal plants. In Europe – he had studied at Salamanca – d'Orta had been so intimidated by the respect for the ancient Greeks that he said he had never dared to question their authority;[19] but now in the very different, non-academic environment of Portuguese India he felt freer and above all was armed with fresh knowledge based on direct observation. His *Coloquios* was intentionally composed in dialogue form to give full effect to the contradiction of received wisdom by empirical data. Throughout the book his observations correct or explode ancient opinions on medicinal plants voiced by Ruano, a fictitious graduate of Salamanca steeped in reverence for Classical authority. In firm, dismissive replies d'Orta declared that 'for me the testimony of an eye-witness is worth more than that of all the physicians and all the fathers of medicine who wrote on false information' and that 'you can get more knowledge now from the Portuguese in one day than was known to the Romans after a hundred years'.[20] Another Portuguese *converso*, Christovão da Costa, later provided illustrations of plants d'Orta had described and added more Asian flora, observed during travels in Portuguese Macao and Malacca, in a treatise published in Burgos in 1578.

In Spain interest had been aroused in the flora and fauna of the New World ever since the first voyage of Columbus. By the 1510s American *guaiacum* was being used in central Europe to treat syphilis, one of many examples of fanciful expectations of discovered panaceas from America. And around the time of Philip II's accession, Las Casas was so lavish in his praise of medicinal virtues of balsams extracted from the aromatic trees of the New World that he saw them as treasures of greater value than bullion.[21] The systematic collection of information on flora and fauna in Spanish America was specified as a part of the duties of the royal cosmographer-chronicler, a new officer added to the Council of the Indies in 1571. This information, part of an extensive inquiry into all aspects of the resources of the Indies and designed to secure stronger control from Madrid, was solicited by printed questionnaires despatched throughout America.[22] And simultaneously Philip II commissioned a scientific expedition, sending one of his court physicians, Francisco Hernández, to undertake a full survey of the medicinal plants of New Spain and Peru. The aim was to establish reliable information on the habitat and virtues of these plants through first-hand observation and experiment. He arrived at Vera Cruz in 1571 and over the next five years travelled by mule over much of New Spain accompanied by interpreters, Indian herbalists and artists to sketch plants. And in various hospitals he experimented on the sick with plant extracts. His health suffered and prevented the survey of Peru. But his account of

3,000 flora of Mexico has never been bettered. Volumes of manuscripts with illustrations, seeds of exotic plants and tubs with young specimens were shipped to Spain. Hernández was overjoyed that he had discovered a treasure house of medicinal plants completely unknown to the ancients. Justifiably proud of his advance beyond Dioscorides he promised Philip even greater fame than Alexander the Great had secured from his patronage of Aristotle's natural history. But his exhilaration was soon destroyed by the decision to publish only a small part of his results.[23] It was instead another physician, Nicolás Monardes, who was responsible for familiarizing Europeans with American plants. A physician of Seville, that nerve-centre of trade with the Indies, he imported American flora as part of a commercial enterprise which also involved sending textiles and slaves to the Indies. His *Historia medicinal de las cosas que se traen de nuestras Indias Occidentales* (Seville, 1565–74) would run through forty-two editions in six languages. Sassafras and jalap were described for the first time; and accurate descriptions given of Peru balm, Tolu balm and tobacco.

It was the peculiar fauna of Spanish America which most attracted the attention of José de Acosta during his residence in Peru (1572–86) as a Jesuit missionary. His faith in the ancient authorities he had been taught to revere was weakened soon after he disembarked. Tropical America, far from being uninhabitable, was teeming with Amerindians. And he made fun of Aristotle's assertion that the upper atmosphere was blazing with fire; in Peru's Andean heights he was struggling to keep warm. The first reports of the strange fauna of the New World had been accommodated to existing knowledge; the iguanas Columbus had seen being roasted on spits were interpreted as crocodiles of the Nile. Acosta was amazed by the richness of fauna unknown in the Old World and was at a loss to explain their existence. But he speculated that Amerindians and beasts had crossed from the Old World by land; he was convinced future exploration world reveal that the two continents were a short distance apart. Acosta's observations and theories were published in a much-read book; his *Historia natural y moral de las Indias* (Seville, 1590) within fifteen years was translated into Latin and five European languages.

Spain profited from its trade in American medicinal plants and especially the insect dye, cochineal. But American silver was far more important, one of the principal revenues the crown relied on to pay for the monarchy's huge military expenditure. Rumours of fabulous wealth had been spread by the *conquistadores* after plundering the gold and silver objects from Aztec and Inca temples. The richest of America's silver deposits were discovered in the 1540s at Zacatecas, New Spain and the silver mountain of Potosí in Peru. And it was the determination of monarchs, viceroys and settlers to exploit this great natural wealth to the full that stimulated Spanish metallurgy in the early modern period. More efficient furnaces and ventilators for mines were designed and tested. But the greatest success came from a new technique of extracting silver from its ore, the amalgamation process.[24] Details are lacking, but it is thought probable that when Bartolomé de Medina sailed in the 1550s to New Spain from his native Seville he took with him knowledge of the amalgamation process imparted by contacts with German metallurgists. Medina's achievement was to work the process successfully with American ore. When the process was later introduced at Potosí in the 1570s it caused a revolution in output; there in 1592 some 200 tons of silver were produced. Continuing experiments at Potosí led to the discovery in 1587–8 that the process worked more efficiently by the addition of iron fillings, a metal catalyst.

FROM STAGNATION TO ENLIGHTENMENT

Iberian scientific and technological activity, once so conspicuous, collapsed towards the end of the sixteenth century and remained unimportant for most of the seventeenth century when elsewhere in Europe there was a cluster of scientific talent and discovery. So complete was the collapse that it is difficult to find a single Iberian contributor to the European Scientific Revolution of the seventeenth century. The pattern is the same for both Portugal and Spain: sixteenth-century activity, seventeenth-century stagnation followed by a campaign to rescue the countries from the darkness of scientific backwardness. What was the cause of this intellectual deterioration? Iberian historians have continued to give the explanation favoured by the philosophers of the Enlightenment: the cause was religious fanaticism. This can be supported but the issues are complicated.

It is argued that the most active scientific group in Portugal and Spain, the Jews, was destroyed by the expulsions of 1492 and 1497, and by the subsequent persecution of the converts who remained. It is true that some distinguished Jewish scientists were among those who went into exile, and also that *converso* scientists were killed, like Lluís Alcanyís, Valencia's first professor of medicine, who was burned alive in 1506. But it is also true that numerous *conversos* like Pedro Nuñes managed one way or another to avoid persecution and continue to do important scientific work in the peninsula. The Inquisition (established in Spain 1480; in Portugal 1536) had concentrated its attacks on the *conversos*, and although its persecution became erratic, its survival maintained an atmosphere of fear; still in the eighteenth century it could pounce on suspected Judaizers like the physician Diego Zapata.

There was also the drive against Protestantism, particularly in Spain where fears ran high in the 1550s with the discovery of Lutheran cells in Valladolid and Seville. The Spanish monarchs Charles V and Philip II saw themselves as the champions of Catholicism dedicated to the defeat of heretical Protestantism and Islam. Charles, the emperor who had warred against German Protestant princes, instructed his son to do his utmost to keep Spain free of the Protestant infection. And after Charles' abdication his stern policies were implemented in measures to control contacts with foreign ideas. In 1558 the death penalty was introduced for importing foreign books into Spain without permission and for un-licensed printing. And in 1559 the Inquisitor General, Fernando de Valdés, issued the first Spanish Index of prohibited books; on the list were some scientific works: the important botanical work of Leonhart Fuchs and the zoological treatise of the great Swiss naturalist Conrad Gesner, both now banned in Spain because the authors were Protestant. And in the same year, in another move to keep the Protestant menace at bay, Philip prohibited his subjects from studying at any university abroad except for the 'safe' Catholic centres of Rome, Naples and Bologna. The effect of this at Montpellier is striking: the numbers of Spanish students who matriculated at this French centre of medical teaching fell dramatically from 248 in 1510–59 to a mere 12 in 1560–99. An assessment of the effect of the ban on Spain's scientific development depends on one's view of the importance of Europe's universities; that is debatable, and Spanish historians have argued from the hidebound conservatism of those institutions that the Spanish were not missing much.

The subsequent Spanish Indices of 1583–4 and especially those of 1612 and 1632 extended the ban on foreign authors, eventually including almost the entire works of Paracelsus and his followers, regarded as influenced by Protestantism. But the Index of 1640 permitted the works of Kepler and Brahe after slight expurgations. The effects of the Indices are not easy to assess because of the unknown degree of clandestine circulation of prohibited works, and the impossibility of achieving complete control of imported books.[25]

Nor was Counter-Reformation Spain cut off from European science. How could it have been when the Netherlands and half of Italy were part of the Spanish Monarchy, when European traders were established in Seville and close relations maintained with German subjects of the Habsburg emperor? Netherlandish scientists like Clusius visited Spain and maintained contact with Spanish physicians into the early seventeenth century. Germans also came to the peninsula as mining experts and gunfounders, though attempts were made to screen them for Protestant beliefs. But teaching in seventeenth-century Spain's universities had become stagnant, increasingly dedicated to the production of bureaucrats and dominated like Italy by Counter-Reformation Aristotelian philosophy. The number of scientific books published in seventeenth-century Spain shows a sharp drop. Whether that is to be attributed to the atmosphere of fear generated by the Inquisition is one of several problems associated with the unresolved question of Spain's scientific stagnation whose debate is certain to continue.

From the end of the seventeenth century, criticism of their countries' scientific backwardness was increasingly voiced by individual Spaniards and Portuguese, and culminated in vigorous attempts at reform by ministers of Enlightenment régimes. In Portugal the process was initiated by men with experience of conditions abroad: diplomats and emigré *converso* physicians.[26] Accustomed to the freer intellectual life of London or Amsterdam, these migrants became all the more convinced that Portuguese society was suffering from the evils of censorship, religious fanaticism and racial prejudice. For them the remedy was to substitute modern ideas, especially modern science, for the prevailing Aristotelianism. And this drastic reform of education was later implemented by the enlightened despotic government of the marquis da Pombal (1750–77). The Jesuits were expelled (1759) removing the principal promoters of Aristotelianism. At the university of Coimbra Musschenbroek's Newtonian texts replaced Aristotelian physics. And professors from Padua were brought over to establish experimental-science teaching at Coimbra and at Lisbon's newly founded Royal College of Nobles.

The same campaign for educational reform and the new science occurred on a larger scale in Spain. In the 1680s Juan de Cabriada, a Valencian physician, was quarrelling in Madrid with Galenist physicians, trying to persuade them to accept Harvey's discovery of the circulation of the blood and to open their eyes to recent developments. Disgusted with hidebound physicians enslaved to the ancients, Cabriada wrote his *Carta filosófica, médico-chymica* (Madrid, 1687) in which he expressed his shame over Spanish stagnation; it was 'as if we were Indians, always the last' to hear of progress in Europe.[27] There was also confrontation between supporters of traditional and new learning in Seville. Cartesian physics had won some ground there through the *Cursus philosophicus* (1673) of Manuel Maignan, a French minim. Physicians imbued with corpuscular philosophy secured royal recognition to found

Spain's first modern scientific society, the Regia Sociedad de Medicina y demás ciencias of Seville (1700). The rector of the university of Seville tried in vain to dismantle the new society with accusations of heretical philosophy.[28]

The belief that modern science was incompatible with Catholicism was the source of Spanish backwardness according to Feijóo, Benedictine and professor of theology at Oviedo. From the 1720s his influential essays attacked Spain's educational system calling for a new scientific curriculum based on experiment and observation, especially modelled on the philosophy of Francis Bacon and Isaac Newton. Newton may have come from heretical England but it was ignorant to assume that the Protestant venom had been conveyed to his physics.[29]

The political climate in Spain changed markedly with the accession of Charles III, who had previously ruled over the Kingdom of the Two Sicilies with the assistance of an enlightened minister, Tanucci. Motivated by the policy to maximize the power of the crown, the Jesuits were thrown out of Spain (1767) so removing a pillar of Aristotelian education. The king's ministers were appointed directors of the universities and soon the crown was trying to introduce modern courses; plans were devised for replacing Galen with Boerhaave, Aristotle with Newton.[30] There was some temporary success; at Granada Aristotelian physics was no longer taught to theology students. But generally academic conservatism was victorious, a result guaranteed by the outbreak of the French Revolution which brought a change in crown policy through fear of subversive ideas. In the Indies the story was the same. In the 1760s Mutis was teaching Copernicanism and Newtonianism – he even translated the *Principia* – in Colombia. In Guatemala in the 1780s a Franciscan, Goicoéchea, was using apparatus to teach courses based on Boyle, Nollet and Boerhaave. And at a seminary in Lima Rodríguez de Mendoza introduced the philosophy of Descartes, Gassendi and Newton while the university remained staunchly Aristotelian.

But the most distinctive feature of the Spanish Enlightenment was the *Sociedades Económicas de Amigos del País*, local economic societies dedicated to regional economic development through the promotion of scientific and technical education; by 1788 forty-eight of these institutions had been founded throughout Spain. Their manifesto had been supplied by the *Discurso sobre el Fomento de la Industria Popular* (1774) of Campomanes, a minister of the crown. This text – a copy was sent to every parish – called on nobility and clergy to found local societies for fostering useful knowledge; the goal was to match the prosperity of England and Holland. The recommendations included the formation of a cabinet of natural history to display the local resources of raw materials and stimulate manufactures. Many answered the call. At Lugo, Bishop Armañá became the director of an economic society, persuaded that fostering agriculture and industry would best defeat poverty in his diocese. In the Basque country the count of Peñaflorida, acutely aware since his student days in France of Spain's backward science, founded an economic society which sponsored technical studies abroad. The Elhuyar brothers were sent to study chemistry with Rouelle in Paris and metallurgy with Werner in Freiberg; one of them also studied chemistry in Sweden with Bergman and Scheele. The fruits of this were their discovery of tungsten and the creation of Mexico's Colegio de Minería (1792), a distinguished centre of mining education where pupils used specially translated editions of works by Werner and Lavoisier. Madrid's Economic Society wanted agrarian reform and believed this could best be achieved by universal education in the exact sciences and natural history, enlightening the noble landlord and the humblest peasant – special technical manuals for peasants were envisaged for the dissemination of chemistry stripped of its 'mysterious jargon'. But because the plan also required a redistribution of land, criticizing the evils of amortization including inalienable ecclesiastical estates, it was condemned by the Inquisition as an attack on the clergy. The overall failure of the Economic Societies was due to the powerful forces of Spanish conservatism, which proved insurmountable until the liberal revolution of the nineteenth century. By then the Scientific Revolution had made deep inroads in Spain, Portugal and Spanish America.

NOTES

1 The collected papers of a recent symposium on the *Alfonsine Tables* and related astronomical texts have been published in M. Comes, R. Puig and J. Samsó (eds.), *De astronomia Alphonsi Regis* (Instituto Millas Vallicrosa de Historia de la Ciencia Árabe, Barcelona, 1987). The papers in Spanish, English and French deal mostly with technical details, but there is also some discussion of the importance and influence of the Alfonsine astronomical texts.

2 An inventory of the Escorial's Arabic collection and Urrea's description of his appointment are published in N. Morata, 'Un cátalogo de los fondos árabes primitivos de El Escorial', *Al-Andalus* 2 (1934), 87–181.

3 J. M. López Piñero, *Ciencia y técnica en la sociedad española de los siglos XVI y XVII* (Barcelona, 1979), p. 298. This is the best survey of Spanish science for those centuries.

4 L. García Ballester, *Historia social de la medicina en la España de los siglos XIII al XVI. La minoría musulmana y morisca* (Madrid, 1976).

5 J. Fournel-Guerin, 'La Pharmacopée morisque et l'exercice de la médecine dans la communauté morisque aragonaise (1540–1620)', *Revue d'histoire*

maghrebienne 6 (1979), 53–62; M. García-Arenal, *Inquisición y moriscos. Los procesos del Tribunal de Cuenca* (Madrid, 1983), p. 110.

6 V. Navarro Brotóns, 'Zacut', in J. M. López Piñero *et al.* (eds.), *Diccionario histórico de la ciencia moderna en España*, 2 vols. (Barcelona, 1983), II, 441–3. This biographical dictionary is an indispensable reference work for Spanish science from the late fifteenth to the early twentieth century.

7 Y. Baer, *A History of the Jews in Christian Spain*, trans. L. Schoffman, 2 vols. (Philadelphia, 1978), I, pp. 289–305.

8 D. C. Goodman, *Power and Penury. Government, Technology and Science in Philip II's Spain* (Cambridge, 1988), p. 219.

9 J. Simon Díaz, 'La Inquisición de Logroño (1570–1580)', *Berceo. Boletín del Instituto de Estudios Riojanos* 1 (1946), 89–119; p. 94.

10 Quoted by J. Caro Baroja, *Los judios en la España moderna y contemporánea*, 3 vols. (2nd edn; Madrid, 1978), I, pp. 102–3.

11 D. Waters, 'Science and the Techniques of Navigation in the Renaissance', in C. Singleton (ed.), *Art, Science and History in the Renaissance* (Baltimore, 1967), pp. 198–9.

12 The revised interpretation can be seen in P. E. Russell, *Prince Henry the Navigator: The Rise and Fall of a Culture Hero* (Oxford, 1984); and M. Newitt, 'Prince Henry and the Origins of Portuguese Expansion', in Newitt (ed.), *The First Portuguese Colonial Empire* (Exeter, 1986), 9–35.

13 Waters, 'Science and the Techniques of Navigation', pp. 205f.

14 Goodman, *Power and Penury*, pp. 74–81.

15 See the intelligent discussion of the problem by Alonso de Santa Cruz, a cosmographer consulted by Charles V and Philip II, in his *Libro de las longitudes*, first published in Seville in 1921.

16 R. Hooykaas, *Science in Manueline Style* (Coimbra, 1980), pp. 111–12, discusses João de Castro's studies on magnetism.

17 E. Goldschmidt, 'Not in Harrisse', *Essays honoring Lawrence C. Wroth* (Portland, 1951), 129–41. For European scholars' reluctance to accept the New World see the stimulating account in J. H. Elliott, *The Old World and the New 1492–1650* (Cambridge, 1970), pp. 13f.

18 This Portuguese exhilaration is illustrated in R. Hooykaas, *Humanism and the Voyages of Discovery in Sixteenth-Century Portuguese Science and Letters* (Amsterdam and Oxford, 1979).

19 Garcia d'Orta, *Colloquies on the Simples and Drugs of India* (trans. C. Markham; London, 1913), p. 274.

20 *Ibid.*, pp. 125 and 127. A recent assessment of d'Orta, along with a collection of papers of very variable quality on all aspects of Portuguese science from the Middle Ages to 1900 can be found in a publication of the Academia das Ciências de Lisboa: *História e Desenvolvimiento da Ciência em Portugal. 1 Colóquio: até ao Século XX*, 2 vols. (Lisbon, 1986).

21 B. de Las Casas, *Apologética historia sumaria*, ed. E. O'Gorman, 2 vols. (Mexico, 1967), I, pp. 97 and 106.

22 Goodman, *Power and Penury*, pp. 68–72.

23 Goodman, 'Philip II's Patronage of Science and Engineering', *British Journal for the History of Science* 16 (1983), pp. 62–5.

24 Goodman, *Power and Penury*, pp. 172–94.

25 For some views on the relations between the Spanish Inquisition and science see S. Muñoz Calvo, *Inquisición y ciencia en la España moderna* (Madrid, 1977), and the special issue of *Arbor*, 124 (1986).

26 D. Goodman, 'Portugal', in J. Yolton (ed.), *The Blackwell Companion to the Enlightenment* (Oxford, 1991).

27 J. de Cabriada, *Carta filosófica, médico-chymica* (Madrid, 1687), pp. 230–1. For the introduction of modern science in Spain see López Piñero, *Ciencia y técnica*, pp. 371–451.

28 R. Ceñal, 'Cartesianismo en España. Notas para su historia (1650–1750)', *Revista de la Universidad de Oviedo*, special issue (1945), 5–97.

29 D. Goodman, 'Science and the Clergy in the Spanish Enlightenment', *History of Science* 21 (1983), 111–40.

30 A recent survey of Spain's scientific Enlightenment is provided by M. Sellés, J. Peset and A. Lafuente (eds.), *Carlos III y la ciencia de la Ilustración* (Madrid, 1988).

7

THE SCIENTIFIC REVOLUTION IN ENGLAND

JOHN HENRY

ENGLAND has always figured prominently in efforts to explain the Scientific Revolution. An intellectual backwater in the sixteenth century, it more than made up for this in the seventeenth century, so that by 1660 it became, arguably, 'the major centre for organized scientific activity in Europe'. Accordingly, it has continually drawn the attention of, and provided fertile ground for, historians seeking to explain the changing approach to the natural world and the burgeoning of natural philosophy which constitute the Scientific Revolution. Indeed, the two earliest attempts to reveal the driving forces behind the new science – Boris Hessen's Marxist account of 'The Social and Economic Roots of Newton's "Principia"', and Robert Merton's Weberian thesis, 'Science, Technology and Society in Seventeenth-Century England' – both focused on the English scene.[1]

In Hessen's case, however, concentration upon England was merely a matter of historiographical expediency. Although the problems of mechanics and hydrostatics which Newton dealt with in his *Principia mathematica* could be made to support Hessen's claims, and although 'the English revolution gave a mighty stimulus to the development of productive forces', Hessen's thesis was by no means confined to late seventeenth-century England. 'The brilliant successes of natural science during the sixteenth and seventeenth centuries', Hessen wrote, 'were conditioned by the disintegration of the feudal economy, the development of merchant capital, of international maritime relationships and of heavy (mining) industry.'[2] Clearly, these were Europe-wide phenomena. Consequently, whatever the merits of Hessen's thesis it can be of little help in trying to understand what, if anything, characterized the Scientific Revolution in England and we need not dwell upon it.

Robert Merton accepted Hessen's premise that economic and military necessities proved to be the mother of scientific inventions but, following Max Weber, he related the rise of capitalism to the ascendancy of the

'Protestant ethic'. He developed his ideas in the English context, arguing that the Puritan ideas and values of early seventeenth-century England provided a context within which the new science could flourish. Even so, it is by no means clear from Merton's account whether there was anything specific to English Puritanism which made it more conducive to the development of natural science than other forms of European Protestantism, and from our point of view, therefore, Merton's thesis is not much of an advance on Hessen's.

The major problem with the Merton thesis is that it relies too much on prosopographical claims about religious orientation in an area which is notoriously difficult, if not impossible, to define. Much of the criticism of the Puritanism and science thesis is concerned with denying not only that individual thinkers were Puritans but also that Puritanism can be defined in any useful and meaningful way. Indeed, Charles Webster, the historian who has been more successful than anyone else in promoting and extending Merton's thesis, has admitted that the complexities of English Puritanism present an 'insuperable barrier' to analysis by 'headcounting'.[3] Such difficulties might have been circumvented if Merton had been able to explain why Puritanism should prove so amenable to scientific study and achievement, but Merton's efforts in this direction are disappointingly vague. For all his talk of natural philosophy as a means of demonstrating the glory and benevolence of the Creator while simultaneously bringing comfort and relief to man's estate, we nowhere come across a really convincing reason why Puritans were more concerned about, more successful or more productive in, science than any other religious group.

Charles Webster's monumental *Great Instauration* goes a long way to filling this lacuna in Merton's thesis, but only with the help of some special pleading. The key to understanding the Puritan concern with science, according to Webster, is the millennial idea of progress. The thousand-year rule of the Protestant saints in the last age of the world was to take place on earth, but an earth returned to a paradisiacal state thanks largely to man's renewed dominion over nature. Commitment to this view of the development of science necessitated an emphasis on pragmatic and technological matters at the expense of theoretical concerns. For the Puritans, Webster tells us, 'There was little point in engaging in highly abstract metaphysical disputes about the nature of the ether, or entering into long term scientific investigations.' Webster's *Great Instauration*, therefore, is a consummate study of various pragmatic, reformist endeavours in education, medicine, agriculture and other commercial concerns. To a large extent, however, it leaves unanswered the questions of why and how a recognizably 'modern' science consolidated itself and began to flourish in Interregnum England. Although 'The Puritans evolved a comprehensive system of science consistent with their millennial ideology', Webster went on to acknowledge that 'Modern science has evolved in the context of a quite different, even alien ideology.' Within its own terms Webster's study is an unassailable survey of the Puritan origins of what could be called Puritan science, but it does not help us to understand the achievements of thinkers like William Gilbert, Thomas Harriot, William Harvey, Robert Boyle, Robert Hooke, Isaac Newton and others which can be seen with hindsight to be prototypical, in various ways, of all subsequent science.[4]

In raising this last point, however, we are immediately confronted with another problem. What kind of explanation of the origins of modern science are we looking for? It is all too clear, even from a superficial glance, that neither Hessen nor Merton have anything to say about the details of scientific theories or practices pursued by the natural philosophers they discuss. It is one thing to show a correlation between the content of Newton's *Principia* and the historian's view of 'the tasks of the epoch, which were raised for accomplishment by the class entering into power', but it is quite another to explain precisely how Newton might have arrived at his solutions to these tasks. How did he arrive at his methodology? How was it that he came to rely upon concepts of attractive and repulsive forces operating between bodies at a distance from one another? Similarly, it is one thing to argue, as Merton does, that Puritanism provided a motive and a sanction for experimentalism, and it is another to show how particular experiments were devised and conducted, and how their conclusions were received.[5]

Even those historians who have extended Hessen's or Merton's work by indulging in much more detailed scrutinies of actual scientific work have failed to provide a full understanding of early modern science. The Marxist historian Edgar Zilsel, for example, in trying to account for the sophisticated experimental method used by William Gilbert in his study of magnetism pointed to the contemporary flourishing of elite craftsmen. The work of miners, smelters, metalworkers, practical chemists, navigators, mapmakers and others was mentioned by Gilbert in his *De magnete* and it is from them and their alleged 'experimentalism' that Gilbert is said to have taken his cue. Zilsel's study contains valuable material and he succeeds in showing that Gilbert did indeed borrow some experiments from the navigator Robert Norman. Nevertheless, he misses an important element in Gilbert's experimentalism by dismissing Gilbert's 'magnetic philosophy' as a kind of 'medieval vitalism'. Gilbert goes far beyond Norman, for example, in his experimental investigation of magnetic 'dip' (a perfectly balanced iron pointer will dip, and point below the horizon after it has been magnetized). By reproducing the phenomenon of dip with small magnetized needles suspended just above the surfaces of specially turned spherical lodestones, Gilbert is able, not only to explain why dip takes place (the pole of the magnetized pointer points directly to the magnetic pole of the earth, ignoring the earth's curvature), but also to insist that the earth itself must be a giant spherical lodestone. Gilbert does this, not merely (perhaps not even primarily) to develop a way of determining latitude when no stars are visible, but in order to provide him with a physical basis for upholding the Copernican theory of the earth's rotation on its axis.[6]

Zilsel's neglect of the pro-Copernican intentions of Gilbert's *De magnete*, was almost certainly a direct result of his own historiographical commitment to the belief that early modern science was driven by more immediate social and economic changes in Gilbert's milieu. We can see, therefore, the danger of such ideological commitments to a sound historical understanding. This does not mean, however, that we should turn away from Zilsel's, Hessen's and Merton's kind of 'externalist' history of science to a supposedly more rigorous 'internalist' history, concentrating only on technical and intellectual considerations which are supposed to develop 'naturally' as part of the problem-solving process. The time is long overdue for historians of science to recognize that the externalist/internalist distinction is in itself pernicious to good historiography. Although A. Rupert Hall was correct in his early critique of the Merton thesis, 'Merton Revisited', to point out that historians who focused upon the social and economic relations of science were more concerned with the scientific movement, the public face of science and the public reaction to it, than with the systematic details of scientific knowledge, it does not have to be this way. Conversely, it should be possible to think with Hall that science is 'a deep intellectual enterprise whose object is to gain some comprehension of the cosmos' while recognizing that the enterprise is conducted by men and women who cannot possibly pursue this object in a single-minded way, divorced from all other preconceptions, preoccupations, values and intentions.[7]

The internalist/externalist distinction is valid as an excuse for circumscribing the extent of one's historical research. We all have to draw a line somewhere. It is a serious error, however, to make the distinction, as it were, a philosophical as opposed to a historiographical one. Just because science is a complex, interconnected network of systematic knowledge does not mean that the internalist approach is the only valid way of understanding its development. The ways in which we arrive at an understanding of the physical world are complex in the

extreme and a full analysis of the processes involved requires anthropological, sociological and psychological insights as well as those of
the historian and philosopher of science. Perhaps this ideal is still some
way off, but the best recent work in the history of science has at least
demonstrated that externalist and internalist approaches can be
combined to give an account of scientific development which can show
the relevance of the broader social, religious and political context to both
the discovery and the establishment of even the most recondite
experimental and theoretical niceties.[8]

Ideally, then, if we wish to understand what made English science
characteristically different from Continental science in the seventeenth
century, we need to take into consideration not only the general context
within which it was evolving but also the specific technical problems that
were being confronted by its practitioners. Needless to say, in a short
essay we will have to depend upon restricted examples, and brief
indications. Previous historiography points to two major factors which
are characteristic of the formation of science in England. Whatever else
may be said about the Puritanism and science thesis, the historical
studies which it has provoked have led to the establishment of an
undeniable link between the development of science in England and
contemporary religious developments which were uniquely English.
The other characterizing feature is most clearly acknowledged in the
history of philosophy: English philosophy since John Locke is usually
classified as 'empiricist', and it is routinely acknowledged that Locke
modelled his own philosophy on the science of Robert Boyle, Isaac
Newton and other contemporary English natural philosophers. English
natural philosophy was fundamentally empirical in a way that set it
apart from other European countries. Although Continental natural
philosophers experimented, only English natural philosophers can
be said to have been experimentalists. The beginnings of English
empiricism can be seen in the tendency for natural philosophers to come
together in informal collaborating groups. As we shall see later,
empiricism went hand in hand with the concurrent theological demands
on natural philosophy, and arguably received its most forceful encouragement from that quarter, but first we will briefly consider the
nature of these groups.

FROM THE THREE MAGI TO THE ROYAL SOCIETY: THE ORGANIZATION OF SCIENCE IN ENGLAND

With the notable exception of Bacon, most natural philosophers in late
sixteenth- and seventeenth-century England can be seen to have worked

in close association with like-minded colleagues, collaborating over particular problems, the methods required to solve those problems and the theoretical assumptions implicit in their methods. One of the earliest of these groups, coming together at the turn of the century, was the trio of mathematicians and philosophers described by John Aubrey, in *Brief Lives*, and Anthony Wood, in *Athenae Oxonienses*, as 'the Earl of Northumberland's three Magi'. Although the coherence of this group has been greatly exaggerated there can be little doubt that Thomas Harriot, Walter Warner and Robert Hues shared interests in mathematics, the revival of atomism and alchemy. Sir Charles Cavendish and his brother William, earl of Newcastle, also gathered a group of natural philosophers into a loose community at Welbeck Abbey. The Welbeck circle included Thomas Hobbes, Robert Payne and John Pell, all of whom shared an interest in mixed mathematics, and especially optics. In the 1640s, a group of young physicians, excited by the anatomical researches of William Harvey, gathered around their mentor in Oxford and extended his work.[9]

There were, of course, links between these separate groups. A letter from Hobbes to William Cavendish reveals that he was well acquainted with the details of some of Warner's speculations, and contemporary accounts suggest both that Hobbes plagiarized Warner, and that Harvey had 'his hint' about the circulation of the blood from Warner. These claims have not been substantiated but it is easy to see from Warner's papers why contemporaries who had the opportunity to read them might have thought that the genius of the older man was insufficiently acknowledged. Furthermore, there were links between these early English groups of philosophers and Continental thinkers like Descartes and Gassendi, usually through the mediation of the Minim friar, Marin Mersenne, who made himself the centre of an extensive network of natural philosophers.[10]

In spite of these European connections, however, the English scene, at least in some important respects, remained characteristically different. Although these early English thinkers entered enthusiastically into the atomist revival of the late Renaissance, their own experimental knowledge in alchemy or animal physiology tended to prevent them from accepting the kind of strict mechanistic philosophy being developed by Descartes. The pre-Cartesian systems of natural philosophy produced by Warner and Hobbes, for example, both involve assumptions that particles of matter have certain active faculties analogous to the Galenic faculties of parts of the human body, such as the 'pulsific' faculty.[11] Similarly, because of their direct collaboration with Harvey, Oxford physiologists like Nathaniel Highmore and Ralph Bathurst were

unlikely to accept Descartes' strict mechanistic account of the operation
of the heart, with its concomitant distortion or rejection of some of
Harvey's experimentally determined conclusions. Nevertheless, Harvey's followers were sufficiently affected by the nascent mechanical
philosophy that they did not wish to uphold the more extreme of
Harvey's own vitalistic opinions. The resulting hybrid philosophy, part
mechanistic and part chemical or vitalistic, can be seen subsequently in
the theorizing of a number of Harvey's followers. Walter Charleton and
Thomas Willis, for example, tempered their mechanical philosophies
with suggestions that the particles of matter, or at least some particles of
matter, could be endowed with activity. Glisson, who became Regius
Professor of Physick at Cambridge, began to work much more in isolation
from his earlier colleagues and developed a philosophy in which matter
was said to be intrinsically self-motive, perceptive and possessed with
certain appetites. Glisson's case is extreme but it can be seen to have had
its origins in the same experimental Harveian tradition as the other non-
mechanical medical theorists who sought to extend Harvey's work in the
1640s and 50s.[12]

The continuity of various theoretical and experimental traditions can
also be seen in the cosmological use of the 'magnetical philosophy'
which was first developed by William Gilbert and his collaborator
Edward Wright at the very end of the sixteenth century. Gilbert
developed the sophisticated experimental method, for which he is
renowned in the history of science, in order to establish that the earth is
a giant lodestone, and that like all lodestones (as Gilbert saw them) it has
the power to rotate while maintaining its axis of rotation in a fixed
orientation in space. This effort to provide physical arguments in
support of Copernicus' mathematically based contention that the earth
was in motion was explicitly animistic, but Gilbert's later followers chose
to speak instead in terms of 'Attractive or Magnetique Virtue',
'magneticall vigor', 'intrinsic energy' and so forth. Such notions were a
far cry from Descartes' own account of magnetism and, indeed, from
any explanation that he would have considered to be valid in the
mechanical philosophy. Nevertheless, as J. A. Bennett has shown, these
ideas continued to be invoked alongside more mechanistic hypotheses,
right through to the 1680s, by a number of leading English theorists such
as John Wilkins, Christopher Wren and Robert Hooke. Perhaps the
most significant aspect of this tradition for subsequent developments was
Wren's and Hooke's belief that planetary motions could be explained on
the assumption that a tangentially moving planet has an attraction for
the sun 'in the same manner as the load-stone hath to Iron, and the Iron
hath to the load-stone'. It was Hooke's communication of this idea to

Newton in 1679 which enabled Newton, previously ignorant of the traditions of 'magnetical philosophy', to break free from the Cartesian assumption that planetary motions must be explained in terms of constrained centrifugal tendencies. As is well known, in the hands of Newton, this idea led on to the universal law of gravitation.[13]

If Newton, as a Cambridge don, was isolated from the group of magnetical philosophers in London, there was another intellectual and experimental tradition in which he took an active part. Although virtually nothing is known about his collaborators, there can be no doubt that Newton was part of a circle of alchemical adepts in Cambridge, London and, possibly, Stoke Park in Northamptonshire. Much of Newton's alchemical activity was confined to copying out unpublished alchemical treatises for his own use, but he also performed his own alchemical experiments. In a rare alchemical composition of his own, describing the 'Vegetation of Metals' (c. 1669), Newton spoke of a subtle spirit of the aether which is 'Nature's universall agent, her secret fire, ye onely ferment and principle of all vegetation. The material soule of all matter...' He went on to hypothesize that this spirit 'perhaps is ye body of light becaus both have a prodigious active principle both are perpetuall workers'.[14] Closely similar speculations were carried over into Newton's 'Hypothesis of Light' of 1675, which was read before the Royal Society, and in the immensely influential 'Queries' appended to the *Opticks*. Query 30 of the third (1717) and subsequent editions, for example, asks: 'Are not gross Bodies and Light convertible into one another, and may not Bodies receive much of their Activity from the Particles of Light which enter into their Composition?' Apart from the direct influence of Newton's knowledge of alchemy on his views about light and active principles within matter, it seems reasonable to suppose that his ready acceptance of Hooke's magnetically inspired suggestion that there might be an attractive force operating between the sun and planets derived from his own non-mechanistic ways of thinking. In a draft fragment entitled 'De aere et aethere' (c. 1673–5) Newton had already invoked repulsive forces between particles of matter (itself an idea inspired partly by Boyle's and Hooke's experimental work with the air pump) and had likened a putative active aether to magnetic effluvia.[15]

All the major contributors to the new science in seventeenth-century England can be shown to have developed their ideas within the context of one group or another, collaborating within a particular tradition. Even the more idiosyncratic thinkers, like Thomas Hobbes and Francis Glisson, can properly be understood only by locating their early work within the traditions of the groups from which they emerged. Some of these groups, such as the circle of natural philosophers who gathered around Richard Towneley in Lancashire or the 'Traventane Philosophers' in Carmarthenshire, whose leader Sir William Lower corresponded with Harriot, were clearly defined but other groupings were so diffuse and shifting that they are perhaps best regarded as communities of like-minded thinkers.[16] There are two obvious examples of such wider communities: those linked by a common interest in mathematics and the mechanical arts, and those with an interest in alchemy or chemistry.

J. A. Bennett has recently made a persuasive case for the role of comparatively humble mathematical practitioners in stimulating the development of new techniques for understanding the physical world, and thereby providing new inspirations in natural philosophy. Certainly, the mechanical arts and mathematical sciences brought together a wide range of social and intellectual types. An important site for the meeting of mathematical instrument makers and the writers of textbooks and instruction manuals, with university-trained natural philosophers, was Gresham College in London. Although the professors of Gresham College were university men they were expected to lecture on practical issues, relevant to the tradesmen, merchants and seamen of London. The College's value as a teaching establishment seems to have been poor but it was undoubtedly an important centre for scientific research and innovation.[17]

An interest in chemistry can also be seen to cut across social and intellectual barriers. From Harriot to Newton and beyond chemistry was regarded as the best way of discovering what Bacon referred to as 'the true textures and configurations of bodies'. The inescapably empirical nature of chemical studies often led English thinkers to conclusions which could not easily be explained in Cartesian or other mechanistic terms. 'Chemistry', wrote Sir Christopher Wren, 'often times gives light enough to contradict mechanical hypotheses that otherwise seem well grounded'. The resulting experimental natural philosophy was a hybrid: a mechanical philosophy in which it was accepted that the fundamental particles of matter could have special chemical properties. Foreshadowing later notions of chemical affinities, for example, Robert Hooke wrote of particles of matter which are 'congruous' to one another and 'incongruous' to other particles, while Newton speculated about 'some secret principle of unsociableness' between particles.[18]

However, we cannot hope to understand why such a hybrid form of 'new philosophy' developed in England and not elsewhere merely by pointing to the empirical results of chemical research. There were, after all, chemists working on the Continent. The full story is, of course, complex and wide-ranging but one major aspect of the story derives from the perceived success of Paracelsian medical reforms. Paracelsians, followers of the Swiss autodidact who called himself Paracelsus, had shown the remarkable possibilities for curing disease by 'chemical', as opposed to the more usual herbal, remedies. In England, however, Paracelsianism first became prominent during the Interregnum period when it was associated with the more radical reformist elements in society. Recognizing, from their own empirical researches, the validity of many Paracelsian principles, the less radical, or more conciliatory, English thinkers incorporated some of those principles into their more conservative mechanical philosophy. The politico-religious conservatism of the mechanical philosophy, or rather the 'experimental philosophy', was itself being carefully managed at this time, as we shall see later. The collaborative group most responsible for this assimilation of iatrochemical ideas into the mechanical philosophy was the Royal College of Physicians.[19]

The most significant, influential, and indeed the most extensive, group of collaborating natural philosophers was, of course, the Royal Society, but this cannot be regarded as merely a larger version of the kind of close-knit working groups we have already considered. Michael Hunter has rightly cautioned against glib assumptions that the Society was an organization of like-minded thinkers with a clear corporate identity and a coherent 'ideology'.[20] In fact, the Society was deliberately established in order to bring together all manner of different thinkers from different traditions, in the hope of bringing to fruition the reform of natural philosophy which was widely perceived to be already well under way. Even so, providing we bear in mind Hunter's warnings about the artificiality of its constitution, it is nonetheless possible to speak meaningfully of a characteristic type of Royal Society science. A comparatively small group of natural philosophers were responsible for instituting the Society and setting its main agenda. It was this initiating group who decided, for example, that the way to reform natural philosophy was by a huge collaborative effort of many hands and minds. In this they can be seen to be endorsing Francis Bacon's views as to the best means of achieving the 'Great Instauration', and rejecting Descartes' belief that 'as a rule there is not such great perfection in works composed of several parts, and proceeding from the hands of several artists, as in those on which one man has worked alone.'[21] The key to understanding the main, characteristic, thrust of the Royal Society is to trace it back to the less formally constituted groups of the Interregnum from which it was born in the Restoration.

The prime movers in the establishment of the Royal Society seem to have belonged to two separate but overlapping groups of philosophers based in London and Oxford. In 1645 a group devoted to 'the New Philosophy or Experimental Philosophy' began to meet, either in Gresham College or the home of one of its members. Initially comprised of John Wilkins, John Wallis, Theodore Haak, George Ent, Francis Glisson, Christopher Merrett, Jonathan Goddard, Charles Scarburgh and the Gresham Professor of Astronomy, Samuel Foster, the 'numbers encreased' so that soon 'many others' attended. This London group continued to meet even after Wilkins, Wallis and Goddard were intruded into Oxford after Parliamentary ejections of royalists. Wadham College, where Wilkins was the newly appointed Warden, now became a second centre for the study of natural philosophy, proceeding 'rather by action, then discourse; chiefly attending some particular Trials in Chymistry, or Mechanicks'.[22] The experimentalist emphasis of both these groups is unsurprising given the fact that many of the members had collaborated in earlier groups on various experimental research programmes. Harvey's followers were well represented in both groups, as were the 'magneticall philosophers'. The Gresham College Professors brought their pragmatic concerns to the London group, while Robert Boyle, William Petty and others brought their Baconianism to the Oxford group.

The profound influence of Francis Bacon's ideas on various social reformers of the Interregnum period and the subsequent adoption of a kind of Baconianism by the Oxford 'experimentall philosophicall clubbe' and then the Royal Society is one of the most characteristic aspects of the Scientific Revolution in England.[23] Bacon himself seems to have pursued natural philosophy not only, as William Harvey said, *like* a Lord Chancellor, but also *because he was* Lord Chancellor: extending the Renaissance humanists' emphasis on the moral duty of Christians to live the *vita activa* to his own more pragmatic and political concerns with 'the enlarging of the bounds of Human Empire, to the effecting of all things possible'.[24] Bacon's ideas for the reform of natural philosophy were taken up by Samuel Hartlib, John Dury and Jan Amos Comenius, who were united by their belief in the need for social, educational and ecumenical religious reform. Similarly, Robert Boyle began his career in natural philosophy as a member of an aptly named 'Invisible College' whose members, whoever they were, were united not only by an interest in experimental chemistry but also by a belief that knowledge should benefit mankind. Bacon's name, and sometimes even his philosophy, were increasingly invoked during the Interregnum to justify the pursuit of natural philosophy. When the Royal Society was founded in 1660 its leading Fellows quickly developed a Baconian rhetoric in support of the

Society and its work, and even, to some extent, carried out research programmes which were recognizably 'Baconian'.[25]

The salient features of Royal Society Baconianism were an emphasis on collaborative effort to be carried on over a long time period, an insistence (in keeping with Bacon's own legalistic concerns) upon gathering and establishing 'matters of fact', a concomitant refusal to indulge in 'premature' speculative theorizing, and a fondly held belief, often anachronistically referred to as 'utilitarianism', that natural philosophy should be a means of obtaining 'a Dominion over Things, and not onely over one anothers Judgements'.[26] In many ways these features, together with an emphasis on the experimental method, can be seen to be characteristic of late seventeenth-century English natural philosophy. Certainly it has to be acknowledged that not all English natural philosophers were Fellows of the Society, and by no means all those who were Fellows subscribed personally to such Baconian precepts. Nevertheless, the public image of the Society, propagated by its leading Fellows in the prefaces to their publications, in their correspondence at home and abroad, in the *Philosophical Transactions*, and in the more explicit manifestoes of the Society such as Thomas Sprat's *History of the Royal Society* and Joseph Glanvill's *Plus Ultra*, often seemed to contemporaries, and to many since, to be representative of English science as a whole.[27] And, in so far as the Society can be seen to have grown quite naturally out of the earlier, less formal, groups of collaborating experimental scientists which were typical of the English scene, this judgement is not so very wide of the mark.

So far we have tried to indicate that, for a proper understanding of the development of science in England, we need an account that pays attention not only to the empirical and physico-mathematical conclusions to which seventeenth-century natural philosophers were led, but also to the microsociology of their immediate milieu, their interactions with collaborators or with rivals. These should not be seen as two easily separable strands. Scientists are led to empirical conclusions not just by the nature of the physical world but by the nature of their own mental world (their individual psychologies) and by the nature of their social world; all these things are inextricably linked. But even this provides only part of the picture. Scientists operate, as scientists and as persons, within a broader culture and they cannot fail to reflect that culture in everything they do. The implications of this are potentially endless, of course, but it is also possible to discern salient features of the cultural landscape which can be shown to have affected the development of science. If we wish to understand what made seventeenth-century English science characteristically different from contemporary

European science there can be no doubt that we must consider the powerful effect of religion.

SCIENCE AND SOTERIOLOGY: THE ENGLISH CHURCH AND ENGLISH NATURAL PHILOSOPHY

The earliest, and still the most persistent and influential, of attempts to account for the nature and vigour of the Scientific Revolution in England focused on the roughly contemporaneous 'Puritan Revolution' as the major driving force. In spite of some impressive support, however, the Puritanism-and-science thesis is debilitated by criticism on two major fronts. Robert Merton, in the first really forceful presentation of this thesis, relied to a large extent on a prosopographical survey in which, as critics were quick to point out, the designation 'Puritan' was far too loosely distributed. The only result has been increased awareness of the difficulty of deciding who counts as Puritan and who does not. This difficulty might have been easily surmounted if Merton had been able to *explain* why Puritans should have been more concerned about and more successful in natural philosophy than any other Christian group, but his attempts to do so remain unconvincing.[28]

Charles Webster's magisterial survey of Interregnum reform movements in cultural philosophy and medicine, *The Great Instauration*, has argued that the key to understanding the Puritan concern with science is the millennial idea of progress. Unfortunately, millennial expectations cannot be used to distinguish between Puritans and non-Puritans. Furthermore, as we saw earlier, the kind of reforms sought after by the groups Webster discusses, by his own admission, contributed very little to the 'Scientific Revolution' as it is generally understood by historians of science and which is our concern here.[29]

The major rival to the Puritanism-and-science thesis emphasizes the role of Latitudinarian Anglicanism in stimulating late seventeenth-century natural philosophy.[30] This fares little better than the earlier thesis from the prosopographical point of view; whether someone is to be considered a Latitudinarian Anglican is almost as open to interpretation as judging Puritans. The clear advantage here, however, is that it is possible to understand why Latitudinarianism might have proved amenable to, and encouraging of, work in natural philosophy. Latitudinarianism embraced a particular kind of theological epistemology and methodology as the safest way of ensuring salvation and both the epistemology and the method was carried over into studies of God's other book, the natural world. A further advantage of this thesis is that, once the link between theological and natural-philosophical approaches is recognized, it becomes easy to extend this beyond the ranks of alleged Latitudinarians and so escape the prosopographical objection. The epistemology and methodology of the Latitudinarians are characteristic of them, but were not confined exclusively to their ranks; to a greater or lesser extent the same precepts were advocated by all the major factions of the English Reformed Church. In order to understand this we must begin with a brief account of the Church in England.

It is generally accepted that Anglicanism is best characterized not as a fixed and fully worked-out system of theology but as a tendency, a set of rules designed to point believers in the right direction. As one church historian has put it, Anglicanism is 'not a theology but a theological method'.[31] Furthermore, this methodology was worked out in response to tensions between the Anglo-Catholicism which was a legacy of the Henrician Reformation (the only reformation which did not have its origin in doctrinal differences with the Roman Church), and English Lutheran and Calvinist reformers. The Protestant Reformation in England did not really begin until Edward VI's reign, and the issuing of the Forty-two Articles under Archbishop Thomas Cranmer (1553). These Articles formed the basis of the Elizabethan Thirty-nine Articles (1563), drawn up after the Catholic intermezzo of Mary's reign. But the Articles were by no means intended to provide a comprehensive and fully competent account of Anglican doctrine. Both sets of Articles were intended as a guide only on those controversial matters which separated Catholics and Reformers. The express aim of Cranmer's Forty-two was 'for avoiding of controversy in opinions, and the establishment of a godly concord, in certain matters of religion'. Similarly, the Thirty-nine Articles were intended to indicate the basis for agreement on controversial issues such as the authority of the Church, the means of justification, 'Of Works before Justification', predestination, the validity of the Seven Sacraments, and the real presence of the Body and Blood of Christ in the Eucharist. They cannot be seen as the equivalent of Calvin's *Institutes*, since they are highly selective in their coverage and, in spite of their supposedly deterministic role in controversy, are often so abruptly stated that their meaning is obscure and equivocal. They do not display anything like the definitive rigour to which Calvin aspired.[32]

This was the result of deliberate policy. Born out of tensions between conservative Anglo-Catholics and radical Reformers, the Anglican Church was conceived as a means of uniting the two extremes. Faced on each side by the extremes of Romanism and Calvinism, both of which laid claims to truth based on rigorous and 'irrefutable' logic, the constructors of Anglicanism sought a *via media*. Inevitably, there were those, principally among the radicals, who saw this as mere compromise.

Some apocalyptic commentators regarded the English Church as the 'luke-warm', Laodicean Church, mentioned (in unfavourable terms) in the *Revelation of St John* (3:14–16). For committed Anglicans, however, the Elizabethan compromise was the *aurea mediocritas*, the golden mean. Not just a means of sitting on the fence, the middle way revealed that elements which seemed contradictory were, in fact, complementary, mutually illuminating and cross-fertilizing. The approach was seen as a liberation from the narrow concerns of men to universal truths of God. For Bishop Lancelot Andrewes, for example, the Calvinist *Lambeth Articles* of 1595 raised problems for the faith that seemed incapable of solution. Few people were capable of handling them, much less of profiting by them, and so it was safer for one's salvation to concentrate on universally accepted matters of the faith.[33]

Influenced strongly by the German Reformer, Martin Bucer (who spent the last months of his life in England, as Edward VI's Regius Professor of Divinity at Cambridge), the founders of Anglicanism came to share not only his desire for ecumenism, but also his beliefs about the best way to avoid dissension and promote unity. Accordingly, the Church of England embraced Bucer's notion of *adiaphora*, things which are indifferent to salvation, and therefore to faith. So, the laconic nature of the Thirty-nine Articles was not due to the authors' failure of nerve, much less to failure of intellect; it was the result of a deliberate policy of doctrinal minimalism. The success of their enterprise can be gleaned from the fact that historians have tended to emphasize the Calvinist elements of the Articles (and have no trouble doing so), while Christopher Davenport, alias Franciscus a Sancta Clara, in his *Deus, natura, gratia* (1634), could use the Articles to argue that there were no serious doctrinal differences separating Anglicans from Romanists.[34]

The hallmark of Anglicanism, then, was the ability to steer a middle course between Rome and Geneva by insisting upon the distinction between what was fundamental for belief and what was not. Commitment to the ecumenical and irenical benefits of this approach caused a number of influential thinkers to gather together, in the troubled years of the 1630s, at the home of Lucius Cary, Viscount Falkland, who was himself said to have 'such a latitude of opinion, he believed nothing in the Church could not be dispensed with'. The so-called Great Tew Circle included Edward Hyde, William Chillingworth, Robert Sanderson, John Hales and Gilbert Sheldon, and its subsequent influence on the course of Anglicanism can hardly be doubted. Reacting against the increasing clamour of Calvinistic Puritans and the supposed excessive Romanism of the Laudian Party, this circle of thinkers returned with renewed vigour to the original Anglican method of mediation. Their re-

emphasis of the distinction between fundamentals and non-funda-
mentals of belief gave rise to the Latitudinarian or Low Church Party
which was to prove so successful in the Restoration. The aim of
Latitudinarianism was to determine the method for establishing the
minimum requirements for the true faith.[35]

William Chillingworth, perhaps the greatest theologian in the circle,
insisted that 'nothing is necessary to be believed, but what is plainly
revealed'. It is important to note, however, that by 'revealed' he did not
simply mean what is written in the Bible – he was no biblical
fundamentalist. For Chillingworth, some things were plainly revealed to
us by our commonsense or by our intuitions. 'Unity of opinion', he
believed, would follow from 'right reason, grounded on divine revelation
and common notions written by God in the hearts of all men'. But it was
perfectly obvious, given the amount of disagreement between the
different confessions and sects, that the 'common notions' were limited
in number. It was clear, for example, that divine scripture could not be
taken in its entirety as an unproblematic source of what must be
believed. Similarly, the 'hearts' of men did not necessarily provide a sure
guide, and nor did man's reason.[36]

The trouble with 'reason', as was clear from the fact that both
Calvinists and Papists could claim it for their side, was that it could be
made to subserve virtually any cause. So, the use of reason came to be
regarded as thoroughly untrustworthy. Subtlety of reasoning was
beguiling and treacherous. And yet intelligent and highly educated men
did not want to reject rationality altogether – that way madness lies.
The result, therefore, was a distinction between 'reason' and 'right
reason'. There is much talk of both of these among seventeenth-century
English intellectuals and it is important to understand what was meant.
Of course, much of the distinction is merely rhetorical: one man's 'right
reason' is another man's 'corrupt reason'. But it is not just that. There
is a discernible consistency in the use of 'right reason' by contemporary
writers, which suggests that it was used (no doubt naively) to mean what
we might call 'common-sense' arguments, claims which were 'obviously' true without having to indulge in the complex, and therefore
suspect, intellectual manoeuvring of mathematicians, logicians, or
scholastics. In general, Chillingworth and the other members of the
Great Tew Circle strove to avoid 'disputation', by which they meant the
formal, technical dialectic of scholastic debate. They always regarded
such disputation as a means of exacerbating the differences between
people rather than dissolving them. It was this overriding desire to avoid
religious dispute which led them to adopt a position of doctrinal
minimalism and to defend this, in turn, by recourse to a sceptical

epistemology in which 'moral certainty' was the best that could be hoped for and all that was required. Moral certainty was 'a firm and undoubted assent to a thing upon such grounds as are fit fully to satisfy a prudent man'. Prudence, with its pragmatic concerns, was safer and more reliable than subtle reasoning.[37]

Although the Great Tew Circle can be seen as the precursor of Latitudinarianism it is clear that they were only extending the mediating attitudes that had been introduced into the Church of England by Calvinistically inclined Church leaders during the reigns of Edward and Elizabeth. This irenic attitude, deep-seated and pervasive in English reformed religion and its rhetoric, can be discerned through all the subsequent vicissitudes of the English Church. It even underlies, for example, Cromwell's famous query and plea to the General Assembly of the Kirk of Scotland: 'Is it therefore infallibly agreeable to the Word of God, all that you say? I beseech you, in the bowels of Christ, think it possible you may be mistaken.'[38] But what has this to do with natural philosophy? Why should a theology of compromise (opposed to dogmatism, particularly where chains of disputatious reasoning have to be recurred to, and embracing instead a position of doctrinal mini-malism) affect contemporary natural philosophy?

In order to understand the close links between developments in theology and in natural philosophy we must first remind ourselves that natural philosophy, ever since the thirteenth century in Western Europe, had always been regarded as a 'handmaiden' to the 'Queen' of the sciences, theology. The routine use of natural philosophy, throughout the Middle Ages, for what we might now regard as ideological purposes did nothing to compromise the integrity of natural philosophy. While there was only 'one holy Catholic and Apostolic Church' it seemed perfectly natural, since Truth is indivisible, that the truths of natural philosophy should be compatible or coincident with the truths of religion. After the Reformation, however, natural philosophy came to be used by different factions to support their particular interpretation of the truth. Natural philosophy increasingly came to be seen as a special site for the development of complex chains of reasonings, sometimes even using mathematics, to dupe and beguile the unwary into accepting a false religion.

The close connection between Catholic theology and Aristotelian natural philosophy, brought to everyone's attention by the Galileo affair, led many Englishmen to distrust scholasticism. Thomas Hobbes, for example, pointed out that 'the study of Philosophy it hath no otherwise place, then as a handmaid to the Romane Religion: And...that study is not properly Philosophy, but Aristotelity', while

Joseph Glanvill argued that Aristotle had become an 'Oracle' because the schoolmen had mingled his philosophy with divinity. Similarly, Thomas Sprat in his *History of the Royal Society* emphasized the confusing use of wordy argumentation by Catholic scholastics so that in philosophy, as in religion, men 'were forc'd in all things to depend on the Lips of the Roman Clergy'.[39]

For other English thinkers, however, it was the so-called 'new philosophy' that threatened to undermine the true religion of Englishmen. As Thomas Barlow, later to be the Bishop of Lincoln, remarked, 'the great Writers and Promoters of' the new philosophy were 'of the Roman Religion: (such as Des Cartes, Gassendus, Du Hamel, Maurus, Mersennus, De Mellos, &c.)'. Barlow described how he inquired of friends in Catholic Europe 'whether the Jesuites, in their Colleges, train'd up their young men in the New-Philosophy; or whether (in all their Disputations) they kept them to strict form, and Aristotle's way of ratiocination?' In all cases he received the same answer:

> That none were more strict than they, in keeping all their young men, to the old principles and forms of Disputation. For they well know, that all their Schoolmen, Casuists and Controversy-Writers have so mix'd Aristotle's Philosophy with their Divinity; that he who has not a comprehension of Aristotle's Principles, and the use of them, in all Scholastick Disputes, and Controversies of Religion, will never be able rationally to defend or confute any controverted position, in the Roman or Reformed Religion.[40]

Meric Casaubon was convinced that Descartes' encouragement to systematic doubting was one of the most 'rare inventions to raise the expectations of the credulous, and in the end to send them away pure Quacks or arrand Quakers'. The technique was the same as that of 'Jesuited Puritans', that is, those Jesuits who pretended to be Protestant sectarians in order to confuse and undermine the reformed churches.[41]

Distrust of natural philosophy, whether traditional or new, was running high and any attempt to argue for one at the expense of the other was liable to be seen as a disingenuous subterfuge for purposes of religious (and therefore political) subversion. What was required was a middle way, and one that avoided dogmatism and reliance upon chains of disputatious reasonings. Instead, it should be based upon a mitigated sceptical epistemology, affirming only those propositions which could be seen to be immediately and undeniably true. It must, therefore, eschew speculative theorizing as much as possible and be doctrinally minimalist. In short, if the handmaiden of theology was to regain its integrity as a safe means of determining the truth about the Book of Nature, it had to pursue the same methods which were judged to be the safest means of recovering the true Church and establishing, in Jeremy Taylor's words, what 'will save a man...though it be not infallible'.[42]

It would be a serious mistake to imagine, even for a moment, that English natural philosophers thus embarked upon a conspiracy to turn natural philosophy, by hook or by crook, into an ideological scheme for promoting Anglicanism. This would be like saying that the 'golden mean' of English theology was developed by theologians from Cranmer and Bucer to Chillingworth and Wilkins as a cynical exercise in trying to maintain control of the English Church. There can be no doubt that the theologians who developed the Anglican method of theology really did see it as the best means of restoring the original Christian teachings of the 'Primitive Church', and therefore of establishing the safe way to salvation, and the only way to bring about peace and unity in the Reformed Church. Furthermore, the leading natural philosophers of seventeenth-century England, whatever the precise details of their own personal theologies, were almost to a man convinced of the validity of this very English approach to resolving the difficulties of the reformed Church. This in itself makes it perfectly understandable that they should adopt and adapt (perhaps unconsciously, and certainly as the result of discussion and dispute with colleagues) the prevailing theological epistemology and methodology to their natural philosophy. The aim of irenicism in theology was not merely to arrive at an interim position until something better came along, it was the only sure way to approach the truth. An analogous irenicism in natural philosophy was regarded in the same light.

English natural philosophers rejected a slavish adherence to the word of authority, be it Aristotle or Descartes, just as English theologians rejected the authority of the Pope. Moreover, the philosophers followed the theologians' lead in rejecting logical disputation and so-called apodictic reasoning. 'Reason is nothing but interest', wrote James Harrington, 'there be divers interests and so divers reasons.' Reason had been so abused by different factions in the recent past that almost any claim to its support might prove counter-productive. Emphasis on reason was all too likely to be seen as just another cheat, serving special interests. This is where 'right reason' came in. The trick was to invoke a 'common-sense' view of rationality which was obvious to everyone. 'I affirm nothing', Jeremy Taylor wrote, 'but upon...right reason discernible by every disinterested person.' The conclusions of 'right reason' were not apodictic but much more immediately ineluctable. The immediacy of 'right reason' enabled it to avoid what Walter Charleton called the 'unconstant, variable and seductive imposture of Reason, which he saw as 'the onely unhappy Cause, to which Religion doth owe all those wide, irreconcileable and numerous rents and schismes'. Even here, if reasoning is to be avoided in religion, so it should be in science also. 'Arguing, concluding, defining, judging, and all other degrees of Reason', wrote Robert Hooke, 'are lyable to the same imperfection, being, at best, either vain, or uncertain.'[43]

This proscription against 'meddling with...Metaphysics...or Logick', led Latitudinarians to aspire towards doctrinal minimalism, and here again we can see the natural philosophers professing to do the same. Sprat insisted that the Royal Society was very 'backward from setling of Principles, or fixing upon Doctrines', so much so, in fact, that 'we should grant that they have wholly omitted Doctrines'.[44] Perhaps the best example of this kind of doctrinal minimalism, in order to avoid disputes about *adiaphora*, things indifferent, can be seen in Robert Boyle's refusal to commit himself to Cartesian or Gassendist matter theory. What separated the two schools, according to Boyle, were merely speculative or 'metaphysical' notions, but otherwise 'they might be thought to agree in the main, and their hypotheses might... be looked on as...one philosophy'. He took a similar line with regard to vacuum: refusing to discuss the metaphysical issue of the possibility of space without body, he spoke only of *vacuum Boylianum*, which he defined instrumentally.[45]

The Royal Society's undoubted success in persuading contemporaries that its method almost 'wholly omitted doctrines' stemmed from its spokesmen's constantly reiterated claims that the Fellows deal only with 'matters of fact' – not with the interpretation of those facts, but merely with their establishment. Sprat describes a typical meeting in which, after one or two of the Fellows have performed an experiment, the Assembly takes over to perform its function: 'which is to judg, and resolve upon the matter of Fact'. The Company, according to Sprat, is only concerned with 'the plain objects of their eyes', and not with involved and tendentious interpretations of the experiments. It should be noticed, however, that Sprat revealingly admits that the matter of fact revealed by any experiment has to be judged and decided upon. This emphasis on 'matters of fact', as Paul Wood has argued, was an important element in the irenic ambitions of the natural philosophers who shaped the early Royal Society, and, as Steven Shapin and Simon Schaffer have shown, it became a powerful resource for establishing the objectivity and disinterestedness of the new science.[46]

The English emphasis on 'matters of fact' may have been made most explicit and used to greatest promotional effect by the Royal Society after the Restoration but it can be discerned far earlier, of course, in the enthusiasm for Baconianism. Ideally suited to the eschewing of doctrines,

Bacon's experiments were intended to establish facts for gathering into natural histories. The histories, drawn up in 'Tables of Discovery', were to serve as a basis for the discovery of causes and axioms, but the particular experiments were to be 'of no use in themselves'. This restrictive notion of experiment was essential, Bacon believed, to avoid 'the premature hurry of the understanding to leap or fly to universals and principles of things'.[47]

It would seem, therefore, that there is a great deal of truth underlying Sprat's rhetorical claims in *The History of the Royal Society* that the Church and the natural philosophy of England 'arose on the Same Method'. 'This will be evident', Sprat wrote, 'when we behold the agreement that is between the present Design of the Royal Society, and that of our Church in its beginning.' As we have now seen, they were both anti-dogmatic, rejected disputation and arguments based on complex chains of reasoning, adopted a mitigated sceptical epistemology, and professed themselves to be doctrinally minimalist. English science was not stimulated exclusively by the Puritan wing of the Church, nor by the Latitudinarians, but by a much more general tendency in English reformed religion. As Sprat put it:

> Though I cannot carry the Institution of the Royal Society many years back, yet the seeds of it were sown in King Edward the Sixth's, and Queen Elizabeths Reign: And ever since that time Experimental Learning has still retaind some vital heat, though it wanted the opportunities of ripening itself, which now it injoys. The Church of England therefore may justly be styl'd the Mother of this sort of Knowledge.[48]

By the end of the seventeenth century it was clear that English church leaders had failed to bring about the restoration of the so-called Primitive Church of the early Christians, before it had been corrupted by Romanists and over-zealous Reformers. English natural philosophy, however, not directly affected by the contingencies of state which brought about the Clarendon Code, the Glorious Revolution and other political developments, was able to flourish. The efforts of the former 'handmaiden' to present herself as 'indifferent' to the finer, or more controversial, points of both religion and natural philosophy, to reject dogmatic and uncertain doctrines, and to insist upon only obvious and plain truths to which all men could assent, although modelled on the parallel efforts of churchmen, led not just to a new image of science, but also to a new style of doing science. No longer the handmaiden, whose role was to serve religion, science was now seen to be an unbiased, ideologically neutral, and therefore a safe and trustworthy means of establishing the truth about the natural world. This was a scientific revolution in itself and it surely accounts for the intense interest in seventeenth-century English natural philosophy by the French *philosophes* and subsequent philosophers and historians of science. The success of this new style of science can be seen in countless examples, such as Charles Darwin's proud claim in his *Autobiography* (1876) that he 'worked on true Baconian principles, and without any theory collected facts on a wholesale scale'.[49] But perhaps the greatest measure of its success is the fact that most people, scientist and non-scientist alike, even to this day believe that natural science is ideologically neutral, unbiased and objective.

Let us be clear about the historiographical implications of this view of the links between science and religion. In a sense it can be seen as an exercise in historiographical irenicism. The initial focus on Puritanism as the driving force behind the English Scientific Revolution has always been unconvincing because too many of the 'Puritans' seemed to be Anglicans. This problem was exacerbated by the fact that much of Merton's evidence derived from a survey of the members of the Royal Society – an organization not founded until after the Restoration. Charles Webster has recently acknowledged that 'quantitative methods' are so fraught with difficulty that they will never be able to 'carry as much weight as our present impressionistic assessment'. The trouble is: one man's impressionistic assessment is another man's biased viewpoint.[50]

Providing we accept, however, that the link between religion and natural philosophy did not depend upon a particular set of theological doctrines but rather on a method of arriving at the 'safe way to salvation' we can see the more general affiliation between science and religion. As Hugh Kearney has pointed out, all the factions of the English Reformed Church (with the exception of extreme radical sects) shared a common 'vision of what the Church of Christ ought to be if it were stripped of externals and inessentials'.[51] It can hardly be denied that there were considerable differences between the factions as to just what was external and inessential, but the methodology of sceptical epistemology, anti-dogmatism and doctrinal minimalism was generally acknowledged. Merton, Webster and others, such as Dorothy Stimson and Christopher Hill, were correct in their impressions that Puritanism, loosely defined, had something to do with the flourishing of natural philosophy in seventeenth-century England but it was only part of the picture.[52]

Likewise, Barbara Shapiro was correct to point to Latitudinarianism. But the Latitudinarians only emphasized what was already a strong current in English reformed theology and once again their contribution should be seen as only partial. It is perhaps significant also that church

historians tend to attribute the weakened state of the Anglican Church
in the eighteenth century to the success of the Latitudinarian party at the
end of the seventeenth century. It was at this time that the image of the
Anglican as tantamount to an unbeliever (which, by the way, is still
widely held among many non-Anglican Christians) first became current.
Bearing this in mind we can see why Lotte Mulligan, attributing 'The
predominance of Anglicans in post-Restoration society... to religious
indifference', might have been led to conclude that 'science correlated
less with puritanism or latitudinarianism than with the waning role of
religion.'[53]

Although Anglicanism and particularly Latitudinarianism played a
major role in showing how natural philosophy could shake off its old
image as a mere handmaiden to religion and establish itself as a
supposedly safe way of generating undeniable truths, it was no by means
the only element in the story. It is important to reiterate that what the
natural philosophers borrowed from the English Protestant Reformation
tradition were merely methodological principles which seemed to offer
the best hope of settling disputes and arriving at 'truth'. There is no
reliable evidence, in spite of the efforts of James and Margaret Jacob and
others, to show that the new philosophy was established upon 'a
metaphysics of God and matter' which was 'produced for ideological
reasons' by Anglicans to help restore a stable monarchy and 'outlaw'
radicalism and republicanism.[54] Apart from anything else this thesis
displays the worst faults of an exclusively externalist approach to the
history of science. It utterly fails to acknowledge the dynamics of how
scientific knowledge is arrived at. The implications of the Jacobs thesis
seems to be that Boyle, for example, deliberately forged a particular
account of the physical world in order to promote a specific politico-
religious ideology. Such an artificially constructed account of the
physical world could succeed only with thinkers who shared Boyle's
ideology (or who joined with him in a conspiracy), and so the Jacobs
have had to insist upon the ideological unanimity of the Royal Society.
Their insistence upon this last point, as Michael Hunter has shown,
cannot be supported by the evidence.[55]

Michael Hunter's own view of the early Royal Society is so finely
textured that he would also deny the existence of a unified methodological approach of the kind described in this essay. Certainly there was
dissent within the Society (again parallel with debates in religion) about
the best method for establishing truth, but there can be little doubt
that the successes of Royal Society science, particularly as they were
exemplified by Boyle and Newton, and as they were presented by
Oldenburg in his extensive correspondence and in *Philosophical Trans-*

actions, owed a great deal to their anti-dogmatic 'Baconian' methodology of 'doctrinal minimalism'. Part of the aim of this, as we have seen, was to seem to remove natural philosophy from its former role as servant to the ideology of religion. Where the Royal Society or individual fellows made statements about the religious uses of their natural philosophy they tended to be apologetic, defending their natural philosophy against charges of being irreligious or subversive of the Church of England, rather than positively ideological. Even so, this seemingly ideologically neutral natural philosophy could be used as a powerful resource for supporting religion, and in particular the religion of those who most emphasized the values of anti-dogmatism and doctrinal minimalism – namely, the Latitudinarians.[56] The Jacobs view of the ideological uses of the new philosophy was not unfounded, therefore, but their presentation of the mechanical philosophy as a self-consciously produced political tool is rather wide of the mark.

In a short essay we must confine ourselves to an impressionistic view of the links between science and religion, and not all historians will agree with our impressions. There are more detailed accounts of the close similarities between the method of English theology and English natural philosophy in Henry van Leeuwen's *The Problem of Certainty in English Thought* and in Barbara Shapiro's *Probability and Certainty in Seventeenth-Century England*, although both concentrate unduly upon Anglican thought. Shapiro's account takes natural philosophy as its starting point and misses, therefore, the fact that the probabilism which she discerns in many aspects of early modern intellectual life stems from the anti-dogmatism and sceptical epistemology developed by English Reformers seeking a middle way between the essentially unreformed Church of Henry VIII and the Calvinism of more radical theologians. Nevertheless, her scholarship has provided us with the fullest account so far of the links between contemporary religious and scientific methodology in England. It is hoped, anyway, that the brief account given here can be used to help refine our understanding of the development of natural philosophy in England. Once we accept the prevalence of this characteristically English theological method across all shades of opinion in the English Reformed Church, we can see why some historians associated it with Puritanism, others with Anglicanism, and others with a rise in what they took to be religious 'indifference'. This thesis, unlike that of Merton, cannot be undermined by exercises in 'headcounting'. In the first place, it is easy to see that with regard to this irenic tradition of English theology a Latitudinarian like John Wilkins, a staunch royalist and Anglican like Walter Charleton, the rather more 'Puritanical' Robert Boyle and John Wallis, and the more radical reformers

Samuel Hartlib and John Dury, to pick just a few examples, could all be
in agreement. In the second place, this argument does not depend upon
prosopographical statistics but on a putative *explanation* of how theology
affected natural philosophy. Even if only a small minority of English
natural philosophers embraced and advocated in natural philosophy the
same kind of sceptical epistemology and doctrinal minimalism they saw
in contemporary English theology, the fact remains that the rhetoric and
the reality of this new methodology came to be seen, by French
Enlightenment *philosophes* and later by historians, as the reason for
England's great achievements in science. Moreover, because our claims
are concerned with the origins of a specific scientific methodology which
can be shown to have an intimate connection with the detailed scientific
conclusions that were reached, they are not vulnerable to the charge that
they pay insufficient attention to 'internal' technical demands upon
scientific theory and practice. The scientific methodology described here
was characteristically English; it is hard to see how it could have
developed this way unless it was inspired by the characteristic methodology of English theologians' attempts to find the safe way to salvation.

CONCLUSION

We have seen that science in England was most successfully carried out
in loosely organized groups which emphasized experimental approaches
to natural knowledge. Whether the impetus towards these groupings
and their methods stemmed from patrons like Henry Percy or the
Cavendish brothers with an interest in living the Renaissance ideal of the
vita activa, or from the nature of the subjects under scrutiny (not even the
most traditional thinker of the day would believe that alchemy or
anatomy and physiology could be pursued without empirical investigation), or from millenarian ambitions about the improvement of man's
lot, or simply as a diversion from the tribulations of politics and religion,
the fact remains that their experimental enterprises could easily be
accommodated to efforts to establish the safe way to generate new
knowledge which were inspired by parallel efforts in religion to establish
the 'safe way to salvation'. All these factors mutually encouraged and
reinforced the development of English science with its emphasis on
Baconian fact gathering, and empiricism. The overall result was the
establishment, as Robert Hooke said, of 'the *real*, the *mechanical*, the
experimental Philosophy'.[57]

These factors also help to explain why it was that English natural
philosophers were willing to entertain, to a much greater extent than
Continental philosophers, causes that were not strictly mechanical in

their operations, including attractions and repulsions, and chemical and even vitalistic notions. Cartesian attempts to give a theoretical explanation of magnetic and gravitational attractions and other experimentally demonstrable phenomena were regarded as far too speculative. The simple matter of fact, in such cases, was that magnets have an attractive virtue, or that the wall of the stomach has a perceptive faculty, and so on.[58] Moreover, to deny that bodies could have intrinsic energy, motive faculties, gravitational attraction and the like was not only to deny experimental matters of fact, it was also to elevate dogmatic prejudice above undeniable sensory experience. When Newton declaimed, in the 'General Scholium' which he added to the second edition of his *Principia mathematica* in 1713, that hypotheses 'have no place in experimental philosophy', he made no distinction between kinds of hypothetical explanation, 'whether metaphysical or physical, whether of occult qualities or mechanical'. Freely admitting that he had not been able to discover the cause of gravity 'from phenomena', he unabashedly wrote that 'to us it is enough that gravity does really exist...and abundantly serves to account for all the motions of the celestial bodies and of our sea.'[59] For him, gravitational attraction was an irrefutable matter of fact. Moreover, as we have seen, Newton's initial realization that gravitational attraction could most fruitfully be dealt with as a simple 'matter of fact' was inspired by his own alchemical research, and by the experimental tradition of the 'magneticall philosophers' as communicated to him by Robert Hooke.

It seems clear, therefore, that in order to understand what has been called the 'Newtonian style' of natural philosophy, his methodology and the way that he presented his work to his contemporaries, we must consider not just the technical advances in mathematics and in experimental science which preceded his own work but also the efforts of his older contemporaries to arrive at what they took to be a safe way of generating natural knowledge, free from the ideological associations of Aristotelianism or the kind of mechanical philosophy being propagated by Cartesians or Hobbists.[60] Moreover, if we wish to go beyond Newton's method and try to reach an understanding of how he arrived at the details of his natural philosophy, we must combine our studies of his experiments, his mathematics and his philosophizing, with a microsociological study of his interactions with his peer-group, as well as the broader concerns of the English scientific culture of which he was a part. The overt introduction into his system of attractive and repulsive forces operating at a distance, for example, depended not only upon his private convictions about the import of alchemical experiments, but also upon his awareness that analogous ideas were being discussed in London by

Hooke, Wren, Halley and other members of the Royal Society, and by his realization that the invocation of such forces could be defended on sound methodological grounds which were in harmony with the teachings of religion. It is by no means fatuous to assert that the *Principia mathematica*, in many ways a culminating achievement of the Scientific Revolution, could only have been written by an Englishman.

NOTES

1 Charles Webster, 'Puritanism, Separatism, and Science', in D. C. Lindberg and R. L. Numbers (eds), *God and Nature: Historical Essays on the Encounter between Christianity and Science* (Berkeley, 1986), 192–217, p. 197. B. Hessen, 'The Social and Economic Roots of Newton's "Principia"', in *Science at the Cross Roads* (London, 1931; 2nd edn 1971); Robert K. Merton, 'Science, Technology and Society in Seventeenth Century England', *Osiris* 4 (1938), 360–632; reprinted as a book (New York, 1970; repr. Atlantic Highlands, N. J. and Hassocks, Sussex, 1978).

2 Hessen, 'Social and Economic Roots', pp. 170, 155.

3 Webster, 'Puritanism, Separatism and Science', p. 199. For Merton's Weberian roots see Max Weber, *The Protestant Ethic and the Spirit of Capitalism*, (trans. Talcott Parsons, London, 1930).

4 Charles Webster, *The Great Instauration: Science, Medicine and Reform 1626–1660* (London, 1975), pp. 517, 520.

5 Hessen, 'Social and Economic Roots', p. 204; Merton, *Science, Technology and Society* (1970), pp. 80–111.

6 Edgar Zilsel, 'The Origins of William Gilbert's Scientific Method, *Journal of the History of Ideas* 2 (1941), 1–32, p. 5. William Gilbert, *De magnete*, (trans. P. Fleury Mottelay, New York, 1958), p. 314.

7 A. Rupert Hall, 'Merton Revisited, or Science and Society in the Seventeenth Century', *History of Science* 2 (1963), 1–16, p. 15.

8 See, for example, Steven Shapin and Simon Schaffer, *Leviathan and the Air Pump: Hobbes, Boyle and the Experimental Life* (Princeton, 1985); and R. G. Frank, Jr, *Harvey and the Oxford Physiologists: Scientific Ideas and Social Interaction* (Berkeley, 1980). Further examples, together with commentaries which expand the discussion given here can be seen in S. Shapin, 'History of Science and its Sociological Reconstructions', *History of Science* 20 (1982), 157–211; and Jan Golinski, 'The Theory of Practice and the Practice of Theory: Sociological Approaches in the History of Science', *Isis* 81 (1990), 492–505. For a theoretical discussion of the internal/external distinction see Barry Barnes, *Scientific Knowledge and Sociological Theory* (London, 1974), pp. 99–124.

9 John Aubrey, *Brief Lives*, ed. Andrew Clark, 2 vols. (Oxford, 1898), ii, pp. 285–6. Anthony Wood, *Athenae Oxonienses* (2nd edn, 4 vols. (London, 1721), i, col. 460. Cf. John W. Shirley, *Thomas Harriot, a Biography* (Oxford, 1983). Jean Jacquot, 'Harriot, Hill, Warner and the New Philosophy', in J. W. Shirley (ed.), *Thomas Harriot, Renaissance Scientist* (Oxford, 1974), 107–28; Jean Jacquot, 'Sir Charles Cavendish and his Learned Friends', *Annals of Science* 8 (1952), 13–27, 175–91; R. G. Frank, *Harvey and the Oxford Physiologists* (Berkeley, 1980).

10 See Jacquot, 'Harriot, Hill, Warner, pp. 124–5, 120–4; [John Wilkins and Seth Ward], *Vindiciae Academiarum* (Oxford, 1654), p. 53; H. P. Bayon, 'Allusions to a "Circulation" of the Blood in Manuscripts anterior to *De motu cordis*', *Proceedings of the Royal Society of Medicine* 32 (1938/9), 707–18, pp. 711–12; Charles Webster, 'Harvey's Conception of the Heart as a Pump', *Bulletin of the History of Medicine* 39 (1965), 508–17, p. 516. R. Lenoble, *Mersenne, ou la naissance du mécanisme* (Paris, 1943).

11 Thomas Hobbes, *Thomas White's* De mundo *examined* (ed. H. W. Jones, Bradford, 1976), p. 101; Walter Warner, British Library Additional MSS 4394, fo. 138ʳ.

12 See John Henry 'Occult Qualities and the Experimental Philosophy: Active Principles in pre-Newtonian Matter Theory', *History of Science* 24 (1986), 335–81; and John Henry, 'Medicine and Pneumatology: Henry More, Richard Baxter, and Francis Glisson's *Treatise on the Energetic Nature of Substance*', *Medical History* 31 (1987), 15–40.

13 Stephen Pumfrey, 'Magnetical Philosophy and Astronomy, 1600–1650'; and J. A. Bennett, 'Magnetical Philosophy and Astronomy from Wilkins to Hooke', both in René Taton and Curtis Wilson (eds.), *The General History of Astronomy, Vol. 2: Planetary Astronomy from the Renaissance to the Rise of Astrophysics, Part A: Tycho Brahe to Newton* (Cambridge, 1989), pp. 45–53 and 222–30; J. A. Bennett, 'Cosmology and the Magnetical Philosophy, 1640–1680', *Journal of the History of Astronomy* 12 (1981), 165–77; and R. S. Westfall, *Never at Rest: A Biography of Isaac Newton* (Cambridge, 1980), pp. 382–8.

14 Westfall, *Never at Rest*, pp. 286–301; 304–8.

15 Isaac Newton, *Papers and Letters on Natural Philosophy* (ed. I. B. Cohen, Cambridge, Mass., 1978), pp. 178–99; *idem, Opticks* (repr. with preface by I. B. Cohen, New York, 1952), p. 374. A. R. Hall and M. B. Hall (eds.), *Unpublished Scientific Papers of Isaac Newton* (Cambridge, 1962), pp. 214–28. Cf. Westfall, *Never at Rest*, pp. 374–5.

16 On the Towneley Circle see Charles Webster, 'Richard Towneley (1629–1707), the Towneley Group, and Seventeenth-Century Science, *Transactions of the Historic Society of Lancashire and Cheshire* 118 (1966), 51–76. On the Welsh group see Shirley, *Thomas Harriot*, pp. 388–414.

17 J. A. Bennett, 'The Mechanics' Philosophy and the Mechanical Philosophy', *History of Science* 24 (1986), 1–28. See also E. G. R. Taylor, *The Mathematical Practitioners of Tudor and Stuart England* (Cambridge, 1954); and Mordechai Feingold, *The Mathematicians' Apprenticeship: Science, Universities and Society in England, 1640–1650* (Cambridge, 1984).

18 Bacon, *Works*, 14 vols. (ed. J. Spedding *et al.*, London, 1857–74), IV, p. 125. Christopher Wren, *Parentalia: Or Memoirs of the Family of the Wrens* (London, 1750), p. 221. Robert Hooke, *Micrographia* (London, 1665), pp. 12, 15–16, 21, 31–2. Isaac Newton, 'An Hypothesis explaining the Properties of Light' (1675), reprinted in I. B. Cohen (ed.), *Isaac Newton's Papers and Letters on Natural Philosophy* (Cambridge, Mass., 1978), p. 183.

19 P. M. Rattansi, 'Paracelsus and the Puritan Revolution', *Ambix* 11 (1963), 24–32; Theodore M. Brown, 'The College of Physicians and the Acceptance of Iatromechanism in England, 1665–95', *Bulletin of the History of Medicine* 44

(1970), 12–30. For another discussion of the importance of the College of Physicians see Charles Webster, 'The College of Physicians: "Solomon's House" in Commonwealth England', *Bulletin of the History of Medicine* 41 (1967), 393–412; and R. G. Frank, 'The Physician as Virtuoso in Seventeenth-Century England', in B. J. Shapiro and R. G. Frank, Jr, *English Scientific Virtuosi in the Sixteenth and Seventeenth Centuries* (Los Angeles, 1979), 57–114. On iatrochemists see A. G. Debus, *The English Paracelsians* (London, 1965); and H. J. Cook, 'The Society of Chemical Physicians, the New Philosophy and the Restoration Court', *Bulletin of the History of Medicine* 61 (1987), 61–77.

20 See Michael Hunter, *Establishing the New Science: The Experience of the Early Royal Society* (Woodbridge, Suffolk, 1989), particularly the chapter on 'Latitudinarianism and the 'Ideology' of the Early Royal Society: Thomas Sprat's *History of the Royal Society* (1667) Reconsidered', pp. 45–71.

21 René Descartes, *Discourse on Method* (1637), ch. 2.

22 See Webster, *Great Instauration*, pp. 51–7, 153–74. Thomas Sprat, *History of the Royal Society* (London, 1667), p. 53.

23 Webster, *Great Instauration, passim*. Michael Hunter, *Science and Society in Restoration England* (Cambridge, 1981), pp. 8–21.

24 J. Martin, *Francis Bacon, the State, and the Reform of Natural Philosophy* (Cambridge, 1991). Brian Vickers, 'Bacon's so-called "Utilitarianism": Sources and Influence', in Marta Fattori (ed.), *Francis Bacon: Terminologia e fortuna* (Rome, 1984), 281–313. Francis Bacon, *New Atlantis*, in *Works*, III, p. 156.

25 Webster, *Great Instauration*, pp. 57–67. M. Hunter, *Science and Society, passim*. Walter E. Houghton, Jr 'The History of Trades: Its Relation to Seventeenth-Century Thought', in P. P. Wiener and A. Noland (eds.), *Roots of Scientific Thought* (New York, 1957), 354–81.

26 Sprat, *History of the Royal Society*, p. 62.

27 Joseph Glanvill, *Plus Ultra* (London, 1668). Hunter, *Science and Society*, pp. 32–58. For indications of how Henry Oldenburg, secretary to the Society, tried to disseminate its founders' epistemological and methodological views in his correspondence see Michael Hunter, 'Promoting the New Science: Henry Oldenburg and the Early Royal Society', in *Establishing the New Science*, 245–60; and John Henry, 'The Origins of Modern Science: Henry Oldenburg's Contribution', *British Journal for the History of Science* 21 (1988), 103–10.

28 Merton, *Science, Technology and Society*. For an indication of the continuing influence of Merton and a full discussion of the literature it has generated see I. B. Cohen (ed.), *Puritanism and the Rise of Modern Science: The Merton Thesis* (New Brunswick and London, 1990).

29 Webster, *Great Instauration*, pp. 1–31, and 520.

30 B. J. Shapiro, 'Latitudinarianism and Science in Seventeenth-Century England', *Past and Present* 40 (1968), 16–41; Paul B. Wood, 'Methodology and Apologetics: Thomas Sprat's *History of the Royal Society*', *British Journal for the History of Science* 13 (1980), 1–26; Margaret C. Jacob and James R. Jacob, 'The Anglican Origins of Modern Science: The Metaphysical Foundations of the Whig Constitution', *Isis* 71 (1980), 251–67; Lotte Mulligan, 'Puritans and English Science: A Critique of Webster', *Isis* 71 (1980), 456–69.

31 H. R. McAdoo, *The Spirit of Anglicanism: A Survey of Anglican Theological Method*

in the Seventeenth Century (London, 1965), p. 1; see also P. E. More and F. L. Cross, *Anglicanism: The Thought and Practice of the Church of England* (London, 1935), pp. xx–xxi.

32 For a general history of the Reformation in England see A. G. Dickens, *The English Reformation* (London, 1964). The quotation describing Cranmer's Forty-two Articles is cited from Bernard M. G. Reardon, *Religious Thought in the Reformation* (London, 1981), p. 260, which should be consulted for a brief account of what doctrinal differences there were between the various factions.

33 Lancelot Andrewes, *Judgement of the Lambeth Articles*, cited from McAdoo, *Spirit of Anglicanism*, p. 30; see also p. 312.

34 C. Hopf, *Martin Bucer and the English Reformation* (Oxford, 1946). Franciscus a Santa Clara, *Deus, natura, gratia* (Lyons, 1634); see J. B. Dockery, *Christopher Davenport, Friar and Diplomat* (London, 1960).

35 The comment upon Falkland was given by his friend, Edward Hyde, later Earl of Clarendon, quoted from Victor D. Sutch, *Gilbert Sheldon, Architect of Anglican Survival, 1640–1675* (The Hague, 1973), p. 5. On the Great Tew Circle and the origins of Latitudinarianism see H. G. van Leeuwen, *The Problem of Certainty in English Thought, 1630–1690* (The Hague, 1963), McAdoo, *Spirit of Anglicanism*, pp. 1–23; R. R. Orr, *Reason and Authority: The Thought of William Chillingworth* (London, 1967); J. W. Packer, *The Transformation of Anglicanism, 1643–1660, with special reference to Henry Hammond* (Manchester, 1969); and Hugh Trevor-Roper, 'The Great Tew Circle', in *Catholics, Anglicans and Puritans: Seventeenth-Century Essays* (London, 1987), pp. 166–230.

36 Chillingworth quoted from McAdoo, *Spirit of Anglicanism*, p. 14.

37 On 'right reason' see Christopher Hill, '"Reason" and "Reasonableness"', in *Change and Continuity in Seventeenth-Century England* (London, 1974), 103–26; Robert Hoopes, *Right Reason in the English Renaissance* (Cambridge, Mass., 1962); and Mulligan, '"Reason", "Right Reason", and "Revelation" in Mid-Seventeenth-Century England', in Brian Vickers (ed.), *Occult and Scientific Mentalities in the Renaissance* (Cambridge, 1984), 375–401. The Definition of moral certainty is from John Tillotson, *Works* (9th edn., London, 1728), p. vi, cited from Leeuwen, *Problem of Certainty*, p. 37, which should be consulted for a full discussion of these matters. See also Barbara Shapiro, *Probability and Certainty in Seventeenth-Century England* (Princeton, 1983).

38 Letter to the General Assembly of the Kirk of Scotland, August 3, 1650. W. C. Abbott (ed.), *The Writings and Speeches of Oliver Cromwell* (Cambridge, Mass., 1939), II, p. 303.

39 Thomas Hobbes, *Leviathan* (London, 1655), Pt. IV, ch. 46, p. 370. Joseph Glanvill, 'Letter ... concerning Aristotle', in *Scire/i tuum nihil est: Or, the Author's Defence of the Vanity of Dogmatizing* (London, 1665), p. 79. Sprat, *History of the Royal Society*, p. 14, see also pp. 34–5. See also Joseph Glanvill, *Philosophia pia: Or, a discourse of the Religious Temper, and Tendencies of the Experimental Philosophy* (London, 1671), p. 44.

40 Letter from Barlow to 'Sir J. B.', written in 1675 and published in P. Pett (ed.), *The Genuine Remains of that Learned Prelate Dr Thomas Barlow* (London, 1693), pp. 157–9.

41 Meric Casaubon, *On Learning* (1667), published in M. R. G. Spiller, '*Concerning*

Natural Experimental Philosophie' : Meric Casaubon and the Royal Society (The Hague, 1980) pp. 195–214; p. 205, and 214. On English beliefs that Jesuits pretended to be sectaries, see p. 216. See also Casaubon, *Of Credulity and Incredulity in Things Natural, Civil and Divine* (London, 1668), p. 136. For a fuller account of the association of the new philosophy with Roman Catholicism see Spiller, *'Concerning Natural Experimental Philosophie'* and John Henry, 'Atomism and Eschatology: Catholicism and Natural Philosophy in the Interregnum', *British Journal for the History of Science* 15 (1982), 211–39.

42 John Tillotson, *Works*, (London, 1728), p. v, cited from van Leeuwen, *Problem of Certainty*, p. 44.

43 Jeremy Taylor, *Works* (ed. R. Heber, London, 1828), XI, p. 356, cited from McAdoo, *Spirit of Anglicanism*, p. 53. Walter Charleton, *A Ternary of Paradoxes* (London, 1650), sig. f2; Robert Hooke, *Micrographia* (London, 1665), sig. av. See also J. Glanvill, *The Vanity of Dogmatizing* (London, 1661), pp. 1–16; and Robert Boyle, *Works* (ed. Thomas Birch, 6 vols., London, 1772), IV, p. 164.

44 The unattributed quotation is quoted from C. R. Weld, *A History of the Royal Society* (London, 1848), I, p. 146, who claims it was written by Hooke. But see Michael Hunter and Paul B. Wood, 'Towards Solomon's House: Rival Strategies for Reforming the Early Royal Society', in Hunter, *Establishing the New Science*, 185–244; p. 242, n. 211. Sprat, *History of the Royal Society*, p. 107, see also pp. 31–2, 62.

45 Robert Boyle, *Works*, I, p. 356, and p. 10.

46 Sprat, *History of the Royal Society*, p. 99, see also p. 334. On the crucial importance of the 'matter of fact' in Royal Society rhetoric see Wood, 'Methodology and Apologetics', p. 18; Shapiro, *Probability and Certainty*, p. 20; McAdoo, *Spirit of Anglicanism*, p. 302; Peter Dear, '*Totius in verba*: Rhetoric and Authority in the Early Royal Society', *Isis* 76 (1985), 145–61; and especially Steven Shapin, 'Pump and Circumstance: Robert Boyle's Literary Technology', *Social Studies of Science* 14 (1984), 481–520; Steven Shapin and Simon Schaffer, *Leviathan and the Air Pump: Hobbes, Boyle and the Experimental Life* (Princeton, 1985).

47 Bacon, *Novum organum*, 2nd Part, Book I, Aphorism LXIV, in *Works*, IV, pp. 65, 95. See Sprat, *History of the Royal Society*, p. 108.

48 Sprat, *History of the Royal Society*, pp. 371, 372. The link between English theological method and the methodology of science has been noted before in Douglas S. Kemsley, 'Religious Influences in the Rise of Modern Science: A Review and Criticism, Particularly of the "Protestant-Puritan Ethic" Theory', *Annals of Science* 24 (1968), 199–226; and by Wood, 'Methodology and Apologetics'. Kemsley and Wood, however, seem to believe that the theological method can be identified exclusively with Anglicans; I am arguing that it was common to different factions and shades of opinion within the English Reformed Church as a whole.

49 Francis Darwin (ed.), *The Autobiography of Charles Darwin and Selected Letters* (New York, 1958), p. 42.

50 Webster, 'Puritanism, Separatism, and Science', p. 199.

51 H. F. Kearney, 'Puritanism and Science: Problems of Definition', *Past and Present* 31 (1965), reprinted in Webster (ed.), *The Intellectual Revolution of the Seventeenth Century* (London, 1974), 254–61; p. 256.

52 Dorothy Stimson, 'Puritanism and the New Philosophy in Seventeenth-Century England', *Bulletin of the Institute of the History of Medicine* 3 (1935), 321–34; Christopher Hill, *Intellectual Origins of the English Revolution* (Oxford, 1965). For a full bibliography see Cohen, *Puritanism and the Rise of Modern Science*, pp. 89–111.

53 Shapiro, 'Latitudinarianism and Science'; Mulligan, 'Puritans and English Science'.

54 Jacob and Jacob, 'Anglican Origins of Modern Science'.

55 See Hunter, 'Latitudinarianism and the "Ideology" of the Early Royal Society'.

56 Wood, 'Methodology and Apologetics'.

57 Hooke, *Micrographia*, sig. A2ʳ.

58 For a fuller account of these issues see Henry, 'Occult Qualities and the Experimental Philosophy'.

59 Isaac Newton, *Principia mathematica* (ed. F. Cajori, Berkeley, 1960), pp. 546–7.

60 I. B. Cohen, 'The *Principia*, Universal Gravitation, and the "Newtonian Style", in relation to the Newtonian Revolution in Science', in Z. Bechler (ed.), *Contemporary Newtonian Research* (Dordrecht, 1982), 21–108. For a discussion of the social, religious and intellectual background to the 'Newtonian style' see Henry, 'Occult Qualities and the Experimental Philosophy'. For a fuller discussion of how Newton presented his work to suit the aims and the rhetoric of the Royal Society propagandists see Dear, '*Totius in verba*'; and Simon Schaffer, 'Glass Works: Newton's Prisms and the Uses of Experiment', in David Gooding, Trevor Pinch and Simon Schaffer (eds.), *The Uses of Experiment: Studies in the Natural Sciences* (Cambridge, 1989), 67–104.

8

THE SCIENTIFIC REVOLUTION IN BOHEMIA

JOSEF SMOLKA

'HISTORIANS write about scientific revolutions as automatically as of political, economic or social revolutions' – these are the words with which Roy Porter began his stimulating deliberation on the Scientific Revolution.[1] He is right, of course. Thanks to the intensive work of historians of science over the recent decades, the concept of Scientific Revolution has become deeply embedded in the consciousness of current historiography.

Nevertheless, we shall be going back to the concept of Scientific Revolution again and again. Certainly partly because this concept in itself, although it has now been the subject of tens of monographs and thousands of articles, is still relatively new. However, also because the concept of revolution itself is very flexible and may adopt the most various forms, depending on the field in which the revolutionary changes are taking place.

Let us attempt to present a small parallel between the classical political revolution and the Scientific Revolution. Let us consider two examples, two types of political revolution which are among the best known: the French Revolution of the end of the eighteenth century (and let us ignore the exceedingly strict opinions voiced by the British Prime Minister on the occasion of its 200th anniversary), and the Russian Great October Revolution of 1917. It seems to me that both satisfy the prerequisites already developed with regard to Classical ancient drama and observed, for instance, by Shakespeare, Molière, or even Havel. These amount to the principle of three unities: the unity of place, time and action. The decisive events of both revolutions took place in the streets of the capital cities of the respective countries, and both took place in a relatively well-defined time interval. The fact that, with progressing civilization, the time required for the main revolutionary changes to take place is apparently becoming shorter, changes nothing: in Prague, in 1989, the Velvet Revolution took but hours (naturally, we are justified in asking whether historically this was indeed a real revolution, or whether it is so called just symbolically). However, let us revert to our French-Russian example: the dramatic principles of unity of place and time were adhered to in exemplary fashion in both cases. The unity of action was essentially observed as well. Both revolutions presented relatively comprehensive programmes which ensued from their anti-royalist and anti-Czarist orientations and which did not change substantially during the course of the revolution. As in Classical tragedies of Antiquity the main actors, bearers of revolutionary ideas, and the multitudes of their followers did not change very much either.

We are well aware that every comparison and every parallel of such complicated, as well as widely separated, social processes have their difficulties and generate problems resulting from excessive simplification. Nevertheless – 'tout de même', to quote the French. Let us keep to this comparison a little longer. We have tried to evoke the idea that the three unities of political revolution hold true, although we would surely be able to find a number of examples of the opposite.

Let us now consider the Scientific Revolution, and let us try to deliberate on it from this point of view. What form will the unity of place take, although mention will be made only of the four principal *coryphaei*? Copernicus lived and worked in northern Poland, in the neighbourhood of the sombre Baltic, Kepler perhaps never crossed the frontiers of central Europe. Galileo's name has permanent ties to sunny Tuscany, Newton carried out his research in the seclusion of a Cambridge college. The differences are paramount, in place, but also in lifestyle, organization of social life, etc. Let us take a look at the unity of time. Our foursome is miles apart here as well: Copernicus (1473–1543) lived through nearly half of his life in the fifteenth century, the most fruitful years of Kepler (1571–1630) and Galileo (1564–1642) fall in the beginning of the seventeenth century, whereas Newton (1642–1727) lived a third of his life in the eighteenth century. The mathematician, moreover, would find that the intersection of their lifetimes (assuming the two middle ones to be a single person) forms an empty set. And how about the principle of action? The comparison here would be much more favourable because all of them essentially followed a single main trend. Heliocentrism, at which the first of them, Copernicus, arrived, but not without a certain amount of hesitation, became Kepler's and Galileo's point of departure, whose indubitability they supported with a number of other scientific arguments, whereas Newton was successful in integrating all existing discoveries and upgrading them to a comprehensive theory of gravitation.

Moreover, one should realize that the Scientific Revolution does not

take place in the street, it is not attended by the masses, and apparently
has no immediate consequences. Everything takes place in the heads of
the learned (although they are open to stimuli from without), and in the
sixteenth and seventeenth centuries the propagation of their ideas is
relatively slow, technically speaking, of course, but especially because
time – or if you would prefer social consciousness – is slow to mature,
and one of the favourite sayings of today's youth, 'Change is life', will
still have a very long way to go before it becomes justified.

However, let us leave exaggerated metaphors, the purpose of which
was just to draw attention once again to a certain discontinuity of the
Scientific Revolution in place and time, as well as to the great differences
which distinguish it very substantially from other revolutionary phenomena. At the same time, we wanted to find out to what extent we were
justified in putting on the agenda the problem of studying the processes
of the Scientific Revolution of the sixteenth and seventeenth centuries
and their consequences in the national context, in concrete historical
structures, in individual and unrepeatable, material and spiritual
conditions of the individual countries.

Let us remind the reader of at least two other facts: Copernicus had no
more significant successor in Poland (which also applies to Kepler in
Bohemia and Austria), and Galileo's legendary 'eppure si muove', a
whole century later, which represents the peak of his scientific and
human destiny, remains to this day a symbol of rare personal courage.
Even if this were all we knew about this topic, these two episodical facts
indicate that the problem of propagating scientific knowledge in national
contexts was not simple and deserves the full attention of historians of
science. Moreover, it is in fact surprising that the problem, in its entirety,
was posed as late as it was. We were, therefore, very glad to be able to
respond to the initiative of the editors of this volume in an attempt to
contribute at least briefly in throwing light on the peripeteia which the
main stages of the Scientific Revolution were to encounter during their
propagation in Bohemia.

Bohemia, a small country in the heart of Europe, located roughly
between 15° and 18° east longitude and 49° and 51° north latitude,
consists of two main parts: in the west Bohemia itself, a land of the
crown, and Moravia in the east, an independent margraviate. The
principal centre of Bohemia was Prague with a university founded in
1348, the oldest university in central Europe[2]; the principal centre of
Moravia was Olomouc where the university was, however, founded
much later.[3] Bohemia has long since lost its dynastic rights, its throne
having been occupied by the Austrian branch of the Habsburgs already

in 1526. Nevertheless, Prague had remained a royal seat. In the preceding centuries, the country had experienced the extensive Hussite revolutionary movement, the heritage of which was the surviving, relatively large, religious tolerance which was a marked national characteristic when the Inquisition was at its height. After the defeat of Hussitism, however, feudalism again began to sink deeper roots in Bohemia and Moravia, but its impact was not as hard as it was to become after the year 1620.

This was roughly the situation in the first half of the sixteenth century, which is considered, in the European context, by most to be the beginning of the Scientific Revolution. It did not provide very much incentive to the cultivation of sciences and education in general, both universities being mainly concentrated on educating clergy, or at best teachers.

New elements began to have a greater bearing on the life of the country in the second half of the sixteenth century. The crafts began to undergo a more substantial development. Some of them called for a higher technical standard as well as theoretical knowledge. This concerned for example watchmaking, supported by the increased need to know the exact time. Distances had to be determined as accurately: land is surveyed and levelling is carried out in connection with the founding of fish-ponds. Increased interest was being shown in technology, especially in the manufacture of iron and beer. The advancement of mining and metallurgy in Jáchymov and Kutná Hora was responsible for a number of practical and theoretical treatises (Agricola, Mathesius, Ercker). Increased interest in alchemy and, above all, in astrology can be observed in the houses of the nobility and burghers, in the whole of Europe and in Bohemia alike.

Social life is beginning to pose concrete questions which, perhaps, still do not require science of the highest standard for their answers (no knowledge is required, e.g., of Copernicus, to say nothing of cosmology), but they do create a certain atmosphere in which the numbers of textbooks on arithmetic and geometry, surveying manuals, calendars, pieces of weather lore and various astronomical treatises, specifically concerned with exceptional phenomena, are beginning to increase. People are beginning to show interest in their immediate environment, and the first herbaria are being printed. The important thing is that copywriting is slowly beginning to recede, and that book printing is developing into the principal means of disseminating knowledge. And not in Latin, but in Czech and German, in the colloquial tongue of the common people.

Since practical knowledge is being advanced, one can expect, sooner or later, more interest to be shown in more remote, theoretical problems, not immediately associated with praxis, against this broader background. Of the several people who are steering their activity towards the problem we are interested in, let us name at least two whose significance exceeded the boundaries of the Czech region. First of all, Cyprianus Leovitius a Leocinia (1514–1574), born in Hradec Králové, who, however, spent most of his life in the services of the Fugger family in Augsburg and nearby Lauingen. But he had a permanent connection with Bohemia, and his work drew a relatively large response there. Credit is due to him for the astronomical calculations of the positions of the separate planets, the sun and the moon. For example, he worked out very detailed ephemerides for the planets up to the year 1750, as well as ephemerides of solar eclipses, of the moon, etc. In this particular instance he drew on Regiomontanus' tables, a critical edition of which he published. In accordance with these tables, he essentially based his studies on the traditional geocentric model of motion in the planetary system.[4] However, it is interesting that, in calculating the solar and lunar eclipses, he encountered some discrepancies and, in spite of his critical attitude to Copernicus, he did use his assumptions of the moon's orbit in his calculations.[5]

A substantially more significant personage was Thaddeus Hagecius (1525–1600), or Nemicus, Ageccio in Italian. He studied mathematics and medicine in Prague and Vienna, and later stayed with Hieronymus Cardan in Bologna and Milan. He took part in the war against the Turks as a physician in Hungary and Austria. After 1570 he resided permanently in Prague, although as personal physician of Emperor Maximilian II, later of his successor Rudolph II, he travelled frequently.

Although the initial interests of Hagecius were, to a large extent, connected with astrology, he was able to rise above the standard of contemporary European science and intervene in it thanks to his broad Renaissance background. In 1562 he published the first Czech edition of Mathioli's herbarium. At the same time he devoted himself to surveying: he was perhaps the first to attempt precise measurements using trigonometry. In 1585 he published a short treatise in Frankfurt on manufacturing beer. He collected old manuscripts and indulged in extensive scientific correspondence. For example, the report has been preserved that he sent the Latin translation of al-Choresmi's algebra to Adrian van Roomen. In the calendar disputes he assumed the role of a determined advocate of the Gregorian reform.[6]

His principal interest, however, was in astronomy in which Tycho Brahe, Kepler and Galileo, for example, acknowledged a number of his results. His authorship of a number of calendars and pieces of weather lore apart, it appears that he received his main impulse from a new star which was discovered in the Cassiopeia constellation in November 1572. This was a phenomenon which generated a whole avalanche of astrological and astronomical literature in Europe. Hagecius first reported the results of his observations to Vienna and, a year later, published them in an independent treatise, *Dialexis de novae et prius incognitae stellae ... apparitione* (Frankfurt-am-Main, 1574). The author of the well-known bibliography of astronomical literature, Zinner, has included this work of Hagecius among the most widely read treatises of the end of the sixteenth century.[7] Its importance in the history of science is probably twofold: in it Hagecius introduced – it seems for the first time – a new method of measuring the positions of stars which rests in determining its right-ascension and time at the instant of its meridian passage. Its second and even more important significance is his finding that the new star had no measurable parallax and that, consequently, it must be even more distant from the earth than the moon (whose parallax was known and routinely used), and that it therefore must be a fixed star. This conclusion represented a principal breakthrough into the Aristotelian concept which admitted variations in the so-called sublunar region (between the earth and the moon's orbit), whereas the supralunar, etheric sphere was considered to be quite perfect, i.e. unchanging.

Hagecius reached similar conclusions also in other treatises in which he dealt mostly with comets that appeared in the years 1556, 1557, 1577 and 1580. For the further development of sciences in Bohemia it was very important that Tycho Brahe arrived at the same results as Hagecius. These problems became the subject of their mutual correspondence and formed the foundation of their scientific interrelationship.[8]

Hagecius became acquainted with Tycho personally in Regensburg in 1575, at the coronation of Rudolph II. On this occasion he presented him with a copy of Copernicus' letter to Wapowsky and with a copy of the first unpublished outline of his system of planetary motion[9]: this sketch is immature, still resembling the epicycles of Ptolemy's system. The primary question, as far as Czech historians of science are concerned, is, of course: where did Hagecius get these manuscripts? No fully satisfactory answer has yet been found. One of the hypotheses is that Hagecius obtained them from A. Perlachius, his Viennese teacher.[10]

We know that Hagecius held Tycho in high esteem. He would hardly have given him copies of Copernicus' manuscripts had he not considered them to be important. With a certain amount of probability, therefore, we may assume that Hagecius' relation to Copernicus was positive. This hypothesis is also supported to some extent by Tycho's report that

Hagecius carried out some of the calculations in the revised version of his *Dialexis* by assuming diurnal motion of the earth. Otherwise, Hagecius did not indulge in cosmological problems very much, but one feels that he evidently supported traditional geocentrism. As opposed to Tycho, for example, he did not even attempt to develop some kind of compromise system. Nevertheless, one cannot overlook the fact that he must have known Copernicus' opinions, but did not oppose them. One could also pose the question, why did Hagecius not accept Copernicus in a more determined manner, or at least make some kind of a statement to this effect? Was he bound by religious prejudices? Hardly, because he was a faithful advocate of Huss's opinions and of the party advocating communion in both the bread and wine. Did he hesitate because he was the personal physician of the emperor and thus had close ties to the royal court? The most probable answer is that he was under the strong influence of tradition, namely of astrology, and that, on the contrary, neither his own attention nor that of the scientific milieu, which he was in contact with, was concentrated on cosmological problems.

We have perhaps discussed the period of the second half of the sixteenth century in too great detail. However, we did want to demonstrate that the conditions for scientific work in Bohemia and Moravia were not very favourable. Let us add that, in this period, there was no physicist, astronomer or mathematician, or even more pervasive philosopher who would have been able to compete with, for example, Tartaglia or Francis Bacon – a choice made at random. Thus, not even Hagecius, although the most outstanding among domestic scientists at the end of the sixteenth century, with Copernicus within reach, was able to formulate a standpoint on him, much less on his acceptance.

However, at this point it is necessary to draw attention to the fact that the reluctant attitude to Copernicus' ideas and their slow propagation were quite general. His opinions first prevailed rather as a mathematical tool, more satisfactory than Ptolemy's geocentrism, a fact to which we could have drawn attention in connection with Leovitius as well as Hagecius. The number of convinced supporters of Copernicus, such as Rheticus, Rothmann, Mästlin or Digges, was relatively small in Europe as a whole.[11]

In the last years of the sixteenth century, however, the situation began to change significantly. At the turn of the sixteenth and seventeenth century, Emperor Rudolph II and his undisguised interest in and generous support of all connected with the arts and sciences attracted many foreign artists[12] and scientists to Prague, many of the real ones and no lesser number of those who only posed as such. Hagecius, at that time the emperor's physician and first medical officer of Bohemia, inspired the emperor with the propitious idea of inviting Tycho Brahe to Prague, and providing him with the possibility of establishing a scientific centre similar to his Uraniborg observatory on the Danish island of Hven.

In the learned Europe of the time, Tycho Brahe (1546–1601) had become famous mainly due to his papers on the new star of 1572 and on comets, i.e. similarly to Hagecius, and also as organizer of the Uraniborg observatory, founded in 1576, unprecedented in the history of astronomy and in fact in the history of science in general. The result of the concentrated efforts of Tycho and his collaborators was the unusual improvement of the methods and instruments used in astronomical observations. However, Tycho is also known in the history of science as the author of a planetary system. Tycho had already worked it out in Denmark and had published it in the treatise *De mundi aetherei recentioribus phaenomenis* (Uraniborg, 1588).

At the end of 1599 Tycho arrived in Prague and assembled a group of young collaborators: Longomontanus (1564–1647), a Danish astronomer; his own son George; Francis Gansneb Tengnagel (1573–1636), his son-in-law; but above all Johannes Kepler (1571–1630). The work plan which Tycho laid down was the observation of planets. This was not a new programme; it tied in closely with Tycho's previous efforts. Its purpose was to conclude the calculations of planetary orbits within the scope of Tycho's planetary system, and to work out precise planetary tables.

Tycho's system was, to a certain extent, a compromise: it retained the sun orbiting about a fixed earth, which was the centre of the universe, as in all geocentric models; however, the planets orbited round the sun, as postulated by Copernicus. This was at any rate a breakthrough: in this way Copernicus was at least partly acknowledged.

We may only speculate whether the subsequent development was favourable for science or not. For a certain period of time, observations were conducted in a manor in Benátky (about thirty-five kilometres north of Prague); later an observatory began to be built in the Prague Castle. Disputes between the workers as to the final location of the observatory, financial problems with the court and, finally, Tycho's unexpected death caused the promising astronomical centre to disintegrate.

However, fortunately the right man, Johannes Kepler, remained. He came to Prague in the year 1600.[13] Being Mästlin's pupil, he arrived already as a convinced supporter of Copernicus. He stayed in Prague for twelve years, during which he created most of his scientific works.[14] Tycho entrusted him with elaborating the theory of motion of the planet

Mars, the planet which, apart from Mercury, which was difficult to observe, had the largest eccentricity of the planets then known. This was the reason why its observed motion displayed the largest deviations from theoretical values. Was this also a lucky coincidence?

Kepler used Tycho's observations, he reduced Mars's opposition from the so-called mean positions to the actual positions of the sun and, after tedious and prolonged work, he arrived at the formulation of two laws of planetary orbits in 1605. The first of these laws expresses the fact that planets move along elliptical orbits. This led to a paradoxical situation. Copernicus' idea had not been established, but Kepler was already in fact criticizing it or, if we prefer, continuing to develop it. The idea that planets move along circular orbits was adopted by Copernicus from ancient tradition, which he was unable to overcome. Although the most varied ideas, which anticipated one thing or another, usually quite randomly, as later developments indicated, appeared in the history of astronomy, the idea of the circular orbit remained unaffected. Indeed, the circle, which was the solution to the isoperimetric problem, represented the most perfect pattern during the whole of Antiquity. However, the idea of the circular orbit had now been definitively overcome. The harmonic model was also disrupted by Kepler's second law, which concerns the non-uniform motion of planets. After they had been published in the treatise *Astronomia nova* in 1609, another ten years went by before he produced the third law, which determines the relation between the mean distances of the planets from the sun and their orbiting periods. However, Kepler had then already left Prague and was working in Linz.

Until then, Kepler's feat was unique in the history of science. Armed with the principal idea of heliocentrism and a tremendous volume of observational material, this astronomer, aged thirty to thirty-five, was able to carry out, to use modern terms, mass data processing, the necessary calculations, and derive from them relatively complicated and mathematically precisely formulated laws.

The author of this paper confesses that, in the uninvited competition between the two contemporaries, Kepler and Galileo, he had previously given the larger part of his irrational sympathies to the Italian, whose activity was much more diverse, and therefore also more interesting. Only on re-thinking this 'old-new' subject did he realize the fantastic part Kepler played in history. He is able to visualize another person carrying out the individual experiments or observations of Galileo, and even deducing from them the more general conclusions Galileo drew (we know that a number of scientists had come close to them in various ways); however, he considers Kepler's role to be irreplaceable. At the same time, he realizes that this excursion has put him offside because he has gone beyond the boundaries and violated the rules which a historian has to observe, by psychologizing and conditionally estimating 'what would have happened, if'.

The fact remains, that Kepler's results were accepted in Prague and in the remainder of Europe without more substantial objections, which was quite a rare phenomenon at the time. However, it is also true that they did not draw a larger response, and that Tycho's authority, for example, was felt, at least in Bohemia, for a long time much more than Kepler's. Indeed, Kepler achieved full recognition only half a century later in Newton's *Principia*. Subsuming Kepler's laws into the theory of gravitation simultaneously rectified, to a considerable extent, a certain weakness which history of science had quite rightfully to admit: even Kepler's model was only kinematic and did not solve one of the most topical problems of the seventeenth century, i.e. what the *primum movens* of planetary motion was. And irrespective of whether Kepler thought it to be some kind of force, the seat of which was in the sun, or magnetism (which was most probably due to the influence of Gilbert's treatise *De magnete*, published in London in 1600, which became known in Bohemia and Moravia in a very short time), he was unable to integrate this concept in an acceptable manner in his model and lend it a dynamic character. In this respect, Kepler is indebted, in the negative sense, to Copernicus and, one might also say, to ancient traditions. From this point of view, however, the non-uniform motion of planets is different and new, a thing none of the classics of astronomy would ever have thought of, a thing that paved the way for Kepler's laws and pointed directly towards the theory of gravitation.

However, let us return to Bohemia and try to find further evidence, still very inconclusive, of the response to Copernicus' system. We have already mentioned Tycho who, in spite of not agreeing with it in words on principle, in fact had accepted it in part: the earth is fixed, but the planets orbit the sun. Jan Jessenius (1566–1621) was the author of a slightly different compromise model. He studied in Breslau, Padua and Wittenberg, where he was appointed professor of surgery in 1595. In 1600 he came to Prague and became Rudolph II's royal physician after Hagecius, who died in that year. At the same time, he was professor of surgery at the Prague University. Strictly speaking, he was not even an astronomer. In 1596 he published in Wittenberg the treatise *Zoroaster*, which is an interpretation of his cosmological opinions. In his opinion, the earth revolves about its axis – which is a Copernican element – but the sun and planets orbit the earth. This was a concept which the history of science had already known since the fifteenth century, when it was created, on a philosophical platform which was also Jessenius' platform, by Nicolaus Cusanus. Jessenius added to it his pantheistic concept of the universe, according to which planets affected their own orbits and their motion with their own will. His ideas also include that of Giordano Bruno about the infinity of the universe, as well as a number of elements of the Aristotelian approach.[15]

Jessenius' idea of the universe is thus a mixture of the most varied strands of opinion. However, the author later abandoned it and, under the influence of Tycho, whose close friend he became in Prague, he fully adopted his system. Let it be added that Jessenius did not devote himself to astronomy even in later years. He was rector of the university, he conducted the first public autopsy in Prague (1600, 1605), and he was one of the twenty-seven Czech nobles executed for anti-Habsburg activity in 1621.

Kepler left Prague in 1612; coincidently, Kepler's best friend, or rather his protector due to the difference in age, rector of the university, Martin Bachacius (1539–1612) also died in the same year, the year that Emperor Rudolph II died. However, Kepler left no tradition, nobody continued his work, and nobody worked in the field of celestial mechanics in Bohemia for long years to come. It even seems that Bachacius, although an astronomer by education (true, not a creative astronomer, who never published an astronomical or other scientific treatise) and, to some extent, also Kepler's collaborator, was unable to grasp the significance of his work.

The demise of Rudolph II represents an important milestone in the history of Bohemia. Naturally, this does not involve the year 1612, which is more symbolical. A large number of persons left Prague already in the course of the first decade, because the possibilities of providing sustenance for them dwindled as Rudolph's power gradually diminished. Scientific work deteriorated accordingly.

In the Czech literature, the term 'Rudolphian Scientific Centre' has come to be used for this concentration of more and less significant personalities in the time of Rudolph II. The content of the term 'centre' is not, of course, precisely defined and, consequently, it is difficult to argue it. However, it does seem that the term 'centre' already contains elements of an organized and programmatically concentrated facility. However, we do not encounter anything of the sort, with the exception of the short time Tycho's group was at large. It rather resembled a slightly randomly selected grouping (containing many more artists than real scientists anyway), a grouping of persons who had no common programme but exploiting the advantages of the emperor's court and relatively liberal religious freedom. It is characteristic that none of these persons were connected with the Prague University (which was otherwise in a very poor state[16] nor did they have any influence on its activity.

Zdeněk Horský, my friend and collaborator, once wrote that 'The Rudolphian centre of scientific work was not a mere random result of the activity of foreign scientists in Prague, but was created with the direct participation of Thaddeus Hagecius in an environment in which astronomical research had been developing and becoming more detailed since the middle of the sixteenth century.'[17] One cannot but agree with the second part of his statement: the active participation of Hagecius, who apparently had considerable influence at the court, is indubitable, and the advancement of astronomy in the preceding period is also beyond doubt. The subjective and random features in the selection of persons who, moreover, function practically without any links whatsoever, seem to be too large. This appears to be proved by the rate of disintegration, which was much larger than the rate of creation. Equally important is the fact that this stage had no significant impact on the further development of sciences in Bohemia.

Let us attempt to summarize to what extent the Czech environment had participated in the process of the Scientific Revolution until then, on science's complicated way from Copernicus to Newton. We have seen that the acceptance of Copernicus' ideas created embarrassment, to say the least. Hagecius, as holder of his manuscripts, could perhaps have felt some sympathy for him, but never said so openly. All the others we mentioned worked in Bohemia for a certain limited period of time: Reymarus-Ursus, Tycho and Jessenius adopted an inconsistent approach to Copernicus' system and preferred to create compromise models. Thus, the only undeviating advocate of heliocentrism was J. Kepler who, moreover, substantially improved and developed it with his laws. The fact that Kepler did not become more familiar with the Prague milieu, that he remained on his own and found no successor, had a very unfavourable effect on the further scientific development of Bohemia.

However, one cannot overlook the fact that Galileo Galilei achieved a number of results during the Rudolphian period, which concerns the Scientific Revolution in Italy. It is evident that Galileo's results did reach Prague. However, there was no-one to draw on them or at least propagate them; experimental science did not have very much scope there at the time. The only exception was again Kepler. In his treatises *Dissertatio cum nuncio sidereo* (Prague, 1610) and *Narratio de observatis quatuor Jovis satellitibus* (Frankfurt, 1611) he confirmed the surprising results of Galileo's first historical observation of the sky by telescope. On the basis of observations with a telescope of his own design, Kepler confirmed the existence of sun-spots, the lunar surface, the composition of the Milky Way containing a multitude of stars, and Jupiter's satellites, which Galileo reported in his treatise *Nuncius sidereus* in 1608.

On the other hand there are but few documents on the response to the proceedings against G. Bruno. Two persons from Prague appear to have been present at the auto-da-fé. One of them was San Clemente, the Spanish ambassador to Rudolph's court, representative of the Spanish branch of the Habsburgs, adamant in requiring the consistent re-catholicization of Bohemia. It is ironic that it was to him Bruno dedicated his book on Raimund Lull's science of medieval mysticism in 1588, the book having been published during Bruno's half-year sojourn in Prague. He was surely expecting San Clemente to facilitate his approach to the emperor, which may indeed have happened. However, later San Clemente changed his opinion. He accepted Bruno's martyr death cynically, like a militant Catholic. A record of his remark that 'now Bruno changed to smoke may seek and visit his infinite worlds' has been preserved.

The second person assisting in the drastic act of Bruno's auto-da-fé was also an ambassador, in this case, however, Rudolph's ambassador to Rome. He was Johannes Mathias Wackher de Wackensfels. He was not a specialist scientist but an educated man, close to Thaddeus Hagecius, and was one of the few friends Kepler had in Prague. Wackher was apparently intimately acquainted with Bruno's philosophy; in its spirit, he attempted to find solution to numerous problems even before Galileo was able to provide them with his discoveries. Immediately after the discovery of Jupiter's satellites, for example, he predicted that they would surely orbit in the same direction as the moon orbits the earth, which was later confirmed. Wackher tried to make his younger friend understand Bruno's philosophy. Kepler appreciated the firmness with which Bruno accepted his fate at the stake, but found no greater sympathy for his ideas. In the first place, he was unable to come to terms with the concept that all other stars were the same as our sun, he could not become reconciled with the sun not being the centre of the universe, and to the fact that he would have to abandon one of the principal assumptions of the geometrically harmonic pattern of the universe, which had been his life companion and about which he was very particular. Kepler did indeed devote half of his treatise *Dissertatio cum nuncio sidereo* to the opinions of his friend Wackher; however, he was unable to restrain himself from expressing regret at Galileo's discoveries exciting a new wave of Wackher's admiration for that 'terrible' philosophy of Bruno's.[18]

This is a situation characteristic of the tolerant atmosphere of Prague at this time: the Protestant Kepler is opposed to Bruno's teaching, which the Catholic Church has condemned; nevertheless, he does devote half of his treatise to it; Wackher, a Catholic convert in the service of the emperor, on the contrary, sympathized with it.

However, the whole situation was to change shortly. The exit of Rudolph II from the political scene in 1611 and his death in 1612 indeed constituted a fact to be reckoned with.[19] However, the social events in general which took place in the second decade of the seventeenth century, had a much greater impact on the further development of science in Bohemia and Moravia. These did not only affect science, but the economic and spiritual evolution of the country as a whole for the three centuries to come. The political tension between the emperor and the Czech estates came to a head in 1618 with the uprising of the estates which, however, was not successful and ended with the defeat of the Battle of the White Mountain in 1620. Moreover, the Thirty Years' War had broken out, which, until peace was re-established with the Treaty of Westphalia in 1648, recklessly devastated central Europe: the armies of all participating nations, ranging from France to Sweden, swept through Bohemia several times. This was not the worst, however. The retaliatory measures of the Habsburgs proved to be much more serious with regard to future evolution. It was then that Bohemia was deprived of much of its independence. Prague, which had until then been a royal city and cultural centre, had to give way to Vienna and gradually sank to provincial town status. Serious changes also took place in the economy. The feudal system, disrupted by the preceding events, began to strengthen its position again. These changes were perhaps even more pronounced in the spiritual sphere. Consistent re-catholicization set in, the purpose of which was to liquidate all Hussite and Reformation traditions still at large in the country. It is no wonder that this period of history in the Czech national culture came to be called the 'Dark Age'.

The protagonist in this process was the Catholic Church, whose power and status in Bohemia rose during that period. This applies in particular to the Jesuits, an order which represented the Church's most militant, as well as most reactionary, section. With the aid of the state the Jesuits assumed control of all education, they gradually acquired decisive influence in the Prague and Olomouc universities and, in the last third of the seventeenth century, they practically controlled the whole spiritual life of the country. The conditions then remained unchanged until the middle of the eighteenth century.

The negative features of social evolution were also reflected to no small degree in the development of science. Among the subsequent rulers there was no patron of Rudolph's type and, consequently, the only place where science was able to develop was the university. However, the Prague university was in very poor shape. It lacked professors, means and students.[20] Besides, it was prone to constant attacks from the Jesuits, who were not only attempting to gain control over the faculties of philosophy and theology, which they achieved in 1622, but also over the faculties of medicine and law. The drawn-out struggles reflected the centralist interests of the monarch, the papal court, the Prague archbishopric, the Jesuit Order, and of other church orders and secular professors. They ended after nearly thirty years and in fact represented a Jesuit victory. The Jesuits gained control of the university in Olomouc in a similar manner. Let us remind the reader in this connection that the Catholic Church fought most severely against the advocates of 'new science'. Distinct proof of this is provided not only by Bruno's auto-da-fé, but also by the Church's interdict on the long dead Copernicus in 1616 and the proceedings against Galileo. The conditions for the development of the process which we refer to as the Scientific Revolution were, therefore, greatly restricted in Bohemia and Moravia – to avoid claiming that its acceptance, let alone advancement, were directly excluded.

The educated Czech had to ask himself the question and in answer face the decision – both of which have been topical in his country in recent decades too – whether to preserve one's personal liberty and independence, and emigrate, or stay put and more or less give up, adapt to the given conditions. Comenius, for example, chose the former solution, but there were few scientists who followed suit. Most of them remained and were forced, in one way or another, to give in.

With regard to further evolution, the worst period was perhaps the tens and twenties. After Kepler's departure, not one treatise of natural science was published. An exception is perhaps provided by a few medical dissertations which were of little professional significance and lacked publicity. One such was the dissertation of Joannes Marcus Marci (1595–1667), which was devoted to, among other topics, epilepsy.[21] It presents a review of contemporary scientific ideas on the aetiology of these diseases. It is to be appreciated that there is no mention of the obsession theory, the official attitude of the Church. According to Temkin, a large majority of physicians and scientists of the second half of the seventeenth century believed that epilepsy could be caused by the devil and witchcraft.[22]

In later years, Marcus Marci was to become the most important scientist in these countries, a scientist with wide and all-encompassing interests; he was a physician, biologist, physicist, astronomer, mathematician, pharmacist; he was interested in geography, and could speak a number of languages. However, at the same time he was a kind of live symbol which reflected all the problems of the evolution of Czech science in the post-White-Mountain period.[23]

Marci submitted his dissertation relatively late, when he was already thirty years of age (the reason for this is probably in the adverse conditions prevalent at the Prague university); Francisco Roia de Aquista of Verona was his tutorial professor. A brilliant career followed. A year thereafter he was appointed assistant professor and in 1630 full professor, soon afterwards chief medical officer of the Bohemian Kingdom, and then personal physician to two emperors, Ferdinand III (reigned (1637–57) and Leopold I (1657–1705). He served several terms as dean of the faculty of medicine and, in 1662, he was appointed rector of the Prague, then already the Charles-Ferdinand, university.

This rapid ascent, which took place in an extraordinarily complicated military, political and religious situation, was naturally not a matter of chance. It is very difficult to prove this from historical sources; on the basis of the correspondence recently discovered in Rome, however, it appears that he had the benefit of influential support from several personalities of high standing. First of all, there was Count Bernard Martinic, who was in turn appointed to a number of important government offices, and then Cardinal Ernest of Harrach, who was Prague archbishop from 1623 until his death in 1667, the same year that Marci died. Cardinal Harrach was known for his anti-Jesuit attitude; he attempted to stem the disproportionate growth of their influence to the detriment of the other orders. In the literature, the opinion is maintained that Marci was also involved in the cardinal's efforts to prevent the Jesuits from controlling the Prague university as a whole: he was allegedly a member of the delegation sent to Rome in 1642 to intervene in this sense at the papal court. However, more recent research has so far been unable to support this hypothesis.

Marci's attitude to the Jesuits was not unambiguous: on the one hand, he was an implacable opposer of the opinions of the Spanish Jesuit, Roderigo Arriaga, who was the principal representative of scholastic tendencies at the Prague university;[24] on the other, we know that he frequently visited the Jesuit college in the Clementinum, near which he resided and where he had a number of friends; moreover, for more than twenty years he was in correspondence with Athanasius Kircher, a German Jesuit, who was involved with the Collegium Romanum in Rome.[25] This correspondence indicates that not only did he want to gain as much information as possible about the most various scientific disciplines from Kircher, but that he was also bound to him by profound friendship. One may assume that Marci was apparently under a certain amount of pressure during his whole life to become a member of the Jesuit order (he began his studies at a Jesuit secondary school in 1608). He resisted it literally until the last hours of his life, when he allegedly applied for acceptance into the order. The author of this essay was fortunate to find this application in the archive. After analysing it with his friend Prof. Z. Servít, however, he cannot but declare it to be a spurious document of the Jesuits who, for reasons of prestige, made all efforts to draw this indubitably most significant representative of Czech science in amongst themselves, and to make use of the fact for promotional purposes.

But let us go back to Marci's scientific youth. On the basis of his dissertation on epilepsy he became a physician. That was his only effort as an author for the time being, but nobody else published anything either. Only in 1635 did he publish a book which again dealt with the field of medicine, or, to be more accurate, of philosophical biology. It was called *Idearum operatricium idea*...[26] In it Marci, who shortly before this became a father for the first time,[27] discussed problems of ontogenesis. Given the level of scientific development, he could, understandably, only speculate: he assumed the existence of some kind of latent force, creative and active (*idea operatrix*), which inseminates the seed and controls the gradual development of the individual. In this case Marci was apparently under the influence of some kind of Renaissance neo-Platonism, with remnants of medieval mysticism and other philosophical concepts added. It is claimed that Harvey was acquainted with and appreciated this work.[28] However, in Prague Marci was criticized, not because of the factual content, but mainly because he did not submit his book to the archbishop's censorship. Essentially, however, because of disagreement with Marci's conclusions.

We have arrived at an interesting point here: if we disregard Marci's two books which were published posthumously from his literary remains by his pupil, Dobřenský, *Idearum operatricium idea* is the last work to be published in which Marci expresses his opinions on medical and biological problems. As a physician, aged forty, in his prime, he abandoned his discipline and became a physicist. He mostly dealt with mechanics and optics, but also published papers on astronomy and mathematics. This does not mean that he abandoned his medical profession or his office at the faculty of medicine; he executed both routinely throughout his whole life, but his publications thereafter dealt exclusively with the exact sciences.

Marci thus converted completely. There are, understandably, no documents relating to the reasons for this conversion, so that we may only speculate. This hitherto mostly 'philosophizing' physician switched to the career of an experimenter in physics, to carry out experiments which, apart from Kepler's studies in optics, had no precursor. The experiment, its description, diagram and deductive explanation of the phenomenon, which is based almost exclusively on geometry, division into individual theorems and lemmas – this is the method first encountered in his book of 1639, *De proportione motus seu regula sphygmica* ... ,[29] which he then also maintained in later works. Why did this conversion take place then? Marci was prompted by no domestic model, nor influenced from abroad, and thus one can but speculate that, apart from the intrinsic persuasiveness of the experiment, he was motivated by the effort to avoid, in his own scientific work, ideological conflicts with church as well as secular authorities and, in the end, jeopardizing his quite privileged position. This is indicated not only by the fact that, as author, he abandoned medicine and biology, in which there was considerable danger of committing philosophical heresy, but also by the fact that, in physics and astronomy, he mostly devoted himself to philosophically unexceptionable fields. Marci never adopted an overt standpoint on geocentrism or heliocentrism, his astronomical treatise of 1650 being devoted to a minor problem, the method of correct determination of geographic longitude. Neither at the time his first physics treatise was published, nor in later years, did he openly react to Galileo, although he prepared his first work not long after Galileo published his *Discorsi*.[30]

But let us leave hypotheses, the danger of which was already pointed out by Newton, and go back to the year 1639 when Marci's first treatise of physics, *De proportione motus seu regula sphygmica* ... , on the proportionality of motions, or the rules of impact, was published in Prague. In it Marci analysed motion as such and studied situations which occurred if bodies made contact. This treatise is of exceptional importance to the history of science in Bohemia: not counting Kepler, who was indeed a guest in this area, this is the first purely physics treatise published in Bohemia. It is also important because it is devoted to the analysis of motion, to dynamics, thematically conforming to the standard of its period. The problem of motion of a body, terrestrial or celestial, really was among the most topical problems of the first half of the seventeenth century: Galileo, Kepler, Descartes and a number of others devoted themselves to it, although each in his own slightly different way and from different points of departure. At this point, the author cannot but remind the reader of the words of I. B. Cohen who gave his paper on the problem of the scientific revolution the title 'Dynamics: The Key to the "New Science" of the Seventeenth Century', opening it with the words: 'Dynamics was the pioneer subject to the "new science" of the seventeenth century. Not only did dynamics set a model for all other parts of science, in showing how to combine refined conceptual analysis and the exactness of mathematics with the rough data of experiment and controlled observation, but it led in Newton's *Principia* to a new integrated view of the entire "Systema Mundi" – a world machine that was not run by clockwork or crystalline spheres but by forces acting from and on otherwise inert matter.'[31]

Marci's book starts with numerous definitions and auxiliary lemmas, by which the author attempted to clarify his fundamental positions. Some of them are, of course, quite trivial; however, some are quite interesting. For example, consider his formulation 'virtus agendi et actio inter se sunt aequales, estque idem modus incrementi.'[32] One can hardly avoid thinking that this contains the embryonic form of Newton's second law of motion.[33] Marci then goes on to introduce the concept of 'impulse' acting along a straight line or circle, and then the concept of velocity. He states that velocity increases in free fall, but decreases in 'forced' motion.[34] By comparing free fall and motion along an inclined plane he arrives at the conclusion that the velocity increases with the square of time. He then goes on to circular motion and to the pendulum, where he explicitly formulates the principle of isochronism and proportionality between the length of the pendulum and the oscillation period.[35] Further on he deals with combining notions by means of the parallelogram.[36]

The next section, devoted to impact, is very important. At its beginning Marci makes a few important remarks: he restricts his attention only to the so-called central impact; he then points out explicitly the necessity to differentiate between impact of soft and hard bodies, and the dependence on the quality of the body's material.[37] He then formulates a number of theorems for the impact of spheres. He worked with wooden spheres, which involved the so-called elastic impact. He first deals with the problem in which one of the spheres is at rest, distinguishing the cases – the spheres are identical, the larger is moving, the larger is at rest – then going on to cases in which both are moving. He thus arrives at a number of theorems which are correct, with a few exceptions. Marci emphasized the ratio of masses,[38] unfortunately only in general; he did not weigh the spheres nor measure their velocities.

The next section deals with the free fall of various bodies. Marci concluded that all bodies fall at equal speed, regardless of shape, weight or volume, and if differences do occur, these are due to the medium in which the fall occurs.[39]

The conclusion of the book is devoted to the description of Marci's instrument for pulse measurements or also astronomical measurements: it is based on a small pendulum with a sphere, the length of the pendulum being continuously variable.

Perhaps we have devoted too much time to the contents of the treatise: however, this was necessary in order for us to be able to judge it. His study of impact, which was greatly appreciated, is of great significance, the more so as it is historically one of the first. Galileo published some of his deliberations in his *Discorsi* which, of course, tended toward different conclusions, but these were strictly rejected by Huygens.[40] Marci's efforts preceded Mersenne's, as well as the unfortunate attempts of Descartes conducted in the 1640s, which drew so much critique even from his contemporaries, and, of course, also the studies provoked by the Royal Society (Wallis, Wren, Huygens). Not only are the individual laws important, but also the differentiation of qualities of the bodies – which Descartes, for example, simply ignored.

The older Czech literature highly appreciated the sections on isochronism and on the relation between the length of the pendulum and the oscillation period; it acknowledged Marci's priority to their discovery.[41] Galileo is said to have known about these things much earlier, possibly as early as 1583. However, the law of proportionality of the square of time and the length of the pendulum only appeared in his correspondence of 1637 and then in the *Discorsi*, which were published in 1638, i.e. a year before Marci's book was published. We know that Marci had the opportunity to acquaint himself with the *Discorsi* on his trip to Italy at the end of 1638 or 1639[42], so that the question of the independence of his discovery may be controversial. We are unable to rule out the independence of Marci's discovery, but we are unable to prove it. Marci's reference to the parallelogram of forces in the composition of motions is also interesting. The idea of the parallelogram is considerably older, but was not very widespread at the time. But the most interesting part is that in which Marci discusses free fall. We know that Galileo discovered that the velocity of falling bodies was independent of their weight at the turn of the sixteenth century and seventeenth centuries. This was a great argument against Aristotelian physics and consequently became the object of many attacks by Galileo's opponents. Galileo, therefore, also published them in the *Discorsi*. This was evidently a great confession on Marci's part. We are able to realize how great – although it does not, of course, involve Galileo's name – by remembering that Marci already wrote about this after the Inquisition's second intervention against Galileo, which occurred in 1633. Moreover, he accepted his standpoint unequivocally and unconditionally. This is one of the brightest items of Czech scientific development in the seventeenth century. The alignment with Galileo's standpoint, in this problem, however, also throws a different light on Marci's study of the pendulum: he must have read about this in the *Discorsi*, as well.

Apart from mechanics, Marci also devoted much effort to another field, optics. His findings are summarized in his book *Thaumantias liber de arcu coelesti*, published in Prague in 1648, and also in two smaller polemical treatises of later years.[43] According to the title, the book is devoted to the rainbow, but in it Marci actually deals with the most varied problems. His effort to explain the rainbow led Marci to the problems of the refraction of light, his whole subsequent work being concerned with the field of physical optics, still in its infancy in the seventeenth century. He studied the laws of dispersion of the light ray on passing through a prism: he found that rays of different colours displayed different angles of refraction, and that monochromatic rays on subsequent refraction retain their colour. Marci's discoveries were very important; however, nobody paid them much attention at the time. It was not until twenty-four years later, when Newton dealt with these problems and included them in his theory of light, that they became famous. The question has been posed, in this connection, whether Newton could have been acquainted with Marci's book.[44] Unfortunately, documents are lacking; but Barrow, Newton's teacher,[45] may have known it. Marci's works have again been studied in detail in recent years and further points of interest discovered: he already knew of the diffraction of light on a slit, of colours of thin layers and of other phenomena hitherto unknown.[46]

The question whether Newton could have been acquainted with Marci's studies in optics raised another question, i.e. to what extent Marci was known in England in general. An item of information appeared in the Czech literature that a certain Englishman, who was interested in his physical results and the possibility of applying them to navigation, offered Marci a chair at the University of Oxford in 1662.[47] It is also claimed that Marci was offered a fellowship of the Royal Society. Both these reports are very vague and in no way secure. Nevertheless, it has been possible, in recent years, to clarify objectively some of the facts about his relation to England.[48] In 1669 Edward Browne, a physician from London, was planning a trip to the Continent. On this occasion Oldenburg, Secretary of the Royal Society, asked him to contact Marci. Browne did not know Marci, and consequently Oldenburg was forced to give him further instructions: 'As for Marcus

Marci, I believe you'll hear that he is at Prague where by a Latin letter of yours to him he might doubtless be engaged to a correspondency with us which being but once you began, I shall be able enough to continue afterwards.' After his return, Browne made this laconic report to Oldenburg: He had not forgotten to ask after Marcus Marci in Prague; however, he was given to understand that he had died two years ago. Even so it is interesting that Oldenburg knew of Marci and that he was interested in establishing a correspondence with him.

We have only been able to mention the main points concerning Marci. Much of what is known about him has had to be omitted. However, let us point out that much is still unknown and awaits discovery.[49] Nevertheless, he was a complicated personality who reflected the tremendous controversies of his period, a period he was able to understand in his way and, as one of the very few educated Czechs, to overcome.

We have so far devoted our attention to the work of J. M. Marci, who is the protagonist of the development of science in Bohemia and Moravia, the only person who was able to come close to the 'new science'. Let us mention some of the others, at least briefly, starting with the physicists. Their treatises come nowhere near to Marci's standard, being mostly of a reviewing nature and only occasionally supported by authentic experimental work. Thematically they fall into the traditional branches of physics, which had already been cultivated in Antiquity, avoiding topical problems, or touching on them only sporadically.

In view of this, attention was, of course, devoted to mechanics. Judging by their treatises, the Olomouc Jesuit, G. Boehm, and M. Copylius, who worked in Prague and then in Breslau, devoted themselves to statics. Copylius' principal treatise is an interpretation of and commentary on Archimedes' statics. T. Moretus (1602–1667), a Jesuit from a well-known Belgian family of printers,[50] who was concerned with the interpretation of Archimedes' law in one of his treatises, continued the discussion of ancient problems. A great response was drawn in its time by the attempt to construct a *perpetuum mobile* by Valentin Stansel, a Jesuit, but mainly the author of a number of astronomical works, who is quoted – and this is not common knowledge – in Newton's *Principia*.[51] The essence of his *perpetuum mobile* was two tanks, located one above the other; water flowed from the top tank to the bottom *via* a water-wheel which drove a pump, and this pumped the water back into the top tank. This 'antlia Pragensis' was demonstrated at one of the public discussions in the Prague university. Soon afterwards a critical voice was heard from Germany which claimed that the amount of water flowing down could not be pumped up again, and therefore that this could not be a *perpetuum mobile*. Nevertheless, Stansel's machine was known and appreciated throughout Europe. Marci's pupil, J. J. V. Dobřenský, who devoted himself mainly to medicine, was able to determine the specific weight of numerous substances with great accuracy. Perhaps the only exceptional case, of a treatise coming close to European problems was that of F. E. K. Herberstein, who proved that Galileo's statement that the trajectory of a thrown body is parabolic was correct; however, this treatise is of a later data, from the beginning of the eighteenth century.

More attention was devoted to optics than mechanics. It was mainly concentrated on catoptrics, optics of the reflected ray, a study which was also cultivated in Antiquity. In the 1668 treatise of S. Hartmann, a Prague Jesuit, catoptrics were deified to the extent that a remarkable theory of the structure of mass was created within their scope: its basic construction elements are neither atoms nor other particles, but small mirrors (!). The Jesuits Moretus and J. Hancke also studied the properties of mirrors. A more modern section of optics was dioptrics, the optics of light-ray diffraction; however, it was less frequently studied at that time. The work of Moretus, who studied the diffraction of rays in media of various optical densities, is the most interesting. The treatise of B. Conradus (1599–1660), an Olomouc Jesuit, who attempted to interpret the origin of the rainbow, was renowned; this was then a topical question which one encounters with, for example, Descartes and in connection with which we also spoke of Marci above. It was he who attacked Conradus' tenets; and a sharp polemic followed. Conradus was also author of a treatise devoted to acoustics, which did not draw much attention.

More modern branches of physics, which were only beginning to appear on a worldwide scale – magnetism, electricity or thermics – were then quite unknown in Bohemia and Moravia, or at least nothing was published about them. However, it does seem that Gilbert's treatise of 1600, *De magnete*, was quite widely read there, since copies of it were preserved in a number of libraries.

Astronomy provides a picture similar to that in physics, a number of authors being involved in both. The most pressing problems remain untackled. Nobody is dealing with the fundamental problem, which is still the planetary system. Copernicus' name is out of bounds to such an extent that he is not even criticized. No mention is made of Kepler. Either Brahe's model or another compromise system, whose author was Riccioli, an Italian Jesuit, is being accepted. The interest of astronomers is being concentrated on other areas. It is interesting that telescopes of relatively large size were already being used in Prague and Olomouc in the middle of the seventeenth century. For example, Zimmermann observed sun-spots, and in his treatise *Sol siderum princeps* he tried to explain their origin by changes in the density of solar matter. His conclusion that solar matter is therefore not invariable and that, from this point of view, it is similar to terrestrial matter, was in contradiction with the official Aristotelian view of the unchanging nature of translunar regions. Stansel (1621–1715?) drew similar conclusions in his *Propositiones selenographicae*, having made a whole series of interesting observations of the moon. Later Stansel was sent to Spain by the Jesuits, and then as a missionary to Brazil, where his *Legatus uranicus* was published. However, observations were not made only with the telescope, a great novelty at the time, but also with older instruments. Recently, for example, proof was found in Marci's correspondence with Kircher of the use of Tycho's renowned instruments for astronomical observations. Cometary astronomy, in which the question whether comets were sublunar or translunar was still on the agenda, drew a certain amount of interest as well; but for local astronomers this question still remained unanswered.[52]

At this point, some mention should be made of the astronomers who refused to convert to the Catholic religion, preferring to emigrate. These included Šimon Pertlic (1588– after 1640), who devoted himself to comets in the astrological context too; Martin Horký who did his country poor service during his stay in Italy by attempting to refute Galileo's discovery of Jupiter's satellites; and, finally, John Amos Comenius, who was among the convinced advocates of geocentric ideas.[53] His progressive ideas in other areas were unable to affect astronomy.

In Bohemia and Moravia, therefore, physics and astronomy displayed similar features in the first two-thirds of the seventeenth century: the strong influence of ancient traditions is still being felt, including an Aristotelianism which should by now have been outdated; partial or even marginal problems are being tackled, rather than topical ones, which remain out of bounds; and the 'new science' is neither being introduced nor developed in Bohemia and Moravia. In this respect Marci and his work remain an isolated case.

Considerable stagnation thus set in in Bohemia with the disintegration of the centre at Rudolph II's court. A limited revival began in the thirties, lasting until the sixties. However, by then the ideological hegemony of the Jesuits had become so firm that the limited degree of tolerance – possibly even support – they displayed towards science (to science conceived, of course, in such a way as to demonstrate its traditional rather than its revolutionary features) was no longer necessary, and consequently they were able to create a near-perfect vacuum in our area over the next few decades. It is interesting that a similar development was experienced in the history of Czech literature at the same time. We should not be very far from the truth if we were to claim that, at the end of the seventeenth century, when the 'new science' was triumphant and had reached its peak in Newton's work, the sciences in Bohemia and Moravia became practically extinct.

Learned societies began to appear abroad and a base for publishing journals began to be formed, even in neighbouring Germany, but none of this, unfortunately, penetrated into Bohemia and Moravia. It is difficult to believe, but this state of affairs last until the second half of the eighteenth century. The change that occurred then was not the result of the logic of scientific research itself, but of the intervention of the establishment of the Habsburg empire: Empress Maria Theresia realized that, if the monarchy is to function properly, the state official must have at least a minimal education in the fields of science, technology and agriculture. With the aid of van Swieten, a Dutch physician summoned to Vienna in the capacity of royal adviser, the influence of the Jesuits in universities began to be restricted, experimental sciences began to be cultivated and restrictions on communication with scientifically developed countries began to be relaxed. Only then did Newton reach Bohemia.[54] It is a paradox that his ideas had by then become much more acceptable to the Jesuits, and that his opinions could, to a certain extent, be reconciled with Aristotelianism; whereas Jesuit resistance to, for example, Descartes' philosophical opinions remained quite irreconcilable.

In summarizing the two centuries of scientific evolution in Bohemia and Moravia from the middle of the sixteenth to the middle of the eighteenth century, and in attempting to answer the question, to what extent they participated in the process we refer to as the Scientific Revolution, we come to the conclusion that their evolution was autonomous but very limited, and that it was moulded in a quite decisive manner by the social situation which developed in the Czech area: re-catholicization and the near-absolute ideological hegemony of the Jesuit Order, intellectual oppression and lack of freedom which went hand in hand with complete isolation from modern European scientific trends. And it is in a way paradoxical that whereas the historical conditions for scientific development at the beginning of the period involved were relatively favourable, at its end, when the Enlightenment and rationalism were beginning in Europe, Bohemia and Moravia were as it were starting from scratch, from the very beginning, but only slowly, hesitatingly and uneasily; the consequences, unfortunately, were also carried over into the scientific development of the nineteenth, and perhaps even of the twentieth century.

NOTES

1 R. Porter, 'The Scientific Revolution: A Spoke in the Wheel?', in R. Porter and M. Teich (eds.), *Revolution in History* (Cambridge, 1986), 297–316.

2 For its history, see *Stručné dějiny University Karlovy* ['Short history of the Charles University'] (Prague, 1964).

3 For its history see, most recently *Kapitoly z dějin olomoucké university 1573 – 1973* ['Chapters from the history of the Olomouc University'] (Ostrava, 1973).

4 The general evaluation of the role of C. Leovitius has most recently been attempted by J.-P. Verdet, 'La diffusion de l'héliocentrisme', *Revue d'histoire des sciences* 42:3 (1989), 250–1. His conclusions are, of course, rigorous: '…Leovitius… n'a jamais été considéré comme un calculateur habile. Il est astrologue et uniquement astrologue…'. He also remarks Leovitius' critique of Copernicus' tables.

5 Attention has been drawn to this factor by, e.g., Z. Horský in *Dějiny exaktních věd včeských zemích do konce 19. století* ['History of the exact sciences in the Czech lands up to the end of the nineteenth century'] (Prague, 1961) p. 37.

6 The most numerous biographical data and literature on Hagecius so far have been collected by Q. Vetter, 'Tadeáš Hájek z Hájků' ['Thaddeus Hagecius'], *Říše hvězd* 6:6, 1–16. Of the older literature Č. Zíbrt, 'Tadeáš Hájek z Hájků a učeni Koperníkovo' ['Thaddeus Hagecius and Copernicus's learning'] is of fundamental importance for our topic (*Časopis Musea království českého* (1900), 563–7).

7 E. Zinner, *Geschichte und Bibliographie der astronomischen Literatur in Deutschland zur Zeit der Renaissance* (Leipzig, 1941), p. 414.

8 It is even claimed that Brahe invited Hagecius to Denmark in 1581 (cf. Vetter, 'Tadeáš Hájek', p. 4); however, the visit did not take place. Their mutual correspondence, published by I. L. E. Dreyer, amounts to more than thirty long letters (see *Tychonis Brahe Dani Opera omnia*, VII (De Hague, 1924).

9 The title of this outline reads *Nicolai Copernici de hypothesibus motuum coelestium a se constitutis commentariolus*, abbr. *Commentariolus*. Some authors (e.g. A. L. Birkenmajer, *Mikolaj Kopernik*, I (Cracow, 1900, p. 70)) have voiced the hypothesis that this title is due either to Hagecius or to Tycho. The critical edition of the *Commentariolus* was published by L. Prowe, *Nicolaus Copernicus*, II (Berlin, 1884), 184–202. The fact that he had obtained Copernicus' treatise from Hagecius was explicitly confirmed by Tycho himself: '…quo idem quoque fecit Copernicus in Tractatu quodam de Hypothesibus a se constitutis, quem mihi Ratisbonae aliquando manuscriptum impertiit Clarissimus Vir D. Thaddeus Hagecius, diutina amicitia mihi coniunctissimus: ego vero eundem postea aliis quibusdam in Germania mathematicis communicavi…', Tycho Brahe, *Astronomiae instauratae progymnasmata…* (Prague, 1603), p. 480. A

paradoxical situation: Tycho Brahe is not a supporter of Copernicus; nevertheless, he makes his treatise available to others!

10 Perlachius could have then obtained them through Transtetter, his teacher, from the Olomouc canon and professor of the Vienna university, A. Stiborius, who was a friend of the Pole, Jan Glogowczyk (cf. Birkenmajer, *Mikolaj Kopernik*, pp. 636–7).

11 A. Koyré and E. Rosen were quite justified in writing: '...parmi ceux qui le suivent, il faut distinguer ceux qui acceptent le copernicanisme comme une technique mathématique nouvelle et supérieure à celle de Ptolémée en usant pour la construction des tables et le calcul des éphémérides, de ceux qui acceptent l'héliocentrisme comme exprimant la vérité physique de l'Univers, ainsi que de ceux qui admettent sur le même plan d'hypothèse l'astronomie copernicienne et celle de Ptolémée', and further on: 'On le voit bien, les Coperniciens sont rares au XVIe siècle...' (*Histoire générale des sciences*, II, *La Science moderne* (Paris, 1969), pp. 69 and 71 respectively).

12 The literature on the arts at Rudolph's court from recent years is relatively extensive, e.g., J. Hořejší, J. Krčálová, J. Neumann, E. Poche and J. Vacková, *Renaissance Art in Bohemia* (London, New York, Sydney and Toronto, 1979), and also *Rudolph II and his court, Leids Kunsthistorisch Jaarboek* (Delft, 1982) with a number of articles by Czech and foreign authors.

13 Earlier Kepler was in Austrian Graz, which he was forced to leave because of his religion. His following words are very characteristic for the choice of his new place of work: '...Prague is suitable for my studies, the contact between nations is quite brisk there'.

14 Kepler's sojourn in Prague has been comprehensively discussed by Z. Horský, *Kepler v Praze* ['Kepler in Prague'], (Prague 1980).

15 For details on this problem see Z. Horský, 'Kosmologické názory Jana Jessenia' ['Cosmological opinions of Jan Jessenius'], *Sborník pro dějiny přírodních věd a techniky* 2 (Prague, 1955), 126–47.

16 See, e.g., Z. Winter, 'Na kathedře v Karolinum' ['The Chair in the Carolinum'], *Časopis Musea království českého* (1898), 12–38.

17 *Dějiny exaktních věd v českých zemích do konce 19. století* ['History of the exact sciences in the Czech lands up to the end of the nineteenth century'] (Prague, 1961), p. 47.

18 Here Kepler used the term 'horrida'. On Wackher see Horský, *Kepler v Praze*, pp. 209f.

19 The dramatic events of Rudolph's reign have been described, by, e.g., J. Janáček, *Pád Rudolfa II* ['The fall of Rudolph II'] (Prague, 1975).

20 Even later, in the years 1642–8, when the situation could have been consolidated to some extent, only eight students and one doctor were matriculated, e.g., at the faculty of medicine. See M. Truc, 'Příspěvek k dějinám lékařské fakulty v letech 1638–1954' ['A contribution to the history of the Faculty of Medicine in the years 1638–1654'], *Acta Universitatis Carolinae, Historia Universitatis Carolinae Pragensis*, VII, 1 (1966), p. 9.

21 J. Marcus Marci, *Disputatio medica de temperamento in genere et gravissimorum morborum tetrade, epilepsia, vertigine, appoplexia et paralysi...* (Prague, 1625).

22 O. Temkin, *The Falling Sickness* (Baltimore, 1945), p. 210.

23 For a picture of Marci's life and physics works see J. Smolka, 'Joannes Marcus Marci – His Times, Life and Work', *Acta historiae rerum naturalium necnon technicarum* 3 (Prague, 1967), 5–25. On his medical work see Z. Servít, 'Joannes Marcus Marci. His Contributions in the Field of Medicine and in the Development of Concept relating to Brain Mechanics', *ibid.*, 27–37. Marci's bibliography has been dealt with by D. Ledrerová, *ibid.*, 39–50.

24 For details see J. Klitzner, 'Marcus Marci, der grösste Denker des 17. Jahrhunderts im böhmisch-mährischen Raum', *Zeitschrift für Geschichte und Landeskunde Mährens* 44 (1942), 111–12.

25 For details refer, e.g., to J. Smolka, 'Nové pohledy na J. Marka a jeho dobu. K objevu korespondence s A. Kircherem' ['New approaches to J. Marci and his period. On the discovery of a correspondence with A. Kircher'], *Dějiny věd a techniky* 4 (1970), 44–9. Another very intimate friend of Marci was Juan Caramuel y Lobkovic (1606–82), son of a Dutch noble, who lived at Rudolph's and later at the Spanish court. In 1650 he was appointed vicar-general of the Prague archbishopric; he was one of the most ardent advocates of re-catholicization. Among other things, he studied physics, astronomy and mathematics. For details see A. Denis, *Čechy po Bílé hoře* I, pt. 2 ['Bohemia after the White Mountain'] (Prague, 1931), pp. 12f.

26 *Idearum operatricium idea sive hypothesis et detectio illius occultae virtutis, quae semina faecundat et ex iisdem corpora organica producit* (Prague, 1635)

27 His wife stemmed from the Milan family of the Miseroni who also served at Rudolph's court: Ottavio (d. 1624), for example, was a cutter of precious stones, and Dionysio (d. 1661) administrator of Rudolph's world-famous collections. This fact must have had some influence on Marci's general orientation.

28 See W. Pagel and P. Rattansi, 'Harvey meets the "Hippocrates of Prague"', *Medical History* 8 (1964), 78–84; J. Needham, *A History of Embryology* (New York, 1959), pp. 80f.; V. Kruta, 'Harvey in Bohemia', *Physiologia Bohemo-Slovenica* 6 (1957), p. 433.

29 *De proportione motus seu regula sphygmica ad celeritatem et tarditatem pulsuum ex illius motu ponderibus geometricis liberato absque errore metiendam* (Prague, 1639).

30 *Discorsi e dimonstrazioni matematiche intorno a due nove scienze attentati alla mecanica ed i movimenti locali* (Leiden, 1638).

31 I. B. Cohen, 'Dynamics: The Key to the "New Science" of the Seventeenth Century', *Acta historiae* ... 3, p. 79.

32 Marci, *De proportione motus*, propositiones IV, fo. B 3.

33 'Mutationem motus proportionalem esse vi motrici impressac...'. Attention has also been drawn to the opposite factor, i.e. that in the formulation of 'impressed force', which appears here, Newton was under the influence of an older tradition: '...he seems to have had in the back of his mind the old scholastic dictum: Cessante causa cessat effectus', M. Jammer, *Concepts of Force. A Study in the Foundation of Dynamics* (Cambridge, Mass., 1957), p. 121.

34 'Velocitas continuo augetur in motu naturali, minuitur in moto violento', Marci, *De proportione motus*, propositio IX, fo. E 2.

35 'Perpendiculum ex quolibet puncto eiusdem circuli aequali tempore recurrit in suam stationem', *ibid.*, propositio XXIV, fo. I 1.

36 'Motus perfecte mixtus fit per diametrum parallelogrami, cuius latera constituit
motus simplex…', *Ibid.*, propositio XXXII, fo. K 2.

37 'Corpora percussa alia esse molia, quorum partes percussioni cedunt, inter se
vero unitae manent…Alia dura; et siquidem percussioni nullo modo cedunt,
absolute dura…Corpora autem dura absolute quia neque perfornatur, neque
partes habent percussioni cedentes, aequalem recipiunt atque inferunt plagam,
motum vero ex illa plaga reflectunt, atque eo magis, quo duritie magis
praestant,' *ibid.*, fo. L 3, 4. These words are quite clear. The remark made by
E. Hiebert is therefore not correct: '…G. Baliani, M. Marcus, Toricelli,
H. Fabri, and G. Borelli. In none of these works was there any clarity in the
distinction between elastic and inelastic collision,' *Historical roots of the principle
of conservation of energy* (Madison, 1962), p. 72 n. 30.

38 '…impulsus enim, quo globus ligneus ad motum concinatur, haud quaquam
loco movebit pilam ferream eiusdem molis aut maiorem: at vero si huius
impulsu moveatur globus ligneus, motu agitabitur multo velociore,' *ibid.*, fo. M
1, 2. The following remark is also significant: '…Hanc proportionem motus et
impulsus non a mole, sed a gravitate illorum corporum determinari…', *ibid.*, fo.
M 2.

39 '…motum quatenus a gravitate procedit eiusdem speciei seu gradus, eadem
celeritate fieri in omnibus, quantumvis mole, figura, pondere a se different…illam inaequalitatem motus, quo inaequalia pondera moventur, esse a
medio, in quo fit motus…', *ibid.*, fo. P 1.

40 R. Dugas, *La Mécanique au XVIIᵉ siècle* (Neuchatel, 1956), p. 72, values Galileo
in this respect quite categorically: 'Sur la percussion, Galilée s'est montré très
confus. C'est là, comme l'a noté Huygens, une notion qu'il ne maîtrisera pas.'

41 See for example F. Studnička, *Joannes Marcus Marci a Cronland, sein Leben und
gelehrtes Wirken* (Prague, 1891), pp. 23–4. They were also greatly appreciated by
E. Mach, *Die Mechanik in ihrer Entwickelung historisch-kritisch dargestellt* (Leipzig,
1883), p. 284.

42 For more particulars about this journey see Z. Pokorný, 'Dopis Marka Marci
Galileimu' ['Letter of Joannes Marcus Marci to Galileo,'] *Sborník pro dějiny
přírodních věd a techniky* 9 (Prague, 1964), 7–19; pp. 12. During this trip Marci
met in Graz with Paul Guldin who enabled him to read the *Discorsi*. They
apparently made a great impression on Marci, so that, after his return to
Prague, he sent his book *De proportione motus* and a letter to Galileo. Among other
things he also wrote in the letter: '…verum librum tuum Graecii primum
aspexi, dum Italiam deinde peterem, a Patre Gulden mathematico illius legendi
spatio dumtaxat unius diei mihi copia facta.' However, the blind Galileo did
not respond. Pokorný's translation of Marci's letter was based on the Latin
version published by A. Favaro in *Le opere di Galileo Galilei*, XVIII (Florence,
1906), pp. 267f.

43 They are the *Anatomia demonstrationis…de angulo, quo iris continetur* and *Dissertatio
in propositiones physicomathematicas de natura iridos R. P. Baltharsaris Conradi…* (both
Prague, 1650).

44 This question has been studied by, for example, G. Sarton, 'Discovery of the
Dispersion of Light and of the Nature of Color (1672)', *Isis* 14 (1930), 326–8.
However, he does not admit that Newton knew Marci's *Thaumantias*.

45 The author of Newton's biography, S. I. Vavilov, *Issak Nyuton* (Moscow and
Leningrad, 1945), p. 31, suggests in several places that some opinions of Barrow

published in his 'Optical Lectures' (and reviewed by Newton before they were printed) are reminiscent of Marci, although his name is not explicitly mentioned. See also L. T. More, Isaac Newton. A Biography (New York and London, 1934), p. 80.

46 Most credit for this study is due to Jiří Marek, who published a whole series of papers on Marci's optics, e.g. 'Prvé zprávy o pozorování ohybu světla na štěrbině v českých zemích' ['The first reports of observations of light diffraction on a slit in the Czech Lands'], Sborník pro dějiny přírodních věd a techniky 8 (Prague, 1963), 5–42; 'Pozorování ohybu světla a barev tenkých vrstev u Jana Marka Marci' ['Observations of light diffraction and colours of thin layers by Joannes Marcus Marci'], ibid. 7 (1962), 62–85; 'Vztah Jana Marka Marci k Huygensovu principu ['The relation of Joannes Marcus Marci to Huygens' principle'], ibid. 9 (1964), 71–80; 'The Observation of the Interference of the Light of Higher Orders in 1646 and its Response', Nature 201 (1964), 110, etc.

47 B. Bauman, Filosofické názory Jana Marka Marci ['The philosophical opinions of JMM'] (Prague, 1957), p. 20, quotes this fact, referring to W. R. Newbold, The Cipher of Roger Bacon (Philadelphia, 1928), p. 33.

48 Credit for this valuable finding is also due to J. Marek, 'Jan Marcus Marci a londýnská Royal Society' ['JMM and the London Royal Society'], Sborník pro dějiny...9, (1964), 81–2.

49 In the author's opinion, this mainly concerns the re-evaluation of his philosophical opinions. Marci's sensualism, for example, still remains unappreciated. Long before Locke's Essay concerning Human Understanding he wrote: 'Nihil enim in intellectu, cuius notitia non fuit in sensu' (Pan en panton seu Philosophia vetus restituta (Prague, 1662) p. 412), to which, e.g., Servít, p. 34, drew attention. It is also necessary to re-evaluate his treatise Otho-Sophia seu philosophia impulsus universalis..., (Prague, 1683), published from his literary remains, which is considered to be philosophical but is in fact thoroughly physical – nobody has so far studied it in detail. A considerable task is the analytical processing and publishing of Marci's correspondence with Kircher, Caramuel and others.

50 'Mare Moretus' was named in his memory on the Moon's surface.

51 In hispanicized form Estanzielo; see I. Newton, Philosophiae naturalis principia mathematica (Amsterdam, 1723), p. 474 (prop. XLI, probl. XXI).

52 These questions have been discussed in detail by Smolka and Horský in the appropriate chapters of Dějiny exaktních věd... ['History of the exact sciences...'], pp. 70–82. As regards the biographies and bibliographies of the individual persons, a very useful tool is I. Čorncjová and A. Fechtnerová, Životopisný slovník pražské university (Filosofická a teologická fakulta 1654–1773) ['Biographical dictionary of the Prague University'], (Prague, 1986).

53 In this connection it is interesting that Comenius bought from the widow of Jacob Christmann, a professor at Heidelberg, Copernicus' manuscript of De revolutionibus orbium coelestium, later referred to as the so-called Prague holograph, which became the property of O. Nostic in the years 1626–30. Cf. Birkenmajer, Mikolaj Kopernik, p. 642.

54 Most recently, this topic has been comprehensively discussed by R. Kolomý, 'K přijetí Newtonovy fyziky u nás' ['On the acceptance of Newton's physics in Bohemia'], Zborník dejín fyziky 5 (Liptovský Mikuláš, 1987), 30–45.

9

INSTITUTING SCIENCE IN SWEDEN

SVEN WIDMALM

INTRODUCTION

THE ideas, the organization, and the technology associated with the seventeenth century Scientific Revolution were introduced into Sweden in three steps. First, Cartesian philosophy (with Copernican cosmology) was imported in the course of a prolonged academic row in the second half of the seventeenth century; second, institutions of the continental and British academy type were created in the first half of the eighteenth century, while at the same time Newtonianism and experimental physics made their entry; third, in the decades around the mid-eighteenth century, science reached maturity with Swedish scientists achieving international eminence in a number of fields – especially in natural history, mineralogy and chemistry. Carl Linnaeus (von Linné) and his colleagues made the eighteenth century a golden age for Swedish science (and a favourite topic for latter-day historians of science).[1] Around 1780, however, the position as one of the most active scientific nations in Europe was lost, and toward the end of the century Swedish science had been reduced to relative obscurity.

In the following, the technical or philosophical aspects of Swedish science will be touched upon but lightly; the development will be discussed primarily from the institutional point of view. The seventeenth century will therefore be dealt with briefly, while the organization of the forces of Swedish science, which occurred in part as a response to the disintegration of the forces of the Swedish military, will be given a fuller treatment. We will see that Swedish science flourished when the scientists successfully managed to find support from the temporal powers – the Diet (*Riksdag*), which swayed the country 1720–72, during the so-called Age of Freedom (or Age of Liberty: *Frihetsiden*), when Sweden seemed a republic in all but name. The close relationship between science and the Swedish brand of parliamentarism is borne out by the simultaneous eclipse of both in the 1770s, when the enlightened despot Gustav III reintroduced absolutism and the scientific development in Sweden dwindled.

THE INTRODUCTION OF THE NEW PHILOSOPHY

Cartesianism was first brought to Sweden in the form of René Descartes himself, who died, a guest of Queen Kristina's, in the cold Stockholm winter of 1650. At Uppsala University it was introduced about a decade later, by the professors of medicine Petrus Hoffvenius and Olof Rudbeck, both educated in Leiden. The so-called Cartesian controversies which erupted on account of this followed a pattern of academic dispute established on the continent, beginning in the Netherlands in the 1640s.[2] Cartesianism – together with Gassendi's atomism – aroused the suspicion of theologians and in 1664 the first controversy began. Theologians demanded that the chancellor of Uppsala University should prohibit the philosophy of Descartes – mainly, it seems, because they were upset by the frivolous biblical exegesis put forth by its advocates, and by the threat that the new philosophy posed to the Aristotelian idea of form. The action failed, however, and the theologians were forced to conduct a positional academic war to force Cartesianism out of the curriculum. They temporarily succeeded, largely because Rudbeck and Hoffvenius were the only professors who supported the new philosophy, and only Hoffvenius was prepared to put up a fight for it.

In the 1680s, however, the Cartesians had multiplied, and now it was they who took to the offensive against the theologians. Rudbeck and his colleagues in the faculties of medicine and philosophy denounced the philosophy of papist scholasticism and praised the rationalism of Descartes, the empiricism of Bacon and the experimentalism of the Royal Society and the Académie des Sciences.

This the second Cartesian controversy was a Swedish version of the Battle of the Books; the outcome was a standoff, which in reality spelled defeat for the theologians.[3] In 1689, the absolute king, Karl XI, proclaimed that philosophic speculation could be pursued freely as long as it did not contradict the letter of the Bible. The Bible *per se* was not of great concern for Cartesian natural philosophy, so its adherents could rightly claim victory. Copernican cosmology followed suit and was accepted at about the same time.[4] In the second decade of the eighteenth century, Cartesian physics was taught at the secondary grammar schools. In the 1720s, young mathematicians like Anders Celsius and Samuel Klingenstierna embraced Newtonianism and also the rationalist philosophy of Christian Wolff. Newton's ideas seem not to have caused any strife, whereas the authorities opposed Wolffianism to begin with, but made it the bulwark of orthodoxy in the 1740s.[5]

THE RUDBECKIAN LEGACY

In the second half of the seventeenth century, Uppsala University – by far the most important academic institution in Sweden – was dominated by the imposing personality of Olof Rudbeck Sr, professor of medicine 1660–91. He had made his scientific reputation as an anatomist, by the discovery of the lymphatic vessels in the early 1650s. Later, however, his vast energies were directed elsewhere: botany and history became the main areas of research for this Renaissance figure. With the assistance of his son, Olof Rudbeck Jr, he created a foundation of sorts for the Linnaean science of the next century, and he laboured on the monumental *Atlantica* (1679–1702), a speculative history of Sweden.

Rudbeck was an important ally of the Cartesians though he himself had some qualms about the new philosophy and stayed in the background during the heat of struggle. The *Atlantica*, which took up more and more of his time, was a project of quite another dimension and scope, both more fantastic – truly baroque – and more provincial, than that of natural philosophy. By empirical research in the Baconian vein, Rudbeck claimed to have verified the fundamental tenets of the Gothicist theory of history: that Sweden (or rather the Scandinavian peninsula) was the home of the Goths, who had conquered Rome, and of the Hyperboreans; it was the cradle of Western civilization, and Swedish nature was particularly bountiful, making the country potentially very rich.[6]

Gothicism had been around since the Middle Ages, it received a boost in the sixteenth century, when Sweden became self-governed and Protestant, and its popularity received new impetus with the growth of Sweden's political power in the seventeenth century. Hence, Rudbeck had a long tradition to build on, and the current political situation made the late seventeenth century a timely moment to put forth a historical synthesis of the Gothicist brand. Rudbeck added many stunning new insights to the body of received Gothicist opinion, using etymology, archaeology, astronomy and geology. Among other things, he presented post-diluvian Sweden as the 'womb of the human race' (*vagina gentium*), he identified Sweden with Plato's Atlantis, and Old Uppsala with the magnificent capital of the sunken island (which Rudbeck naturally claimed was a peninsula, sunk, not in the real sea but in that of oblivion).

Rudbeck managed to reinterpret much of the history and the mythology of Antiquity as a story about Sweden's glorious past. Sweden was potentially rich; it was also the original home of many branches of learning, especially astronomy, encouraged by the ancient cult of the Sun. (Knowledge about the zodiac had, according to Rudbeck, been brought from Sweden to Greece by Orpheus.)

With Rudbeck's *Atlantica* Gothicism reach its climax, and it was to hold a grip upon the imagination of patriotic Swedes well beyond the period of political greatness, into the 1740s (to be revived once again with the advent of Romantic nationalism in the early nineteenth century). Gothicism, or Rudbeckianism, was an important ideological backdrop for the attempts to introduce a modern organization for scientific research into Sweden. The notions, that Sweden was particularly well suited to scientific research, and that the country could become wealthy by exploiting its vast natural resources, inspired generations of scientists and economists.

PATRIOTIC SCIENCE[7]

The vision that carried Rudbeck's patriotism further than that of his precursors or successors was obviously fuelled by the contemporary political situation. Never before had Sweden managed to achieve the position of a military Great Power; under Karl XI, the Baltic Sea was a *mare nostrum*, but after his death in 1697 the Baltic empire started to crumble. His son, Karl XII, upheld the military strength of the country for a while, but after his death in 1718 the loss of military importance, apparent since the battle of Poltava in 1709, became definite. The economy was in a sorry state, not only because of the wars but also because of a severe outbreak of the plague, which hit the country in 1710/11.

From 1710 and into the 1730s the sense of having lived through a national disaster of immense magnitude affected the intellectual climate in Sweden. Science was advertised as a possible means to achieve a national revival. The Gothicism of Rudbeck was an important factor in the creation of a patriotic science which would restore the economy and replace Sweden's military notoriety by cultural repute. The sciences of Descartes, Newton and Huygens, as well as the natural history of Rudbeck himself, would prosper under the northern skies. It has been said that mathematics, physics and mechanics were 'ennobled to become primarily patriotic sciences' at this time.[8] This was true also of natural history, and of scholarly disciplines like history and linguistics. It was argued that Sweden offered peculiar advantages for scientific research; in particular its northern part (Lapland) was seen as a scientific resource, advantageous for work in astronomy, physics and natural history.[9]

It was in the first year of plague, when 'hunger and war had brought the country to the utmost brink of destruction', that the first scientific society in Sweden was founded.[10] Uppsala university was temporarily closed down and some members of the staff formed a private club for discussing scholarly, scientific and technological issues. They called themselves the 'Collegium Curiosorum', and the leading members were the university librarian Eric Benzelius Jr, and Christopher Polhem, the eminent mining engineer.

A typical example of the patriotic view of science among the members of this group is found in a list of twenty 'experiments that are necessary to perform in the mountains and valleys of Lapland'.[11] It was drawn up by Polhem in 1711, in preparation for a scientific expedition to Torneå (on the northern board of the Gulf of Bothnia). The expedition was a failure, but the 'experiments' remained central to the program of patriotic science throughout the 1720s. The first was a measurement of an arc of meridian, to determine the shape of the earth through a comparison with Picard's and Cassini's measurements in France. This undertaking had been on the agenda already in 1695, when two mathematicians visited Torneå in the first scientific expedition in Sweden ever. Geodetic measurements in the north remained a central feature in the patriotic program because they constituted a task which combined its essential features: high relevance for international science, and the utilization of peculiar traits of Swedish nature – in this case, accessibility to northern latitudes and frozen waters, thought to be essential commodities for measuring long distances on the earth's surface that would yield decisive information about its shape when collated with data from more southern parts of Europe.

Polhem also suggested experiments in acoustics, that were to capitalize on the great differences in height between mountains and valleys in the north, experiments with the pendulum, investigations of refraction in water and air at different altitudes, and physical experiments with ice. Polhem saw Lapland as a great outdoor laboratory.

Emanuel Swedenborg – being a close associate of Polhem and Benzelius' brother-in-law – was intimately connected with the Uppsala group. He published what may be regarded as the unofficial transactions of the Collegium Curiosorum: the Daedalus Hyperboreus (1716–17), the first scientific journal in Sweden. Here, several of Polhem's experiments were described, 'to show that experiments are more abundant in our country than in others'.[12] Swedenborg proudly wrote about 'experiments that can be performed during winter through our Swedish cold'; he described four such experiments that all involved the study of ice, asserting that 'these and other experiments can be executed in Sweden better than anywhere else in the world'.[13] Swedenborg embraced Rudbeck's teachings, and in his writings from around 1720 the links between Gothicism and patriotic science become conspicuous.[14]

By the help of arguments heavily scented with Gothicist rhetoric Swedenborg advocated the building of an observatory and the creation of a Swedish academy of sciences modelled after the Royal Society. In 1716, he and Polhem met with Karl XII to discuss scientific development in Sweden, but shortly afterwards the king was assassinated.[15] Instead, Benzelius took the initiative of reforming Swedish science. In 1719 he revived his Collegium under a new name, calling it the Science Society ('Bokwettsgillet'; from 1728 'Kungl. Vetenskapssocieteten' or Societas regia literaria et scientiarum). It was anticipated that the new Uppsala society should become a counterpart to those in London, Berlin, Saint Petersburg and Paris: a national academy, but promoting a particularly Swedish brand of science and economically useful research. During the 1720s and the early 1730s the members discussed science and humanities largely in a national context; they set about exploring the natural and human resources of Sweden as a means to aid the recovery of national renown and economy. The Society issued a journal, the *Acta Literaria Sveciae*. Swedenborg's journal, which reflected the activities of Benzelius' society in its early phase, was written in Swedish, the language of the Goths; the new journal was in Latin, which indicated the growing international ambitions of the Uppsala group. The patriotic programme of the Society embodied the urge toward internationalism: Swedish scientists had a responsibility to provide foreign colleagues with information that could be gathered in the north and in the north only.

The Society met two or three times a month. *Sweden*, from just about any perspective, was the dominating theme of discussion. The Fatherland was considered from the aspects of natural history, astronomy, meteorology, history, linguistics and ethnology. Special attention was paid to the vast almost unknown Lapland. Olof Rudbeck Jr was an ardent student of Lapland natural history (he had been a member of the party which went to Torneå in 1695), and of Laplander culture and language. He sought confirmation of his father's Gothicist theories and collected material to prove that the Laplanders were descended from one of the lost tribes of Israel. But he was by no means alone in his preoccupation with Lapland, though his particular line of inquiry was rather unusual. Benzelius, Polhem and others treated the subject from different aspects.[16] A major preoccupation was the need for a natural-history inventory of Sweden. The Society sponsored Linnaeus' early work, above all his seminal expedition to Lapland in 1732. Gunnar Broberg has argued that the young Linnaeus was deeply influenced by Rudbeckian thinking, and his Lapland journey was surely the greatest moment of patriotic science.[17] It resulted in, among other things, the popular *Flora lapponica*, published in Holland in 1737, where Linnaeus mixed Lapland exotica with descriptive botany and discussions on systematics.

Around 1725 intensive efforts were made to strengthen the position of the Society. State institutions like the Board of Mines (Begskollegium) and the Board of Medicine (Collegium Medicum) were approached in order to establish scientific collaboration, as was the university. It was hoped to bring about a transformation of the professorship in poetics at Uppsala into a chair in physics. It was expected that the Society could then make use of the experimental apparatus that had to be purchased by the university if such a chair was established. The university authorities were approached, but no professorship in experimental physics emerged until 1750, with Klingenstierna as its first incumbent.[18] It was the itinerant experimental physicist and steam-engine builder Mårten Triewald who, in 1728, introduced this particular species of science to a Swedish audience.[19]

As a member of the ecclesiastical estate, Benzelius had achieved a strong position in the Diet. In the mid-1720s he used it in order to secure royal charters for his society. More important, he wanted financial support for the building of an observatory in Uppsala and a monopoly of almanac publishing for the Society. The Society had been founded, he wrote, in order to 'serve the Fatherland, to make it famous among foreign nations for learning and science, as, up till now, it has been famous for valour and bravery'.[20] This exemplifies the connection typically made by the members of the Uppsala group between Sweden's past as a warring nation and its future as a scientific nation. Benzelius emphasized the responsibility that Swedish scientists had of carrying out research that depended on 'our position, close to the pole'.[21] He mentioned the study of refraction, observations to determine parallaxes, geodetic measurements to determine the shape of the earth, the study of the Aurora Borealis, meteorology and fact-gathering in natural history. In all of these areas, scientists in England and France eagerly awaited news from their colleagues in the north. That Benzelius' scheme was not just empty rhetoric is shown by the fact that several young scientists did try to make a name for themselves through work of this kind. Linnaeus has already been mentioned; both Celsius and Triewald tried to establish international reputations with scientific studies of the Aurora Borealis.[22]

Benzelius' campaign was nominally successful but in reality a failure. In 1728, royal charters were granted to the Society, Count Arvid Horn, the most powerful politician of the day, agreed to become *praeses illustris*, and honorary members from the nobility were elected. No observatory and no monopoly of almanac publishing were forthcoming, however – the reason apparently being political differences between Benzelius and Horn.[23] The Royal Society of Uppsala therefore had its wings clipped from the start; it was never to amount to much more than a professorial association.

Benzelius left Uppsala in 1726, for an ecclesiastical career which would eventually make him archbishop of Sweden (like two of his brothers and their father before them – kinship was most important for promotions in the church and at the university). Celsius then took over the leadership of the Society. He became professor of mathematics (astronomy) in 1730 (following in the footsteps of his father and his paternal as well as his maternal grandfather), and during the period 1732–7 he was away – first on an educational trip abroad and in 1736–7 in the region of Torneå, as a member of the famous French expedition under Pierre-Louis Moreau de Maupertuis which attempted to measure the shape of the earth. With no money and no leadership, the Science Society lay dormant during these years.

Maupertuis' expedition marked the end of the first attempt to create an institutional setting for modern science in Sweden.[24] Benzelius was disgusted that the Swedish government had not given one iota of support for the work which had been so high on the agenda of patriotic research over the past decades; Celsius explained that his experiences in the north showed that the country was unfit for practical astronomy: in the summer the midnight sun made the sky too bright, and in the winter, 'when you make your observations your fingers freeze till they fall off'.[25]

As it turned out, by the time the ambitions of the Uppsala group were thwarted, modern science in Sweden had really taken off. Shortly after his return to Uppsala, Celsius did manage to get money for an observatory; completed in 1742, it was the first of its kind in Sweden.[26] In 1739, the Royal Swedish Academy of Sciences ('Kungl. Svenska Vetenskapsakademien') was founded in Stockholm, on the initiative of Linnaeus and Triewald. The new academy succeeded (in 1747) in procuring the almanac monopoly which Benzelius had so eagerly desired, and by 1753 it had managed to build the first relatively successful observatory in Sweden (Celsius' by and large being a failure).

The success of the Academy of Sciences was closely related to a major

shift in Swedish politics, the rise to power of the so-called Hat party at
the Diet of 1738–9. The connection was represented in the flesh by
Anders Johan von Höpken, one of the Young Turks in the Hat party,
and also among the six founding members of the Academy. Thirty years
later, Höpken, now an ex-premier, liked to look back at the founding of
the Academy as one of the many blessings brought to the country by the
– then deeply unpopular – Hat party.[27]

In their heyday, the Hats had aimed to make the country rich by
promoting (and subsidizing) trade and industry, to make it strong by
reforming agriculture and increasing the population, and to regain some
of its former military might through an alliance with France directed
against Russia. They differed from the opposition, the Caps, by their
more radical mercantilism, by their pro-French policy, and by their
strong opposition to monarchical rule; in constitutional matters, radical
Hats by mid-century leaned toward republicanism. The rise of Hats and
Caps gave Swedish parliamentarism a party political structure similar to
that of Britain.[28] Politics became polarized, and science benefited from
this as the Academy of Sciences became closely associated with the ruling
Hats. The Academy was seen as instrumental for the implementation
of Hat policy; hence it received strong political support and was able to
raise the level of Swedish science to previously unknown heights.

SCIENTISTS SERVING THE STATE

Lorraine Daston has recently argued that the internationalism typical
of eighteenth century science disappeared under dramatic circumstances
after the French Revolution; especially under Napoleon, French
scientists renounced their membership in the Republic of Letters and put
their services at the state's disposal, provoking a similar reaction among
British colleagues.[29]

In Sweden, however, a comparable situation had emerged already in
the late 1730s. By 1740 an ideological consensus among proponents of
modern science and representatives of the political establishment
(predominantly aristocratic) had emerged; it was founded on the tripod
of physico-theology, mercantilism and utilitarianism.[30] In an important
article on the social functions of the natural sciences in the second half
of the eighteenth century, Karin Johannisson has written that 'the
identification of national economic with scientific goals was the core' of
the activities at the Academy of Sciences around mid-century.[31] Again
and again it was claimed, in the tradition of Ray, Derham and Wolff,
that God had created the world so that man could both comprehend and

extract its manifold riches; in the tradition of Colbert, that the state must encourage manufacturers to exploit and process natural resources in order to increase export and decrease import; and, in the Baconian tradition, that empirical science was the means to make such an exploitation feasible. As one of the most influential Hat ideologists put it: theoretical models 'bear less similarity to the created world than a rotten Lap hut to the most magnificent castle'; science should 'be of use to humankind and, above all, to the Republic'.[32]

By and large this was the usual admixture of elements that went into the fabric of early Enlightenment optimism, but it achieved an especially strong impetus in Sweden because of the near unanimity by which it was adhered to, by academics, engineers, priests, civil servants, businessmen and members of the aristocracy.

The kind of 'science' (*wetenskap* – a wide concept, including technology) which the members of the Academy subscribed to was commonly labelled 'economy' (*oeconomi*), or even 'Divine Economy'.[33] According to Linnaeus, economy was 'the science which teaches us to use the natural objects by means of the elements'.[34] Hence, to Linnaeus, natural history and physics were the two foundations of economy – together they would help increase the wealth of the nation. The economist Anders Berch devised a more complete system of economic science, with natural history, physics, chemistry etc. as important sub-specialities. Berch's views carried much weight; in 1741 he was appointed first holder of the chair in economics at Uppsala – a professorship forced on the university by the government, making Berch a semi-official ideologist for the Hats.[35]

This view of science – not separating it from technology – had social implications. Celsius wrote that in the Academy, a 'minister should not forbear to be seated at the same table as a craftsman', and to some extent this social levelling was realized.[36] The Academy became a platform for a new alliance between members of the professional and the leisured classes, between intellectuals, mechanics, businessmen and aristocracy, who shared the political views of the Hat party. Together they produced a steady stream of publications all written in Swedish, which signifies the reorientation from an audience of international scientists, at which the *Acta* of the Science Society was aimed, to a national audience, which would partake in the creation of a flourishing economy according to Hat precepts. Paradoxically, the effect was that Swedish science for the first time became a concern for scientists in the major European countries. From 1749 the Academy's Proceedings (*Handlingar*) were translated into German in extenso, and volumes of selected articles were published in Latin, Dutch, Italian, Danish and French (by d'Holbach).[37] A modern reader is struck by the blending of articles on science and on technology (with the latter predominating): to contemporaries it was all *wetenskap*. The Academy also published its Presidential Addresses (*Presidietal*), where matters of national economy and technology were often given a broader political treatment; and, like its French counterpart, it published *éloges* of deceased members, which celebrated the promoters of knowledge and industry.

The international attention which the Academy received was due to the fact that many of its members were leading practitioners of their respective fields: Linnaeus and his flock of disciples in natural history; Charles De Geer and Carl Clerck in entomology; Nils Rosén von Rosenstein in paediatrics; Axel Fredrik Cronstedt, Johan Gottschalk Wallerius and others in mineralogy; Torbern Bergman and Carl Wilhelm Scheele in chemistry; Pehr Wilhelm Wargentin in astronomy; Klingenstierna in mathematics and physics; Johan Carl Wilcke in experimental physics. The quality and quantity of Swedish science had increased dramatically since the early decades of the eighteenth century, and the Academy – in particular during Wargentin's term as permanent secretary, 1749–83 – was its institutional focus.

The breakthrough for modern science in Sweden was much indebted to the successful management of the scientific forces of many institutions by the Academy of Sciences, and especially by its secretary Wargentin. He corresponded with all and sundry – humble priests and physicians in the provinces, as well as professors and ministers, and also with a large number of foreign scientists.[38] He was at the centre of a network which coordinated the work of scientific professionals and amateurs in Sweden, and made possible the creation of a united scientific community; the foreign relations kept up by Wargentin, and colleagues like Linnaeus, placed this community squarely at the centre of the European stage.

In a national context, the Academy may be viewed as a cover organization for a number of state institutions. This function is a key to the understanding of its success and, later, its loss of vigour.[39] Under Wargentin's skilful leadership the Academy promoted the interests of the National Land Survey ('Lantmäteriverket', founded in 1628), the Board of Mines (1637), the Board of Medicine (1663), and the universities in Lund, Åbo, Greifswald, and, in particular, Uppsala.

The Academy opened the pages of its publications to professional men associated with all these institutions. They published results of scientific and technological work in the Proceedings and statements on policy in the Presidential Addresses. Through the politically well connected Wargentin, and other influential members, the Academy functioned as a lobby for scientific and technological interests in the Diet. They also maintained good relations with the Lutheran State Church, its clergy constituting a small but important group in the Academy, often with botanical or zoological interests. The church's affiliation with the Academy was manifested on the ideological plane, by physico-theology, and on the administrative plane, by Wargentin's and Linnaeus' membership of the committee that planned a new translation of the Bible in the 1770s. Linnaeus wanted to use the clergy as a subsidiary force for natural history, surveying the flora and fauna of the nation from north to south. In this he was successful. Swedish priests would cultivate Linnaean science for generations to come.[40] Similarly, Berch thought the country priests should disseminate information about modern farming technology to the peasantry.[41]

The Academy took an active part in the running of several minor state institutions. The Office of Tables ('Tabellverker', 1749) was more or less annexed to the Academy. Plans for this Office were drawn up by Wargentin's predecessor Pehr Elvius Jr, and its pioneering work in population statistics was led by Wargentin and his successor Henrik Nicander.[42] As the statistics were based on the parish registers, this work relied on the cooperation of the church. Wargentin also organized geodetic measurements for the admiralty's sea chart. Beginning in the 1750s they provided many a needy astronomer with a temporal occupation. Papers filled with statistical and geodetical data flowed into the Proceedings from these projects.[43]

The Academy supported, and in time took over the management of, several workshops for the manufacture of scientific instruments and maps.[44] Instruments of high quality were produced by Daniel Ekström, an apprentice of George Graham's. His workshop was formally run by the Surveying Office, but it was located in the basement of the observatory of the Academy where Ekström was a respected member. The quality of the output from his workshop was high also by international standards. It was upheld by the means of government subsidies; he was a benefactor of the pro-manufacture policy of the Hats. The same was true of the internationally renowned globe manufacturer Anders Åkerman, who worked under the auspices of the Cosmographical Society ('Cosmographiska sällskapet') at Uppsala and was supported by the Diet as a result of Wargentin's lobbying.[45]

Unlike in Britain, however, there was no expanding home market where the instrument makers could dispose of their products. They did export some instruments and globes, but to survive they had to rely on state subsidies. These sufficed only for a while, and only for a few makers; hence, no tradition of excellence was established in these areas. Ekström died penniless in 1755, and when Åkerman passed away in 1778 he was on the brink of ruin. The Academy took over both workshops, and also that of the lens manufacturer Carl Lehnberg who, by the help of government support, had produced high quality optical glass but left no money at his death in 1768. By the end of the century there were no makers of advanced scientific instruments in Sweden. The fate of instrument making in the Age of Freedom parallels that of science: it prospered and withered away in conjunction with the economic policy of the Hats.

The Academy itself was not providing income for scientists, with a few exceptions: Wargentin himself and Wilcke, who were receiving very modest salaries indeed, as secretary/astronomer and physicist respectively. (Wilcke's position was financed through a donation.) Most of the *active* scientists in the Academy were professional men: many were academics; chemists, geologists and mineralogists were often employed by the Board of Mines; a good number were physicians or priests; technicians and craftsmen were fairly common; only a few were gentlemen of private means, like Charles De Geer. For a while it seemed as if the good will shown toward the sciences by the Diet would result in a steadily growing labour-market for scientific specialists. A few new positions were created at the universities, most notably professorships in chemistry and experimental physics at Uppsala in 1750. These chairs were the result of an otherwise abortive attempt by the Hats to restructure the university in order to change it into an institution for the education, not only of priests, jurists and physicians, but all kinds of civil servants: bureaucrats, military officers, surveyors, mining officials, and so on.[46] This scheme was in line with the utilitarian thinking in Sweden at the time; in a European context it was pretty well unique.

By mid-century the mathematical sciences had become well established through the work of Klingenstierna, Celsius, and his successor Mårten Strömer. Their pupils were competent, and in a few cases brilliant. For a while it seemed as if they would also be able to find employment. The Surveying Office planned to go in for large scale geodetic measurements, but when the enclosure movement gained momentum in the 1750s geodesy was cut out and the Office only employed one astronomer at very low pay.[47] The admiralty employed a handful of astronomers for their hydrographical measurements, but not in permanent positions. At the universities, salaried positions were hard to come by. Even a professor often had to wait for years before he received payment as the salary was reserved for his predecessor until death.

The 1760s brought military fiasco in the Seven Years' War, financial crisis, and political upheavals – all of which contributed to the breaking of Hat power. According to the most radical Hat ideologist, the Hobbistically inclined scientist and bishop Johan Browallius, the Diet was to be considered infallible. But in 1772 the Leviathan of the Hats was replaced by the enlightened despot Gustav III. With his coup d'état the Diet lost its political power, and the fabric of personal and institutional relationships which Wargentin and others had woven, in order to unite science and government, was rent. Johannisson has traced the descent of Swedish science to the 1760s; by the 1770s it was obvious to all; and in the 1780s the scientists complained loud and wide about the state of affairs.[48] To put it bluntly, as contemporaries did, there were no jobs for scientists, especially not for mathematicians and astronomers. Complaints were to no avail. At the turn of the century, a close-knit community of creative Swedish scientists no longer existed. We still find competent practitioners of, in particular, the Linnaean sciences working at the universities; but the sense of common interest which had made scientific life in Sweden in the mid-eighteenth century so lively is gone.

Changes in the constitution of the Academy's membership indicate that utilitarianism lost its hold on Swedish science towards the end of the century.[49] In mid-century, academics made up between 10 and 15 per cent of the membership; between 1765 and 1800 this figure was nearly 25 per cent. Physicians constituted 5–10 per cent of the membership in mid-century; thereafter their number increased, reaching almost 20 per cent by 1800. The percentage of technologically oriented professionals, on the other hand, decreased with time. This group – consisting of e.g. military engineers, mining engineers, architects and surveyors – was very well represented in the crop of members elected in 1739, the first year of the Academy's existence: almost 30 per cent. Between 1750 and 1770 it was slightly less than 20 per cent, and in the last two decades of the century it remained on a level of c. 15 per cent. The percentage of civil servants also decreased, though less markedly, from around 20 by mid century to around 15 in the 1780s and 1790s.

Hence, the membership of the Academy became less diversified with time. Technicians and civil servants were not homogeneous groups, like physicians and academics; they represented many institutions and also private business. Their waning influence within the Academy indicates that it lost its role as a cover organization for different interest groups and that its utilitarian ethos faded. The diminishing utilitarian zeal is readily seen also in the decrease in the number of articles covering economically relevant topics in the Proceedings. Here, a dramatic drop occurs in the 1780s, from 30–40 per cent since mid-century to 10–20 per cent until the 1810s, and after that even lower.[50] It should be emphasized, however, that this was a gradual process. The 1790s did for example see a minor revival of utilitarianism, but in the early nineteenth century the Academy finally turned into an academic rather than an economic society. From the 1770s onward, societies and journals were founded specializing in practically oriented fields like agriculture, military science, medicine, or mining. After the turn of the century, the splitting of *wetenskap* into 'science' and 'technology' had become a fact.

REFLECTIONS ON THE SCIENTIFIC REVOLUTION IN SWEDEN

The concept of Scientific Revolution may be used in different ways. It may denote an unspecified change of scientific thought or practice, in which case it resides in the eye of the beholder: if you are sensitive enough you can detect revolutions everywhere.[51] A revolution in science may also, with Thomas S. Kuhn, be seen as a sudden change in the way of conceiving the world – in the 'world view', as Swedes (and Germans) are apt to put it. It then depends upon the peculiar dynamics of the collective intellectual enterprise of scientists. This paper has adopted a more neutral and socially oriented position: by the consent of historians the major reorientation of scientific thought and organization which took place in the seventeenth century in Europe is called the Scientific Revolution. The breakthrough of the new modes of thinking and organization in Sweden constitutes *its* Scientific Revolution. As the history of Sweden differs from that of England or France, however, the Swedish revolution has peculiarities of its own.

If we accept Roy Porter's view, that a scientific revolution should include the 'overthrow of an entrenched orthodoxy' by protagonists of a new intellectual order, then the Swedish Scientific Revolution was effected by 1689, when the prohibition against Cartesianism was lifted.[52] At that time, however, the scientific *movement* in Sweden was hardly more than a ripple on the surface of the academic duck pond. It would take several decades before it gained momentum and led to a modern scientific institution in Sweden.

In the second decade of the eighteenth century, the engineers Polhem and Swedenborg, who were thoroughly Cartesian in their scientific outlook, and above all the scholar Benzelius, attempted to launch Swedish science onto the international scene by adopting new models of organization, patterned after foreign academies. They put forth an ideal of scientific research which, in this paper, has been termed 'patriotic'. Sweden, and especially Lapland, was made for science, it was claimed; a well endowed academy would be able to harvest the scientific fruits of the land and make Sweden culturally and also economically prominent. Hence, most of the ideas of how and why Swedish science should be supported, that were later to prove successful, were already formulated by the 1720s; it took another two decades before political support was rallied. The members of the Academy at Stockholm emphasized the economic aspect of patriotic science. The Academy was modelled after the Royal Society, but its close alliance with the Hat government made it similar to the academies in France or Russia. It flourished as long as it was politically well connected; when the political system with which it was associated went downhill, so did the Academy.

So much for the organization and ideology of Swedish science. What about its content? Did Swedish science add something *new* to the European development? If so, Linnaean science is the obvious place to look. Linnaeus is one of the few Swedes throughout history who merits a place in the scientific hall of fame, and he was very much at the centre of stage at the Academy of Sciences in the eighteenth century. Sten Lindroth has written that Linnaeus' sexual system rested on scholastic foundations.[53] He strove to create a system by which the Aristotelian essences of plants could be defined by logical rules. This system would ideally be 'natural' and reflect the 'real' order of nature. This analysis seems to put Linnaeus outside of the Scientific Revolution, and therefore it hardly explains his success. Seen in the institutional and ideological context which has been sketched in this paper Linnaeus becomes more a contemporary of his own age.

Linnaeus benefited from the patriotic program of the Science Society, which exhausted its meagre resources by paying for his trip to Lapland in 1732. Just like Rudbeck, Linnaeus worked in the strictly empirical vein and with an uncanny ability to make masses of facts adjust to a pre-established scheme. He also shared the patriotic view of science. Sweden had the *potential*, Linnaeus claimed, to feed a vast population; by the development of agriculture and industry, not least in the northern parts, its potential would be realized. His own travels in the Swedish provinces were carried out in order to make an inventory of useful natural resources. Linnaeus was, most of the time, a reliable supporter of the Hat party, and he was perhaps the most eloquent spokesman for the peculiar ideology which united scientists, politicians and industrialists in mid-century. In a speech held before the royal couple in 1759 he presented a catalogue of arguments in favour of scientific research. The take-home lesson for the royal couple was that the well-being of the country demanded state support for the sciences:

> Without sciences, we would
> bring in *Priests* from Rome.
> *Physicians* from Montpellier.

Architects from Venice...
Clothes from Brabant.
Calendars from Lübeck.
Turnips and *Root-crops* from Hamburg.
...[54]

    The Linnaean method, with its emphasis (manifest in his very rhetoric) on collecting and classifying vast amounts of data characterized Swedish science in general in the eighteenth century. Its most notable achievements, in natural history, chemistry and mineralogy, follow the Linnaean patterns. Swedes became experts in identifying new plants, animals, minerals, and elements; the construction of classification schemes became a favourite occupation not only of biologists, but of chemists and mineralogists like Wallerius, Bergman, and a host of colleagues working in the laboratory of the Board of Mines.[55] We find a similar mind at work behind Wargentin's statistical tables of the moons of Jupiter and of the Swedish population – both achievements of the highest international order.

    Fact gathering and classification, then, were the main characteristics of Swedish eighteenth century science. The Swedish nation was its favourite object of inquiry. Swedish scientists carried out surveys of the land, of its minerals and natural objects, as well as its population. Linnaeus extended the survey of above all plants to a large part of the globe and became the botanical repository of the western world. Scientifically less prominent undertakings, such as the statistically oriented work of the National Land Survey or the amassing of medical information by the Board of Medicine, through its provincial doctors, also fit the picture.[56] It is not so strange, then, that we should find pioneers of both geological mapping (Daniel Tilas) and plant geography (Göran Wahlenberg) in Sweden. In fields such as these Swedish – especially Linnaean – influence on international science was of some importance. The wide application of systematic models in different areas toward the end of the century is one case in point; Swedish eighteenth century science also displayed many characteristics of the 'Humboldtian science' of a somewhat later period.[57]

    Finally, the question of similarities between the Swedish development and the instituting of modern science in other countries should be commented upon. I will only mention one perhaps somewhat obvious point relating to the Merton thesis about the connection between science and religion in seventeenth century Britain. Lately, Merton's ideas have come under renewed scrutiny, and it has been pointed out, by John Heilbron and Steven Harris, that it lacks in specificity (something which

Merton has never denied). (See also John Henry's essay in this volume.) The Puritans may have created a fertile ground for the development of science by emphasizing empiricism and utilitarian values, but so did the Jesuits. Harris in particular shows that the Jesuit 'sanctification of learning and labor' had a similar effect, and Heilbron argues for an 'ecumenical Merton thesis', by also pointing to the scientific work of the Jesuits.[58]

On this very general level, the Swedish Hats merit a place alongside Puritans and Jesuits, because they too valued and sturdily supported empirical science for utilitarian purposes. There is one obvious difference, however: the Hats were not a religious movement or order, and in many instances their politics were quite amazingly secularized.[59]

The obvious point, then, is that science, in Sweden as in other communities, flourished at a time when it received very strong social support – a conclusion which according to Heilbron 'ranks almost as an analytical truth'.[60] Perhaps less obvious, to accommodate the Merton thesis to the case of Swedish eighteenth century science it would have to be not only ecumenical but also secularized. Physico-theology did play an important part in utilitarian ideology, but it was not associated with any particular religious persuasion or organization. The Swedish utilitarians were Lutherans, it is true; but it is hard to see any special connection between their Lutheranism and their physico-theology. They were devoted to God, to *wetenskap*, to national economy, and sometimes to politics. There seems to be no good reason for giving the religious aspects of the utilitarian ideology preeminence over the mundane ones. Science was seen as a means to realize an optimistic, indeed almost utopian, vision of national revival, put forth by Benzelius, Swedenborg and Polhem, and later given political credence by the Hats. The ideology to which eighteenth century Swedish science conformed may therefore, in broad terms, be described as *patriotic* rather than, say, Lutheran. Its eclipse started when political unity was lost, in the 1760s, and it was completed when power was finally seized by a neurotic king who liked to think of himself, not as a promoter of common interests like industry and agriculture, but as the country's 'premier nobleman'.[61]

NOTES

1 Swedish history of science, especially the work by Sten Lindroth and his pupils, has concentrated on the eighteenth century. The main source of information about the period's scientific life is Lindroth's monumental history of the Royal Swedish Academy of Sciences. Crammed with reliable and engagingly presented information, it is perhaps the finest monograph of a scientific academy in any language. Sten Lindroth, *Kungl. Svenska Vetenskapsakademiens*

historia, 1739–1818, 2 vols. (Stockholm, 1967). See also Lindroth's likewise monumental overview of the development of Swedish history of science and ideas: *Svensk lärdomshistoria*, 4 vols. (vol. 4 ed. by Gunnar Eriksson) (Stockholm, 1975–81), where vols. II–III pertain to the period under consideration here.

2 The introduction of Cartesianism is described in detail in Rolf Lindborg, *Descartes i Uppsala: Striden om 'nya filosofien' 1663–1689* (Uppsala, 1965). See also Lindroth, *Svensk lärdomshistoria*, II (Stockholm, 1975), pp. 447–65; Gunnar Eriksson, 'Epikuros i Uppsala', in Gunnar Eriksson *et al.* (eds), *Vetenskapens träd* (Stockholm, 1974), 95–116.

3 This interpretation, which contradicts Lindborg's conclusions in *Descartes i Uppsala*, is persuasively argued by Gunnar Eriksson in a review in *Lychnos* (1965–6), 435–42.

4 On Copernicanism in Sweden, see Henrik Sandblad, 'Det copernikanska världssystemet i Sverige', pt. 1, *Lychnos* (1943) 149–88; pt. 2, *Lychnos* (1944–5), 79–131. This article has been published in English: 'The reception of the Copernican System in Sweden', in *Etudes sur l'audience de la théorie héliocentrique, Colloquia Copernicana* I, *Studia Copernicana* V (Wrocław, 1972), 241–70.

5 On Wolffianism in Sweden, see Tore Frängsmyr, *Wolffianismens genombrott i Uppsala: Frihetsida universitetsfilosofi till 1700-talets mitt* (Uppsala, 1972). No study exists of the introduction of Newtonianism into Sweden.

6 On Rudbeck's Baconianism, see Gunnar Eriksson, 'Olof Rudbeck d.ä.', *Lychnos* (1984), 77–119. Rudbeck's Gothicism is treated in Lindroth, *Svensk lärdom-shistoria*, II, pp. 284–96. See also Lindroth's *Les Chemins du savoir en Suède: De la fondation de l'université d'Upsal à Jacob Berzelius – Etudes et Portraits* (Dordrecht, 1988), pp. 57–82.

7 This section summarizes the content of ch. 4 of Sven Widmalm, *Mellan kartan och verkligheten: Geodesi och kartläggning, 1695–1860* ['Between map and reality: geodesy and surveying, 1695–1860'] (Uppsala, 1990). Detailed references can be found there.

8 Hans Forssell, 'Minne af erkebiskopen doktor Erik Benzelius den yngre', *Svenska Akademiens Handlingar* 58 (1883), 113–476; p. 289.

9 On the role of Lapland in Swedish culture, and in economic thinking, during the eighteenth century, see Sverker Sörlin, *Framtidslandet: Debatten om Norrland och naturresurserna under det industriella genombrottet* (Stockholm, 1988), ch. 2.

10 Quote from Erik Prosperin, *Tal om kongliga Vetenskaps Societeten i Upsala* (Stockholm, 1791), pp. 8–9.

11 Christopher Polhem, *Christopher Polhems brev*, ed. Axel Liljencrantz (Uppsala, 1941–6), pp. 71–4. Cf. Carl-Otto von Sydow, 'Vetenskapssocieteten och Henric Benzelius' lapplandsresa 1711', *Lychnos* (1962), 138–63, esp. pp. 138–154.

12 *Daedalus Hyperboreus Eller Mathematiska och Physicaliska Försök och Anmerckningar För April Månad 1716 beskrifna af Emanuel Swedberg* (1716), p. 10. A facsimile of this short-lived journal has been issued in *Kungliga Vetenskaps Societetens i Upsala tvåhundraårsminne* (Uppsala, 1910).

13 *Ibid.*, pp. 30–1.

14 N. V. E. Nordenmark, *Swedenborg som astronom* (*Arkiv för matematik, astronomi och fysik* 23A: 13) (Stockholm, 1933), pp. 2, 26–7; Tore Frängsmyr, *Geologi och*

skapelsetro: Föreställningar on jordens historia från Hiärne till Bergman (Stockholm, 1969), p. 157. Swedenborg's relationship to the Uppsala context, including the Rudbeckian heritage, is outlined in Gunnar Broberg, 'Swedenborg och Uppsala', *Världarnas möte: Nya Kyrkans Tidning*, 4 (1990), 90–104.

15 Nordenmark, *Swedenborg*, pp. 26–7, 39–42.

16 Widmalm, *Mellan kartan*, pp. 44–6.

17 Gunnar Broberg, 'Olof Rudbeck d y och hans tid', in Tomas Anfält *et al.*, *Fogelboken av Olof Rudbeck d y: Historisk, konstvetenskaplig och ornitologisk kommentar* (Stockholm, 1985), 15–41. (This work has been published in English, as *Olof Rudbeck's Book of Birds* (Stockholm, 1987).)

18 Henrik Schück (ed.), *Bokwetts Gillets protokoll* (Uppsala, 1918), pp. 124, 133–4, 166–8.

19 Svante Lindqvist, *Technology on Trial: The Introduction of Steam Power Technology into Sweden, 1715–1736* (Uppsala, 1984), pp. 183–214.

20 Quoted in Widmalm, *Mellan kartan*, p. 47.

21 Ibid., p. 47.

22 Svante Lindqvist, 'Ett experiment år 1744 rörande norrskenets natur', in Gunnar Eriksson *et al.* (eds.), *Kunskapens trädgårdar: Om institutioner och institutionaliseringar i vetenskapen och livet* (Stockholm, 1988), 40–77; N. E. V. Nordenmark, *Anders Celsius* (Uppsala, 1936), pp. 35, 57. Lindqvist underlines that Triewald used Swedish nature and climate as scientific resources when attempting to establish himself internationally as a physicist.

23 Björn Ryman, *Eric Benzelius d.y.: En frihetstida politiker* (Stockholm, 1978), pp. 195–8.

24 The most detailed treatment of the expedition is Nordenmark's, in ch. 3 of his *Anders Celsius*. Good, internationally oriented treatments may be found in Harcourt Brown, *Science and the Human Comedy: Natural Philosophy and French Literature from Rabelais to Maupertuis* (Toronto, 1976), pp. 167–206; Claude J. Nordmann, 'L'Expedition de Maupertuis et de Celsius en Laponie', *Cahiers d'histoire mondiale* 10:1 (1966), 74–97.

25 Celsius to Benzelius, 28 November 1736; quoted in Widmalm, *Mellan kartan*, p. 52.

26 On Celsius and his observatory, see Lindroth, *Les Chemins du savoir*, pp. 111–20.

27 Bengt Hildebrand, *Kungl. Svenska Vetenskapsakademien: Förhistoria, grundläggning och första organisation* (Stockholm, 1939), p. 244.

28 Through the work of Michael Metcalf and Michael Roberts, high-quality scholarship on the political development of eighteenth century Sweden is also accessible in English. For an up-to-date overview, see Roberts' *The Age of Liberty: Sweden 1719–1772* (Cambridge, 1986).

29 Lorraine Daston, 'Nationalism and Scientific Neutrality under Napoleon', in Tore Frängsmyr (ed.), *Solomon's House Revisited* (Canton, Mass., 1990), 95–119.

30 The term 'utilitarianism' (in Swedish, *utilism* as opposed to *utilitarism*) is used to describe the idea that all knowledge should be aimed to fulfil economically or politically useful purposes. It is not meant to suggest a close similarity with the particular philosophy of e.g. Hutcheson or Bentham. Cf. Sven-Eric Liedman, 'Utilitarianism and the Economy', in Tore Frängsmyr (ed.), *Science in Sweden: The Royal Swedish Academy of Sciences, 1739–1989* (Canton, Mass., 1989), 23–44.

31 Karin Johannisson, 'Naturventenskap på reträtt: En diskussion om natur-
    vetenskapens status under svenskt 1700-tal', *Lychnos* (1979–80), 109–54; p. 111.
    Cf. Gunnar Eriksson, 'Motiveringar för naturvetenskap: En översikt av den
    svenska diskussionen från 1600-talet till första världskriget', *Lychnos* (1971–2),
    121–70.

32 Johan Browallius, *Tankar öfwer naturkunningheten, och huru then bör drifwas wid en
    academia* ['Thoughts on how knowledge of nature should be perpetuated at an
    academy'] (Stockholm, 1737), pp. 4–5.

33 Tore Fränsmyr, 'Den gudomliga ekonomin: Religion och hushållning i 1700-
    talets Sverige', *Lychnos* (1971–2), 217–44. Frängsmyr points out that Rud-
    beckian influences prevailed in the economic optimism of the Age of Freedom.
    For a brief discussion of the term *wetenskap*, see Lindqvist, *Technology on Trial*,
    pp. 15–16.

34 Carl Linnaeus, 'Tanckar om Grunden til *Oeconomien* genom Naturkunnogheten
    ock *Physiquen*', *Vetenskapsakademiens Handlingar* 1740, 405–28; pp. 427–8. Cf.
    Sven Widmalm, 'Gravören och docenterna: Cosmographiska sällskapet i
    Uppsala, 1758–1778', in Eriksson *et al.*, *Kunskapens trädgårdar*, 78–106, esp.
    p. 81.

35 Berch's economic and political views are expounded in Sven-Eric Liedman, *Den
    synliga handen: Anders Berch och ekonomiämnena vid 1700-talets svenska universitet*
    (Värnamo, 1986). Cf. Liedman, 'Utilitarianism and the Economy'.

36 Quoted in Hildebrand, *Kungl. Svenska Vetenskapakademien*, p. 266.

37 Lindroth, *Vetenskapsakademiens historia*, 1:1, pp. 208–16.

38 Nordenmark, the zealous biographer of eighteenth century Swedish astrono-
    mers, printed a catalogue of Wargentin's correspondence in his *Pehr Wilhelm
    Wargentin: Kungl. Vetenskapsakadmiens sekreterare och astronom 1749–1783* (Uppsala,
    1939), pp. 425–49. Nordenmark's book on Wargentin, like his other bio-
    graphies, offers much detail but little historical or human insight.

39 This has been suggested by Henrik Sandblad in his *Världens nordligaste läkare
    1750–1810* (Stockholm, 1979), pp. 16–17.

40 Knut Hagberg, *Carl Linnaeus: Den linneanska traditionen* (Stockholm, 1951), esp.
    pp. 38–51.

41 Liedman, *Den synliga handen*, pp. 92–125.

42 On the Office of Tables, see Karin Johannisson, *Det mätbara samhället: Statistik
    och samhällsdröm i 1700-talets Europa* (Stockholm, 1988), pp. 159–79; 'Society in
    Numbers: The Debate over Quantification in Eighteenth Century Political
    Economy', in Tore Frängsmyr, J. L. Heilbron and Robin Rider, (eds.), *The
    Quantifying Spirit in the Eighteenth Century* (Berkeley, 1990), 343–61, esp.
    pp. 357–60.

43 Widmalm, *Mellan kartan*, ch. 6.

44 The best description of Swedish instrument making in this period is Lindroth's,
    in *Vetenskapsakademiens historia* 1:2, pp. 789–822. See also Gunnar Pipping's
    descriptive catalogue of the instruments preserved at the Academy of Sciences,
    The Chamber of Physics (Stockholm, 1977), pp. 40–52, 60–1.

45 Widmalm, 'Gravören och docenterna'.

46 Torgny T. Segerstedt, *Den akademiska friheten under frihetstiden* (Uppsala, 1971),
    pp. 66–83.

47 Widmalm, *Mellan kartan*, ch. 5.

48 Johannisson, 'Naturvetenskap på reträtt'; Lindroth, *Vetenskapsakademiens historia*, II, pp. 1–8; Widmalm, *Mellan kartan*, ch. 12.

49 The data presented in this paragraph derive from E. W. Dahlgren's catalogue of members elected to the Academy 1739–1915, *Kungl. Svenska Vetenskapsakademien, personförteckningar 1739–1915* (Stockholm, 1915). Lindroth has analysed the *election* of members in the academy 1739–1818. See Lindroth, *Vetenskapsakademiens historia*, I:1, p. 28; II, pp. 28 and 75. Lindroth's figures, like mine, show an increase in the percentage of physicians, but they do not reveal the gradual decrease of technicians or the gradual increase of academics. As Dahlgren gives the year of election as well as that of death (or exclusion) of the members, it is possible to find the constitution of the membership of the Academy at any given time. This analysis builds on data from 1739, 1745, and then from every fifth year up to 1800.

50 Lindroth, *Vetenskapsakademiens historia*, I:1, p. 229; II, p. 186.

51 Hacking shows that Cohen's definition of a scientific revolution has this kind of vagueness. See I. B. Cohen, *Revolution in Science* (Cambridge, Mass., 1985), pp. 26–39; Ian Hacking 'Science Turned Upside Down' (review of Cohen), *New York Review of Books*, 27 February 1986, pp. 21–6. Cf. Tore Frängsmyr, 'Revolution or Evolution or How to Describe Changes in Scientific Thinking', in William R. Shea (ed.), *Revolutions in Science: Their Meaning and Relevance* (Canton, Mass., 1988), 164–73.

52 Roy Porter, 'The Scientific Revolution: A Spoke in the Wheel?', in Roy Porter and Mikuláš Teich (eds.), *Revolution in History* (Cambridge, 1986), 290–316; p. 300.

53 Sten Lindroth, 'Linné – legend och verklighet', *Lychnos* (1965–6), 56–122. This article has been translated into French and English, as 'Linné – légende et réalité', in *Les Chemins du savoir*, 121–83; and as 'The Two Faces of Linnaeus', in Tore Frängsmyr (ed.), *Linnaeus: The Man and His Work* (Berkeley, 1983), 1–62. This book is an excellent introduction to Swedish Linnaeus scholarship.

54 Carl Linnaeus [von Linné], 'Tal vid deras Kongl. Majesteters höga närvaro, hållit uti Upsala ... den 25 septemb. 1759', in Carl von Linné, *Tre tal* (ed. Arvid H. Uggla, Uppsala, 1954), 27–36, on p. 30.

55 On the relationship between Linnaeus' and Bergman's classification schemes, see Marco Beretta, 'T. O. Bergman and the Definition of Chemistry', *Lychnos* (1988), 37–67. Swedish eighteenth century chemistry, and its utilitarian aspects, have been described in a series of articles by Anders Lundgren: 'Bergshantering och kemi i Sverige under 1700-talet', *Med hammare och fackla* 29 (1985), 90–124. 'The New Chemistry in Sweden: The Debate That Wasn't', *Osiris* 4 (1988), 146–68; 'The Changing Role of Numbers in Eighteenth Century Chemistry', Frängsmyr *et al.*, *The Quantifying Spirit*, 245–66.

56 Sandblad, *Världens nordligaste läkare*, pp. 5–12; Widmalm, *Mellan kartan*, pp. 66–70.

57 John E. Lesch, 'Systematics and the Geometrical Spirit', in Frängsmyr *et al.*, *The Quantifying Spirit*, 73–111. On Humboldtian science, see Susan Faye Cannon, *Science in Culture: The Early Victorian Period* (New York, 1978), pp. 73–105.

58 Steven J. Harris, 'Transposing the Merton Thesis: Apostolic Spirituality and the Establishment of the Jesuit Scientific Tradition', *Science in Context* 3:1 (1989), 29–65; p. 51; J. L. Heilbron, 'Science in the Church', *ibid.*, 9–28; p. 9.
59 For secularized attitudes in Hat politics and economics, see for example Johannisson, *Det mätbara samhället*, pp. 13–18; Bo Lindberg, 'Religionens politiska användning – en akademisk doktrin under 1700-talet', in Ronny Ambjörnsson *et al.* (eds.), *Idé och lärdom* (Lund, 1972), 85–108; Eva-Lena Dahl and Nils Eriksson, 'Urborgaren: En studie i en merkantilistisk människo- och samhällsyn', *ibid.*, 109–49.
60 Heilbron, 'Science in the Church', p. 9.
61 For a brilliant analysis of King Gustav's personality, see Erik Lönnroth, *Den stora rollen: Kung Gustaf III spelad av honom själv* (Stockholm, 1986).

THE SCIENTIFIC REVOLUTION IN SCOTLAND

PAUL WOOD

THE subject of this essay is an historiographical minefield. The very concept of the Scientific Revolution has been challenged on a number of fronts in recent years, and there is now little agreement as to who made the revolution, what the exact nature of the revolution was, and when precisely this protracted event occurred.[1] One might also question the validity of focusing on 'national' contexts, for as the distinguished historian J. H. Elliott has warned, the 'besetting sin of the national historian is exceptionalism', that is, the inability or unwillingness to see the wood for the trees.[2] Arguably, the need for a less particularistic historical vision is especially urgent when dealing with the early modern period. Despite the growing use of the vernacular, Latin served as the lingua franca in Europe well into the eighteenth century, and this fostered the existence of a cosmopolitan Republic of Letters in which national identities were to a large extent submerged in the broader European realm of learning. Furthermore, during the early modern era regional loyalties were often more powerful than national ones even in a country like France, which boasted a highly developed and increasingly centralized state apparatus. Hence the notion of a French or an English 'national' context is an extremely problematic one, in so far as it may not in fact address the contextual specificities it was initially intended to capture.

Moreover, Scotland is an anomalous example of a national context because she lost her nationhood through parliamentary union with England in 1707, having already lost her independent crown in 1603. Since the Scottish experience for much of the seventeenth and eighteenth centuries was one of cultural assimilation and political domination by England, the explanatory purchase of national factors would, *prima facie*, seem to be limited. Nor has Scotland figured largely in traditional histories of the Scientific Revolution. Mention might be made of Napier's invention of logarithms, but many scholars would probably agree with Lord Dacre's notorious comment that at 'the end of the seventeenth century Scotland was a by-word for irredeemable poverty, social backwardness, political faction'.[3] Could the Scientific Revolution have impinged on such a small and remote country, which was riven by religious dispute for much of the seventeenth century?

If one thinks that the Scientific Revolution began in 1543 with the appearance of Copernicus' *De revolutionibus* and effectively ended with the publication of Newton's *Principia* in 1687, then the answer to this question would have to be that Scottish participation in this great cultural transformation was limited. There are good reasons not to accept this periodization, however. First, such a chronology begs the issue of whether the Scientific Revolution should be defined primarily in terms of developments within physics and astronomy, as has traditionally been the case. Secondly, the institutional and conceptual continuities between late-seventeenth and eighteenth-century science suggest that we should not regard 1687 as marking the end of an era. Instead, we should consider the seventeenth and eighteenth centuries as marking a distinctive period in the development of the natural sciences which ended with the so-called 'second' scientific revolution, which many scholars would now argue occurred at the turn of the nineteenth century.[4] In doing so, we can rightly see the Enlightenment as being (in part) the culmination of the Scientific Revolution, and thus highlight the centrality of science in Enlightened culture. We can also then recognize that Scotland did indeed contribute in significant ways to the remodelling of the sciences in early modern Europe. For by the close of the eighteenth century, Scotland was a centre for the cultivation of natural knowledge, celebrated by men like Thomas Jefferson, who wrote that as far as science was concerned 'no place in the world can pretend to a competition with Edinburgh'.[5] North Britain had become a 'Hotbed of Genius', and in what follows I hope to show how and why this dramatic change in fortune occurred.

Like Lord Dacre, many Scots in the seventeenth and early eighteenth centuries took a dim view of the state of their country because the traumatic events which followed the signing of the National Convenant in 1638 had left the nation divided and embittered by intense and sometimes bloody religious conflict. These were not the most propitious of times for the pursuit of the sciences, and the Scots' apparent failure to do so moved one contemporary, the mathematician James Corss, to write in 1662:

I Have oftentimes lamented with myself to see so many Learned
Mathematicians to arise in sundry parts of the world, and so few to appear
in our Native Country. In other things we are parallel with (I shall not say
in a superlative degree far above) other Nations; but in Arts and Sciences
Mathematical, all exceed us. And had not that thrice Noble and Illustrious
Lord, viz John Lord Nepper, Baron of Merchiston, &c. preserved the
honour of our Nation by his admirable and more than mortal invention
of Logarithms, we should have been buried in oblivion, in the memories
of Forraign Nations...[6]

Napier was indeed a singular man, but his singularity in Scotland was
partly due to the fact that in this period many Scottish men of science
(including the mathematician and astronomer Duncan Liddell, the
chemist William Davidson, and the botanist Robert Morison) sought
advancement elsewhere.[7] Scottish professors and students had long been
fixtures in institutions of higher learning across Europe, and these
expatriates collectively made a considerable contribution to the advancement of the sciences during the sixteenth and seventeenth
centuries.

With so many Scots on the move, one might well conclude with Lord
Dacre that in the seventeenth century the Scottish universities were 'the
unreformed seminaries of a fanatical clergy'.[8] Yet Scottish academe was
not uniformly hostile to intellectual innovation, even though the Kirk
sometimes discouraged the introduction of new ideas during the first half
of the century. While the teaching of natural philosophy in this period
was confined exclusively to commentaries on works by Aristotle,
from 1600 until 1626 regents (university teachers) in Edinburgh were
questioning certain aspects of Aristotelian cosmology. None went so far
as to endorse the Copernican theory, but they recognized that the
Ptolemaic system was in need of revision, and some of them were
interested in the Tychonic compromise. However, in 1626 the regent
James Reid was attacked by the Moderator of the Edinburgh presbytery
for magnifying the status of philosophy at the expense of theology, and
the university was reluctantly forced to dismiss him the following year.
This clerical intervention apparently checked the regents' enthusiasm
for cosmological speculation, because the ideas of Tycho and Copernicus
were only briefly alluded to in the 1630s and 40s, and it was not until
the 1660s that alternatives to geocentrism were seriously canvassed.
Elsewhere, the absence of such overt harassment left regents and
professors relatively free to query the Aristotelian view of the super-
lunary realm. At Marischal College Aberdeen, for instance, the first
Liddell Professor of Mathematics, William Johnston, lectured on the
details of the Ptolemaic, Copernican and Tychonic accounts of

planetary motions, and on the basis of Tycho's observations denied the existence of solid celestial spheres. Then, in the 1650s, the Marischal regent Andrew Cant affirmed the mutability of the heavens, citing Tycho's work on the nova of 1572 and on comets to justify his claim. Significantly, Cant seems to have read widely in the astronomical and natural-philosophical literature of his day, for he was acquainted with the writings of Kepler, Descartes and Galileo. Yet he rejected their heliocentrism, as did all of the men who taught astronomy and natural philosophy in the Scottish universities during the first six decades of the century. Indeed, like many of his contemporaries Cant criticized the heliocentric hypothesis because it was inconsistent with Scripture, but his response to Copernicanism can hardly be said to be that of a 'fanatical' Calvinist, as Lord Dacre would have it.

Following the Restoration, however, the curricula of the Scottish universities changed dramatically. In the late 1650s and in the 1660s, most regents who cited Descartes did so critically, but in the 1670s Cartesianism, as well as heliocentrism, displaced the Aristotelian world-view in the classrooms of St Andrews and Marischal College. By the early 1680s regents at King's College Aberdeen and Edinburgh were also championing Cartesianism in their lectures, despite rearguard action by older men loyal to Tycho, Aristotle and even Ptolemy. Only Glasgow resisted this swing to Descartes' system of the world, in so far as the regents there summarized for their pupils the main tenets of Aristotelian, Epicurean and Cartesian natural philosophy, without expressing a preference for any of them. Yet while the majority of the Scottish regents teaching in the 1680s subscribed to some form of Cartesian mechanism, they were highly eclectic when it came to explaining particular phenomena such as the tides or the nature of light and colour, and for their theoretical ideas and empirical information they drew on a broad range of authors including Robert Boyle, whose researches were widely regarded as embodying the true principles of the experimental philosophy.[9] Alongside the general fascination with Cartesianism, therefore, went an enthusiasm for experimentalism, and a recognition of the achievements of the experimental philosophers associated with the Royal Society of London.

A number of factors account for the swiftness with which Aristotelianism was swept aside by new ideas following the Restoration. First, after 1660 the virtuosi in Scotland were more in touch with the latest trends in natural philosophy and medicine. In part this was due to the fact that the Scots continued to seek educational opportunities abroad, with medics in particular benefiting from their studies at centres like Padua, and especially Leiden, where Scotsmen went in growing numbers as the century progressed.[10] But these European contacts were now being increasingly supplemented by closer links with the English scientific community. Symptomatic of these new ties with England is the fact that two Scots, Sir Robert Moray and the earl of Kincardine, were among the founder members of the Royal Society of London, and Moray in particular provided inspiration, information and patronage for friends like Sir Robert Sibbald north of the Tweed.[11] For their part, Sibbald and his circle were in touch with other prominent English virtuosi with whom they shared natural-historical and antiquarian interests.[12] Moreover, Scottish mathematicians corresponded with the London-based intelligencer John Collins, who provided them with news about the informal transactions within the English (and continental) mathematical community. Nor were the newly established contacts restricted to men based in Edinburgh, for the correspondence network between Scotland and England incorporated savants working in the university towns of Glasgow, St Andrew's and Aberdeen. Because the English were at the forefront of scientific advance in this period, the new philosophical commerce between Scotland and England was thus a potent catalyst for change which helped to trigger the relatively sudden transformation of the Scottish intellectual landscape during the second half of the seventeenth century.

Secondly, institutional innovations both inside and outside the universities fostered the growth of the new science. In Edinburgh, Sibbald and his associates established a physic garden in 1675 and, more importantly, founded the Royal College of Physicians of Edinburgh in 1681. Sibbald and his friends also gained academic credibility during these years. The town council granted the keeper of the physic garden, James Sutherland, a college salary in 1676 and subsequently made him professor of botany in 1695; the council also added to Sibbald's many honours by appointing him a professor in the university in 1685, along with Drs James Halket and Archibald Pitcairne. As early as the mid-1680s, therefore, the institutional infrastructure was in place which would later facilitate the meteoric rise to prominence of the Edinburgh medical school.[13] Moreover, chairs in mathematics were either revived or established in St Andrews (1668), Edinburgh (1674) and Glasgow (1691), and the universities also acquired telescopes and other pieces of experimental apparatus.[14]

The activities of the man elected to the newly founded Glasgow chair of mathematics and experimental philosophy, George Sinclair, tell us much about the outlook of the typical Scottish virtuoso at this time. Sinclair's career had in fact begun in Glasgow in 1654, when he was appointed a regent, but in 1666 he was forced to resign for political reasons, and he subsequently moved to Edinburgh, where he taught mathematics and supervised various civic improvement schemes sponsored by the town council. During his Edinburgh years, he published a number of works which show that he shared the scientific enthusiasms of the age. Thus he studied pneumatics, hydrostatics, astronomy, meteorology and the technicalities of coal mining, and was interested in such paraphernalia as diving bells, barometers, hygroscopes and air pumps. Moreover, as his exchanges with the St Andrews professor of mathematics, James Gregory I, in the early 1670s well illustrate, Sinclair was a dedicated Baconian who insisted that the principles of natural philosophy had to be grounded in natural history, and who sought to apply natural knowledge for the purposes of material improvement.[15] Yet his Baconianism had a credulous streak, for like Joseph Glanvill and Henry More, Sinclair was deeply worried by the atheistic and materialistic implications of Cartesian mechanism, and he too collected 'relations' which he claimed demonstrated empirically the existence and activity of spiritual beings.[16] Furthermore, mathematics had for Sinclair a quasi-mystical and theological meaning, and he apparently believed that comets and other celestial phenomena were of astrological significance.[17] Hence Sinclair's writings register the tensions between the *mentalité* of the new science and older modes of thought which were manifest in the works of the virtuosi more generally, and they alert us as well to the religious preoccupations which conditioned the reception of Cartesianism in Scotland during the second half of the century.[18]

The 1680s also saw the formation of clubs devoted to the cultivation of natural knowledge. The Royal College of Physicians for example, grew out of a medical club which began meeting fortnightly in Sibbald's lodgings in 1680, consisting of Sibbald, Pitcairne, Andrew Balfour, Archibald Stevenson and Thomas Burnet. The proceedings of this group were typical of the many clubs which flourished across Europe in this period, for Sibbald recalled in his autobiography that he and his cronies met to discuss 'letters from ... abroad, giving account of what was most remarkable a doing by the learned, some rare cases [that] had happened in our practice, and ane account of Bookes, that tended to the improvement of medicine or naturall history, or any other curious learning'.[19] While Sibbald's coterie was probably the first instance of such a body in Scotland, similar clubs dedicated to the study of antiquities, medicine, and natural history sprang up in Edinburgh during the 1680s.[20] These different ventures culminated in Sibbald's unsuccessful bid in the years 1698–1702 to create a Royal Society of Scotland modelled on the learned academies of Italy and France. His failure in this enterprise indicates that the institutional basis for natural knowledge outside the universities was still somewhat fragile even in Edinburgh, while in the provinces the virtuosi did not organize themselves into clubs until well into the eighteenth century.[21]

These developments all bore fruit in the rapid assimilation of Newton's work in Scotland at the turn of the eighteenth century. During the 1670s and 80s Newton's early papers on light and colours were widely discussed in the Scottish universities, but it was only after the publication of the *Principia* in 1687 that his ideas really began to take hold north of the Tweed. The currency which Newton's system quickly gained in Scotland was due in no small part to the proselytizing zeal of members of the Gregory family. James Gregory II (1666–1742) was the first Scottish academic to expound the central themes of the *Principia* in a set of graduation theses from 1690, which he published while serving as a regent at St Andrews. But Gregory had to leave his post there because of his Jacobite sympathies, and in 1692 he succeeded his kinsman David Gregory (1659–1708) as professor of mathematics at Edinburgh, where he continued to champion Newton's ideas. For his part, David Gregory was not as enthusiastic an expositor of Newtonianism as James, although he did introduce his students in Edinburgh to certain aspects of Newton's writings. Yet even without David Gregory's whole-hearted advocacy, Newton's system of the world soon found an audience among the Edinburgh regents, and by 1705 at the latest Newtonianism had displaced Cartesianism in the classroom. Elsewhere, the regents and professors were similarly quick to absorb Newton's work, and by 1710 the Newtonian system was firmly entrenched in the natural philosophy courses given at Glasgow, St Andrews, and the two Aberdeen colleges. Thus the Scottish universities incorporated Newton's theories into their curricula far more readily than did academic institutions in England or on the Continent, and in doing so they laid the groundwork for the scientific achievements of the Scottish Enlightenment.[22]

The enthusiastic reception given to Newton's doctrines in Scotland was conditioned by a number of factors. First, Newton's emphasis on God's providential control of the creation was more congenial to Calvinist sensibilities than was Descartes' apparent concentration on the purely mechanical interaction of matter in motion. Whereas Cartesianism seemed to many to open the door to materialism, Newtonianism (particularly as it was expounded in the Boyle Lectures and other popularizations of the period) offered a seemingly conclusive demonstration of the existence and operation of non-material powers in the natural order.[23] Hence it was perceived as making a potentially vital contribution to what was widely regarded as the main aim of the universities, namely the inculcation of morals and religion. Most educated Scots valued natural knowledge more for its moral than its material utility, and they would have endorsed Colin Maclaurin's statement that 'natural philosophy is subservient to purposes of a higher kind, and is chiefly to be valued as it lays a sure foundation for natural religion and moral philosophy'.[24]

Secondly, the introduction of Newtonianism into Scotland occurred at a time when the landed and professional classes pressed for the reform of the university system, so that young Scots (and their money) would remain at home. In the wake of the Glorious Revolution, a Parliamentary Visitation Commission was struck in 1690 to raise the standards of university education and to enforce loyalty to the new régime. In the end, the Commission itself accomplished little on either front, but its efforts did serve to highlight the need for change, and the universities responded to this need by updating their curricula and upgrading their facilities. Mathematics, medicine and natural philosophy benefited greatly from these reforms. During the years 1690 to 1715, new chairs were established in mathematics and medicine, while instruments were purchased by King's College Aberdeen, St Andrews, and Glasgow; the last also founded a physic garden and a teaching position in botany. Then, after the Jacobite uprising of 1715, a Royal Visitation Commission made a clean sweep of Jacobites teaching in the universities, and installed a new generation of men who promoted the study of the natural sciences.[25] Because of these changes, natural philosophy and mathematics came to occupy an increasingly central role in the curricula of the Scottish universities, and this shift in educational priorities in turn contributed to the institutionalization and wider dissemination of the Newtonian system.

A third reason for the swift rise of Newtonianism in Scotland lay in the fact that the Scots established a highly developed network of patronage and communication centred on Isaac Newton himself.[26] Beginning in 1670 James Gregory I corresponded indirectly with Newton through John Collins, and his nephew David likewise tried to begin a mathematical correspondence in 1684. David Gregory's associate, the mathematician John Craig, travelled to Cambridge in 1685 where he visited Newton; Craig later settled in England and published works on fluxions, as well as the idiosyncratic *Theologiae Christianae principia mathematica* (1699).[27] David Gregory artfully cultivated Newton's support, a ploy which paid dividends when Gregory was elected to the Savilian Chair of Astronomy at Oxford in 1692. Once installed there, Gregory became one of Newton's most energetic disciples, and gathered around him men dedicated to advancing the Newtonian cause in the fields of natural philosophy and medicine, including the expatriate Scots

John and James Keill. Following Gregory's departure, the most prominent Newtonian resident in Scotland was his close friend Archibald Pitcairne, who returned from a brief sojourn in Leiden as an enthusiastic advocate of a Newtonian form of iatromechanism, which he promptly expounded in the dispute then raging in Edinburgh over the nature and treatment of fevers.[28] Pitcairne's intervention in the debate, however, proved inflammatory, for he was suspended from the Royal College of Physicians in November 1694 and remained *persona non grata* until 1704, when peace was finally declared between the rival factions led by Sibbald and himself.[29] Within the Edinburgh medical fraternity, therefore, the introduction of methods and concepts derived from Newton was highly politicized, but the embattled Pitcairne continued to advance his brand of Newtonian physiology until his death in 1713.

During the first two decades of the eighteenth century, key university posts in mathematics and the natural sciences were filled by men who were connected with Newton and his disciples. The first professor of mathematics at King's College Aberdeen, Thomas Bower, had moved within the ambit of Gregory's circle in Oxford prior to his appointment in 1703 and owed his chair partly to Pitcairne's efforts on his behalf. Scotland's most accomplished mathematician of the eighteenth century, Colin Maclaurin, cultivated Newton's favour while teaching at Marischal College, and subsequently reaped the benefits when Newton helped him obtain the Edinburgh mathematics professorship in 1725. John Stewart, who succeeded Maclaurin at Marischal, may have lacked English connections, but he was no less committed to the Newtonian cause, as can be seen in his annotated translation of Newton's two major mathematical tracts aimed at the teaching market.[30] Moreover, Maclaurin's would-be successor in Edinburgh, James Stirling, first rose to prominence as a mathematician in the 1710s by extending Newton's work on cubic curves and the differential method; when he returned to London after a period in Venice, Stirling was befriended by Newton, who secured his election to the Royal Society in 1726 and found him employment.[31]

At Glasgow, the distinguished geometer Robert Simson lived in London for a year prior to taking up the mathematics chair in 1711, and while in the metropolis Simson fraternized with Edmond Halley among others. As a devotee of Newton and of ancient geometry, Simson had a profound impact on the course of eighteenth-century Scottish mathematics, not least because he counted among his students Maclaurin, Matthew Stewart (professor of mathematics at Edinburgh 1746–75), William Trail (professor of mathematics at Marischal College Aberdeen 1766–79), and John Robison (professor of natural philosophy at

Edinburgh 1774–1805). Yet it must be said that his legacy was somewhat ambiguous, in so far as he had little time for the powerful analytic methods of continental mathematicians, preferring the purity of geometrical techniques. His predilection for the Greeks may have harmonized well the strong element of Classicism in Enlightened Scottish culture, but it also checked the growth of advanced mathematics in Scotland for much of the century; as a result the Scots were not as receptive to foreign innovations in areas like mathematical physics as they might otherwise have been. Indeed, it was not until a new generation of men led by John Playfair began to champion the work of French mathematicians and natural philosophers at the turn of the nineteenth century that the Scots were able to shake free of the philosophical prejudices inherited from Simson and his protégés.[32]

Nevertheless, on balance the Newtonian revolution in Scotland had fruitful consequences for the cultivation of natural knowledge. Until his premature death in 1746, Colin Maclaurin was the leading champion of Newton's writings north of the Tweed. Maclaurin stoutly defended the Newtonian cause in the controversies surrounding the conceptual basis of the method of fluxions and *vis viva*, and both he and James Stirling endeavoured to demonstrate Newton's claim that the earth is shaped like an oblate spheroid.[33] Maclaurin also assembled a network of astronomers across Scotland who periodically collaborated with him in observing various celestial phenomena. The surviving members of this group later tracked the two transits of Venus in the 1760s; these were of symbolic significance for the Newtonian camp because Edmond Halley had first shown how such transits could be used to ascertain the mean distance of the earth from the sun, and hence establish the size of the solar system.[34]

Through the researches of the Astronomer Royal James Bradley, published in 1728, stellar aberration became a phenomenon of considerable theoretical moment within both astronomy and optics and subsequently attracted the attention of Scottish natural philosophers like Thomas Melvill, Patrick Wilson, his Glasgow colleague Thomas Reid, and John Robison. Moreover, by the late 1780s the theoretical stakes involved had been raised considerably, because in 1785 Roger Boscovich proposed what was seen as an *experimentum crucis* between the projectile and undulatory theories of light, involving the measurement of terrestrial aberration. For committed Newtonians aberration thus became a test for their basic theoretical postulates, and consequently they expended considerable intellectual effort in reconciling their principles with the apparent phenomena.[35] Nor was aberration the only problem area in physical optics which generated significant research among the Scots during the eighteenth century. Thomas Melvill's critique of Newton's account of refractive dispersion was debated by the expatriate Scottish instrument maker James Short, the Edinburgh professor of medicine William Porterfield, and the young Henry Brougham.[36] Furthermore, the Scots were extremely active in the overlapping field of the theory of vision, where the work done was often presented as being Newtonian in method if not in content.[37]

Apart from medicine, chemistry was probably the subject for which Scotland was best known in the eighteenth century, and here too the Newtonian corpus helped shape the Scottish chemical tradition. Having been given a copy of 'De natura acidorum' by Newton in 1691, Archibald Pitcairne was the first Scottish savant to apply Newton's concept of attraction to chemical phenomena, and Pitcairne's example was followed in Edinburgh by Andrew Plummer, who taught chemistry during the formative years of the Edinburgh medical school.[38] But the most significant (and indeed the most complex) use of the theoretical resources of Newtonianism is found in the seminal work of William Cullen and Joseph Black.[39]

By the mid-eighteenth century, Newtonianism was far from being a monolithic body of doctrine, and the researches of Cullen and Black well illustrate the divergent applications of Newton's ideas in the period. First, the pathbreaking study of fixed air by Joseph Black continued a line of experimentation begun in Stephen Hales' *Vegetable Staticks*, where Hales investigated the properties of 'this now fixt, now volatile *Proteus* among the chymical principles', namely 'air'.[40] Yet Hales' brand of Newtonianism differed radically from that of one of the formative influences on Cullen's theoretical outlook, the Dublin physician Bryan Robinson. For whereas Hales invoked the operations of attractive and especially repulsive forces to explain the behaviour of aerial particles, Robinson took up Newton's speculations in the queries added to the 1717 edition of the *Opticks*, and postulated the existence of an etherial fluid to account for a broad range of phenomena, including fermentation. Cullen in turn derived his explanations of the states of matter and of elective attraction from Robinson's ether theory, and thereby effectively placed the science of heat on an etherial basis. Black too theorized about such imponderable fluids after the manner of Cullen and invoked the authority of Newton in doing so, although he differed significantly from his teacher in identifying phlogiston as the medium responsible for the phenomena of light, heat, magnetism, electricity and gravitation.[41] Philosophical chemistry in Scotland thus brought together the form of Newtonianism exemplified in Hales' writings and associated with Newton's immediate disciples, and that more speculative mode found in the works of Robinson and other ether theorists of the mid-eighteenth century.

But the Scottish chemical tradition did not simply spring from the various brands of Newtonianism like Pallas Athena from the head of Zeus. At the theoretical level, the science of heat in Scotland also had its roots in the chemical system of Hermann Boerhaave, whose concept of fire as an active principle was routinely elided with Newton's ether hypothesis from the 1740s onwards.[42] Moreover, many of the problems addressed by Scottish chemists in the eighteenth century were prompted by the practical concerns of medical therapy and economic improvement. Because chemistry promised such utilitarian benefits the subject was given a secure place in the universities by patrons who controlled positions and purse strings.[43]

The science of chemistry was also shaped by its pedagogical context. Dissatisfied with previous teaching practices in Scotland, William Cullen set out at Glasgow to present chemistry as a polite, rational, systematic and independent science of more than narrowly medical interest, and his realization of these aims had two important consquences for the cognitive content of his course. To make his subject intelligible for his pupils Cullen imposed order on the amorphous mass of material he needed to teach by deploying the classificatory methods of the natural historian, and thereby reinforced the already close links between chemistry and natural history in Scotland. Secondly, as an academic Cullen faced the task of identifying a discrete body of knowledge for which he was responsible. Consequently, he challenged the hitherto dominant reductionist view that chemistry was a branch of the mechanical philosophy, and defined his subject in such a way as to emphasize that it was a theoretically independent branch of science possessing its own distinctive range of phenomena and investigative techniques, rather than being simply ancillary to medicine or to the Newtonian system.[44]

Furthermore, the researches of Cullen and Black required precise measurements which could only be obtained using good quality instruments, such as the thermometers and other hardware produced by James Watt or the Glasgow professor of practical astronomy, Alexander Wilson, who had been an associate of George Martine's in St Andrews. The craft of the instrument maker thus played a vital part in the birth of the science of heat, as indeed it did in the advance of the other sciences cultivated in eighteenth century Scotland.[45]

Another field which thrived institutionally because of its intimate connections with medicine and improvement (and which owed little to the rise of Newtonianism) was natural history. As Geographer Royal, Sir Robert Sibbald wanted to catalogue the human and natural resources of his country and to chart her contours in order to promote the economic interests of the nation, and particularly those of his associates among the landed classes. At his death in 1722 his dream was still unrealized, and it was not until Sir John Sinclair published *The Statistical Account of Scotland* during the 1790s that something approaching Sibbald's scheme actually appeared in print.[46] In the interim, however, Scottish naturalists made some progress in surveying their native land, for they compiled collections of Scottish plants, investigated coal seams and mining techniques, and toured the Highlands to collect information about the inhabitants, the socio-economic conditions in which they lived, and their physical environment.[47]

But the Scots were by no means preoccupied solely with local issues. They were in touch with natural historians throughout Europe and the Americas, and received specimens, news and intellectual stimulus from their contacts abroad. Like their continental counterparts, Scottish natural historians debated such questions as the sexuality of plants, the theory of generation and the nature of Trembley's polyp, the merits of artificial as opposed to natural systems of classification, the origins of racial differences among humankind and the history of the earth. Significantly, the Scots were among the first to adopt the Linnaean system of classification in their teaching and they were also quick to assimilate the contents of Buffon's *Histoire Naturelle*, although Scottish academics rejected Buffon's critique of artificial taxonomic systems because it challenged their teaching practices and they dutifully warned their students against Buffon's heterodox ideas.[48] Moreover, from the 1770s onwards, university courses in natural history typically included a considerable amount of detail about the terraqueous globe, and it was out of this natural-historical matrix that the science of geology was born.[49] Thus James Hutton is perhaps best seen not as the father of modern geology, but as Scotland's consummate natural historian of the eighteenth century.[50]

Given the great cultural prestige enjoyed by the natural sciences in the Enlightenment and the fact that most learned Scots believed that natural and moral philosophy were but two branches of the same tree of knowledge, it is not surprising that natural history and Newtonian science provided methodological models for the emerging science of man in eighteenth-century Scotland. Whereas previous commentators have celebrated the application of introspective and inductive methods to the study of the human mind by Scottish moral philosophers in the period, it is clear that the moralists were also inspired by the classificatory and descriptive procedures of the natural historians. Influenced by the writings of Bacon, Locke, Buffon and Rousseau (among others), figures such as Adam Ferguson and John Millar attempted to compile natural histories of our mental faculties and of the progress of human societies.[51] But, as good Baconians, the Scottish moralists also believed that the compilation of natural histories was a prelude to the application of the method of induction, and here they turned to Newton's methodological dicta for guidance. This 'Newtonian turn' in Scottish philosophy received its most cogent formulation in the writings of Thomas Reid, but Reid's teacher at Marischal College, George Turnbull, was perhaps the first to urge his countrymen to follow Newton's suggestion in Query 31 of the *Opticks* that both natural and moral philosophical inquiries should be conducted according to the same methodology. From at least the 1720s on, therefore, scientism sustained the belief that the sciences of man and nature were intimately connected in terms of method, and hence that moral philosophy had to be reconstructed using empirical and inductive techniques.[52] However, the conceptual traffic between the two branches of learning was not in one direction exclusively, for Scottish men of science were closely attuned to methodological and metaphysical issues and thus shared a common philosophical culture with the moralists.[53]

Intellectual prestige and cognitive structures do not exist in a social vacuum; rather, they represent processes of collective cultural affirmation and of institutionalization. Natural knowledge was valued in the Scottish Enlightenment because the architects of this historical episode, namely the political magnates and their allies in the professional and landed classes, believed that the sciences were morally and materially beneficial. Power brokers like the duke of Argyll and Lord Bute (who were both keen naturalists) remodelled the universities and other institutions to reflect their own intellectual priorities, which meant that the natural sciences and medicine flourished under their patronage.[54]

Within academe, the most important single initiative was the founding of the Edinburgh medical school in 1726. Created in the image of the Leiden school by the canny Lord Provost of Edinburgh, George Drummond, and the anatomist Alexander Monro I, the medical school provided a further impetus for the support of the natural sciences in the university.[55] As a result, subjects like botany, chemistry and natural history prospered, and new chairs in natural history (1767) and agriculture (1790) were established.[56] Rival efforts to found medical schools in Glasgow and Aberdeen were conspicuously less successful, but in Glasgow there was sufficient support as the century progressed for funding lectureships in chemistry (1747), materia medica (1766), and midwifery (1790).[57] Natural history on the other hand fared much better than medicine outside of Edinburgh, for it was added to the reformed curricula of the two Aberdeen colleges in 1753 and taught as part of the natural philosophy course at Glasgow beginning in 1755.[58] As for the physical sciences, astronomy received a boost with professors in practical astronomy appointed at Glasgow (1760) and Edinburgh (1785), and observatories built in Glasgow and Aberdeen.[59] Moreover, the provision of education in mathematics and the natural sciences expanded well beyond the universities in this period. In addition to the itinerant lecturers who occasionally made their way north of the Tweed, private tutors as well as teachers in the burgh schools and newly established academies attempted to give their pupils elementary instruction in the different branches of mathematics, navigation, and even natural philosophy, and from its inception in 1796 Anderson's Institution in Glasgow featured natural philosophy and chemistry courses open to men and women of the town.[60] Finally, if one adds to these institutional innovations the plants, models, instruments, books, museum specimens and other paraphernalia acquired by the Scottish universities and academies during the course of the eighteenth century, one sees that by 1800 Scotland possessed facilities for the study of the natural sciences which were equal (and in some cases superior) to those found anywhere in Europe or America.

The Scottish professors and their students were a remarkably clubbable group in the Enlightenment, and many of their societies provided a forum for the discussion and dissemination of natural knowledge. The most long lasting of the professorial groups was the Edinburgh Philosophical Society (1737–83), which was grafted on to the rump of a defunct medical society (fl. 1731) by Alexander Monro I and Colin Maclaurin. After an initial period of vigorous activity, the Society alternated between serious decline and periodic renewal, so that by the 1770s its considerable reputation abroad did not correspond to the moribund reality of its proceedings at home.[61] But its demise was not brought about so much by internal weaknesses as by the cultural and political conflicts dividing Edinburgh in the early 1780s, which also left their impress on the proceedings of the Royal Society of Edinburgh from its inception in 1783.[62] Outwith Edinburgh, university men founded philosophical and literary societies in Aberdeen and Glasgow (wherein they discoursed *inter alia* about mathematics, natural history and natural philosophy), as well as an Aberdeen club devoted to agricultural improvement.[63] Scottish students were no less active, with the Medical Society formed in Edinburgh in 1737 (Royal Charter, 1778) being the most enduring monument to the combination of student sociability and antagonism towards academic authority.[64] Other notable student groups included chemistry societies in Edinburgh and Glasgow, the

Edinburgh Society for the Investigation of Natural History (f. 1782), the Academy of Physics (fl. 1797–1800), and the Aberdeen Medical Society (fl. 1789).[65]

The proceedings of this array of societies tell us much about the culture of science in the Scottish Enlightenment, for on the whole they demonstrate the power of the ideology of scientism, and many of them embodied the Baconian map of learning presupposed by most learned Scots in the eighteenth century. The most explicit statement of the ethos of scientism comes in the rules agreed to by the original members of the Aberdeen Philosophical Society in 1758. These specified that contributions to the meetings were to be exclusively 'Philosophical', where 'Philosophical Matters are understood to comprehend Every Principle of Science which may be deduced by Just and Lawfull Induction from the Phenomena either of the human Mind or of the material World; [and] All Observations & Experiments that may furnish Materials for such Induction'.[66] Moreover, in most of the societies formed during the course of the century, the members ranged over much the same topics canvassed by the virtuosi of Sibbald's generation, namely medicine, the physical sciences, natural history, antiquities and improvement. The men of the Enlightenment thus instantiated in practice Bacon's vision of the filiation of the sciences, and in particular the close connections between natural and civil history.[67]

By 1800, however, Bacon's map of learning was being redrawn. The first signs of this transformation are noticeable in the 1780s, with evidence of incipient specialization in the single-subject student societies and in the Royal Society of Edinburgh, where the Fellows were divided into physical and literary classes. Significantly, the proceedings of the Society were soon devoted entirely to natural knowledge since the literary branch ceased to function by 1798, signifying the Society's break from the virtuoso ideal of the unity of knowledge which had thus far held sway. Furthermore, Newton's legacy had become increasingly fragmented after the 1740s, since ethers and imponderable fluids (which had been anathema to many of the early Newtonians) were now a standard theoretical resource. With the advent of the chemical revolution, Scottish naturalists also experienced their first moment of profound conceptual change, which was to be followed by the rise of the wave theory of light in the early decades of the nineteenth century.[68] All of these trends were registered in the teaching of the sciences, for the courses given in the universities became less generalized in scope and far more eclectic in content.[69]

Broader social and political changes also impacted on the culture of

science at this time. When Henry Dundas consolidated his control of
Scotland during the 1780s, he typically rewarded political loyalty rather
than merit. Consequently, university posts were increasingly filled by
undistinguished men, and the quality of teaching declined.[70] The role
played by the Moderate Party within the Scottish Kirk also altered
dramatically in this period. Whereas under the distinguished leadership
of the historian William Robertson (who served as Principal of
Edinburgh University from 1762 until 1793), the Moderates had promoted the ends of Enlightenment, under Dundas and his ecclesiastical
manager, Principal George Hill of St Andrews, the party became a less
positive force in Scottish letters. In the fiercely contested election of John
Leslie to the chair of mathematics at Edinburgh in 1805, for example,
the Moderates were more concerned to defend their political interest in
the town than academic standards, and against Leslie they backed a
lacklustre candidate, the Rev Thomas Macknight, who was the son of a
leading Moderate clergyman.[71] The Leslie affair illustrates that the
religious tensions between the Moderates and the Evangelical party,
which had been contained for the most part in the previous century,
were once again becoming a significant factor in Scottish public life, and
the growing divide between rational and Scripture-based theologies in
this period rendered problematic the prevailing relations between
natural knowledge and religion[72]

Part of the reason why Henry Dundas was able to gain complete
political control of Scotland was that he skillfully exploited the fears of
sedition which had been aroused by the French Revolution. Initially,
many of the literati welcomed the events of 1789, but with the onset of
the Terror most Scottish savants turned against the Revolution, and
their anti-Jacobinism was given voice in John Robison's *Proofs of a
Conspiracy against all the Religions and Governments of Europe* (1797). In the
troubled decade of the 90s heterodox ideas like those of James Hutton
regarding the age of the earth were tainted with suspicions of subversive
intent, and the 'theophobia gallica' coloured perceptions of French
science.[73] Instead of being mobilized in the service of moderate reform,
therefore, the natural sciences were now deployed in the defence of the
established order, and this conservative use of scientific knowledge was
to become more conspicuous as class tensions heightened within the
industrial society of nineteenth-century Scotland.[74]

The years from roughly 1790 to 1810 therefore mark a genuine
watershed in Scottish intellectual life. Contemporaries recognized that
an era had passed, and some saw only decline ahead.[75] Yet Scottish
science did flourish in the nineteenth century, although in very different
circumstances. Scottish savants still travelled abroad, but they no longer

flocked to the Continent; instead they were lured to the metropolis or they migrated to far-flung corners of the world as servants of the British Empire. At home, the virtuoso was being displaced by the 'scientist' because the Baconian ideals of the seventeenth and eighteenth centuries were crumbling in the face of specialization and the division of intellectual labour. Newton and the great figures of the Enlightenment were still worshipped, yet their ideas were selectively transformed by a generation preoccupied with problems of its own.[76] Most troubling of all, however, was the fact that the Scots were only beginning to realize the tragic costs of improvement in deserted Highland crofts and squalid Glasgow tenements. Scotland was once again divided, only science was now as much a part of the illness as it was a part of the cure.

NOTES

1 For a lucid introduction to these issues see Roy Porter, 'The Scientific Revolution: A Spoke in the Wheel?', in Roy Porter and Mikuláš Teich (eds.), *Revolution in History* (Cambridge, 1986), 290–316.

2 J. H. Elliott in 'The Missing History – A Symposium', *TLS*, 23–9 June 1989, p. 699.

3 Hugh Trevor-Roper, 'The Scottish Enlightenment', *Studies on Voltaire and the Eighteenth Century* 58 (1967), 1635–58; p. 1636.

4 The case for a 'second' scientific revolution at the turn of the nineteenth century is summarized in I. B. Cohen, *Revolution in Science* (Cambridge, Mass., 1985), ch. 6.

5 Thomas Jefferson to Dugald Stewart, 21 June 1789, J. P. Boyd *et al.* (eds.), *The Papers of Thomas Jefferson*, 19 vols., continuing (Princeton, 1950–), xv, p. 204.

6 Quoted by D. J. Bryden, *Scottish Scientific Instrument-Makers 1600–1900* (Edinburgh, 1972), p. 1.

7 John Read, 'William Davidson of Aberdeen: The First British Professor of Chemistry', *Ambix* 9 (1961), 70–101; A. George Molland, 'Duncan Liddell (1561–1613): An Early Benefactor of Marischal College Library', *Aberdeen University Review* 51 (1985–6), 485–99.; S. H. Vines, 'Robert Morison and John Ray', in F. W. Oliver (ed.), *Makers of British Botany: A Collection of Biographies by Living Botanists* (Cambridge, 1913), 8–43.

8 Trevor-Roper, 'Scottish Enlightenment', p. 1636. My discussion of the natural philosophy curriculum in what follows summarizes John L. Russell, 'Cosmological Teaching in the Seventeenth-Century Scottish Universities', *Journal for the History of Astronomy* 5 (1974), 122–32, 145–54, and Christine King, 'Philosophy and Science in the Arts Curriculum of the Scottish Universities in the Seventeenth Century', (Ph.D. thesis, University of Edinburgh, 1974), ch. 6.

9 This eclecticism was encouraged to some extent by the structure of natural philosophy courses, which were divided into general and special physics. In general physics, the regents discussed such general issues as the scope of physics and the nature of space, time and matter, whereas in special physics they dealt with specific celestial and terrestrial phenomena. For an indication of the range

of topics covered in courses of general and special physics see King, 'Philosophy and Science', pp. 244–7.

10 Scottish students may have been attracted to Leiden by the presence of their countryman Adam Stuart, who was appointed as a professor of philosophy in 1644, and who soon became embroiled in the controversies surrounding Cartesianism, which he vociferously opposed. Eventually, Leiden became an important centre for the teaching of Cartesian natural philosophy; see Edward G. Ruestow, *Physics at Seventeenth and Eighteenth-Century Leiden* (The Hague, 1973), chs. 3–6.

11 On Moray see especially David Stevenson, 'Masonry, Symbolism and Ethics in the Life of Sir Robert Moray, FRS', *Proceedings of the Society of Antiquaries of Scotland* 114 (1984), 405–31. For his contacts with James Gregory I and Sibbald see R. G. Cant, *The University of St Andrews: A Short History* (rev. edn., Edinburgh and London, 1970), p. 74; Roger L. Emerson, 'Sir Robert Sibbald, Kt, the Royal Society of Scotland and the origins of the Scottish Enlightenment', *Annals of Science* 45 (1988), 41–72; p. 44. A list of Scottish Fellows of the early Royal Society is found in Roger L. Emerson, 'Natural Philosophy and the Problem of the Scottish Enlightenment', *Studies on Voltaire and the Eighteenth Century* 242 (1986), 243–91; p. 289.

12 Emerson, 'Sibbald', p. 58 (n. 72).

13 Harold R. Fletcher and William H. Brown, *The Royal Botanic Garden Edinburgh 1670–1970* (Edinburgh, 1970), pp. 3–10; W. S. Craig, *History of the Royal College of Physicians of Edinburgh* (Oxford, 1976), chs. 2 and 3. As Craig points out (p. 64), of the twenty-one original Fellows of the College, eleven had studied at Leiden, and a further six at other continental universities. Sibbald owed his great influence in Edinburgh to the patronage of the duke of York; Hugh Ouston, 'York in Edinburgh: James VII and the patronage of learning in Scotland, 1679–1688', in John Dwyer, Roger A. Mason and Alexander Murdoch (eds.), *New Perspectives on the Politics and Culture of Early Modern Scotland* (Edinburgh, 1980), 133–55. Sibbald was amply rewarded by his patrons: he was made Geographer Royal and Physician to the King in 1680, and he was knighted in 1682.

14 James Coutts, *A History of the University of Glasgow: From its Foundation in 1451 to 1909* (Glasgow, 1909), p. 195; Cant, *University of St Andrew's*, p. 75. Cant notes that an observatory was begun at St Andrews in the 1670s, but following James Gregory I's departure for Edinburgh, it apparently fell into disuse and was eventually torn down in 1736. An observatory was also built at King's College Aberdeen in 1675; Cosmo Innes (ed.), *Fasti Aberdonenses: Selections from the Records of the University and King's College of Aberdeen 1494–1854* (Aberdeen, 1854), p. lix.

15 George Sinclair, *Natural Philosophy Improven by New Experiments* (Edinburgh, 1683), p. 316; idem, *The Principles of Astronomy and Navigation*... (Edinburgh, 1688).

16 George Sinclair, *Satans Invisible World Discovered* (Edinburgh, 1685). In his preface, Sinclair notes that he believed students should be taught the principles of Cartesianism even though he considered this system to be heterodox. Significantly, Sinclair refers here to the works of Dutch Cartesians.

17 Sinclair, *Natural Philosophy*, pp. 5–8; *Principles of Astronomy*, pp. 15–19.

18 For a discussion of these tensions in the English context see Michael Hunter, *John Aubrey and the Realm of Learning* (London, 1975), ch. 2. Many Scottish regents thought that Cartesianism had irreligious implications; see King, 'Philosophy and Science', pp. 211, 216, 217, 225, 240–1, 255.

19 Quoted by Craig, *History*, p. 70. Sibbald stated that these meetings ceased once the College was founded.

20 Emerson, 'Sibbald', p. 72.

21 Emerson, 'Sibbald', *passim*, and 'Natural Philosophy', pp. 267–9.

22 On the reception of Newton in Scottish academe see Christine M. Shepherd, 'Newtonianism in Scottish Universities in the Seventeenth Century', in R. H. Campbell and Andrew S. Skinner (eds.), *The Origins and Nature of the Scottish Enlightenment* (Edinburgh, 1982), 65–85.

23 Newton's declared nescience about the physical causes of gravitation and other forces also harmonized well with Calvinist views about the limitations of human knowledge, which were strikingly reformulated in the epistemologies of David Hume and Thomas Reid; Roger L. Emerson, 'Calvinism and the Scottish Enlightenment', in J. Schwend (ed.), *Festschrift für Horst Drescher* (Mainz, 1991).

24 Colin Maclaurin, *An Account of Sir Isaac Newton's Philosophical Discoveries, In Four Books* (London, 1748; New York, 1968), p. 3; see also Colin Maclaurin to Rev Colin Campbell, 12 September 1714, in Stella Mills (ed.), *The Collected Letters of Colin Maclaurin* (Nantwich, 1982), 159–61, for Maclaurin on the moral uses of natural philosophy and mathematics.

25 In Aberdeen a chair of mathematics was established at King's College in 1703, and a chair of medicine founded at Marischal College in 1700. Medical chairs were also endowed at Glasgow (1703; Regius Chair 1713) and St Andrews (1720); Emerson, 'Natural Philosophy', pp. 248–58; A. D. Boney, *The Lost Gardens of Glasgow University* (London, 1988), chs. 2 and 3. On the legacy of the 1690 Commission see also Ronald G. Cant, 'Origins of the Enlightenment in Scotland: The Universities', in Campbell and Skinner, *Origins*, 42–64.

26 My account of Newton's relations with the Scots in what follows is based on Anita Guerrini, 'James Keill, George Cheyne, and Newtonian Physiology, 1690–1740', *Journal of the History of Biology* 18 (1985), 247–66; *idem*, 'The Tory Newtonians: Gregory, Pitcairne, and their circle', *Journal of British Studies* 25 (1986), 288–311; *idem*, 'Archibald Pitcairne and Newtonian Medicine', *Medical History* 31 (1987), 70–83.

27 Richard Nash, *John Craige's Mathematical Principles of Christian Theology* (Carbondale and Edwardsville, 1991).

28 Andrew Cunningham, 'Sydenham versus Newton: The Edinburgh Fever Dispute of the 1690s between Andrew Brown and Archibald Pitcairne', in W. F. Bynum and V. Nutton (eds.), *Theories of Fever from Antiquity to the Enlightenment* (London, 1981), 71–98.

29 Craig, *History*, pp. 408–19; W. B. Howie, 'Sir Archibald Stevenson, his Ancestry, and the Riot in the College of Physicians at Edinburgh', *Medical History* 11 (1967), 269–84.

30 The Aberdeen careers of Bower, Maclaurin and Stewart are described in my

Aberdeen and the Enlightenment: The Curriculum of the Aberdeen Colleges 1717–1800 (Aberdeen, 1991), introduction and ch. 1.

31 On Stirling see Charles Tweedie, *James Stirling: A Sketch of his Life and Works along with his Scientific Correspondence* (Oxford, 1922), and Ian Tweddle, *James Stirling: 'This about series and such things'* (Edinburgh, 1988). Although Stirling enjoyed the support of the patrons of the Edinburgh chair, his Jacobitism prevented him from taking up the appointment.

32 Despite his significance, there is unfortunately no modern study of Simson; in lieu of such a work see Rev. William Trail, *Account of the Life and Writings of Robert Simson, MD, Late Professor of Mathematics in the University of Glasgow* (London, 1812).

33 Mills, *Letters of Maclaurin*, pp. 287–302, 304–13, 336–8, 425–35; Tweddle, *James Stirling*, pp. 101–39, 169–71; James Stirling, 'Of the Figure of the Earth, and the Variation of Gravity on the Surface', *Philosophical Transactions* 39 (1735–6), 98–105; P. B. Wood, 'Thomas Reid, Natural Philosopher: A Study of Science and Philosophy in the Scottish Enlightenment', (unpublished Ph.D. dissertation, University of Leeds, 1984), p. 54.

34 Wood, 'Thomas Reid', pp. 93–4, 144. The various international attempts to observe the transits of 1761 and 1769 are described in Harry Woolf, *The Transits of Venus: A Study of Eighteenth-Century Science* (Princeton, 1959). Woolf does not mention the fact that Scottish astronomers were among the first to lay plans for observing the 1761 transit.

35 'A letter from Mr T. Melvill to the Rev James Bradley, DD FRS with a Discourse concerning the Cause of the Different Refrangibility of the Rays of Light', *Philosophical Transactions* 48 (1753), 261–70; Thomas Melvill to the Rev Dr Bradley, 2 June 1753, *Miscellaneous Works and Correspondence of The Rev James Bradley, DD FRS Astronomer Royal, Savilian Professor of Astronomy in the University of Oxford*, ed. S. P. Rigaud (Oxford, 1832), 483–7; Wood, 'Thomas Reid', pp. 248–59; Kurt Moller Pedersen, 'Roger Joseph Boscovich and John Robison on Terrestrial Aberration', *Centaurus* 24 (1980), 335–45; Geoffrey Cantor, *Optics after Newton: Theories of Light in Britain and Ireland 1704–1840* (Manchester, 1983), pp. 75–6. Significantly, while Reid, Robison, and Wilson accepted Boscovich's contention that terrestrial aberration could provide an *experimentum crucis*, they all rejected his interpretation of the phenomena.

36 Cantor, *Optics after Newton*, pp. 64–8. The Edinburgh professor of practical astronomy Robert Blair also published an important paper on refractive dispersion in the *Transactions of the Royal Society of Edinburgh* for 1794.

37 This is especially true of Thomas Reid's *An Inquiry into the Human Mind, On the Principles of Common Sense* (Edinburgh, 1764).

38 Andrew Plummer is briefly discussed in A. L. Donovan, *Philosophical Chemistry in the Scottish Enlightenment: The Doctrines and Discoveries of William Cullen and Joseph Black* (Edinburgh, 1975), pp. 36–9.

39 On the achievements of Cullen and Black see *inter alia* Donovan, *Philosophical Chemistry*, and A. D. C. Simpson (ed.), *Joseph Black 1728–1799: A Commemorative Symposium* (Edinburgh, 1982).

40 Stephen Hales, *Vegetable Staticks* (London, 1727; London and New York, 1969), p. 180.

41 Arnold Thackray, *Atoms and Powers: An Essay on Newtonian Matter-Theory and the Development of Chemistry* (Cambridge, Mass. and London, 1970), pp. 135–41; P. M. Heimann, 'Ether and Imponderables', in G. N. Cantor and M. J. S. Hodge (eds.), *Conceptions of Ether: Studies in the History of Ether Theories 1740–1900* (Cambridge, 1981), pp. 74–5; J. R. R. Christie, 'Ether and the Science of Chemistry: 1740–1790', in Cantor and Hodge, *Conceptions of Ether*, pp. 96–104. Black's notion of phlogiston is nicely discussed in Carleton E. Perrin, 'Joseph Black and the Absolute Levity of Phlogiston', *Annals of Science* 40 (1983), 109–37.

42 Heimann, 'Ether and Imponderables', pp. 60–70.

43 Donovan, *Philosophical Chemistry*, ch. 5; Christie, 'Ether and Chemistry', pp. 94–5; Charles W. J. Withers, 'William Cullen's Agricultural Lectures and Writings and the Development of Agricultural Science in Eighteenth-Century Scotland', *The Agricultural History Review* 37 (1989), 144–56. Archibald and Nan L. Clow's *The Chemical Revolution: A Contribution to Social Technology* (London, 1952) is an older survey of the economic applications of chemistry in eighteenth-century Scotland which has yet to be superseded. On Cullen's manipulation of the language of utility see J. V. Golinski, 'Utility and Audience in Eighteenth-Century Chemistry: Case Studies of William Cullen and Joseph Priestley', *The British Journal for the History of Science* 21 (1988), 1–31.

44 Donovan, *Philosophical Chemistry*, pp. 93–115.

45 Patrick Wilson, 'Biographical Account of Alexander Wilson, MD, Late Professor of Practical Astronomy in Glasgow', *The Edinburgh Journal of Science* 10 (1829), 1–17; p. 2; R. G. W. Anderson, *The Playfair Collection and the Teaching of Chemistry at the University of Edinburgh 1713–1858* (Edinburgh, 1978), pp. 20–2. 26. Both Cullen and Black were indebted to Martine's careful experiments on heat published in his *Essays Medical and Philosophical* (London, 1740).

46 Emerson, 'Sibbald', pp. 53–6; Sir John Sinclair, *The Statistical Account of Scotland* (ed. Donald J. Withrington and Ian R. Grant, 20 vols. Wakefield, 1983; first published 1791–9). On Sinclair as an improver see Rosalind Mitchison, *Agricultural Sir John: The Life of Sir John Sinclair of Ulster 1754–1835* (London, 1962).

47 Emerson, 'Science and the Scottish Enlightenment', pp. 344–5; B. P. Lenman and J. B. Kenworthy, 'Dr David Skene, Linnaeus, and the Applied Geology of the Scottish Enlightenment', *Aberdeen University Review* 47 (1977–8), 231–7; A. G. Morton, *John Hope 1725–1786: Scottish Botanist* (Edinburgh, 1986), pp. 17–18; Charles W. J. Withers, 'Improvement and enlightenment: Agriculture and Natural History in the Work of the Rev Dr John Walker (1731–1803)', in Peter Jones (ed.), *Philosophy and Science in the Scottish Enlightenment* (Edinburgh, 1988), 102–16; Margaret M. McKay (ed.), *The Rev Dr John Walker's Report on the Hebrides of 1764 and 1771* (Edinburgh, 1980).

48 See my 'Buffon's Reception in Scotland: The Aberdeen Connection', *Annals of Science* 44 (1987), 169–90; *idem*, 'Jolly Jack Phosphorus in the Venice of the North: Or, Who Was John Anderson', in Andrew Hook (ed.), *Glasgow and the Enlightenment* (Edinburgh, forthcoming).

49 At Edinburgh, the professor of natural history John Walker was among the first to include lectures on geology in his course, and his example was followed in the

Aberdeen colleges by James Beattie at Marischal and Robert Eden Scott at King's; see John Walker, *Lectures on Geology* [*sic*]: *Including Hydrography, Mineralogy, and Meteorology with an Introduction to Biology* (ed. Harold W. Scott, Chicago and London, 1966); James Ritchie, 'Natural history and the Emergence of Geology in the Scottish Universities', *Transactions of the Edinburgh Geological Society* 15 (1952), 297–316; Wood, *Aberdeen and the Enlightenment*, ch. 4.

50 The constellation of Hutton's interests in meteorology, plant physiology, agricultural improvement, mineralogy and the theory of the earth is best seen in the context of the development of natural history during the Scottish Enlightenment. Various lesser known aspects of Hutton's activities have recently been explored in Jean Jones, 'James Hutton: Exploration and Oceanography', *Annals of Science* 40 (1983), 81–94; *idem*, 'The Geological Collection of James Hutton', *Annals of Science* 41 (1984), 223–44; *idem*, 'James Hutton's Agricultural Research and his Life as a Farmer', *Annals of Science* 42 (1985), 573–601.

51 See my 'The Natural History of Man in the Scottish Enlightenment', *History of Science* 28 (1990), 89–123.

52 L. L. Laudan, 'Thomas Reid and the Newtonian Turn of British Methodological Thought', in R. E. Butts and J. W. Davis (ed.), *The Methodological Heritage of Newton*, (Oxford, 1970), 103–31; P. B. Wood, 'Science and the Pursuit of Virtue in the Aberdeen Enlightenment', in M. A. Stewart (ed.), *Studies in the Philosophy of the Scottish Enlightenment*, (Oxford, 1990), pp. 127–49. For the influence of Scottish methodological thought on nineteenth-century British physics see G. N. Cantor, 'Henry Brougham and the Scottish Methodological Tradition', *Studies in History and Philosophy of Science* 2 (1971), 69–89; *idem*, 'The Reception of the Wave Theory of Light in Britain: A Case Study Illustrating the Role of Methodology in Scientific Debate', *Historical Studies in the Physical Sciences* 6 (1975), 109–32. A highly problematic study of this issue is Richard Olson, *Scottish Philosophy and British Physics 1750–1880: A study in the Foundations of the Victorian Scientific Style* (Princeton, 1975).

53 For studies which map this common culture see Wood, 'Thomas Reid'; Michael Barfoot, 'James Gregory (1753–1821) and Scottish Scientific Metaphysics, 1750–1800', (unpublished Ph.D. dissertation, University of Edinburgh, 1983); *idem*, 'Hume and the Culture of Science in the Early Eighteenth Century', in Stewart, *Scottish Enlightenment*, 151–90; John P. Wright, 'Metaphysics and Physiology: Mind, Body, and the Animal Economy in Eighteenth-Century Scotland', in Stewart, *Scottish Enlightenment*, 251–301.

54 The significance of the landed interest for the development of the sciences in the Scottish Enlightenment is emphasized in Steven Shapin, 'The Audience for Science in Eighteenth-Century Edinburgh', *History of Science* 12 (1974), 95–121; on the importance of the ethos of improvement see John R. R. Christie, 'The Origins and Development of the Scottish Scientific Community, 1680–1760', *History of Science* 12 (1974), 122–41.

55 The medical school also stood as a monument to the mercantilist ideology shared by Drummond and those pressing for university reform.

56 On the relevant developments within the university of Edinburgh during the eighteenth century see Sir Alexander Grant, *The Story of the University of*

Edinburgh During its First Three Hundred Years, 2 vols. (London, 1884), 1, 344–8, 11, 431–3; R. G. Anderson and A. D. C. Simpson (eds.), *The Early Years of the Edinburgh Medical School* (Edinburgh, 1976); J. B. Morrell, 'The University of Edinburgh in the Late Eighteenth Century: Its Scientific Eminence and Academic Structure', *Isis* 62 (1970), 158–71.

57 Coutts, *University of Glasgow*, pp. 489–90, 495–6, 500–1.

58 Wood, *Aberdeen and the Enlightenment*, ch. 3; David Murray, *Memories of the Old College of Glasgow: Some Chapters in the History of the University* (Glasgow, 1927), p. 111.

59 Grant, *University of Edinburgh*, 1, 338–40, 378–80; Coutts, *University of Glasgow*, pp. 229–30; John S. Reid, 'The Castlehill Observatory, Aberdeen', *Journal of the History of Astronomy* 13 (1982), 84–96. For the sorry story of the abortive attempts to found an observatory in Edinburgh see D. J. Bryden, 'The Edinburgh Observatory 1736–1811: A Story of Failure', *Annals of Science* 47 (1990), 445–74.

60 John A. Cable, 'The Early History of Scottish Popular Science', *Studies in Adult Education* 4 (1972), 34–45; *idem*, 'Early Scottish Science: The Vocational Provision', *Annals of Science* 30 (1973), 179–99; Donald J. Withrington, 'Education and Society in the Eighteenth Century', in N. T. Phillipson and Rosalind Mitchison (eds.), *Scotland in the Age of Improvement: Essays in Scottish History in the Eighteenth Century* (Edinburgh, 1970), 169–99; James Muir, *John Anderson: Pioneer of Technical Education and the College He Founded* (Glasgow, 1950), ch. 4. It should be noted that the universities also tried to reach a wider educational market by opening up courses to non-matriculated students and by offering extra-mural classes in the sciences.

61 The history of the society is reconstructed in Roger L. Emerson, 'The Philosophical Society of Edinburgh, 1737–1747', *The British Journal for the History of Science* 12 (1979), 154–91; *idem*, 'The Philosophical Society of Edinburgh, 1748–1768', *The British Journal for the History of Science* 14 (1981), 133–76; *idem*, 'The Philosophical Society of Edinburgh, 1768–1783', *The British Journal for the History of Science* 18 (1985), 255–303; *idem*, 'The Scottish Enlightenment and the End of the Philosophical Society of Edinburgh', *The British Journal for the History of Science* 21 (1988), 33–66.

62 On the genesis and early years of the Royal Society of Edinburgh see Emerson, 'End of the Philosophical Society'; Steven Shapin, 'The Royal Society of Edinburgh: A Study of the Social Context of Hanoverian Science', (unpublished Ph.D. dissertation, University of Pennsylvania, 1971); *idem*, 'Property, Patronage, and the Politics of Science: The Founding of the Royal Society of Edinburgh', *The British Journal for the History of Science* 7 (1974), 1–41.

63 See my 'Science and the Aberdeen Enlightenment', Jones, *Philosophy and Science*, 39–66; pp. 52–6.

64 James Gray, *History of the Royal Medical Society, 1737–1937* (Edinburgh, 1952).

65 James Kendall, 'The First Chemical Society, the First Chemical Journal, and the Chemical Revolution', *Proceedings of the Royal Society of Edinburgh* 63A (1949–52), 346–58, 385–400; Douglas McKie, 'Some Notes on a Students' Scientific Society in Eighteenth-Century Edinburgh', *Science Progress* 49 (1961), 228–41; G. N. Cantor, 'The Academy of Physics at Edinburgh 1797–1800',

Social Studies of Science 5 (1975), 109–34; E. H. B. Rodger, *Aberdeen Doctors at Home and Abroad: The Narrative of a Medical School* (Edinburgh and London, 1893), pp. 54–70.

66 Quoted in my 'Science and Aberdeen', p. 55.

67 In the early years of the Edinburgh Philosophical Society, for example, Maclaurin and his friends discoursed about subjects like astronomy, mining, Trembley's polyp and Roman remains in Scotland; Emerson, 'Philosophical Society of Edinburgh, 1737–1747', pp. 175–80; see also Wood, 'Jolly Jack Phosphorous'.

68 On the chemical revolution in Scotland see C. E. Perrin, 'A reluctant Catalyst: Joseph Black and the Edinburgh Reception of Lavoisier's Chemistry', *Ambix* 29 (1982), 141–76.

69 For an illustration of this shift see my *Aberdeen and the Enlightenment*, ch. 4.

70 On this point see Roger L. Emerson, *Professors, Patronage and Politics: The Aberdeen Universities in the Eighteenth Century* (Aberdeen, 1991).

71 The dynamics of the Leslie affair have been explored in Ian D. L. Clark,'The Leslie Controversy, 1805', *Records of the Scottish Church History Society* 14 (1963), 179–97; John G. Burke, 'Kirk and Causality in Edinburgh, 1805', *Isis* 61 (1970), 34–54; J. B. Morrell, 'The Leslie Affair: Careers, Kirk and Politics in Edinburgh in 1805', *Scottish Historical Review* 54 (1975), 63–82.

72 A similar pattern is discernible in England; see John Gascoigne, *Cambridge in the Age of the Enlightenment: Science, Religion and Politics from the Restoration to the French Revolution* (Cambridge, 1989), ch. 8.

73 Morrell, 'Robison and Playfair'; Wood, 'Science and the Aberdeen Enlightenment', pp. 57–8; J. R. R. Christie, 'Joseph Black and John Robison', in Simpson, *Joseph Black*, 47–52.

74 Steven Shapin, '"Nibbling at the Teats of Science": Edinburgh and the Diffusion of Science in the 1830s', in Ian Inskter and Jack Morrell (eds.), *Metropolis and Province: Science in British Culture 1780–1850*, (London, 1983), 151–78; J. V. Smith, 'Manners, Morals and Mentalities: Reflections on the Popular Enlightenment of Early Nineteenth-Century Scotland', in Walter M. Humes and Hamish M. Paterson (eds.), *Scottish Culture and Scottish Education 1800–1980* (Edinburgh, 1983), 25–54.

75 For a perceptive treatment of the declinist laments of the period see J. R. R. Christie, 'The Rise and Fall of Scottish Science', in Maurice Crosland (ed.), *The Emergence of Science in Western Europe* (London, 1976), 111–26.

76 For examples see P. B. Wood, 'The Hagiography of Common Sense: Dugald Stewart's *Account of the life and writings of Thomas Reid*', in A. J. Holland (ed.), *Philosophy, Its History and Historiography* (Dordrecht, 1985), 305–22; John R. R. Christie, 'Sir David Brewster as an Historian of Science', in A. D. Morrison-Low and J. R. R. Christie (eds.), *"Martyr of Science": Sir David Brewster 1781–1868* (Edinburgh, 1984), 53–6.

INDEX

Aberdeen, 267, 277; Medical Society, 278;
  Philosophical Society, 278; *see also*
  King's College; Marischal College
Åbo, university of, 250
absolutism, political, 11, 15, 21–39 *passim*,
  48 n. 78, 49 n. 89, 71, 73, 241
Academia Naturae Curiosorum, 96, 138
Académie des Sciences, Paris, 80, 81, 85 n.
  30; experimental philosophy of, 63, 70,
  71–4, 136, 138, 241; Louis XIV and,
  23–5, 29, 31, 41 n. 21, 46 n. 60, 49 n.
  89, 69, 76–7; and mechanical
  philosophy, 76–8
academies, scientific, *see* societies
Accademia del Cimento, 12, 14–15, 25–32,
  35, 37, 47 n. 71, 138
Accademia dei Lincei, 15
Acosta, José de, *Historia natural y moral de las
  Indias* (1590), 170
acoustics, 108, 232, 244
Acta eruditorum, 102, 103, 108, 139
Acta Literaria Sveciae, 245, 249
Acta Medica Hafniensia, 138
African exploration, 165, 166, 168
Agricola, Rudolph, 94, 96, 116, 213
agricultural improvement, Scotland, 276,
  277, 280, 284 nn. 43, 46 and 47, 285 n.
  50
Agrippa, Cornelius, 94, 96, 118
Aguilera, Hernando, 159
air pressure, demonstration of, 60, 62
air pump, 30, 49 n. 88, 96, 135, 185, 268
Aix, scientific coterie at, 61
Åkerman, Anders, 251
Al-Choresmi (Al-Khwarizmi), 214
Alcalá de Henares, university of, 159, 160
Alcanyís, Lluís, 171
alchemy, 94–5, 96, 183, 186, 213; Newton's
  knowledge of, 185, 203
Alexander VI, Pope, 167
Alexander the Great, 170

Alfonsine Tables, 159, 175 n. 1
Alfonso the Wise, king of Castile, 159
almanac, 159, 246, 247
Alpers, S., 141
Alsted, Johann, 95
Altdorf, university of, 92, 93, 96, 97, 102,
  107
Amélie, Empress, 105
Amerindians, 170
Amsterdam, 123, 126, 129, 131–4, 135;
  Athenaeum, 132, 134; botanical
  garden, 132, 133–4; Collegium
  Medicum, 132, 134, 139; Collegium
  Medicum Privatum, 133, 139; *hortus
  medicus*, 134
anatomy: in Bohemia, 220; English, 183;
  French, 58–9, 60, 61, 71, 72; Italian,
  15–16, 18–21, 22, 42, n. 25, 44 nn. 36,
  38 and 42, 45 n. 43; in low countries,
  117, 122–4, 126, 132, 133, 135, 137–9;
  public dissections, 18, 19–20, 45 n. 44,
  132, 138–9, 148 n. 94, 220
Andala, Ruardus, 136
Anderson's Institution, Glasgow, 277, 286
  n. 60
Andreae, Johann, 95
Andreas, Valerius, 128–9
Andrewes, Lancelot, 192
Angers, 81, 89 n. 85
Anglicanism, 5, 190–4, 196–202, 208 n. 48;
  see also Latitudinarianism; physics
Anglo-Catholicism, 191
animals/animal physiology, 133, 138, 183
Antitrinitarian denominations, 153
Apianus, Peter, *Cosmography*, 117
Arabic science, 158–61
Aragon, 160, 161
Archimedes, 231
Argyll, Archibald Campbell, 3rd duke of,
  276
Aristotle/Aristotelianism, 87 n. 70, 92–3,